Stern
Bgm

A Century of Subways

A Century of Subways

Celebrating 100 Years
of New York's Underground Railways

BRIAN J. CUDAHY

Fordham University Press
New York
2003

Library of Congress Cataloging-in-Publication Data

Cudahy, Brian J.
A century of subways : celebrating 100 years of New York's underground railways / by Brian J. Cudahy.
p.   cm.
ISBN 0-8232-2292-6 (hard cover : alk. paper)
1. Subways—New York (State)—New York—History
2. Railroads—New York (State)—New York—History.
3. Interborough Rapid Transit Company—History.   I. Title.
TF847.N5C73   2003
388.4′28′097471—dc22

2003017034

Printed in the United States of America
07 06 05 04 03 5 4 3 2 1
First edition

CONTENTS

INTRODUCTION

A Century of Subways: Celebrating 100 Years of New York's Underground Railways has been written to help celebrate the centenary of the New York Subway. A hundred years ago, on the afternoon of Thursday, October 27, 1904, New Yorkers walked into various entrance kiosks of the city's new Interborough Rapid Transit Company, headed down a flight or two of stairs, and took their very first rides under the sidewalks of New York aboard a fleet of new, electric-powered, rapid-transit trains.

The subway line that opened for business on October 27, 1904, was 9 miles from one end to the other and included twenty-seven separate stations. On October 27, 2004, when the New York Subway celebrates its centenary, the system will encompass 247 miles, and passengers will be able to board trains at 468 different stations.

Mere growth, however it is measured, is not the principal accomplishment that characterizes the first hundred years of subway service in New York. More so than in any other city on the face of the earth, during its first century of service the subway has woven its way into the fabric of this exciting metropolis to the extent that one simply may not imagine New York, with all of its vitality and all of its dynamism, without the all-important mobility that is provided to the city's denizens day after day by electric-powered subway trains speeding passengers uptown and downtown through a network of underground tunnels.

A Century of Subways is not a single narrative story. Rather, in an effort to present a sense of the context within which New York's mass-transit achievement in 1904 should be appreciated and understood, it is a collection of five separate and different stories.

The book's opening chapter, "August Belmont and His Subway," talks about the Interborough Rapid Transit Company, its president, August Belmont, Jr., and the construction of the city's first subway in 1904. It also traces the development of that initial subway into the IRT Division of today's much larger and more comprehensive subway system. As a matter of usage, I have restricted the popular term "IRT" to the post-1940 period, when the Interborough Rapid Transit Company became the IRT Division of the Board of Transportation of the City of New York. I recognize that "IRT" was used in New York prior to 1940, but I trust my distinction is helpful. (I have also restricted the term "City of New York" to the municipal entity that came into existence, through amalgamation, on January 1, 1898, while its less extensive predecessor is referred to as "New York City.")

Chapter 2 tells the story of the only American subway that predated New York's, a wonderfully diverse system whose initial element opened in 1897 in Boston. (Major elements of this chapter initially appeared in my 1972 book, *Change at Park Street Under.*) Boston and New York enjoy a wonderfully rich relationship that incorporates such diverse elements as the New York, New Haven and Hartford Railroad, Babe Ruth and Bill Buckner, the old Fall River Line, Fordham versus Boston College, Central Park and the Public Garden. Chapter 2 advances the proposition that the Massachusetts Bay Transportation Authority (MBTA) and the IRT are also part of this shared heritage.

Even Boston's accomplishment of 1897 was not the world's first subway system. Chapter 3 tells of an underground railway in London, England—powered initially by soot-spewing steam locomotives—that began hauling Queen Victoria's subjects a full three decades earlier in the year 1863, and how it grew and developed into what came to be called the London Underground in subsequent decades. To provide further context for the centenary of the New York Subway, this chapter also presents a broad-gauge look, in both words and pictures, at the general estate of subway systems in Europe at the beginning of the twenty-first century.

Chapter 4 allows the development of the Interborough Subway to be seen in yet another perspective by examining a parallel style of electrified railway in New York—short-haul service into nearby suburban territory operated by railroad companies whose principal markets are intercity in nature. Neither of the two major intercity railroad companies that inaugurated such service in New York in the early years of the twentieth century—the Pennsylvania Railroad and the New York Central—remain in business in the twenty-first century. But their traditions certainly live on in such public agencies as the Metropolitan Transportation Authority and New Jersey Transit. Two other important railroads whose electric operations into the New York suburbs have also passed into the hands of public agencies are the Long Island and the New York, New Haven and Hartford. Furthermore, in surviving such a shift from the private sector of risk and reward to the public sector of subsidy and service, the commuter railroads of New York have followed the same path that was earlier pioneered when the privately owned Interborough Rapid Transit Company of 1904 evolved into a public entity on the eve of America's entry into the Second World War. (As a further matter of usage, in the pages that follow the abbreviation NYC will refer exclusively to the New York Central Railroad, never New York City.)

The fifth and final chapter in this centenary tribute to the New York Subway sketches out the general development of rail rapid transit throughout North America during the hundred-year interval that began in the plaza outside City Hall in downtown Manhattan on a quiet October afternoon in 1904. It has been, certainly, a quiet revolution and one that has been remarked upon but rarely. But the fact remains that during the final quarter of the twentieth century, urban rail transit saw explosive growth from one end of North America to the other, in cities as different as Baltimore and Buffalo, San Juan and San Francisco, Montreal and Los Angeles.

The legacy of the IRT that began on October 27, 1904, is both substantial and profound. It is also extraordinarily beneficial to the health of urban America. Best of all, though, as the world enters the twenty-first century, it is a legacy whose full dimensions have yet to be revealed.

Burke, Virginia
July, 2003

STONEHENGE VIA SUBWAY

A few summers ago, my wife Mary Lou and I were driving west to east across southern Britain. We were traveling from the Welsh port city of Swansea after a delightful ferry crossing from Cork, Ireland, and our destination was Southampton, England, where we would board the cruise ship *Royal Princess* for a two-week voyage back to New York.

After pausing for lunch that day in the city of Bath, mid-afternoon found us driving down a two-lane country road in Wiltshire for a visit to Stonehenge. As we approached the historic site, the famous circle of haunting stone loomed large in an open field off to our right; a parking lot was on the left. We pulled in, locked the car, and tried to get our bearings. And that's when we saw the sign. Accurate, brief, and helpful, it read in its entirety: "Stonehenge, Via Subway."

The "subway" that one uses to reach the ancient wonders of Stonehenge operates neither local nor express service; it has no third rail, no high-level platforms, no multicolor route maps. It is, of course, a simple pedestrian underpass that tourists in the parking lot may use to cross the two-lane road without having to worry about the perils of traffic (British traffic, I might add, which operates on the "wrong" side of the road). But the utter incongruity of a contemporary sign directing one to a historic site that is over five thousand years old "via subway" was simply delightful. That evening, as we enjoyed a fish-and-chips dinner in a Southampton waterside restaurant mere yards from the spot where RMS *Titanic* departed on her famous voyage, I kept thinking back to mid-afternoon: "Stonehenge, Via Subway."

I tell this story as a prelude to a centenary tribute to the New York Subway to underscore the point that language is not always our ally when precision is the goal. We shall be discussing subways, and while it will be easy enough to distinguish an enterprise like the Interborough Rapid Transit Company of 1904 from the pedestrian tunnel at Stonehenge, in the contemporary world of mass transportation, it is not always as simple a matter to say what is—and, as important, what is not—a true subway. A proliferation in recent years of what is generally called light rail transit has blurred a number of older distinctions. Is it appropriate to refer to a surface-running streetcar system whose service terminates downtown at a small underground facility as a true subway? What about an electrified commuter rail service that cuts across the heart of a central city, operates high-platform cars that look for all the world like ordinary subway cars, controls access to its stations with turnstiles or fare gates, and even markets its service to short-haul patrons? May it properly be called a subway? Should it be?

The answers to all of these questions are, in no special order: absolutely, yes; positively, no; and it all depends.

In the chapters that follow we shall be using, perforce, descriptions like "the first subway in North America," and "the oldest subway in the world," and "the second largest subway in Europe." There will be an unavoidable measure of ambiguity in the use of the word "subway" in all of these situations, though, and few absolute assertions will not be subject to some kind of qualification.

With a little luck and a lot of patience, our centenary celebration of New York's Interborough Rapid Transit will clarify and amplify the colorful heritage of those specialized urban railways that are called subways. But full and perfect clarity will often lie beyond just our horizon, and imprecision will continue to emerge at unexpected times and in utterly surprising places. Like on a cloudy summer afternoon at the end of a parking lot off a two-lane road in the British countryside where a sign affirmatively proclaims: "Stonehenge Via Subway."

1

August Belmont and His Subway

THE SUBWAY that opened in the City of New York on the afternoon of Thursday, October 27, 1904, was of modest proportions when compared to the massive rail rapid-transit system that would be carrying New Yorkers on their appointed rounds a hundred years later, on Wednesday, October 27, 2004. In 2004, for example, there are important north-south trunk lines in Manhattan—four-track subways allowing both local and express service—under Eighth Avenue, Seventh Avenue, Broadway, Sixth Avenue, and Lexington Avenue. Add to this a modest but separate two-track north-south subway under portions of Sixth Avenue that is part of the Port Authority Trans-Hudson (PATH) system, three crosstown subways that intersect the north-south trunk lines while remaining separate from them, a difficult-to-describe loop line through the financial district in lower Manhattan, various feeder routes into the north-south trunk lines, and, finally, segments of a new two-track subway under Second Avenue on the East Side that was begun some decades ago, abandoned and left incomplete in the face of fiscal constraints, but stands on the verge of being activated again, and one has a sense of how popular the single line that opened in 1904 eventually became.

In October 1904, when service was inaugurated on New York's first subway, the route its trains followed was located entirely on Manhattan Island. In 2004, subways in New York serve four of the city's five boroughs, and there are no fewer than thirteen two-track crossings of the East River between Manhattan and Long Island and four separate crossings of the Harlem River linking Manhattan with the Bronx.

Because of this growth and development, contemporary accounts of the New York Subway understandably—and quite properly—focus on its totality and speak in terms of the overall system's three divisions, the IND, the BMT, and the IRT. There is, however, a discreet identity to something called the Interborough Rapid Transit Company, the corporate predecessor of today's IRT Division and the entity that inaugurated subway service in New York in 1904. The Interborough and the IRT deserve attention on their own terms.

CONTRACT ONE AND CONTRACT TWO

A quarter-century before New York inaugurated service on its first subway line in 1904, a quartet of north-south elevated railways was built to link business districts in Lower Manhattan with residential neighborhoods to the north. Constructed entirely with private capital, protected by franchise contracts authorized by state legislation enacted in 1875, and with trains powered by small steam locomotives, this first form of true rapid transit to serve New York City included lines over Second Avenue and Third Avenue on the East Side, Sixth Avenue in the center of Manhattan, and Ninth Avenue on the West Side. The Second Avenue and Sixth Avenue lines were part of an enterprise that was eventually known as the Metropolitan Elevated Railway Company, while the lines over Third and Ninth Avenues were managed jointly as the New York Elevated Railroad Company.

In 1879—before the Metropolitan's Second Avenue Line had even been completed, in fact—the two elevated companies were merged into a single system called Manhattan Railways, and it was also at this time that financier Jay Gould entered the New York elevated picture, a man whose manipulation of railroad securities had triggered a full-blown financial panic in 1869. As described by historian David McCullough, in his acquisition of the Manhattan elevated lines Gould's plan was "to harass and intimidate the existing owners at every opportunity, drive the stock down below its true value, then begin buying."[1] Under Gould—perhaps even despite him—the four Manhattan elevated lines became an important element of mass transport in New York City during the final quarter of the nineteenth century.[2]

In 1891, Manhattan Railways added a third elevated company to its expanding empire: the Suburban Rapid Transit Company, whose route extended northward from the banks of the Harlem River into the central Bronx—or the "Annexed District," as it was often called in the 1890s. Suburban operated its first train in 1886 and provided connections at its southern end to both the Second Avenue and the Third Avenue lines. Once acquired by Manhattan Railways, Suburban became a northward extension for both Second Avenue and Third Avenue services.[3]

The era that saw the emergence of elevated railways in New York was a time when memories of the Civil War were still vivid in America, and veterans of that awful conflict occupied important positions of trust in business and politics. Transatlantic steamships grew larger and faster year after year, and New York solidified its position as the nation's principal seaport for trade and commerce with Europe. To the west, in the nation's heartland, the mining of coal and the conversion of iron ore into finished steel had become major industries that helped sustain the national economy.

But if industrial growth was an important dynamic in shaping the final decades of the nineteenth century, so, too, was the ever-present possibility of political corruption. Tammany Hall, an organization within the Democratic Party of New York City, was particularly associated with such corruption, especially during the late 1860s when Tammany's leader was the notorious William Marcy ("Boss") Tweed.

Tweed saw the emerging elevated railways as an opportunity and took pains to thwart any rival ventures that might represent competition for the predecessors of Manhattan Railways. The Tweed era would end in the early 1870s, though. "Boss" Tweed was convicted in 1873 and died in prison in 1878, and Manhattan Railways was left to sink or swim without his assistance. The fact remains, however, that one cannot understand the culture of New York City during the age of the elevated railways without paying some attention to the unusual style of politics that was distinctive to the era.[4] Politics and high finance aside, the elevated merger of 1878 was quite sensible, since the two predecessor companies never operated in total independence from each other. All four lines used the same South Ferry terminal at the southern tip of Manhattan Island, for instance, and the Metropolitan's Sixth Avenue Line operated over Ninth Avenue trackage north of 53rd Street. Following the merger in 1878, sections were completed of the various elevated lines that had been authorized but not yet constructed.

Elevated railway service proved popular with New York passengers. In 1881, Manhattan Railways carried 75.6 million riders. A decade later, in 1891, this had grown to 196.7 million.[5] And while the elevated lines clearly represented a major advance in both speed and comfort over surface-running streetcars, the merger of the elevated companies in 1879 did not produce a sound and stable system that could accommodate future patronage growth. A 1900 report in the journal *Municipal Affairs* claimed that in addition to uncertainties associated with Gould's questionable financial maneuverings, the elevated lines soon became inadequate as providers of needed mass-transport services, noting that for "a number of years following its construction, the elevated railroad seemed to deal satisfactorily with the question of rapid transit. The population, however, kept growing beyond these facilities."[6] So just as elevated railways emerged when streetcars proved inadequate for New York's transportation needs, when the capacity of the elevated system was reached, what began to be heard in New York was a "strong demand for an underground road by which passengers could be transported from the Battery to Harlem in fifteen minutes."[7]

Abram S. Hewitt was born in Haverstraw, New York, in 1822, and after graduating from Columbia College sought his fortune in America's rapidly expanding iron and steel industry. This background made him especially useful during the Civil War, and he was dispatched to Britain to help secure weapons for the Union Army from foundries there. After the war, Hewitt turned his attention to public life and as a reform member of New York's Democratic Party fought the abuses of the Tweed ring and Tammany Hall. After serving five terms in the U.S. House of Representatives, in 1886 Hewitt unexpectedly bested Republican Theodore Roosevelt and was elected mayor of New York City, a post he held for a single two-year term from 1887 through 1889.[8]

On January 31, 1888, midway through his term, Mayor Hewitt delivered a message to the city's Board of Aldermen outlining needed municipal improvements in a variety of transportation areas—the harbor and docks, the streets, but most important, rapid transit. "The time has come when the growth of the city is seriously retarded by the want of proper means of access to and from the upper and lower portions of the city," the mayor wrote. Unless a proper system of rapid transit is constructed, "the population which ought to increase at the upper end of the city will be driven to Long Island and New-Jersey."[9]

The mass-transit system that Hewitt proposed would include both subway and elevated segments, and given the fact that electric traction was then in its infancy, the mayor was open to the new system's being powered by either electricity or steam locomotives, while day-to-day operation of the new railway would be handled under contract by a private company. In fact, Hewitt believed that the New York Central and Hudson River Railroad was the obvious choice in this regard.[10] But building the infrastructure itself, Hewitt argued, should be a public-sector responsibility. "[I]t will be proper for the city itself to undertake to make the provision, because the citizens as a body will thus get the benefit of the increase in the value of properties which these facilities will create."[11]

This was a new and very different public policy option—municipal construction of needed rapid-transit facilities. The *New York Times* gave the mayor's proposal strong editorial endorsement, and while the paper quibbled over some specifics of the routes Hewitt had suggested, the "essential feature of the Mayor's plan . . . which provides for the construction of the new rapid-transit system at the expense of the city itself," was something the *Times* welcomed, since it could well serve to keep the project "free from waste or extravagance for private profit."[12]

Hewitt had been associated with a civic association that advocated municipal construction of an underground urban railway for New York as early as the 1870s, so the idea itself was not new. But it achieved an important new level of maturity when it became a formal recommendation of the city's chief executive officer in January 1888.

The decade and a half following Hewitt's message, when the New York Subway progressed from conceptual proposal to concrete-and-steel actuality, was one of extraordinarily fundamental political change and realignment in metropolitan New York. In addition, it was an interval when the mass-transport industry would experience the most important and profound technological advances in its entire history. A mere *two days* after Mayor Hewitt delivered his message to the Board of Aldermen on January 31, 1888, 335 miles south of New York City, in Richmond, Virginia, a one-time naval officer by the name of Frank Sprague completed work on the electrification of the Union Passenger Railway there, an achievement widely regarded as the first truly successful deployment of electric traction as the source of power for any kind of commercial railway service.[13] Between them, Hewitt's call for municipal construction of mass-transport facilities and Sprague's "subjugation of the subtle and hitherto illusive force of electricity" for mass-transport purposes were both necessary preconditions for what would happen in New York on October 27, 1904.[14]

That subway proponents in New York were able to marshal the political, the financial, and the technical consensus that their project necessarily required precisely at a time when basic frames of reference in all three areas were anything but stable is further testament to the extraordinary achievement the 1904 subway truly was. Consider, for example, the fact that January 1, 1898, was the culmination of the single most profound political shift that New York had ever seen—and likely ever will see. In a lengthy effort that was motivated, at least in substantial part, by a desire to dilute the often-corrupt influence that Tammany Hall exercised on New York City politics, this date saw the amalgamation of the five-borough City of New York out of a variety of formerly independent cities and towns. Prior to January 1, 1898, New York City included only Manhattan and the Bronx. From that day on, the City of New York has been a five-borough colossus that also includes Brooklyn, Queens, and Staten Island. And yet the newly amalgamated city executed the first contract for subway construction less than two years after it had been formerly established, and the various commissions and boards out of whose work the technical specifications for the subway emerged were conducting their deliberations at the very same time that municipal amalgamation was also under active deliberation and debate.

It is entirely plausible, of course, that subway proponents in New York welcomed the diversion that amalgamation provided, and had overall political matters been more stable in the years leading up to 1904, the business of seeing the subway through to completion and developing its specifications might have been subject to hopeless compromise from political quarters that were more than preoccupied by the business of amalgamation. Such a possibility aside, though, a strong measure of admiration is in order for advocates in New York who were able to forge a decision to build a subway and proceed with its construction at the very same time when fundamental political realignment of unprecedented dimensions was also under way.

The era defined by Hewitt's message to the Board of Aldermen in January 1888 and the opening of the city's first subway in October 1904 was no less tumultuous in national and world affairs. In politics, Grover Cleveland would be elected to the only nonconsecutive second term in presidential history in 1892, while in 1901 William McKinley became the third U.S. president to suffer the terrible fate of assassination. In February 1898, the battleship USS *Maine* exploded in Havana Harbor, and before the year was over the United States had declared war on Spain. Germany, Austria-Hungary, and Italy created the Triple Alliance in 1902, sowing the seeds of world conflict in years to come, and the eventual dissolution of the mighty British Empire was foreshadowed when separate colonies in Australia were united into a self-governing commonwealth in 1901.

It was also an interval that saw Henry Ford perfect assembly-line production of automobiles in 1903, the same year that two brothers from Dayton, Ohio, traveled to Kitty Hawk on North Carolina's Outer Banks and confidently left the face of the earth in a vehicle that was heavier than the air through which it flew. Back in New York City, in 1902 architect Daniel H. Burnham's Flatiron Building was constructed on a triangular piece of land at the three-way intersection of Broadway, Fifth Avenue, and 23rd Street. On June 16, 1904, mere months before the new subway opened for business, the excursion steamboat *General Slocum* was heading up the East River with a church group from the Lower East Side. The vessel caught fire, flames quickly engulfed its wooden superstructure, and 1,029 souls lost their lives in a disaster whose horror would not be eclipsed in New York until September 11, 2001. As for the man Abram S. Hewitt defeated in 1886 to become mayor, on the day subway service was inaugurated in New York in 1904, former mayoral candidate Theodore Roosevelt was serving as the twenty-sixth president of the United States. Indeed, October 27, 1904, the day the subway opened, was President Roosevelt's forty-sixth birthday.

Amid all this change and upheaval, a number of benchmarks can be identified that helped define a path from Mayor Hewitt's 1888 message to the inauguration of subway service in 1904. They include the following:

- In April 1890, Hewitt's successor as mayor of New York City, Hugh J. Grant, appointed a five-member commission to prepare preliminary recommendations for the city's rapid-transit needs. The chair of this ad hoc commission was an immigrant banker by the name of August Belmont, and under his leadership a recommendation was sent to the mayor in July of 1890 calling for the construction of a four-track underground railway from lower Manhattan to the Bronx.[15]

- Next the mayor appointed a new and different commission to carry the matter forward. Presided over by William Steinway and popularly known as the Steinway Commission, it drew up more detailed transit plans, which were approved by the Board of Aldermen in 1891.[16]

- On the assumption that a private company would be willing to build the new subway with its own resources in exchange for a long-term franchise to operate the facility, the recommendations of the Steinway Commission were put out for bid, but "capital was afraid of the enterprise under the conditions offered," and no bids were received.[17] Hewitt's earlier proposal of municipal funding for the project was still too radical an idea for serious consideration, and the work of the Steinway Commission seemed destined for oblivion.

- When further progress appeared least likely, the Chamber of Commerce of New York State took the initiative to secure passage of a bill by the legislature in early 1894 that established a new Rapid Transit Commission. The bill was signed into law by Governor Roswell P. Flower on May 22, 1894, and the new commission was given statutory authority to draw up final plans for a subway and then either "sell the franchise or . . . provide for ownership by the city."[18] Hewitt's notion of municipal financing was not assured by this action, but at least it was now in play as a legislatively approved possibility.

- A referendum was held on November 6, 1894, that revealed a strong preference on the part of New York voters for municipal ownership of the new subway. The vote was 132,647 to 42,916, and it was conducted on the very same Election Day when voters also gave their approval to the creation of the amalgamated City of New York.[19]
- The Rapid Transit Commission was not bound by the results of the 1894 referendum, however, and as late as the spring of 1899, a proposal was before the commission from the city's largest streetcar operator, the Metropolitan Street Railway, that might have resulted in the franchise being sold outright and the subway built with private capital, namely the Metropolitan's.
- On April 17, 1899, representatives of the Metropolitan withdrew their offer, and public construction—and ownership—of the proposed subway became the only option.[20]
- After reaching a final determination with respect to routes and engineering specifications, the Rapid Transit Commission issued on November 13, 1899, a formal call for bids for the construction of a municipally owned subway. Construction of New York's first subway was about to begin.[21]

If one identifies Hewitt's call for a municipally financed transit network on January 31, 1888, as the start of the process, it took New York eleven years and ten months to complete its deliberations and shift into an action mode by advertising for bids. Until the very end of this multiyear deliberation, it was generally assumed that New York's first north-south subway would be built primarily under Broadway, with a major junction in the vicinity of Union Square and separate East Side and West Side branch lines north of that point. When final specifications were completed and bids were sought, however, an alternative route had emerged—which will be described presently. Although more vigorous bidding was expected, only two New York companies, both skilled in heavy construction work, submitted formal bids on the contract.[22]

A firm headed by Andrew Onderdonk submitted a bid of $39.3 million, while the bid of a rival company headed by John B. McDonald came in lower at $35 million. Onderdonk's bid also included a provision to share annual subway profits in excess of $5 million with the city government, while McDonald's did not. The Rapid Transit Commission evaluated the two bids at a meeting on January 16, 1900, and voted that very day to accept Mc-Donald's offer.[23] A contract was signed with McDonald on February 24, and a groundbreaking ceremony was held to kick off the project on Saturday, March 24, 1900.

Shortly before noon on that day, municipal workers carefully removed a slab of pavement directly in front of City Hall to expose a patch of bare earth, and at exactly 1:48 P.M. Mayor Robert A. Van Wyck took hold of a ceremonial shovel with a silver blade and broke ground for the city's new underground railway. The assembled crowd broke into a wild and lusty cheer, and fireworks were set off from the tops of nearby buildings. Feeling it would be inappropriate to toss the dirt he had just dug onto the pavement of City Hall Plaza, the mayor put his own silk hat on the ground and used it as an impromptu container for the new subway's first excavated material.[24]

Initially, McDonald saw his role as solely that of subway builder, not subway operator, even though the contract on which he had successfully bid called for both constructing the new railway and operating it for a period of fifty years—with an option for an additional twenty-five years. "I am a contractor, not a railroad man, and I guess I had better stick to my business. The road will be leased, and it will be in good hands, but it is too early now to say anything about that," McDonald said.[25]

McDonald ran into some difficulties in having proper security bonds posted to cover his performance of the contract, and this led him to form a partnership of sorts with August Belmont, Jr., a man whose father was the chair of the commission appointed by Mayor Grant in 1890.[26] Together, McDonald and Belmont formed the Rapid Transit Subway Construction Company, and if McDonald himself had little interest in handling the operations of the new subway once it was built, Belmont was of an entirely different mind. In 1902 Belmont established the Interborough Rapid Transit Company, an entity that would take over from Rapid Transit Subway Construction once the line was built and would operate the new underground railway.

To underscore the degree to which August Belmont saw his involvement in New York rapid transit as a long-term venture, in 1902 the new Interborough acquired the assets of Manhattan Railways under the terms of a 999-year lease and was thus able to develop coordinated subway and elevated services, particularly in the northern reaches of the Bronx. Under Belmont, the electrification of the formerly steam-powered elevated lines was continued, and as a result the Interborough was able to use the elevated lines to test its new subway equipment and develop a degree of familiarity with electric railway operations even before the new subway ran its first train.[27] Following its lease to Belmont, Manhattan Railways was generally known as the Manhattan Division of the Interborough Rapid Transit Company, while the new underground system was called the Subway Division. (In later years, the Manhattan Division came to be called the Elevated Division.)

In cooperation with the Rapid Transit Commission, Belmont and McDonald assembled an extraordinarily talented team of technical experts to help design, build, and operate the new subway. Some decades later, President John F. Kennedy would address a group of Nobel laureates from the Western Hemisphere who had been invited to a Washington dinner. It was, the president said, "the most extraordinary collection of talent . . . that has ever been gathered together at the White House, with the possible exception of when Thomas Jefferson dined alone."[28] In a similar vein, while dedicated men and women continue to design and build new rapid-transit systems throughout the world today, they compare to Belmont's turn-of-the-century team in much the same way those Nobel laureates from the early 1960s stood in the shadow of Thomas Jefferson.

First mention must go to William Barclay Parsons, promoted to the position of chief engineer by the Rapid Transit Commission in 1894 with responsibility for all aspects of the overall construction project.[29] Then there was George Gibbs, a multitalented individual whose exceptional skills were brought to bear in the development of the Interborough's new rolling stock as well as its wayside signal system, while L. B. Stillwell was primarily responsible for ensuring that the subway's electrical networks were properly designed and built. E. P. Bryan, a man with an impressive railroad background who ensured that the new company's operating practices were safe and sound, was retained by Belmont as the first president of the Interborough, while Frank Hedley, the Interborough's first general superintendent and later to become its president, was a man whose passion for the company was without equal. There was also Belmont himself, of course, whose affiliations through his father with the House of Rothschild in Europe ensured that the enterprise was soundly financed, and while not a formal member of the Interborough team, Frank Sprague, then in the prime of his career, was ever willing to share his expertise by offering ideas and suggestions.

Given such talent, it is little wonder that when the Interborough opened for business in the fall of 1904, the new subway featured cutting-edge rapid-transit technologies that proved to be sound and workable but were in their very infancy and could in no sense be described as conventional. From the outset, the Interborough operated eight-car trains of electric-powered multiple-unit cars that were built out of steel. But consider how utterly novel, even revolutionary, such an arrangement was:

- The world's first all-steel passenger car was built in 1903, the year before the Interborough inaugurated service.
- Frank Sprague demonstrated the workability of multiple-unit control in Chicago in 1898, six years before the Interborough inaugurated service.[30]
- The world's first electrified underground transit line opened in London in 1890, fourteen years before the Interborough inaugurated service.
- The world's first successful electrification of a city streetcar service was in Richmond, Virginia, in 1888, eighteen years before the Interborough inaugurated service.

In the contemporary world of mass transportation, eighteen years is not an unreasonably long period of time for a new rapid-transit line to proceed from initial proposal to operational actuality. Eighteen years before the Interborough inaugurated service, most of the basic hardware it would later utilize had yet to be invented. There were underground railway lines that opened for service in the years before the Interborough's 1904 inaugural, namely London (1863), Budapest and Glasgow (1896), Boston (1897), Paris (1900), and Berlin (1902). But none of these systems incorporated the degree of forward-looking design and technology that the Interborough did, and all would be subject to fundamental upgrading of one sort or another in later years, as will be seen in subsequent chapters. True enough, the Interborough's 1904 line would also receive the benefit of later investment that improved its performance and expanded its capacity. But to a degree that is true for none of the pre-1904 subways, from the very outset the Interborough was a high-performance and high-capacity subway system, even when judged by the standards of a later era. It was, without any question, a generation or more ahead of its predecessors and contemporaries.

Even the decision to construct a four-track underground system that offered both local and express service was a bold advance of extraordinary proportion, as it not only provided for swifter travel into and out of the city's business districts but also produced a subway of much greater capacity than a more conventional two-track system. Contemporary New Yorkers have grown accustomed to the idea of four-track subways that offer both local and express service, and the very sound of an express train roaring past a local-only station has become one of the city's many distinctive auditory signatures. But the novelty this represented in 1904 can all too easily be overlooked. Consider, for instance, that of all the subway lines and systems that have been constructed in world cities since 1904, while there are frequent examples of four-track transfer stations and multiple lines that run together for short distances, there is but a single instance in all the world outside New York of a four-track subway line that features both local and express service. As we shall learn in Chapter 5, that subway operates under Broad Street in nearby Philadelphia.[31]

What remains an elusive piece of historical information, though, is how the idea of a four-track subway originated. Clearly the decision to specify four tracks was the product of consensus; it was incorporated into the final recommendations of the 1890 commission, it was discussed by Mayor Hewitt in his 1888 message to the Board of Aldermen, and more than likely it will never be possible to call any one individual the "inventor" of the four-track subway. But there was an important transit pioneer who examined the problem of transit capacity and performance at roughly the same time the 1890 commission was drafting its recommendations and who advanced technical reasons why any underground rapid-transit system New York might build should accommodate four tracks. Not surprisingly, that individual was Frank Sprague.

In early 1891, an extensive interview with Sprague was published in the *Street Railway Journal* on the general topic of underground rapid transit. While his reflections were not restricted to problems in New York City, in discussing north-south transportation on Manhattan Island Sprague made a strong case that any underground facilities the city would build should include four tracks for the provision of both express service and what Sprague referred to as "way service"—trains that would stop at more stations than the express trains and would later come to be called locals.

Sprague performed a series of calculations, based on measurements he had taken on the Manhattan elevated lines, of the extraordinary energy savings that would be possible if some proportion of the trains did not have to stop and restart at every station along the line. Sprague also advanced an interesting concept—which would not be adopted in the design of the original Interborough but would be realized in two instances when the municipally operated Independent Subway System was built in New York several decades later—that called for the express tunnels to proceed in a straight line from one express station to the other, while the tunnels used for "way service" followed a less direct course to tap important sources of patronage along the way.[32]

Sprague was self-effacing when discussing New York rapid-transit matters. Called upon to address the Electric Club in New York on February 26, 1891, he began by saying that for him "to talk of the Rapid Transit Situation in New York is like a young bachelor indulging in a description of the joys of matrimony."[33] But nothing ever stopped Sprague from promoting the benefits of electric-powered mass transit. "Motors by the tens of thousands are singing songs of victory," he told the 1891 meeting, and in the same interview in which he advocated both local and express service for any future New York Subway, he used much the same musical metaphor: "Electricity will unquestionably be the motive power. The hum of an electric motor is a song of emancipation."[34]

In any event, while the Interborough of 1904 was clearly the first instance of a subway line that featured both local and express service, it may also be the case that Frank Sprague is the person who, among his many other mass-transit innovations, initially advanced a technically detailed recommendation for such an option.

THE ROUTE OF THE 1904 SUBWAY

The 1904 subway would begin in Lower Manhattan at a loop terminal adjacent to City Hall and a single-track City Hall station that incorporated far grander and more elaborate design themes than any of the system's other stations.[35] The basic four-track alignment would begin nearby at an express station adjacent to the Manhattan end of the Brooklyn Bridge, where passengers could transfer to transbridge streetcars and elevated trains bound for points across the river in Brooklyn.[36] From Brooklyn Bridge the four-track line headed north, under thoroughfares that were then called New Elm Street, Lafayette Place, and Fourth Avenue, to a major express station at 42nd Street, adjacent to Grand Central Depot. Here the subway turned sharply to the west (in fact, the subway's station at Grand Central was on an east-west alignment under 42nd Street), tunneled across town to Times Square on the West Side, then resumed its northward trek under Broadway.

North of a major express station at 96th Street, the new subway would diverge into two separate northern branches. One would continue along Broadway—partly as a subway, partly as an elevated line, with some of it a two-track line, some of it a three-track—and terminate on the north side of the Harlem Ship Canal in the Bronx.[37] The other branch would swing eastward at 96th Street, tunnel under the northwest corner of Central Park, and proceed north through Harlem under Lenox Avenue as a two-track subway. North of 135th Street, this line would itself diverge, one short branch leading immediately into a terminal at 145th Street, the other tunneling under the Harlem River and emerging onto a three-track elevated line that continued into the central Bronx and a terminal in the West Farms section at 180th Street, adjacent to Bronx Park.

Thanks to the Interborough's long-term lease of Manhattan Railways, Belmont was able to build a connecting link to and from the combined right-of-way used by the Second Avenue and Third Avenue lines at a point where the new subway emerged from below ground just beyond the final underground station at 149th Street. Between this subway-el junction and 180th Street–Bronx Park, both subway and el trains served the new line. Indeed, el trains began using this structure almost six months before the link with the subway was ready for service.[38]

Along the subway's basic four-track main line between Brooklyn Bridge and 96th Street there were only four intermediate express stations: at 14th Street–Union Square, at 42nd Street–Grand Central, and at 72nd Street. In addition to these express stations, the new subway included sixteen local-only stations. Express platforms could accommodate eight-car trains, while local-only platforms were only long enough to handle five-car trains.

Light maintenance and storage facilities for subway rolling stock would be provided adjacent to both northern terminals in the Bronx, while the principal heavy maintenance base was along the banks of the Harlem River just beyond the terminal station at Lenox Avenue and 145th Street. (The terminal station was underground; the maintenance base was aboveground.) A small underground storage yard was incorporated in the tunnel just north of the subway station at Broadway and 137th Street.

With only minor exceptions, the four-track portion of the line between Brooklyn Bridge and 96th Street was built using a construction technique called "cut and cover." As the name suggests, a thoroughfare would be excavated ("cut"), the underground tunnel was built immediately below ground, and when work was completed, the street would be restored atop the tunnel ("cover"). On tangent track, the interior space provided for each of the four tracks was 12 feet, 6 inches wide, and 12 feet, 4 inches high, measured from the top of the rail.[39] While this construction technique may sound simple enough—dig a hole and build a linear structure—it was surely anything but. Before workers could open a surface excavation sufficient for the construction of a subway tunnel, gas mains, sewer lines, water pipes, and other subterranean utilities had to be identified, exhumed, and routed into temporary facilities. After the new subway was

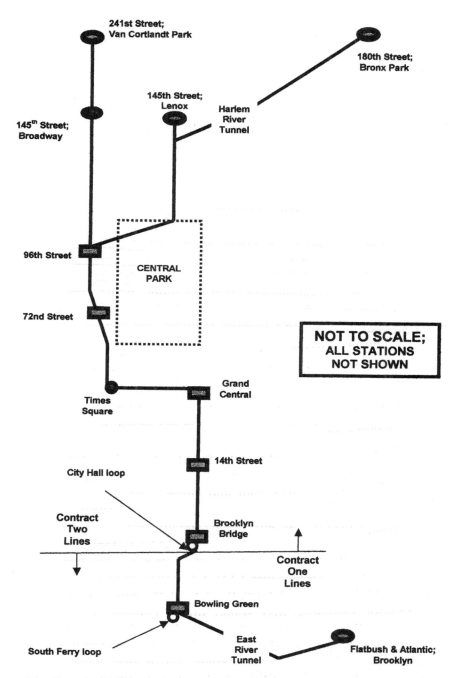

The Contract One and Contract Two subway and elevated lines of the Interborough Rapid Transit Company.

built, all these services had to be restored. Also tricky was ensuring the integrity of buildings and other structures adjacent to the route of the subway as well as taking special precautions at five locations where the subway had to tunnel under one of the city's elevated railways.[40] Nor was the underlying geology of Manhattan Island terribly conducive to underground construction. Engineers had to deal with everything from solid rock to quicksand as they laid out the new subway.

Under Broadway north of the junction at 96th Street, deep-bored tunnels were required for a portion of the subway's route, not cut-and-cover construction. Indeed, in the Washington Heights section of upper Manhattan, a station under Saint Nicholas Avenue at 191st Street measures 180 feet from street level to track bed and remains to this day the deepest station on the entire New York subway system. To tunnel beneath the Harlem River and into the Bronx on the subway's other northern branch, Parsons and his staff decided to assemble sections of prebuilt cast-iron tunnel aboard a barge, lower them into an excavation on the soft river bottom, then connect the underwater structure with subway tunnels on each bank of the river.

Progress in building the new line was steady, though. On the afternoon of March 14, 1903, a ceremony was held in a newly built section of tunnel adjacent to a station at 59th Street–Columbus Circle. Before an invited group of guests, contractor John McDonald handed a long-handled hammer to New York Mayor Seth Low and then removed a special silver-plated railroad spike from his pocket. "Mr. Mayor, this is the first spike to be driven for the tracks of this railroad," McDonald said.[41] The spike was then inserted in a predrilled hole in one of the crossties, and Mayor Low deftly wielded the hammer and drove the spike home. A new phase of subway construction—the laying of track—was under way.

The route the city's first subway followed, though, included a number of compromises that many believed were serious flaws. An important reason for this can be found in provisions of the enabling legislation under which the line was built. By law, the city was prohibited from borrowing in excess of $50 million for subway construction, and hence when a final plan was adopted, it was not as expansive as earlier discussions assumed it should be.

The southern limit of the new line would be adjacent to City Hall in Lower Manhattan, a terminal that failed to provide subway service to important centers of business and commerce between City Hall and South Ferry. Proceeding north and serving both Union Square and Grand Central was sensible enough, but when the route took a right-angled turn to the left into East 42nd Street and proceeded crosstown to Broadway before resuming its northward journey, the East Side areas north of 42nd Street that it failed to serve became all too obvious, and residents there were especially vocal in decrying the fact they were denied subway service, particularly since most subway proposals advanced during the 1890s included such an option.

People who lived in the more populous Upper West Side, which the new subway did serve, were also upset, though, because their journey downtown would not be a direct one and would require a detour, so to speak, as trains headed east across 42nd Street before continuing southward. In addition, before the subway opened in 1904, plans were announced by the Pennsylvania Railroad to construct a massive new Manhattan passenger terminal at Seventh Avenue and West 33rd Street, a section of the city the new subway conspicuously avoided. Consequently, even while construction of the new subway was under way, active proposals were being advanced to correct these shortcomings and expand the system.[42]

A southward spur under Broadway from Times Square to Union Square was regarded as a likely early addition to the new subway, as was a line into the Upper East Side north of 42nd Street, plus a southward extension beyond City Hall to South Ferry, with an even more dramatic continuation under the East River to Brooklyn, a borough of the newly amalgamated City of New York since 1898. The extension to South Ferry and Brooklyn in fact became the first expansion of the original subway, a section of the Interborough that is generally referred to as the Contract Two lines, with the original subway identified as the Contract One system.

Several interesting aspects of Contract Two have often been overlooked. One is the fact that when the Rapid Transit Commission sought bids for its construction in 1902, it was neither automatic nor obvious that Belmont's Interborough would be awarded the contract for its construction—and operation. Two companies submitted bids; Belmont's Interborough, expectedly enough, but also a streetcar and elevated railway operator from Brooklyn called the Brooklyn Rapid Transit Company (BRT).[43] While Belmont was able to offer through-service over the new Brooklyn extension from the Contract One lines and could charge a single five-cent fare for a trip from Brooklyn to the Bronx, the BRT proposal offered free transfers to and from almost all of its surface and elevated lines in Brooklyn, even though the BRT would not be able to offer continuing service over Interborough trackage.

The respective bids submitted by the two companies to build this Brooklyn extension were dramatically different. Belmont would later claim that the true out-of-pocket cost of building an East River tunnel to Brooklyn approached $10 million, and the $7 million bid submitted to the Rapid Transit Commission for the project by the BRT was not out of line with Belmont's later assertion. When the Interborough submitted its bid to build the Contract Two extension, though, it underbid the BRT by a massive $5 million. It proposed to build a two-track extension from the end of the original subway just beyond the Brooklyn Bridge Station southward under Broadway to South Ferry, including a tunnel beneath the East River to Brooklyn and through downtown Brooklyn to a terminal at Flatbush and Atlantic Avenues, for $2 million.

The Interborough also submitted an alternative bid of $3 million. Were it to be accepted, Belmont would not only build the extension to Brooklyn, he would also include the often-discussed spur down Broadway from Times Square south to Union Square. In reporting on these bids, the *Street Railway Journal* noted that since the true cost of building the Broadway spur alone would be in the range of $2.5 million, the Interborough's $3 million bid amounted to an offer to build the entire extension to South Ferry and Brooklyn for a mere $500,000.[44] Belmont, it seems safe to say, was determined to pay any price to maintain an Interborough monopoly on subway service in Manhattan. In his book *Tunneling to the Future,* Peter Derrick maintains that this "low bid, well below the actual cost of construction, reflected the [Interborough's] expectation that operation of this line would be extremely profitable."[45]

Attorneys for the Rapid Transit Commission advised against accepting the alternative bid, since it involved construction work that had not been solicited.[46] The Interborough's primary bid of $2 million for the Brooklyn extension was readily accepted, though, and a contract was executed in the fall of 1902. Ground was broken for the extension in front of the Chesebrough Building near Bowling Green on November 8, 1902, and serious construction began that very afternoon.[47]

As was common in the early electric railway industry, the Interborough Rapid Transit Company built its own powerhouse to generate the current that ran its trains. Commercial electric power first came to New York in the early 1880s, but the Interborough's anticipated demand would have overwhelmed turn-of-the-century electric suppliers. The company's facility was a large building with four tall smokestacks built along the Hudson River to allow easy delivery of coal by barge. It faced Eleventh Avenue and ran between 58th and 59th Streets. Designing and building this powerhouse was totally an Interborough responsibility; it was not part of the city's effort in building the underground railway itself.

Sanford White of the architectural firm McKim, Mead and White—designers of such notable New York landmarks as Penn Station—volunteered his services to the Interborough and assisted in perfecting a French Renaissance theme for the building's exterior. On the inside, the new facility was equipped with both reciprocating and turbine steam engines, and these generated 11,000 volts of triphase, 25-cycle alternating current that was then distributed to a series of eight substations strategically situated along the subway's route. At each substation, the high-voltage AC was stepped down and converted into direct current at a potential of 625 volts, then fed into a third rail adjacent to each track.[48]

The third rail itself was rolled from a special soft steel to ensure maximum conductivity. To protect its own workers—and anyone else who might wander along the subway's right-of-way—the Interborough adapted a wooden cover-board for its third rail that had been developed two years earlier by a suburban railway in Pennsylvania, the Wilkes-Barre and Hazelton. Trains make contact with the third rail by means of an insulated metal "shoe" that extends outward from each of a car's two trucks and slides along the top of the third rail—but under the cover-board. As was common on most electrified railways, the electrical circuit back to the powerhouse was completed through the regular running rails, which served as a ground.[49]

(The design of the Interborough's new generating station and electric distribution system was closely modeled on an earlier powerhouse the company acquired by virtue of its lease of Manhattan Railways in 1902. Steam-powered trains on the Manhattan els were converted to electric traction starting with the Second Avenue Line in December of 1901 and concluding with Ninth Avenue el in early 1903. Manhattan Railways built its powerhouse along the East River between 74th and 75th Streets.)[50]

The Interborough also installed an extensive system of automatic signals designed and built by the Union Switch and Signal Company—under the supervision of L. B. Stillwell—to ensure safe operation of the new subway. Perhaps no aspect of New York subway operations has been subject to more improvement and advancement over the years since 1904 than its signal operations, but from the very outset the Interborough "decided to install a complete automatic block signal system for the high-speed (i.e., express) routes, block protection for all obscure points on the low-speed (i.e., local) routes, and to operate all switches both for line movements and in yards by power from central points."[51] Automatic block signals include a trackside device that is raised when a signal displays a "stop" indication, and should a motorman pass such a signal, the raised device makes contact with a valve on the undercarriage of the lead car and automatically throws the train into an emergency stop.

Tables 1.1 and 1.2 identify the various elements of the Interborough's Contract One and Contract Two lines and indicate when revenue service began over each segment.

ROLLING STOCK FOR THE NEW SUBWAY

As William Barclay Parsons devoted his attention to building the right-of-way for the new railway—for both the Contract One and

TABLE 1.1
CONTRACT ONE

Date	Segment	Style	No. of Tracks	Length (miles)
10-27-04	City Hall Loop	subway	1	0.1
10-27-04	Main Line: Brooklyn Bridge to 96th Street & Broadway	subway	4	6.5
10-27-04	Main Line: 96th Street & Broadway to 145th Street	subway[a]	3	2.5
11-12-04	Main Line: 145th Street to 157th Street	subway	2	0.6
3-12-06	Main Line: 157th Street to Dyckman Street	subway[a]	2	2.1
3-12-06	Main Line: Dyckman Street to 215th Street	elevated	3	0.8
1-14-07	Main Line: 215th Street to 225th Street	elevated	3	0.4
8-1-08	Main Line: 225th Street to 242nd Street	elevated	3	1.2
11-23-04	Lenox Branch: 96th Street & Broadway to 145th Street & Lenox	subway	2	3.0
7-10-05	Lenox Branch: 135th Street & Lenox to Jackson Avenue	subway[a]	2	1.1
11-29-04[b]	Lenox Branch: 149th Street & 3rd Avenue to 180th Street-Bronx Park	elevated	3	3.2

a. Primarily subway construction, but short portion on elevated structure.
b. Date shown indicates start of elevated service by Manhattan Division, not subway service.

TABLE 1.2
CONTRACT TWO

Date	Segment	Style	No. of Tracks	Length (miles)
1-16-05	Main Line: Brooklyn Bridge to Fulton Street (Manhattan)	subway	2	0.3
6-12-05	Main Line: Fulton Street to Wall Street	subway	2	0.2
7-10-05	Main Line: Wall Street to South Ferry	subway	2[a]	0.5
1-9-08	Main Line: Bowling Green to Borough Hall (Brooklyn)	subway	2	1.6
5-1-08	Main Line: Borough Hall to Atlantic Avenue (Brooklyn)	subway	4	0.9

a. Single-track loop from Bowling Green to South Ferry.

the Contract Two segments of the effort—George Gibbs and L. B. Stillwell were equally hard at work developing a proper subway car to run on the new underground system. The Wason Manufacturing Company of Springfield, Massachusetts, delivered two pilot cars in the spring of 1902 that incorporated many features that would characterize Interborough subway cars for the next half-century. Unlike typical elevated cars of the era, which passengers boarded by way of open, porchlike platforms at either end, the two new cars featured enclosed end vestibules and full-length doors. Interior seating copied a design that was popular on Manhattan Railways, namely four sets of cross-seats on either side of the center aisle in the very middle of the car, but longitudinal seating along the sidewalls closer to the vestibules. The more commodious cross-seats would entice early-boarding passengers to move into the center of the car, while benchstyle seating closer to the vestibules accommodated larger numbers of standing passengers.

One of these pilot cars was called the *August Belmont,* the other the *John B. McDonald.*[52] Each was 1½ inches over 51 feet in length—4 feet longer than typical rolling stock used by Manhattan Railways—and ⅛ inch less than 9 feet wide, dimensions that can be expressed in rounded form as 51 feet long and 9 feet wide. Based on the two prototypes, the Interborough quickly placed orders for 500 reasonably similar production-model cars that have come to be called the Composites, a term whose meaning has often been misunderstood. Like the two pilot cars of 1902, the new cars were built with a strong steel underframe, while their car bodies were made of wood. But the "composite" feature of the new Interborough cars was not primarily a reference to this combination of wood and steel. It was based, rather, on the fact that layers of asbestos protected the wooden car bodies to render them less susceptible to fire. "The floors are double with asbestos roll felt sandwiched between, and the floor sheathing is of white pine completely covered on the underside with ¼-inch asbestos transit board," reported the *Street Railway Journal.*[53] The same publication also editorialized about the new subway cars, particularly praising the Interborough's efforts "to guard against accidents through fire, collision or derailment."[54]

Also contributing to the composite character of the new cars was the fact that a portion of their exterior was sheathed with thin copper plating, although in later years, inspectors from the New York Fire Department suggested that this plating was little more than a thick coat of metallic-like paint. When all is said and done, though, the unavoidable fact is that the Interborough's Composites were passenger cars whose bodies were built out of wood. The fleet included underbody truss rods, for instance, typical of other wooden railway cars of the era.

Of the 500 Composite cars that the Interborough ordered, 340 were motorized units and 160 were motorless trailers. Motorized cars each featured a pair of 200-horsepower electric motors, both mounted on one of the car's two trucks. After extensive testing and evaluation, L. B. Stillwell and his staff decided to split the order for motors between the country's two leading electrical suppliers, General Electric and Westinghouse.[55] Over the years, the Interborough would develop something of a penchant for converting motorized cars into trailers as well as installing motors in previously motorless units. Many motorized Composites were thus converted to trailer cars later in their careers.[56]

Because time was running short and the Interborough needed rolling stock quickly, the order for the Composites was split among four separate car-building firms: Wason, Jewett, John Stephenson, and the Saint Louis Car Company.[57] The first five cars—part of the Wason order—were delivered in August 1903, and since no subway facilities were yet available, they were sent to the 98th Street shops of the Manhattan Division's Third Avenue Line. (Shortly afterward, new subway rolling stock would primarily be housed at the 129th Street shops of the Manhattan Division and operate some limited revenue service over the Second Avenue Line, pending completion of the subway.) The Composites featured an interesting exterior color scheme. "The woodwork on the car body and the vestibules is painted a Tuscan red, the Pennsylvania Railroad standard having been adopted," reported the *Street Railway Journal*.[58] This basic Tuscan red was accented by orange trim around the window sash.

Despite the considerable pains that George Gibbs had taken in designing the Composites, these cars represented a decided compromise on what he would have preferred. Gibbs, who was also working with the Pennsylvania Railroad to develop a new generation of passenger cars for service through the Hudson River tunnels it was building, desperately wanted to specify a steel-bodied car for Interborough service. The simple fact of the matter, though, was that no car builder had ever turned out an all-steel passenger car before, and such firms were reluctant to risk the uncertainties that bidding on such an unusual order might entail when there was considerable money to be made turning out conventional wooden cars for the nation's railroads.

Alexander J. Cassatt, the president of the Pennsylvania Railroad from 1899 through 1906 and the man most identified with pressing forward the railroad's bold effort to tunnel beneath the Hudson River and terminate its New York–bound trains in midtown Manhattan, asked Gibbs to relay a message to August Belmont.[59] The Pennsylvania would be pleased to build a pilot-model all-steel subway car for the Interborough in its Altoona (Pennsylvania) shops—and would even do so at cost. Gibbs carried the message to Belmont, the offer was accepted, and in December 1903 a new subway car was delivered that would be carried on the Interborough's roster for over fifty years as No. 3342. Such an unassuming number, however, must not mask something very exceptional about this car. It was the world's very first all-steel passenger car.[60]

Because it was built largely with standard sizes and shapes of steel, No. 3342 was a bit on the heavy side, was less than striking in its appearance, and would spend its days on the Interborough in such nonrevenue service as carrying pay envelopes to the company's workers. Furthermore, not everyone in the Interborough hierarchy was impressed with No. 3342. Belmont held a meeting of his senior staff in January 1904, shortly after No. 3342 had been delivered, to discuss the matter of ordering production-model cars of a similar all-steel design. Many important Interborough people were dead set against the idea and preferred acquiring more Composite cars, Gibbs alone making the case for steel equipment. The wooden bodies of the Composites were felt to deaden sound much better than a largely steel car possibly could, and there was also concern that on an electrified railway a steel car could pose serious problems of a safety nature when high-voltage cables were routed under the floor mere inches away from unsuspecting passengers.

Belmont remained noncommittal and listened attentively to both sides of the issue. Finally, he turned to E. P. Bryan, who had remained silent during the debate, and sought his view. When Bryan said he agreed with Gibbs, that was enough for Belmont.[61] Gibbs went back to work and "perfected his plan, shaving off pounds by the use of pressed shapes and aluminum panels."[62] An order was then placed with American Car and Foundry (ACF) for a fleet of 300 steel subway cars, many of which were delivered in time for the inauguration of subway service in October 1904.[63]

A major structural difference between the Composites and the steel cars was this: while the basic strength of the Composite cars came from a rigid steel underframe on top of which the wooden car body was built, the strength of the steel cars was found in the way the frame and steelwork of the car body combined to form a single, unified structure. More important, though, never again would any wooden subway cars be acquired for service in New York. Even the 1903 Composite cars failed to live out their service life in the subway and were transferred to the elevated lines of the Manhattan Division in 1916. The Interborough's first all-steel subway cars would be popularly known as the "Gibbs Cars" for all of their days. (In Chapter 4 we shall discuss how the Long Island Rail Road inaugurated its own electrified service in 1905 with a fleet of virtually identical Gibbs Cars.)

In addition to the force of Gibbs's arguments, something else that may very well have helped influence Belmont on the question of steel subway cars was the fact that in August 1903, four months before No. 3342 was delivered to the Interborough, a terrible fire on the three-year-old subway in Paris, France, claimed eighty-four lives and demonstrated the peril that wooden cars represented in a belowground environment. We shall learn more about this disaster in Chapter 3.

OPENING DAY

The sun rose in New York at 6:22 A.M. on Thursday, October 27, 1904. It was a brisk but sunny day, the temperature at noon was a bracing 46 degrees, and the city attended to its usual and varied tasks. Steamships sailed in and out of New York Harbor that day, as they did every day, maintaining trade and commerce with foreign lands. Among arriving passenger liners was a Cunard vessel of 13,603 gross tons that docked along the Hudson River waterfront after a nine-day crossing from Liverpool. Eight years later, in 1912, the same RMS *Carpathia* would have a rendezvous with destiny when she rescued survivors from the *Titanic* disaster and returned them safely to New York.

The two lead stories in the *New York Times* on October 27, 1904, reflect the perennial concerns of news media: politics and foreign affairs. Secretary of State John Hay had been the feature speaker at a Republican rally held the previous evening in Carnegie Hall in support of President Theodore Roosevelt's campaign for reelection, while overseas, Great Britain was on the verge of dispatching a Royal Navy squadron from Gibraltar to the North Sea in response to contretemps there between the Russian Navy and an unarmed British fishing vessel.[64] In more mundane matters, the dry-goods store Smith, Gray and Company, at Broadway and West 31st Street, was running a special; it was offering a "new imported English top coat with gray velvet collar" for a mere twenty-eight dollars.[65]

Revenue subway service for the general public began in New York at 7:00 P.M. on October 27, 1904, and the entirety of the first day's receipts—$5,594.05, representing 111,881 nickel fares—was donated to a number of hospitals throughout the city. Earlier in the afternoon, the City of New York held a formal but restrained ceremony to commemorate the day in proper fashion.[66] Matters got under way in the City Council chambers in City Hall at 1:00 P.M., and an estimated crowd of 600 invitees was on hand. With Mayor George B. McClellan serving as master of ceremonies, an opening prayer was led by Bishop David H. Greer, the coadjutor bishop of the Episcopal Church in New York. Half a dozen individuals who had been involved in the subway's design and construction then offered remarks.

August Belmont spoke at some length and outlined financial developments that were vital to the subway's construction, while Alexander E. Orr, the president of the Rapid Transit Commission, paid tribute to key individuals who had seen the project through to completion. "As long as this subway is made to render service to the people of New York," Orr said, "the Chamber of Commerce, Abram S. Hewitt, John B. McDonald, August Belmont and William Barclay Parsons should be held in remembrance as household words."[67] Hewitt, sad to say, was not at the City Hall ceremony. While he lived to see construction of a municipally financed subway get under way in New York in 1900, the former mayor passed away in 1903.[68]

What was intended to be an hour-long ceremony ran considerably longer than planned, thanks in large measure to the extended nature of Belmont's presentation. And so when Mayor McClellan introduced John B. McDonald to say a few words, the hands on the clock were pointing to two o'clock, and guests in the Council chambers could hear the sounds of bells and sirens outside City Hall, which, by prearrangement, were celebrating the opening of the new subway, albeit prematurely. Eventually, a final benediction was given by Archbishop (and later Cardinal) John M. Farley, the leader of the Roman Catholic Archdiocese of New York, and at 2:19 P.M., guests began to leave City Hall, walk across the plaza, enter the ornate kiosk that protected the stairway down to the City Hall Station of the new subway, and board several inaugural trains.

The principal dignitaries rode on the very first train, of course, and Mayor McClellan himself accepted an offer to handle the controls of New York's first subway train. Although the Interborough had obviously operated earlier test trains over the new subway, the train that departed from the City Hall Station at thirty-five-and-a-half minutes after two o'clock on the afternoon of Thursday, October 27, 1904—with His Honor, the mayor, handling the controls—can rightly be regarded as the official inauguration of subway service in New York.

Not all of the mileage called for in the 1900 contract was ready for service on October 27, 1904, and so the inaugural train operated only from City Hall to 145th Street and Broadway. Still to be completed was a further northward extension of the line up Broadway and into the Bronx, as well as the Lenox Avenue branch which would lead into the central Bronx; service would be extended over these lines in subsequent weeks and months. By the end of 1905, the full order of 300 Gibbs Cars had been delivered by ACF to expand the Interborough fleet, and before the new subway celebrated its first anniversary, the first elements of the Contract Two extension had been phased into service. In July 1905 trains began operating beyond Brooklyn Bridge to South Ferry, where a turn-back loop similar to the one at City Hall had been built. On January 8, 1908, service was extended through the new Joralemon Street Tunnel under the East River to Brooklyn, and Interborough trains reached Flatbush and Atlantic Avenues, the site of the Long Island Rail Road's Brooklyn terminal, on May 1, 1908.

Extending subway service to Brooklyn meant that the Interborough needed even more subway cars. Consequently, in 1908 ACF began to deliver a small order of fifty units that incorporated several important improvements over the company's earlier rolling stock. All-steel construction was again specified, of course, but the passenger doors were wider (50 inches versus 39 inches) for easier and faster boarding and alighting of passengers. In addition, the new cars were designed to permit the later installation of a door in the middle of the car's side to facilitate passenger entry and exit even further. On the inside of the new cars, double sliding doors that separated the end vestibule from the interior on the earlier Gibbs Cars were eliminated entirely, but a sliding door was included across the very end of the car. In New York Subway argot, these end doors would eventually come to be called "storm doors." The earlier Gibbs Cars had no such feature, and as a result their vestibules were not totally weatherproof. Passenger compartments were comfortable enough thanks to the sliding doors at the back of the vestibules, but the vestibules themselves, particularly at midtrain positions, were quite drafty, and when trains left the confines of the subway and operated in the open air along elevated structures, vestibules were vulnerable to rain or snow swirling in through the open end of the car.

When a motorman established his operating position in the lead car of a train, a floor-to-ceiling door that otherwise protected the control station was swung across the end of the car and this, in conjunction with the sliding doors between the vestibule and the interior of the car, turned the vestibule into a full-width motorman's cab that was reasonably weatherproof—even without a true "storm door." On the fifty new ACF-built cars that were acquired for the Brooklyn extension, though, the motorman's cab utilized only the right side of the end vestibule, and this became the new Interborough standard.[69] Like the Gibbs Cars and the Composites before them, passenger entry doors on the new cars continued to be manually operated, and a separate conductor or guard had to be stationed at the point where cars were coupled to each other to operate the doors in the vestibules adjacent to his position manually with a lever-style handle. An eight-car express train, in other words, required a motorman at the front and seven guards to open and close the doors, while a five-car local train needed a motorman and four guards.

The fifty new cars acquired in 1908 to 1909 also featured a unique roof profile. In lieu of a standard "railroad roof," where a raised center section containing air vents called a monitor curves gently down into the end of the car, the newcomers featured what is generally known as a "deck roof," popular at the time in streetcar construction; on a deck-roof car the monitor ends abruptly and does not curve downward over the car's end vestibules. These fifty cars would be the only deck-roof rolling stock the Interborough ever ordered. Popularly known as the Gibbs deck-roof cars, they continued in daily service until the mid-1950s. To add another element of innovation that was brought to the Interborough by this relatively small order of fifty cars, they were thought to be the system's first rolling stock to forsake the older Tuscan-red color scheme and adopt a darker hue of Pullman green that would become the new Interborough standard.[70]

In 1906—with all of Contract One in operation, plus the Manhattan portion of Contract Two between Brooklyn Bridge and South Ferry—the Interborough carried 149,778,370 passengers. December proved to be the subway's busiest month that year, with 15,609,516 paying customers, and December 24 was the year's heaviest single day, when 605,246 passengers were transported. In contrast with December, August saw the lightest travel of 1906, when the passenger count was 8,555,795. Brooklyn Bridge was the busiest single station on the new system, followed, in order, by Grand Central, 14th Street, Times Square, and Fulton Street.[71]

With the completion of the Contract Two extension to Brooklyn in 1908, the Interborough had grown to a system of 24.7

miles in length. From Flatbush and Atlantic Avenues in Brooklyn to the northern limits of the system's two branch lines, only 6.7 miles—from Brooklyn Bridge to 96th Street—were of four-track configuration. The rest of the system featured either three tracks (7.4 miles) or two tracks (10.5 miles).[72]

Contract Three and Beyond

With the inauguration of subway service in New York in 1904, an important dynamic that would continually shape the Interborough Rapid Transit Company for the next quarter-century was the need for subway expansion—or "subway relief," to use a phrase popular in newspapers of the era. Major expansion would eventually come in the form of the Dual Subway Contracts of 1913, when the Interborough and the Brooklyn Rapid Transit Company (BRT) would be awarded rights to build equivalent and almost side-by-side trunk-line subways in Manhattan, with feeder branch lines tapping important residential sections of the city's outer boroughs.

Before the Dual Contracts finally settled matters, though, various proposals were put forward to expand the Interborough Subway. East Side service north of 42nd Street and a West Side spur down either Broadway or Seventh Avenue south of Times Square often seemed on the verge of construction in the years between 1904 and 1913. In 1904, Parsons advanced a recommendation to the Rapid Transit Commission that would have seen the Interborough's Brooklyn Line probe deeper into that borough and connect with one of the surface railways that operated to the oceanfront at Coney Island.[73] For a variety of reasons, though, no expansion of the Interborough would come to pass until the execution of the Dual Contracts.

The fact that additional subway lines were needed in New York was totally consistent with a clearly perceived performance characteristic—some might call it a liability—of the city's original subway. Namely, its trains were too crowded, its platforms were too congested, and passengers were getting in each other's way. Theodore P. Shonts, the Interborough's first president, summarized matters this way: "The passenger business in the New York subway increased so rapidly immediately after the road was placed in operation that there was considerable unpleasant conflict between passengers boarding and alighting from the cars."[74]

Short of building new lines to relieve such conditions, the Interborough explored more modest ways in which the 1904 line could be made to function more efficiently. Minor extensions to station platforms allowed slightly longer trains to be operated, and six-car locals and ten-car expresses became the new norm after 1910. Two options were also explored to speed the loading and unloading of trains at busy stations.

The Interborough favored adding a sliding center door to its cars, a technique that had earlier been used in New York by a cable railway operating across the Brooklyn Bridge to speed the loading of its trains at the busy Park Row terminal at the Manhattan end of the famous span and which the Interborough's fifty deck-roof cars of 1908 to 1909 were designed to allow. But an eminent transit consultant, a man by the name of Bion Arnold, whose work is most associated with mass transit in Chicago, had a different idea: Add an extra door at the end of each car immediately inboard of the original vestibule door, and designate the vestibule door for loading, the new door for unloading.

Regulatory control over New York Subway matters had shifted to a new state agency in 1907, the Public Service Commission (PSC), and under PSC direction the Interborough outfitted a test train with the style of extra doors that Arnold advocated. A carefully monitored twelve-day test was conducted in late February of 1909, and the results were quite clear. The test train with the extra doors required more time to make a trip over the line than a train with no extra doors.[75] This cleared the way for the Interborough's own concept of adding an extra center door to speed boarding and alighting, and starting in 1909, all new rolling stock the company purchased would include such center doors. For that matter the older fleet, including the Composites, was retrofitted with similar center doors. To compensate for any reduction in body strength that cutting a full-width center door might entail, Interborough subway cars were also equipped with supporting girders under the center doors, devices that the Interborough's engineer of car equipment, Norman Litchfield, referred to as "fish-belly" girders.[76] Whatever they were called, though, they helped create what would long be identified as the basic car profile of the Interborough Rapid Transit Company. Another change that the inclusion of center doors brought to the Interborough was the elimination of cross-seats in the center of a car. From the delivery of the Interborough's first center-door cars in 1909, only longitudinal seating would be available aboard Interborough trains.

The story of the negotiation and execution of what have come to be called the Dual Subway Contracts has been told often and involves a good deal of political and economic pulling and hauling.[77] There was an interim effort called the Triborough Subway System, on which some construction was actually begun, but all such work was eventually absorbed into the more comprehensive Dual Systems.[78]

From the perspective of the Interborough, the Dual Subway Contracts represented both a victory and a rebuke. August Belmont initially thought that the Interborough—*his* Interborough, so to speak—had earned the right to be awarded contracts for the construction of any and all subway lines the city might elect to build, particularly in Manhattan. But a new era had dawned in New York, a progressive climate that was not favorably disposed toward the kind of public-private partnership that was responsible for the construction of the original Interborough. Legislation had been enacted in Albany expressly prohibiting the long-term leases that the Interborough held under Contract One and Contract Two, for instance. The new state agency, the PSC, was established in 1907 with broad regulatory and oversight control over rapid-transit matters, and it was the PSC that assumed the lead role in the negotiation of the Dual Subway Contracts.[79]

In his book *722 Miles,* Clifton Hood characterizes the climate that produced the Contract One and Contract Two lines as one where the city's merchant class—he calls it a "mercantile elite"—exercised considerable sway in the development of public policy.[80] But, Hood argues, "the Interborough's opening changed the political landscape," and before New York could build any new or expanded subway lines, the role formerly played by the city's merchant class was taken over by a new generation of political leaders who were distrustful of, if not hostile toward, the earlier arrangements.[81]

Out of the Dual Contracts would emerge a massive subway system for New York that would be operated by two separate companies, Belmont's Interborough and the BRT. The negotiations leading up to the Dual Contracts were protracted and not at all free from acrimony. In the end what evolved, however, was the basic configuration of an Interborough Rapid Transit System that would later become the IRT Division of the New York City's Board of Transportation. Save for the eventual phaseout of the elevated lines that constituted the company's Manhattan Division and the periodic replacement of subway rolling stock, the Interborough would see little change of any fundamental sort once its Dual Contract lines were built and in service.

Continuing the numerical sequence that was begun in 1900, the Interborough's Dual Contract lines were built under the authority of Contract Three. (The new BRT subway system was Contract Four.) Unlike Contract One and Contract Two, where municipal capital alone was used to construct the subway, both Contract Three and Contract Four called for joint investment by the city and the respective transit systems. Under the terms of Contract Three, the Interborough would contribute $58 million, as would the city, but any cost escalation over these two contributions would be wholly a city responsibility.[82] As was the case with the original subway, the transit system had to supply rolling stock and other equipment, and despite the fact that the Interborough and the BRT were investment partners with the city in the construction of these new subway lines, once completed they would be owned by the city alone. And in a separate but parallel agreement, the Interborough would invest $25 million of its own resources to improve various elevated lines of its Manhattan Division. This primarily involved adding a third track to the Second Avenue, Third Avenue, and Ninth Avenue lines to permit one-way express service during rush hours, as well as a few modest elevated extensions in the Bronx. (With the exception of its joint operation over the Ninth Avenue el north of 53rd Street and a few short sections along its own route, the Sixth Avenue el would remain a two-track operation.)

Under the terms of Contract Three, the Interborough was reconfigured in a manner that addressed two critical shortcomings that were identified even before the original Contract One Subway opened in 1904. Instead of a single line that served the East Side below 42nd Street and the West Side above it, separate East Side and West Side trunk lines were established, and the connecting link across 42nd Street was converted into an unusual three-track shuttle service.[83]

Because a new BRT Manhattan Subway would be built under Broadway as part of the Dual Contracts, on the West Side the Interborough proceeded south from 42nd Street primarily under Seventh Avenue. When the four-track West Side Line reached Chambers Street, local and express tracks diverged. Local tracks continued southward under West Broadway and were linked into the same South Ferry loop that had been built as part of Contract Two. (An additional South Ferry loop interior to the original one was also constructed and used primarily by a shuttle service between there and Bowling Green on the Contract Two Line.) South of Chambers Street, West Side express trains followed a twisting two-track route through the heart of the downtown financial district under Park Place and William Street. West Side express trains then tunneled under the East River to Brooklyn, where they linked up with the Interborough's original line to Brooklyn.

The Dual Contracts also gave the Interborough a deeper incursion into Brooklyn beyond the 1908 terminal at Flatbush and Atlantic Avenues. A four-track subway continued south under Flatbush Avenue to the southern rim of Prospect Park.[84] It then turned east under Eastern Parkway and eventually emerged from belowground to become a typical three-track elevated line that continued to New Lots Avenue. A separate, two-track subway branched off this line at Franklin Avenue and continued south into Flatbush under Nostrand Avenue.

Looking to the north, the Interborough's East Side Line proceeded up Lexington Avenue from 42nd Street, although, unlike most other four-track subways in New York, this segment featured its two local tracks on an upper level and the two express tracks in a separate tunnel below. Linking the new Lexington Avenue Line with the older Contract One subway in the vicinity of Grand Central involved some intricate engineering work, including the first use in New York of rotary boring machines to drill the connecting tunnels. A new subway station at Grand Central was also an engineering challenge and was eventually built deep belowground on a diagonal alignment under 42nd Street, where the subway shifted its right-of-way from the Contract One route under Park Avenue south of 42nd Street to the new Contract Three Lexington Avenue Tunnel north of there. (In various PSC working papers, this facility was often referred to as the "diagonal station.") Between the time the Contract One Subway reached Grand Central Depot in 1904 and when work began on the Dual Contracts in the years after 1913, the New York Central and Hudson River Railroad had replaced its older New York station with the magnificent new Grand Central Terminal. We shall learn more about the New York Central—and Grand Central—in Chapter 4.

Once the Lexington Avenue Line crossed under the Harlem River and reached the Bronx, it branched into three separate elevated feeder lines. Following a pattern that was earlier used for the elevated sections of Contract One, these new elevated elements were of three-track configuration. Two outside tracks were used for conventional service, while the interior center track could be used for peak-hour express service in a single direction. Two of the elevated branch lines in the Bronx that were connected to the Lexington Avenue Line—Woodlawn-Jerome and Pelham Bay—were newly constructed at the time of the Dual Contracts, while the third was an extension of the same central Bronx elevated route that had been built under Contract One. The extension branched off the original line just before the terminal at 180th Street–Bronx Park and proceeded north over White Plains Road to a new terminal at 241st Street just below the Westchester County line. Indeed this terminal was—and is likely forever to remain—the northernmost station on the entire New York City Subway system.

In order for trains from the new Lexington Avenue Line to switch onto this older central Bronx branch line, a wonderfully complicated underground junction was built where the two lines intersect. The new Lexington Avenue Line runs north-south under Grand Concourse at this point, while the older Contract One Line runs east-west under 149th Street but at a deeper level than the newer line. The junction is fully grade separated but involves a set of twisting tunnels that bear some resemblance to a typical "cloverleaf" entrance to a limited-access highway; trains must navigate this trackage at dead slow speed.

In addition to feeding subway trains into the Interborough's two Manhattan trunk-line subways—the East Side Lexington Avenue Line and the West Side Broadway–Seventh Avenue Line— the new Bronx feeder routes were also linked to the Interborough's Manhattan Division elevated lines. The Third Avenue el was extended northward through the Bronx over Webster Avenue and a connection with the White Plains Road Line at Gun Hill Road, while the jointly operated Ninth and Sixth Avenue els were extended beyond their original northern terminal adjacent to the Polo Grounds at 155th Street in northern Manhattan across the Harlem River and to a junction with the Jerome Avenue Line just below 167th Street.[85] As mentioned above, a connection at 149th Street and Third Avenue allowed el trains of both the Second Avenue and the Third Avenue lines to use the central Bronx elevated feeder line that was built as part of the Contract One network.

Something that became standard on most four-track Dual Contract subway lines was construction of all four tracks immediately below the street in areas where local-only stations were built; ticket booths and prepayment areas for such stations were typically at platform level, and internal access was rarely possible between uptown and downtown platforms. A different design was used for express stations, though. In order to permit easy transfer between uptown and downtown services, a mezzanine was included between the street and the platforms, and fare collection took place here. Tracks and platforms had to be built at a slightly lower level to allow room for the mezzanine, though, and such a design permitted uptown local and express services to use one platform, downtown trains another. To this day express stations on the Contract One and Contract Two lines such as 72nd Street in Manhattan and Nevins Street in Brooklyn remain immediately below street level and include awkward fare collection arrangements.

When Interborough engineers attempted to use the newly adopted design standard for an express station at 34th Street on the West Side Line, there was a problem; namely, the new terminal built by the Pennsylvania Railroad between 31st Street and

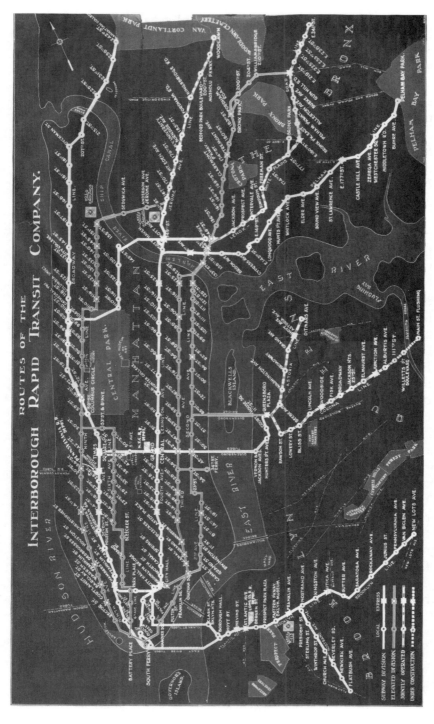

Traditional passenger map developed by the Interborough Rapid Transit Company.

33rd Street precluded the subway from being built at a level that would permit the inclusion of a mezzanine. The answer was a unique express station built immediately below the street with separate outside platforms for the two local services and a common center platform for the two express services that passengers could reach via walkways carefully built around and through the Pennsy facility. (Some years later, the Independent Subway System was forced to use similar construction when a station for its Eighth Avenue Line was built adjacent to Penn Station.)

Tunnel dimensions used for new Interborough Subway construction under the Dual Contracts differed slightly from those of Contract One and Contract Two. Where the original subway featured tunnels that were 12½ feet wide, the company's Dual Contract tunnels were typically a full foot wider. The width of Interborough rolling stock remained the same, though, and station platforms on the company's Dual Contract lines were positioned at the same distance from the track as were those on the original subway. Dual Contract lines designed for the rival BRT, on the other hand, followed more generous dimensions, and the BRT was able to acquire a fleet of subway cars that were wider than those used on the Interborough. This disparity remains a defining characteristic of the New York subways to this day—and likely always will.

More Rolling Stock

With respect to rolling stock, it has often been suggested that the basic Interborough Subway car saw little change or improvement from the time the first all-steel Gibbs Cars were delivered in 1904 until 1938. Such a perspective is quite understandable, particularly from the point of view of subway passengers, who had an opportunity after 1915 to contrast Interborough equipment with rolling stock designed by the rival BRT. Interborough equipment continued to feature passenger entry and exit via end vestibules, although center doors were added to speed passenger flow. New BRT Subway cars, by contrast, were built without end vestibules at all, and as a result they struck many New Yorkers as far more modern.

Once aboard an Interborough train, passengers sat on longitudinal seats along the car sides, and if an Interborough Subway rider wished to confirm what service a train was operating—and where it was headed—such information was displayed on old-fashioned line and destination signs that were made out of metal, not the more modern curtain-roll signs that the BRT featured.[86] (As an Interborough train approached its destination, it was common practice for guards and conductors to walk through the train noisily removing signs for the destination about to be achieved and replacing them with signs for the opposite terminal to which the train would soon be returning. Unused line and destination signs were kept in a small box immediately below the brackets on which active signs were displayed.)

After the PSC assumed regulatory control over city subway services in 1907, it held a public hearing in early 1909 to address the "lack of adequate signs in the New York subway trains."[87] Frank Hedley testified and announced that over the next three months the company would improve its practice of having line and destination signs displayed only at the "corners of alternate cars" by adopting a new policy that would place such signs in the diagonal corners of each and every car. Hedley also noted that Interborough trains displayed distinctive codes on the head end by the use of four-color marker lights mounted at roof level that identified what service a train was operating and what its destination was. Hedley was forced to concede, though, that "only employees are furnished with cards explaining the markers."[88] (See Table 1C in the Appendix for a list of marker-light codes from a somewhat later era.)

One creative form of passenger communication that the Interborough did pioneer was a series of signs in the form of a pseudo-newspaper designed for transit riders and called the *Subway Sun*. The first *Subway Sun* was posted aboard Interborough trains on July 22, 1918, and in subsequent years and decades it would become a popular and entertaining diversion that subway riders enjoyed.[89]

Another design feature of Interborough rolling stock that did little to generate a sense that the company's technology was state of the art was the use of a system of manual bells actuated by pulling on a length-of-the-car rope that guards and conductors used to pass signals to the motorman, rather than any kind of electric-powered device—such as the BRT used. And if one were to give the head end or the tail end of an Interborough train a careful examination, one would see that floor-level signal lamps continued to feature kerosene lanterns, not electric lights—such as the BRT used.

All of these appearances, though, were profoundly misleading. Under the leadership of Frank Hedley, who was general superintendent of the Interborough on October 27, 1904, and served as president from 1919 through 1934, the company could never be called one that took pains to cultivate an image of being passenger-friendly. What Hedley and the Interborough did do, however, was to pay strict and steady attention to running a sound and dependable urban railway. Even as its rolling stock continued to reflect many of the visible specifications that were initially developed by George Gibbs in 1904, in such critical areas as propulsion and braking systems, as well as the installation of automatic devices for opening and closing a train's doors, the Interborough was continually testing, advancing, and adopting new concepts. Hedley himself is widely recognized as the inventor of an important device called an anti-climber, a knuckled piece of wraparound steel attached to the end of a subway car that prevented one car from riding up over another in the event of a rear-end collision, and he was also instrumental in developing an automatic system so all the doors on a ten-car train could be opened and closed by one person, although the state PSC required that at least two conductors be assigned to each ten-car train. With the onset of the multiple-unit door control, or MUDC, an improved operating station was established for conductors and guards. Instead of working at floor level, conductors were able to mount small steel pedestals and gain an improved view of boarding and alighting passengers up and down the station platform.

When the Interborough converted most of its rolling stock to MUDC, an additional safety feature Hedley incorporated was a set of contacts inside the rubber edge of all doors that automatically reopened a closing door if a passenger were to interrupt its closing. Some Interborough passengers expressed misgivings about remotely controlled doors and voiced concerns that closing car doors might trap elderly and disabled travelers. Hedley pointed out that the door-reversing devices were sensitive enough to reopen if they merely brushed against someone's nose—and he quickly volunteered his own nose and demonstrated the claim.[90] After the Second World War, when New Yorkers became more accustomed to automatic doors on their subway trains, these door-reversing devices were removed, as they were contributing to excessive delays at busy stations.[91]

One basic change—in technology as well as nomenclature—that can be used to distinguish Interborough cars acquired before, roughly, 1915 from those acquired afterward is the use of low-voltage battery current to operate a train's multiple-unit control apparatus on later equipment. Prior to 1915, high-voltage traction power was used for such purposes, and cars so rigged are generally referred to as high-voltage cars, or Hi-Vs, while newer rolling stock, with low-voltage control circuits, are known as Lo-Vs. Not surprisingly, Hi-V and Lo-V cars could not operate in the same train.[92]

The Interborough fleet also featured bewildering variety in the way of motorized units, unpowered trailers, cars equipped with one cab, two cabs, or no cabs at all, and a seemingly incurable tendency on the company's part to convert cars from one configuration to another.[93] From the perspective of an Interborough passenger, subway cars acquired in 1925 may have looked very similar to cars that had been in service since 1904. Most assuredly, however, they were not, and if one category of Interborough employees could be called on to offer "expert testimony" on the subject, it would be the various drill motormen whose job it was to couple cars together into trains in the yards and who had to know and respect the incompatible features of the various classes of rolling stock.

INTERBOROUGH SERVICE

After the completion of its Contract Three network—the Interborough inaugurated service over its Dual Contract lines as they were completed between 1915 and 1928—a stable pattern of operations developed that would characterize Interborough trunk-line subway services well into the era of municipal ownership and through the Second World War. West Side operations were identified under one of two service names. Trains that continued north of 96th Street on the Broadway Line were identified as the Broadway–Seventh Avenue service, while trains that branched off at 96th Street and operated via Lenox Avenue were called the Seventh Avenue service. The Seventh Avenue Line and the Broadway–Seventh Avenue Line both offered local and express service.

The Seventh Avenue express used 180th Street–Bronx Park, one of the limits of the Contract One system, as its northern terminal, and Flatbush Avenue, Brooklyn, as its southern terminal, while the Broadway–Seventh Avenue express operated out of 241st Street–Van Cortland Park in the north, and New Lots Avenue, Brooklyn, in the south. (On Sundays, Interborough schedules often called for these two West Side express services to swap their southern terminals.) All West Side locals used the South Ferry loop as their southern terminal; the Broadway–Seventh Avenue local operated to 137th Street in the north, while the Seventh Avenue local terminated at 145th Street and Lenox Avenue.

On the three Bronx branch routes served by Lexington Avenue trains, the Pelham Line was the province of Lexington Avenue locals, which terminated in the south at the original City Hall loop. During rush hours, alternate trains operated an express service on the three-track elevated portions of the Pelham Line and carried a seemingly contradictory message on their metal-plate line and destination signs:

LEXINGTON AVE. LOCAL
EXPRESS
PELHAM BAY PARK

The southern terminal for Lexington Avenue express service was in Brooklyn—Atlantic Avenue during midday, Utica Avenue at most other times. (South Ferry was also available as an alternative southern terminal for the Lexington Avenue express.) On the northern end, alternate Lexington Avenue express trains used the Jerome Avenue branch and terminated at Woodlawn-Jerome, while the other terminal was 241st Street and White Plains Road. In addition to these various mainline services, shuttles were operated between Grand Central and Times Square as well as between Bowling Green and South Ferry.

Equipment assignments on the Interborough varied from year to year, but as a general rule, once the last of the cars needed for Dual Contract service were delivered in 1925, the system's older Hi-V cars were used on various local services, while newer Lo-Vs were retained for express service. One general exception to this rule was the Broadway–Seventh Avenue Line, which tended to be the sole express service where Hi-Vs predominated.

An interesting car assignment practice permitted older Hi-V rolling stock that was never equipped with MUDC to operate in trains that were so equipped. It worked like this: The first and last units of a ten-car train would not have MUDC, although the other eight would. Two conductors would be assigned to such trains, the same compliment required on ten-car trains that featured all-MUDC cars. One conductor was stationed between the first and second car, the other between the ninth and tenth. All doors on cars two through nine were remotely controlled by MUDC, each conductor being responsible for his half of the train. In addition, each conductor would open and close the vestibule door on the non-MUDC car adjacent to his operating station with a hand lever, while a separate remote-control button that was independent of the MUDC system operated the center door in these cars. In keeping with standard IRT practice, the side doors leading to the front and rear vestibules of a train were not used at all, and thus older Hi-V cars that were not rigged for MUDC were able to operate in trains that were, and into the mid-1950s one could get some sense of what subway service must have been like on the Interborough in the days when conductors and guards opened and closed all the doors on a train by muscle power alone, not by pushing buttons. Because none of the deck-roof Hi-V cars from 1908 to 1909 were ever equipped with MUDC, many of them continued to hold down important assignments as lead cars on the Broadway–Seventh Avenue Express for virtually their entire service life.

(Hedley and the Interborough also outfitted many el cars used on the company's Manhattan Division with MUDC. Because these cars were originally built with open end platforms, the con-

version included building an enclosure around the open platforms and converting them essentially into closed vestibules.)

THE STEINWAY TUNNELS—AND STEINWAY CARS

There was one very different element that was added to the Interborough at the time of the Dual Contracts and that has not been
discussed so far. It involves a very different kind of subway
route—and it was served by slightly different kinds of Interborough Subway cars.

In 1907, a group of investors completed work on a pair of
tunnels under the East River between Long Island City and midtown Manhattan, through which they planned to run trolley cars
from various neighborhoods in Queens. The project had a long
and complicated history; work was actually begun in 1892, and
at one time Long Island City piano manufacturer William Steinway was the project's principal investor. (Steinway had also
chaired New York City's Rapid Transit Commission of 1891.)
Work on the tunnel was halted shortly after it began, though, and
the project remained inactive until 1902, when August Belmont
and the Interborough Rapid Transit Company took title to the
unfinished works, soon afterward acquired an electric street railway in Queens, and completed the East River tunnels. A fleet of
fifty new, steel-bodied trolley cars that could be operated in
multicar trains was acquired for tunnel service—ten from Brill,
forty from American Car and Foundry—and in 1907, ceremonial
trips were made through the newly completed tubes that were
still popularly known as the Steinway Tunnels. For a number of
complicated legal reasons, revenue service was never inaugurated, and the tunnels remained unused for another span of
years.[94]

During the negotiation of the Dual Contracts, these East River
tunnels were recognized as a valuable rapid-transit resource; they
were acquired by the city and identified as part of the expanded
Interborough Subway network. At the Queens end of the tunnels,
a pair of new elevated lines would be built into growing residential communities, one to Astoria and another to Jackson Heights,
Elmhurst, and eventually Flushing. On the Manhattan end, this

new Interborough Line from Queens crossed midtown Manhattan and terminated at Seventh Avenue and 41st Street, adjacent to Times Square, but with no physical track connections to either of the company's north-south Manhattan trunk lines.

A roundabout connection was established, though, between these new Queens routes and the rest of the Interborough system. A branch of the Manhattan Division's Second Avenue Line was extended across the Queensboro Bridge, and passengers using the two new Interborough routes in Queens were able to reach Manhattan by subway trains operating through the Steinway Tunnels as well as by elevated trains using the Queensboro Bridge and the Second Avenue el. In fact, passengers along these two new lines in Queens enjoyed a third option, since alone among all Dual Contract projects, the Queens lines were jointly operated by the Interborough and the BRT, with each company operating its own trains over both lines. At a massive elevated transfer station at the Queens end of the Queensboro Bridge, the Astoria Line and the Corona/Flushing Line came together, as did three connections from Manhattan: Interborough Subway trains operating via the Steinway Tunnels, Interborough elevated trains operating via the Queensboro Bridge, and BRT Subway trains operating via a new 60th Street tunnel that had been built under the terms of the Dual Contracts.[95]

Because the Steinway Tunnels under the East River featured grades as steep as 4.5 percent—much steeper than the rest of the Interborough system—subway cars assigned to Queens service, while otherwise similar to the rest of the company's fleet, had to be equipped with a different gear arrangement, and efforts were made to make them as light in weight as possible. As a result they could not operate in multiple units with the company's more conventional cars, and rolling stock so rigged came to be called Steinway cars—Steinway cars to run through the Steinway Tunnels. They could be readily identified by a red line that was included underneath their exterior car numbers. In addition, Steinway cars used in Queens service were all motorized units, another concession to the steep grades in tunnels that were originally intended to be the domain of trolley cars. (One other distinctive feature of the Interborough's Steinway cars was a slightly different style of metal-plate signs for train identification that included arrows pointing in the direction of travel.)

DUAL CONTRACT SUMMARY

Table 1.3 identifies the various route segments that were added to the Interborough Rapid Transit Company's system under the terms of the Dual Subway Contracts of 1913.

TABLE 1.3
INTERBOROUGH RAPID TRANSIT COMPANY DUAL CONTRACT SEGMENTS

Segment	Style	No. of Tracks	Length (miles)
West Side Lines			
Times Square to Chambers Street	subway	4	3.0
Chambers Street to South Ferry[a]	subway	2	1.09
Chambers Street to Borough Hall (Brooklyn)	subway	2	2.3
East Side Lines			
Grand Central to 125th Street	subway	4	4.19
125th Street to Pelham Bay Park[b]	elevated	3	7.73
125th Street to Woodlawn-Jerome[b]	elevated	3	6.62
177th Street to 241st Street	elevated	3	4.97
Brooklyn Lines			
Atlantic Avenue to Utica Avenue	subway	4	2.83
Utica Avenue to New Lots Avenue[b,c]	elevated	2	2.90
Franklin Avenue to Flatbush Avenue[d]	subway	2	3.0
Queens Lines			
Times Square to Hunters Point Avenue (Queens)	subway	2	2.4
Hunters Point Avenue to Queensboro Plaza	elevated	2	0.9
Queensboro Plaza to Main Street–Flushing	elevated	3	6.2
Queensboro Plaza to Astoria	elevated	3	2.5

    a. Between Cortlandt Street and South Ferry this line could be regarded as a single-track loop, not a two-track subway. Station at South Ferry was originally built as part of Contract Two (see text).
    b. Initial station of this segment located in a subway tunnel, although line is principally built on an elevated structure.
    c. Elevated structure designed and built to accommodate three tracks, although only two were ever installed.
    d. Line begins at a junction slightly to the east of Franklin Avenue station.

Table 1.4 identifies the principal subway services operated by the Interborough once the company's full Dual Contract network was in operation.

THE END OF THE INTERBOROUGH

A delicately balanced fiscal compromise at the heart of the Dual Contracts—joint capital investment by the city and the two transit systems, with fare-box income expected to generate a sinking fund to service all debts—came completely apart in the years following the First World War. The two decades that followed the 1918 Armistice saw a gradual realization in New York that something radically different was needed for city mass transit. If any one factor can be cited as being the principal contributor to the collapse of the Dual Contracts, it was the unanticipated scourge of inflation that swept the world after the First World War. And if inflation was the culprit, a further factor that exacerbated its effect was a requirement in the Dual Contracts that stipulated a five-cent subway fare for the forty-nine-year life of the agreements. Operating expenses—salaries, equipment, fuel— reflected this inflationary spiral and continued to rise year after year. But the Interborough—and the BRT as well—experienced no parallel increase in passenger revenue to offset such cost escalation, because the subway fare remained fixed at a nickel.

Raising transit fares is never popular—in New York or anywhere else. But in few places other than New York did retaining the "nickel fare" become quite so dramatic and volatile a political issue. The era between the two world wars would be characterized by such interesting and varied developments as Prohibition, the emergence of Murder Incorporated, the crash of the New York Stock Exchange, Charles Lindbergh's flight to Paris, and Babe Ruth's sixty home runs. Still, it can surely be said that no local political issue generated quite so much fire and bluster in New York during this same colorful period as did the matter of preserving the nickel fare on the city's subways, elevated trains, and street cars.[96]

Renegotiation of the Dual Subway Contracts to give the Interborough and the BRT some relief by way of a fare increase was

TABLE 1.4

INTERBOROUGH RAPID TRANSIT COMPANY BASIC SERVICE PATTERNS:
SUBWAY DIVISION

Service	Northern Terminal	Southern Terminal
Broadway–Seventh Avenue Express[a]	241st Street–Van Cortlandt Park	New Lots Avenue–Brooklyn
Broadway–Seventh Avenue Local	137th Street–Broadway	South Ferry
Seventh Avenue Express[a]	180th Street–Bronx Park	Flatbush Avenue–Brooklyn
Seventh Avenue Local	145th Street–Lenox	South Ferry
Lexington Avenue Express[b]	Woodlawn–Jerome Avenue	Atlantic Avenue–Brooklyn or Utica Avenue–Brooklyn
Lexington Avenue Express	242nd Street–White Plains Road	Atlantic Avenue–Brooklyn or Utica Avenue–Brooklyn
Lexington Avenue Local[c]	Pelham Bay Park	City Hall
Flushing Local	Times Square	Main Street–Flushing
Flushing Express[d]	Times Square	Main Street–Flushing
Astoria Local	Times Square	Astoria
Shuttle	Times Square	Grand Central
Shuttle	Bowling Green	South Ferry

Only basic Interborough services are shown. Additional variations were often operated at various times of day. See Table 1C in the Appendix for a more comprehensive list of such variations.

a. On Sunday, Broadway–Seventh Avenue Express and Seventh Avenue Express "swapped" southern terminals.

b. At certain hours, Lexington Avenue Express trains from Woodlawn-Jerome used South Ferry as southern terminal.

c. During peak hours, alternate trains operated express over three-track Pelham Line in direction of dominant travel and used Pelham Bay Park as northern terminal. During such hours, conventional local service used 177th Street as northern terminal.

d. Peak-hour service over three-track line in direction of dominant travel.

something the city's political establishment was totally unwilling to entertain, and yet the longer the two companies were forced to retain the nickel fare, the worse their economic outlook became. The BRT entered receivership at the end of 1918 and, following reorganization in 1923, emerged as the Brooklyn-Manhattan Transit Corporation (BMT).[97] Subway travel was vital to the economic health of the city and more subway lines were desperately needed. Yet the economic condition of the city's two subway providers was deteriorating rather alarmingly. A series of factors eventually combined to address the question of subway stability in New York.

In 1932, the first elements of a new, municipally owned and operated subway system carried its first passengers in New York. Known as the Independent Subway System, or the IND, it was built to the same general specifications as the older BMT.[98] Building the IND was only the first step, though, in solving the problems, fiscal and otherwise, of the BMT and the Interborough. The second step was the unification of the city's three separate subway systems—the new IND, the BMT, and the Interborough. Given the perilous financial position in which both the BMT and the Interborough found themselves, unification could be achieved only by the City of New York's acquiring the assets of the two private companies and converting their operations into public-sector responsibilities. This would happen during the month of June in the year 1940, as a new world war was raging in Europe across the North Atlantic. Before we discuss the unification of 1940 in greater detail, though, a brief look at one of the Interborough's final achievements as a private company is in order.

NEW CARS FOR THE WORLD'S FAIR

The basic external dimensions—51 feet long and 9 feet wide— and the general physical appearance that were pioneered when the Interborough opened in 1904 continued to define IRT rolling stock through the 1930s. With the advent of the New York World's Fair in 1939 and 1940—the site of which, in Flushing Meadows, was adjacent to a station on the Interborough's Flushing Line—the company ordered a small fleet of fifty new cars that were unique in a number of ways: They were the last cars to be designed and built for the Interborough Rapid Transit Company before municipal acquisition of the company in 1940 and they were the only Interborough-built subway cars to stray from the traditional company profile.

These "World's Fair cars," as they have been called, were hardly cutting edge in their design or technology. They did feature illuminated roll signs at the head end, but line and destination signs inside the cars used the same metal plates as did earlier Interborough equipment. The new cars did not include end vestibules, though, and in this they were indeed different from older Interborough equipment. But mechanically, the new cars were identical with older Steinway-type cars and would operate in trains with them.[99]

Some would say it was unfortunate that the final series of Interborough-designed cars made so halfhearted an effort at upgrading the company's basic rolling stock specifications. Better to have retained the company's classic look for these final fifty cars and wait for a new day when adequate resources were available for a proper upgrade. In any event, when the Saint Louis Car Company delivered car No. 5702 to the Interborough Rapid Transit Company in 1938, it was the very last time that the company created by August Belmont, Jr., in 1902 would ever take title to a new subway car. From the experimental cars *August Belmont* and *John B. McDonald* of 1902 through the Composites, the Gibbs Cars, and all the Hi-Vs and Lo-Vs that followed, a wonderful urban-transit heritage would develop. As No. 5702 entered Flushing Line service on the eve of the Second World War, though, the Interborough Rapid Transit Company itself was a mere two years away from surrendering its corporate identity and becoming a division—the IRT Division—of the Board of Transportation of the City of New York.

JUNE 1940

In 1932 the Interborough had entered receivership; shortly afterward Frank Hedley, then a robust seventy years of age, stepped down as the company's president, and day-to-day control of the railway was assumed by a court-appointed receiver, Thomas E. Murray, Jr. Murray was wise enough to retain Hedley as a paid consultant,[100] but it was Murray who represented the Interborough during the protracted negotiations that led to municipal acquisition in June 1940.

At two o'clock in the afternoon on June 12, 1940, contracts were signed in City Hall—at the same hour and in the same building where, thirty-six years earlier, Mayor George B. Mc-Clellan had presided at a ceremony to mark the inauguration of subway service in the city. Mayor Fiorello H. LaGuardia was handed the Interborough's copies of Contracts One, Two, and Three, and for a consideration of $146,173,855.18, the City of New York took title to the entirety of the company's mass-transit assets, including what remained of the elevated lines. The mayor characterized the three contracts as "footballs"—footballs that had been kicked around by several generations of New York politicians.[101] When Van Merle-Smith, representing a bondholders' committee of Manhattan Railways, handed the mayor the deed to the elevated properties, he said: "We are occupied with an occasion representing civic improvement against a background of Europe clouded with civic destruction."[102]

According to the agreement signed in City Hall on June 12, the handover would formally happen at 11:59 P.M. that very evening, when the Interborough Rapid Transit Company became the IRT Division of the city's Board of Transportation. In addition, 15,500 company employees were converted to municipal workers with civil service standing. A similar ceremony had been held to mark the city's acquisition of the BMT two weeks earlier on June 1.

Under the new order, IRT subway service would exhibit a strong sense of continuity, and few operational changes would be made. Service on the Interborough's Elevated Division, though, was substantially curtailed. The Sixth Avenue Line had been abandoned outright in 1938, even before municipal takeover, while the entire Ninth Avenue Line and the Second Avenue Line north of 57th Street were phased out of service late on the evening of June 11, 1940, the day before the city acquired the company's other assets. Once abandoned, the elevated structures were acquired by the city through condemnation procedures, and shortly afterward they were torn down. (A number of BMT elevated lines in Brooklyn had met a similar fate when that system had been acquired by the City of New York several days earlier.)

The final Ninth Avenue el train was scheduled to depart from South Ferry at 11:10 P.M. on June 11 and reach 155th Street at 11:50 P.M. (Ninth Avenue service between 155th Street, immediately behind the Polo Grounds, and the Jerome Avenue Line would be retained as a shuttle until 1958.) Elements of the Second Avenue Line below 57th Street, including the link across the Queensboro Bridge to the Flushing and Astoria lines at Queensboro Plaza, survived the onset of municipal operation, but they were abandoned in 1942.

The Third Avenue el continued to operate through the Second World War and for a decade afterward, since the IRT Lexington Avenue Line was the only north-south Manhattan Subway on the East Side, and the Third Avenue Line was thought to be needed until a planned new Second Avenue Subway could be built. Key segments at the southern end of the Third Avenue el were eliminated after VJ Day—South Ferry to Chatham Square in 1950, City Hall to Chatham Square in 1953. By 1955, the Third Avenue el was too outmoded to warrant retention, even though the proposed Second Avenue Subway had yet to be built. Service was abandoned on the last of the Manhattan els on May 12, 1955. A segment of the line in the Bronx—up Webster Avenue from 149th Street to a junction with the White Plains Road Line at Gun Hill Road—remained in service for some years afterward, but in 1973 it too was abandoned.[103]

Table 1.5 identifies all major segments of the elevated lines of the Interborough's Manhattan Division and the dates when services were abandoned.

THE IRT AFTER VJ DAY

In the years immediately after the Second World War, the Board of Transportation acquired some new and substantially improved rolling stock for its newly unified municipal subway system. Because the IRT Division retained its limiting dimensions, though, it would always require unique equipment. The other two subway divisions, the IND and the BMT, were built to similar dimensions, and common specifications were developed for their new rolling stock.

Cars acquired by the City of New York for IRT service reflected substantial improvement in the way of propulsion and braking systems—four motors per car, for example, rather than two—not to mention such passenger amenities as fluorescent

TABLE 1.5

ABANDONMENT OF ELEVATED LINES

Line	Segment	Route Miles	Service Suspended
Third Avenue	42nd Street spur to Grand Central	0.18	12-06-23
Sixth Avenue	53rd Street to 58th Street[a]	0.31	6-16-24
Third Avenue	34th Street spur to East River Ferry	0.31	7-14-30
Sixth Avenue	Morris Street to 53rd Street & Ninth Avenue[b]	5.10	12-04-38
Second Avenue	57th Street to 129th Street	3.50	6-11-40
Ninth Avenue	South Ferry to 155th Street	10.23	6-11-40
Second Avenue	South Ferry & City Hall to 57th Street & across Queensboro Bridge to Queens Plaza[c]	6.89	6-13-42
Third Avenue	South Ferry to Chatham Square	1.16	12-22-50
Third Avenue	Bronx Park spur	0.26	11-14-51
Third Avenue	City Hall to Chatham Square	0.35	12-31-53
Third Avenue	Chatham Square to 149th Street[d]	8.60	5-12-55
Ninth Avenue	155th Street to 167th Street & Jerome Avenue[e]	0.73	8-31-58
Third Avenue	149th Street to Gun Hill Road[e]	5.38	4-29-73

a. Original northern terminal of 6th Avenue Line was at 58th Street and 6th Avenue; in 1879 a connection was built along 53rd Street to the 9th Avenue Line, and both lines continued northward via 9th Avenue trackage.

b. First abandonment of a north-south elevated trunk line.

c. Abandonment of 2nd Avenue trackage across Queensboro Bridge served to isolate Interborough's Queens Lines from the rest of the system; see text.

d. Final north-south elevated trunk line in Manhattan.

e. Because elevated structure on this segment could accommodate heavier subway equipment, final years of service were operated with subway equipment, not lightweight elevated cars.

lighting and the use of curtain-roll signs in lieu of the Interborough's old metal-plate system for the display of line and destination information. (Actually, roll signs along the sides of the initial postwar cars were criticized for being too small and inconveniently located at the top of the sidewalls.) In addition, the front end of the new cars displayed a panoply of passenger information, similar to a design developed for the new IND cars in the 1930s—destination signs to tell passengers where a train was going, a line sign to indicate the route it was following, a set of backlit signs to indicate whether the train was an express or a local, and a pair of four-color marker lights. In addition to the hefty power of four motors per car, when the City of New York began to replace older subway rolling stock, no motorless trailer cars were acquired and all trains featured motorized units only.

In general, the new postwar IRT cars were not dissimilar from equally new BMT-IND cars—except they were a little smaller. Subway cars acquired for use on either the BMT or the IND were 10 feet wide and at least 60 feet long. (More recently, some BMT-IND cars have been 75 feet in length.) Rolling stock for the IRT, though, continued—and continues—to observe the same external dimensions pioneered in 1902 on the pilot cars *August Belmont* and *John B. McDonald,* 51 feet long and 9 feet wide. (To be a bit more precise, the two 1902 experimental cars measured 51 feet, 1½ inches in length, while the Interborough-IRT standard became 51 feet and ½ inch.)

A number of technical factors rendered the IRT's basic Manhattan trunk lines as a less likely place to deploy the limited number of new cars the City of New York acquired for the IRT Division immediately after the Second World War. One of these was the placement of platform gap-fillers at various Contract One stations that were built on curves, such as Brooklyn Bridge, 14th Street–Union Square, and a few other places. (If a station is built on a curve, the platform has to be positioned sufficiently far back from the track so that passing trains do not scrape against it. This creates a gap, of course, between the platform and car doors. A gap-filler is a mechanical device that moves out from the platform to close the gap once the train comes to a stop.) Since new IRT rolling stock would eschew end vestibules and feature different door placement from classic Interborough equipment, the platform gap-fillers would have to be repositioned, and furthermore, replacement of older stock with new cars would have to be done completely and virtually simultaneously.

So when the city ordered 350 new cars for IRT service in 1948, the obvious line on which to run them was the now-isolated Flushing Line. With the elimination of Second Avenue elevated service across the Queensboro Bridge in 1942, IRT service on both the Flushing and Astoria lines enjoyed no physical track connections with the rest of the former Interborough system, and while there was a light-maintenance facility at the end of the Flushing Line, heavier work on IRT cars used on the Queens lines was shifted to the BMT's Coney Island shops once they were denied access to the Interborough's principal maintenance shop. Smaller IRT cars could make deadhead moves over BMT trackage, since both systems featured standard-gauge track and compatible electrical systems.[104] In addition, no stations on the Flushing Line used mechanical gap-fillers, and accommodating this line to handle a different style of rolling stock turned out to be the proverbial "piece of cake." Certain railings that the Interborough used to separate boarding from alighting passengers on station platforms had to be removed, since, like the gap-fillers, they were oriented around the door locations on the company's basic rolling stock. But this was a simple task.

With the arrival of these new cars—designated the R-12, R-14, and R-15 units, continuing a notation that was originally developed by the Board of Transportation for the IND, whose initial cars in the early 1930s were called the R-1 units—the mechanically different Steinway cars, including the Interborough's small fleet of fifty cars that were acquired for service to the 1939 and 1940 World's Fair, were transferred to the IRT's basic Manhattan-Bronx network, although their unique mechanical systems restricted their use to trains composed only of similar rolling stock.

In addition, under Board of Transportation auspices, service on both the Flushing and Astoria lines was rationalized in 1949, and the practice of serving each line with both BMT and IRT trains was discontinued. The Astoria Line had its platforms shaved back and it became an extension of the BMT's Manhattan service, while responsibility for operating the Flushing Line was assigned solely to the IRT.

In 1953, the New York subways were placed under a new governance structure. The Board of Transportation, a city agency, was superseded by a newly created state agency, the New York City Transit Authority. Under Transit Authority (TA) auspices, a major car replacement program for the IRT's basic Manhattan-Bronx system was soon begun. Given the constraints of older stations and their platform gap-fillers, major alterations were effected coincident with the acquisition of the new rolling stock. Local stations above 42nd Street on the West Side Line and below it on the East Side Line—the Contract One lines—were still able to accommodate only six-car trains. A major program was undertaken to correct this shortcoming by expanding (almost) all of these local stations so they could handle ten-car trains. In addition, the best way to solve the gap-filler problem at certain express stations was to move platforms north or south so that the curves that required gap-fillers were no longer within the confines of the station. All of this lengthening and stretching and moving shortened the distances between certain stations, and in four instances the wiser course of action was to close a few local-only stations on the Contract One lines, namely City Hall, Worth Street, and 18th Street on the East Side Line and 91st Street on the West Side.

As for the new IRT rolling stock, it much resembled cars that were also being ordered for the wider tunnels of the BMT and IND divisions, except that it continued to respect the original Interborough dimensions—51 feet long, 9 feet wide. One external difference that immediately identifies a postwar IRT car, though, apart from its reduced external dimensions, is the inclusion of three sets of sliding passenger doors along a car's sides. New rolling stock acquired for use on the BMT and IND feature four sets of doors.

Over a ten-year period that began in 1955, a total of 2,510 new subway cars were acquired for IRT service from the Saint Louis Car Company and American Car and Foundry, beginning with 400 Saint Louis–built R-17 units in 1955 to 1956 that replaced older cars on the Lexington Avenue Local and allowed the Gibbs Hi-V cars from 1904 to be retired. With the arrival of 423 new R-36 units from the Saint Louis Car Company in 1964, the complete replacement of all Interborough-era rolling stock was achieved, and the subway system begun by August Belmont was being operated entirely with "second-generation" rolling stock. The last day on which a train composed of older, "first-generation" Interborough Subway cars was used in revenue passenger service was November 3, 1969, a little less than four months after astronaut Neil Armstrong became the first human being to walk on the surface of the moon. The line on which the IRT operated the last of its classic old cars in November 1969 was the remaining Bronx segment of the Third Avenue el, between 149th Street and Gun Hill Road.[105]

In 1964 and 1965, another New York World's Fair was held at

Flushing Meadows, site of the 1939-to-1940 fair, and like the Interborough's fifty World's Fair cars of 1938, the TA's new R-36 units—featuring a colorful two-tone blue paint scheme—were assigned to the Flushing Line for World's Fair service.[106]

SERVICE CHANGES

During the postwar era, a number of service changes were implemented on the IRT. Two relatively small changes—one an addition to the system, the other a subtraction from it—are of interest. The original Contract One terminal, at 180th Street–Bronx Park in the West Farms neighborhood and adjacent to the famous Bronx Zoo, was eliminated in 1952. When this line was extended to 241st Street–White Plains Road at the time of the Dual Contracts, the extension left the original right-of-way just south of the 180th Street terminal, and an at-grade junction at this point was a source of many delays. The easiest solution was to abandon the stub-end terminal outright, even though passengers headed for the Bronx Zoo must now walk an additional three or four blocks. (The abandoned section was a mere 0.2 miles in length.)

A 0.3-mile extension was added to another portion of the Contract One network in 1968 when trackage leading into a surface storage yard north of the 145th Street–Lenox terminal was converted into revenue service and a new at-grade terminal established at 148th Street–Lenox.

IRT expansion on a much larger scale included the incorporation of something called the Dyre Avenue Line in the Bronx into the IRT System and the operation of through-service to Dyre Avenue from the basic Manhattan trunk lines. The Dyre Avenue Line was once part of a suburban electric railway called the New York, Westchester and Boston, which was a subsidiary of the New York, New Haven and Hartford Railroad, but had been abandoned outright in early 1938.[107] (The New York, Westchester and Boston is discussed further in Chapter 4.) In April 1940, the City of New York acquired 4 miles of the line's right-of-way, all within city limits, for $1.8 million and in the spring of 1941 inaugurated shuttle service, using old el cars, between Dyre Avenue and a connection with the IRT at East 180th Street. After the war, the Dyre Avenue shuttle was upgraded into a branch of the IRT Subway network.[108]

Another major postwar service change on the IRT Division was a simplification of service to points on the Broadway Line north of 96th Street. A problem with the traditional service pattern was a serious bottleneck at double crossovers just north of the 96th Street station. All Broadway–Seventh Avenue express trains and all Seventh Avenue locals had to use the crossover, and even when schedules were perfectly maintained, delays were common. With the arrival of new, higher-performance cars in 1959, the TA realigned West Side IRT service to eliminate the need for any routine use of the 96th Street crossover. All Broadway–Seventh Avenue trains coming south from 241st Street–Van Cortlandt Park would continue south of 96th Street as locals; all Seventh Avenue trains from the Lenox Avenue Line would operate as expresses below 96th Street.

The new Broadway–Seventh Avenue service was referred to in TA publications as a "high-speed local," and the usage was not illegitimate. The new subway cars acquired for the line had much better acceleration and braking rates than the older cars they were replacing. In addition, older signals were replaced by a more modern system that allowed trains to operate more efficiently.[109] In later years, the TA would institute "skip-stop" service on the Broadway–Seventh Avenue Line as a further effort to provide swifter service. Under current train-identification rubrics, service that makes all stops between South Ferry and 241st Street–Van Cortlandt Park is primarily called the No. 1 train. During peak rush hours, though, No. 1 trains alternate with No. 9 trains, and although both offer the same service south of 96th Street, between 96th Street and 241st Street, the two services make some common stops but each train also bypasses alternate stations in an effort to speed the overall flow of traffic.

A final postwar service change was the elimination of shuttle operations between the Bowling Green station of the Lexington Avenue Line and South Ferry. Trackage remains in place, and certain Lexington Avenue trains continue to use the South Ferry loop to reverse direction. But such trains show Bowling Green as their southern terminal, and the route formerly used by the shuttle no longer sees revenue service.[110]

Terminology such as Broadway–Seventh Avenue express is no longer accurate with respect to contemporary IRT operations, and a system of number and color codes has been developed to identify the city's various subway services. Colors are derived from the Manhattan trunk line a service utilizes, and there is no repetition of colors throughout the entire subway system—BMT, IND, or IRT. Numbers derived from the Bronx branch line that a train uses further identify IRT services. (Trains on the combined BMT-IND division use a similar letter system.)

Table 1.6 identifies IRT services circa 2004.

As the City of New York celebrates the centenary of subway service in 2004, a new generation of IRT rolling stock has entered service. A fleet of 1,550 new cars identified as the R-142 and the R-142A units began carrying passengers in 2000, and with their arrival most—if not all—of the cars that were acquired in the 1950s and 1960s were identified for retirement.[111] Suddenly, R-62 and R-62A units that joined the fleet between 1984 and 1988 came to be regarded as vintage rolling stock.

Kawasaki Heavy Industries, a Japanese car builder, built the 325-car fleet of R-62 units in 1984 and 1985, and they were both the first IRT cars to be designed and built with onboard air conditioning and the first IRT equipment to feature car bodies of stainless steel. They were quickly followed in 1985 to 1987 by 825 similar R-62A units which were the product of a Canadian manufacturer, Bombardier.[112] And while the R-62s and R-62As were the first IRT cars to be built with onboard air conditioning, coincident with their arrival the TA initiated a massive program of rebuilding its older cars, work that included the installation of air conditioning. The arrival of the R-62s and the R-62As permitted the retirement of many older cars—the R-12 through R-22 units—while the R-26s through R-36s were rebuilt for additional years of service. All rebuilt cars were painted a very attractive color scheme that included a deep red body, and as a result the

TABLE 1.6
IRT SERVICES CIRCA 2004

Number	Color Code	Service	Northern Terminal(s)	Southern Terminal(s)
1[a]	red	Broadway Local	242nd Street & Broadway	South Ferry
2	red	Seventh Avenue Express	241st Street & White Plains Road	Flatbush Avenue; Brooklyn
3	red	Seventh Avenue Express	148th Street; Lenox Terminal	New Lots Avenue; Brooklyn
4	green	Lexington Avenue Express	Woodlawn–Jerome Avenue	Utica Avenue; Brooklyn
5[b]	green	Lexington Avenue Express	Dyre Avenue	Bowling Green
5[c]	green	Lexington Avenue Express	Dyre Avenue or Nereid Avenue	Flatbush Avenue; Brooklyn
6[d]	green	Lexington Avenue Local	Pelham Bay Park	Brooklyn Bridge
7	purple	Flushing Local	Times Square	Main Street
7[c]	purple	Flushing Express	Times Square	Main Street
9[a]	red	Broadway local	242nd Street	South Ferry
S	black	Shuttle	Times Square	Grand Central

Only basic Interborough services are shown. Additional variations were often operated at various times of day. See Table 1C in the Appendix for a more comprehensive list of such variations.

a. No. 1 train operates 24/7, No. 9 train rush hour only. When No. 9 train is operating, No. 1 train and No. 9 train operate "skip-stop" service north of 96th Street.

b. Operates midday, evenings, and weekends only.

c. Operates rush hour only.

d. During rush hour, some trains operate express service between 138th Street and East 177th Street, inbound in the morning, outbound in the evening; some trains also terminate at East 177th Street during rush hour.

rebuilt cars came to be called "redbirds" during their final years of service.

The new R-142 and R-142A units are state-of-the-art in all respects and will provide dependable IRT service well into the twenty-first century. Following a design that was initially executed on a ten-car prototype train built by Kawasaki in 1992 and designated the R-110A, the IRT's newest cars operate as semipermanently coupled five-car sets. The R-110A experimental actually tried to imitate an old Interborough practice, and of its

five-car sets, the two end units were each powered by four motors, cars two and four featured two motors each, while the middle car was a motorless trailer. The R-142 and R-142A units do
not include motorless trailers, but each five-car set does involve
combinations of two-motor and four-motor cars. The end or cab
cars are the four-motor units; the three interior units each feature
two motors.

The R-142 and R-142A units are equipped with rather different kinds of electric motors from traditional New York Subway
cars. In place of traditional direct-current motors, alternating-
current motors power the new cars. Trains continue to draw direct current from the third rail, but onboard equipment converts
this to alternating current to allow the use of newly designed AC
motors. In subsequent chapters, we shall learn more about classic
debates in the early years of the twentieth century over the relative merits of AC and DC for railway electrification purposes.
While DC motors long held the edge for toughness and dependability in applications such as subway service, the development
of new and improved kinds of electronic controls have made contemporary AC motors the new choice for mass transit and electric railway purposes.

The idea of five-car sets means that only two styles of trains
will routinely be operated—five-car trains or ten-car trains. New
York City Transit (NYCT) feels this supplies all the flexibility
it needs. For much of its history, the New York Subway—the
Interborough, the BRT/BMT, or the IND—would alter the length
of trains several times during the course of a day, adding and
subtracting cars in response to changes in demand. Coupling
extra cars onto in-service trains is both a time-consuming as well
as a labor-intensive exercise, and cost-effectiveness analysis has
shown that it is a far wiser course to leave trains intact as much
as possible and to respond to fluctuations in demand by adding
or removing full trains. With respect to the IRT, this means that
most trains will be ten cars in length, with five-car sets operating
certain shuttle services.[113]

The new cars incorporate what must be regarded as an absolute
maximum in the way of automatic systems to keep IRT passengers informed. On the head end of every train, there is merely a
number, illuminated in red, to indicate the service that is being

operated. Gone from the head ends of contemporary IRT trains are the backlit line and destination signs that were first used on the R-12 units in 1948 and gone, too, are the four-color marker lights that Frank Hedley once championed as an adequate system of train identification. (See Table 1C in the Appendix for a list of marker-light codes from days gone by.)

But if the head end of an IRT train now carries only brief identification, elsewhere there is more than ample information. An illuminated exterior sign along the side of each R-142 unit alternately flashes the train's route and its destination, while on the inside each car includes a set of signs suspended from the ceiling that inform passengers of route, destination, and the next station the train will serve. Furthermore, incorporated into space that in the past was reserved for paid advertising, passengers will observe a strip-map showing all stations along the line that the train is working, with a system of lights to indicate the train's actual location along the line. (Apparently, with its R-142 and R-142A units, the IRT does not plan to shift trains routinely from one line to another, since it would take a team of mechanics several hours to remove these maps and replace them with different ones.)

But even all these signs and maps are not the full story. Recorded messages—clearly articulated by professional radio announcers—are broadcast at intervals to keep passengers fully informed about a train's route, its destination, when the doors are about to close, and the next station coming up along the line. One can only imagine, of course, what crusty old Frank Hedley would have said had he participated in the meetings and deliberations that designed these betterments.

Passenger information systems are not the only forms of new technology designed into the new R-142 and R-142A units. Propulsion and braking systems are linked to onboard computers to ensure smooth and efficient operation and to conserve energy as well. The operator's cab aboard an R-142 unit compares to the motorman's cab in a classic Interborough Lo-V subway car in much the way that the cockpit of a new jet airliner contrasts with that in a First World War biplane. Finally, what surely falls into the nothing-new-under-the-sun category is the fact that passenger doors on the R-142 and R-142A units are almost a foot wider than those on earlier IRT rolling stock such as the R-62 and R-62A units—to speed the flow of boarding and alighting passengers, of course.

When August Belmont's Interborough Rapid Transit Company supplemented its original Gibbs Cars of 1904 with the distinctive deck-roof cars of 1908, the newer stock also featured wider passenger doors—and for the very same reason.

August Belmont, Jr. (All photos are from author's collection unless otherwise indicated.)

The ornate City Hall Station from which New York's first subway train departed on its inaugural trip on October 27, 1904.

A block signal mounted on a tunnel wall in the Interborough Subway and the trackside trip which, when in a raised position, automatically applies the brakes should a train pass a stop signal.

The classic look of an Interborough Subway train.

One of the Interborough's original Composite cars operating on the Third Avenue El after its subway days were over.

Hi-V car No. 3815 is leading a Broadway–Seventh Avenue Express bound for New Lots Avenue in Brooklyn.

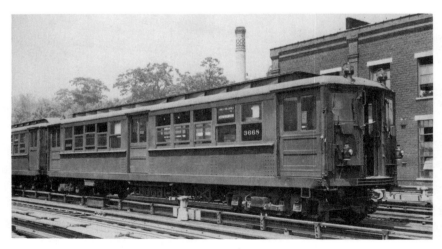

One of the Interborough's distinctive "deck-roof" cars, which were acquired in 1908–1909.

Passengers face each other on longitudinal seats in a typical
Interborough—or IRT—subway car.

Car No. 9558 is an R-36 unit acquired for service over the Flushing
Line to the 1964–1965 World's Fair.

Bound for Pelham Bay Park, a northbound Lexington Avenue Local stops to load and unload passengers at Grand Central.

With R-33 unit No. 9150 in the lead, a southbound Lexington Avenue Express rounds a curve on an elevated portion of the Contract One lines in the Bronx. Called "redbirds" during their final years of IRT service, the cars were about to be replaced by new R-142 and R-142A units when this photo was taken in mid-2002.

South Ferry station, where trains of the No. 1 Line and the No. 9 Line terminate. Note the mechanical "gap-fillers" on the platform that allow passengers to board trains more conveniently from platforms built on curves. Cars No. 1732 and No. 1733 are R-62A units operating in Broadway Local service.

A ten-car train of experimental R-110 units was the prototype for subsequent production model R-142 units and hence represents the contemporary look of an underground railway system that inaugurated subway service in New York in 1904.

2

Change at Park Street Under

THE SUBWAY opened by the Interborough Rapid Transit Company
in New York on the afternoon of September 27, 1904, would
become the nucleus of the largest urban mass-transit system in
America—and by some measures, the largest in the world. But
whatever else one may choose to say about the Interborough in
particular and New York subways in general, it may not be said
that New York was the first city in the Western Hemisphere to
build and operate an underground mass-transit system. That
honor forever belongs to Boston. On the day in 1904 when passengers first boarded Interborough trains for swift rides between
City Hall and Harlem, citizens of Boston were veritable subway
veterans with seven years of subway-riding experience under
their belt.

The Boston Subway shares many similarities with that of New
York. But there are also important differences in the way rapid
transit developed in the two East Coast cities. A brief examination of mass transit Boston style—before 1904 and afterward—
provides an interesting counterpoint to the Interborough Rapid
Transit Company as part of the centenary observance of subway
service in New York.[1]

PARK STREET VIA SUBWAY

Before Boston was able to steal a march on the nation and open
America's first subway in the waning years of the nineteenth
century, a number of preliminary scenarios in both the technical
and the political arenas first had to be acted out. Not the least of
these on the technical side was that the basic hardware necessary
to operate an underground subway successfully—for example,

electric-powered railway cars—had to be invented. On the political side, elected officials at both the state and local level had to develop a consensus to allocate large sums of public money for the construction of an underground railway.

An experimental installation at the Berlin Industrial Exposition in 1879 is widely acknowledged to be the first successful carriage of passengers aboard an electric-powered vehicle. The overseer of this technological breakthrough was a gentleman by the name of Werner Siemens, and following his pioneering work in Germany, others went to work to solve a range of practical problems that had to be addressed before electricity could be safely and successfully deployed on a large scale to carry passengers into and out of the downtown business district of a major city on a daily basis.

Things moved swiftly enough, though. Less than a decade after the Siemens demonstration in Berlin, in early 1888 the city of Richmond, Virginia, could boast that an entire fleet of electric-powered streetcars was hauling its citizens on their appointed rounds. While there were earlier electric streetcars both in the United States and abroad, the Richmond installation is commonly regarded as the first truly successful deployment of the new energy source on a large scale.

A Connecticut-born Annapolis graduate by the name of Frank Sprague—who would later play a supporting role in the development of the New York Subway—was the out-and-out genius who did more than any other score of people in the field. Sprague not only managed the successful Richmond streetcar electrification of 1888 and was responsible for the development of many intricate devices needed to operate an electric street railway, his later invention of a system called multiple-unit control enabled a motorman at the head end of a multicar train to operate the electric motors in all the cars in the train, an achievement that was central in allowing electric-powered trains to run through underground subway tunnels. Measured against the high-tech standards of a later era, Sprague's work at the turn of the century may seem crude and unimpressive. But the technical and engineering difficulties he faced were real in the 1880s and the 1890s, and his success in overcoming them should not be discounted.[2]

During the summer of 1888, as word of the success in Richmond spread through the street railway industry, the president of one of the largest horse-car companies in the country traveled south to inspect Sprague's work. His name was Henry H. Whitney, and the firm he headed up, Boston's West End Street Railway, owned 1,481 streetcars, operated them along 253 miles of track, and carried over 100 million passengers annually.

During the previous year, the Massachusetts legislature had enacted a bill that enabled the West End company to emerge as a consolidation of previously independent street railways.[3] Prior to this legislative action, competition among multiple street railways operating in and around Boston was having a decidedly negative impact on the quality of transit service provided, and legislative intervention to merge the separate and competing firms was deemed necessary. One of the first items of business Whitney felt obliged to address was finding an efficient and reliable form of mechanical power to replace the 7,728 horses the West End company stabled to haul its railway cars along the streets of Boston.

But which form of mechanical power? Cable cars, while gaining popularity in many important American cities, were very expensive and furthermore might prove singularly impractical over the twisting and narrow street of Boston.[4] So Whitney boarded a train in Boston and journeyed south to Richmond, willing to be influenced by what he might find there.

Serious doubts plagued him on first seeing Sprague's work. In the peaceful, almost rural precincts of the quiet southern city, the new electric trolleys performed their routines with leisurely ease. Would they prove equally practical in brisk, congested Boston? Could, say, a large number of cars be started all at once? Would the slim overhead wire safely carry the electrical load needed under such circumstances? Whitney, in other words, was not an instant convert to streetcar electrification Sprague-style.

Like any good salesman, Frank Sprague decided to address the concerns of his potential customer and demonstrate what his product could do. As the cars completed their runs one summer's evening in the year of 1888, they were brought together at one end of the line. Power from the generating station was maintained at peak level and Whitney was summoned from his hotel—unexpectedly, in fact—to witness a truly remarkable demonstration. Shortly after midnight and at a lantern signal from Sprague, twenty-two streetcars were started up—not quite simultaneously, as has sometimes been reported, but each car moved out as soon as the one ahead of it was in the clear, until all twenty-two were moving down the track. No motors melted, no fuses blew, and the system performed exactly as Sprague knew it would. Whitney, for his part, was totally convinced, and Sprague was awarded a contract to electrify Boston's West End system.

In January of 1889, slightly over six months after Whitney visited Richmond, people in Boston were taking their first rides aboard electric-powered trolley cars, and in little more than a decade, all horse-drawn streetcars in the city were withdrawn from service.[5] So popular did the new electric cars quickly become that no less a distinguished Bostonian than eighty-year-old Oliver Wendell Holmes took note of the new order with this little bit of verse:

> Since then on many a car you'll see
> A broomstick plain as plain can be;
> On every stick there's a witch astride—
> The string you see to her leg is tied.

The conversion of its streetcars to electric operation promoted the growth of the West End Street Railway and facilitated the extension of its lines into nearby suburbs.[6] But mere electrification did not allay all of Boston's transportation woes. Indeed, in many important respects, matters grew decidedly worse. Narrow streets in the city's business district were simply incapable of providing sufficient room for all the cars ferrying passengers into Downtown. Tremont Street often saw trolleys lined up "bumper to bumper," to borrow a later phrase. In the words of one Boston official: "The cars on that line dragged their slow length along the mournful processions and at the hours of greatest traffic, especially between five and six o'clock in the afternoon, it was not unusual for cars to take fifteen minutes to go half a mile, and sometimes they were even longer than that."[7]

In 1892, a mere three years after Boston began operating its first electric-powered streetcar, a state commission prepared a comprehensive analysis detailing the extent of Boston's transportation woes. It called for the construction of a network of elevated railways—Boston had none at the time—plus a publicly financed underground tunnel so that West End trolley cars might be removed from city streets and operate belowground in the city's downtown areas. For its time, this was a breathtaking proposal, not likely to win quick, much less universal, approval from ever-conservative Bostonians. Even the management of the West End Street Railway did not welcome the idea of a subway—especially with the kind of lease arrangements the commission was proposing to charge for the use of any such public facility by the privately owned railway company. And the West End was not alone. Certain old-line residents viewed the notion of a subway with only slightly less alarm than a report of Attila the Hun marching east through Dedham. In a more practical vein, some downtown property owners were convinced that their Tremont Street buildings would be undermined by the construction of a subway and eventually collapse. By far the most emotional response, though, was generated by the thought of common laborers digging up sacred Boston Common. Be-whiskered gentlemen shook their heads in horror over the prospect as they squeezed lemon wedges over luncheon entrees of broiled scrod at various private clubs on Beacon Hill.

Further negativism of undetermined proportion was the feeling, reflected in the newspapers, that many potential passengers would surely be uneasy about riding through tunnels below ground, a Stygian territory generally associated with such things as sewers and gas mains and the less sociable members of the rodent and reptile families.[8]

While these misgivings were certainly real, so too was the terrible congestion that continued to plague the streets of downtown Boston. In July 1894, the Massachusetts General Court—the proper name of the state's legislature, not its judiciary—enacted a measure that authorized the incorporation of a new firm that would be called the Boston Elevated Railway, and also the formation of a new public agency, the Boston Transit Commission. The new commission was authorized to make a final determination about the proper solution to the area's transit problems, with the concept of a subway clearly among the options to be considered. Furthermore, the commission was empowered to see its plan through to fruition. Precisely what the Boston Elevated Railway was all about will emerge anon.

The legislation was enacted during the final days of the General Court's 1894 session, a style of last-minute statecraft that many Bostonians regarded as at least suspicious and more likely downright devious. One disconsolate Back Bay resident, a staunch believer in the inviolability of the status quo, remarked that if the legislation had not been enacted "at a time when the best people were away for the Summer," it never would have passed.[9]

Those who were not "away for the Summer," of course, were various factions who were championing so iconoclastic a notion as a downtown subway. Citizens of Boston accepted the legislation, though, in a special referendum that the new law required. The final tally was very close—15,369 to 14,298. There followed several attempts to stop the subway in the courts, but all were unsuccessful.

When the new Transit Commission was impaneled and got down to work, a subway was not a foregone conclusion, and several alternative possibilities were reviewed.[10] One was to rely on a mass-transit concept that had already been applied in New York, Brooklyn, and Chicago—an elevated railway built atop iron or steel support columns. Boston would soon build an elevated railway, but not in the heart of its business district adjacent to the Public Garden and Boston Common. Indeed, when overprinted photographs were prepared superimposing an el structure with a steam-powered train rumbling over Tremont Street and past Park Street Church, the idea earned swift oblivion.

One plan, seriously considered, proposed a surface-level "alley" right-of-way for West End streetcars between and parallel to Tremont and Washington streets. Its chief flaw was operational—too many grade crossings. On top of that, it would require extensive land taking in an area where real estate was extremely valuable.

Hence Boston veered to an underground railway, or the "European transit system," as area newspapers put it—and it was surely a valid description, since London had an operating subway system at the time, with Budapest, Glasgow, and Paris on the verge of such status (more on European subways in Chapter 3).

The Boston Subway project, headed up by chief engineer Howard A. Carsen, called for a subway tunnel for trolley cars that would lead into the central downtown district from three different directions: two from the south and one from the north. The northern "incline"—the term for a subway entry ramp that streetcars would use—was located just beyond Haymarket Square and led up to North Union Station. One of the southern inclines was along Boylston Street at the Public Garden, the other at Tremont and Broadway. (The latter thoroughfare was called Pleasant Street at the time.)

It was anticipated that trolley cars could run through the subway from the northern incline to either of the two southern ones, while in addition three underground loops would enable trolleys to reverse direction inside the subway and return to their point of origin. As to its length, "the subway will comprehend a distance of one and one-third miles."[11] Under the provisions of a twenty-year lease negotiated between the West End Street Railway and the Transit Commission in 1896, the annual rental for the subway was 4 7/8 percent of the subway's construction cost, plus a five-cent toll for each trolley car using the facility.

European engineers had developed two noteworthy but very different styles of subway construction. In London was perfected a deep underground "tube" concept that was constructed by tunneling deep belowground, in mole-like fashion, without disrupting surface traffic and without posing any threat to the foundations of buildings along the route. Glasgow was on the verge of imitating London in this regard.

Paris, on the other hand, even though its initial subway would not open until 1900, was pioneering the use of masonry arches in its subway construction. Such tunnels were located immediately below ground level, requiring surface excavation for the length of the route. But the Paris method had a potentially serious drawback in that because of its reliance on masonry work, it would not tolerate underground disruption adjacent to its right-of-way. It would hardly do, for instance, if the construction of a new office building adjacent to the proposed Boston Subway caused the tunnel to sag.

So a hybrid concept of subway construction evolved—a tunnel built chiefly in open excavation, like Paris, but with adequate steel support to make it "independent of lateral ground support, in the sense that it can stand by itself if the earth is removed from about it," as *Scientific American* reported.[12] The technique, later called the "cut and cover" method, became standard on most subsequent American subway projects. As noted in Chapter 1, it was used in New York for most of the Interborough's underground route, although London-style deep-tunnel construction would be used from time to time when surface excavation was not feasible.[13]

During construction, efforts were made to ensure as normal a flow of surface traffic as could be managed; indeed, it was legally stipulated that during daylight hours Tremont Street had to be available for regular use. As a result, much construction work on the new subway was performed at night.

On March 28, 1895, ground was broken for the new subway in the Public Garden opposite the Providence Railway Depot, close to Boylston Street, thus launching the three-year project. Many unexpected problems cropped up, such as incorrect maps that were supposed to lay out the precise location of sewer, water, and gas lines. Beds of quicksand also caused problems, while an explosion in the subway excavation at Boylston and Tremont streets on March 4, 1896, brought death to nine unfortunate souls. A rather macabre duty was reinterment of the remains of 910 bodies that were exhumed as subway excavators worked their way through Colonial-era burial grounds.

Ventilation of the tunnels was a very serious concern to the designers of America's first subway. Such concerns may seem extreme today, but it must be remembered that at the turn of the century pulmonary disease was mankind's most dreaded killer, and worries about the quality of air passengers would breathe in the underground tunnels was a manifestation of nothing less than the human survival instinct. After the Boston Subway was completed, most gave it very high marks in this regard. Ventilation shafts sunk at several points along the route provided air of a much better quality than older European subways, for example, as rated by no less an authority than the *New York Times*.[14] There was also some worry about the temperature inside the tunnels. The Transit Commission was fearful that the subway would be too cool during the hot days of summer and actually considered efforts to heat the stations, the assumption being that it was un-natural and injurious to have the subway more than a few degrees different from the outside temperature.

The subway cost $5 million to build, and the initial segment that was ready for service connected a terminal under Tremont and Park streets with the incline at Boylston Street adjacent to the Public Garden. It received uniformly, if not universally, favorable comment.

"The air is good, the temperature is comfortable, and the light-hued walls reflect the glow of many hundreds of incandescent lamps that brightly illuminate it," one magazine noted.[15] The *Boston Journal* modestly proclaimed that "our park system, our union stations, and now our subway have opened the eyes of the country to the fact that this city is more than a center of literary and historic associations, and that it has an eye on the future as well as to the past."[16] Among those whose eyes were definitely opened by the new subway was the *New York Times*. "That so conservative an American town should happen to be the pioneer in adopting this is viewed as remarkable," the newspaper saw fit to note.[17]

The aboveground entrances to the new Boston Subway were subject to some criticism, with the kiosk design used along Tremont Street said to resemble a mausoleum.[18] And while most commentators gave the overall project high marks in virtually all respects, *Harper's Weekly* felt the work's "engineering character . . . is too boldly manifest, and the architectural opportunities have not been sufficiently improved."[19]

Other than work cars of various sorts, the first conventional streetcar to enter the subway did so on May 27, 1897. It was a trial trip that operated from the Public Garden incline as far as Temple Place.[20] Additional test runs were conducted throughout the summer of 1897, until finally everything was ready for the inauguration of revenue passenger service.

Early on the morning of Wednesday, September 1, 1897, four-wheeled open-bench trolley car No. 1752 moved out of the Allston car barn in the presence of crowds gathered at the depot in tribute to the extraordinary event. On the front of the car a new yellow sign read: "Subway to Park St." Conductor Gilman T. Trufant and motorman James Reed, two West End veterans, were to pilot car No. 1752 into the new Tremont Street Subway. If they kept to their schedule, they would get to the incline ahead of a Cypress Street streetcar from Brookline and hence would be the first car to carry passengers into the new facility.

Trufant freely admitted that he had slept little in nervous anticipation of the big event, and as soon as Reed intoned "All aboard for the subway and Park Street," things were under way. In the colorful language of the *Boston Globe,* the motorman "compelled the pent-up lightening to do his bidding," and "the trolley hissed along like a brood of vipers."[21] Suspense mounted as No. 1752 was delayed on its run and started to fall behind schedule; surely the Cypress Street rival would get to the subway first. But it did not. As No. 1752 passed the intersection of Boylston and Huntington with no competition in sight, its destiny was assured. At 6:01 A.M., with a huge throng lining both sides of the incline, the car swung off Boylston Street and headed down the grade. Three minutes later the car was abreast of the platform at Park Street, discharging its passengers. Boston had done it—had planned, financed, built, and on this day opened the first subway in the New World.

Once it was in operation, the new subway did exactly what it was intended to do—it lessened street traffic in downtown Boston and allowed streetcars to make their way into the city with greater facility. "The effect was like when a barrier is removed from the channel of a clogged up river," noted *Harper's Weekly* in analyzing the new subway's impact.[22] Service into the subway via the Pleasant Street incline was inaugurated on October 1, 1897, and nearly a year later, on September 3, 1898, the final leg of the original project, from Park Street to the northern incline beyond Haymarket Square, was finished.

THE MAIN LINE EL

The Transit Commission of 1894 was not content with undertaking the construction of the Tremont Street Subway so trolley lines of the West End Street Railway could be funneled into downtown Boston more efficiently. Also part of its master plan for mass-transit improvement was a new elevated line that would

link the Charlestown section of Boston in the north with a neighborhood called Roxbury in the south. Exactly how this new el
would make its way through downtown Boston is an especially
interesting chapter in Boston's transit history.

Boston's Tremont Street Subway of 1898 made use of two of
three important technological innovations that were available to
turn-of-the-century transit planners: electric-powered rail cars
and underground tunnels. The third development was Frank
Sprague's multiple-unit (MU) control which permitted the operation of multicar trains of electric-powered cars. It was first deployed on the South Side Elevated in Chicago in 1897, in the
same year the Tremont Street Subway opened for business.[23]
Boston's next transit project would incorporate all three innovations. August Belmont's Interborough Rapid Transit Company of
1904, of course, also operated electric-powered trains featuring
Sprague-style MU control. But in keeping with its pioneering
tradition, Boston was running such multicar subway trains four
years before the Interborough carried its first passengers.

The agency that would build most of this route and operate
all of it was the Boston Elevated Railway Company (BERY), a
corporation created by the same enabling legislation as for the
original subway. Such a new company was needed, it was believed, because the West End company was unwilling to build
and operate any elevated lines.

The new elevated line would make its passage through downtown Boston via the Tremont Street Subway, so within months
of the subway's opening in September 1897, there began a series
of complex legal moves that culminated in the takeover of the
West End company by the new Boston El.[24]

The idea of an elevated railway was hardly new in urban
America. New York City opened its first el in 1870 and by the
early 1880s it boasted four steam-powered lines running the
length of Manhattan Island, as discussed in Chapter 1. Two other
large U.S. cities also built elevated railways, Brooklyn (in 1885)
and Chicago (in 1892).[25]

But elevated railways were a kind of progress that many Bostonians regarded as downright retrogressive, given the demonstrated practicality of a subway. Els were much cheaper to build,
though, and that, really, was the nub of the matter. BERY tried

to sweeten the pill by taking pains with the design of station structures along the new el—the company actually held a design competition among architects before adopting a basic plan—but as reported in the *Street Railway Journal,* "the people of Boston are proud of their city, and . . . greatly oppose the putting up of an elevated railroad in any of the principal streets."[26] Construction, however, would not be deterred.

In early June of 1901, Colonel William A. Gaston, chairman of the board of directors of the Boston El, petitioned the state's railroad commissioners for formal authorization to open the company's newest rapid-transit line—with the route name Main Line El—to public use. Such permission was quickly granted, and Monday, June 10, 1901, was set as the day when service would begin.

Official permission was not the final step in readying the new route for service, though. Although elevated segments of the Sullivan-Square-to-Dudley Line were complete, an essential linkup with the four-year-old Tremont Street Subway through which the new el trains would operate could not be completed until the last possible moment. Routing of el trains through the trolley subway would exclude large numbers of surface cars from the 1897 facility. The new el trains would use the outside tracks of the subway in locations where there were four tracks, while over a critical two-track stretch between Park Street and Scollay Square, all streetcars would be excluded and only el trains would operate. Streetcars would continue to use the subway's inside tracks, with cars entering via the Public Garden incline terminating at Park Street, and cars entering via the northern incline beyond Haymarket Square terminating at either Adams Square or Scollay Square. The subway's third incline, at Pleasant Street, would be used only by el trains under the new arrangements. In numerical terms, the routing of el trains into the subway would force the elimination of 1,500 daily trolley trips from the underground facility. Plans were made to effect the changeover on the weekend of June 8–10.

At 8:15 P.M. on Saturday evening, June 8, 1901, trolley car No. 2369 on the Franklin Park–Humbolt Avenue Line emerged from the subway's Pleasant Street incline. Motorman Thomas McAvoy and Conductor Alexander Anderson had sixteen passengers in their charge; it would be the last trolley car to use that incline for the next seven years. The car had scarcely moved out onto Pleasant Street than waiting crews set to work tearing up trackage and installing the final connecting rails to a ramp leading up to the recently built elevated structure. Just outside the tunnel portal, a wooden center-island platform would now serve as the Pleasant Street station for the new MU el trains.

In the tunnel itself, additional frantic activity was under way to meet the weekend deadline. Carpenters' hammers echoed from station to station, as new wooden platforms were "superimposed over the regular platforms—to bring passengers on a level with the cars."[27] These were placed along the subway's outside tracks, where the multiple-unit "elevated" trains would run as they made their way through downtown Boston on their runs between Roxbury and Charleston. Final work was also needed in the subway to install and energize the third rail from which the new MU trains would draw electric current.

The southbound track was pronounced ready at five o'clock on Sunday morning, and at 7:00 A.M. BERY Superintendent S. S. Neff ran a test train over the entire line—from Sullivan to Dudley. For the rest of that day, "school trains" were sent up and down the line to acquaint operating employees with the route, even as tunnel gangs were finishing off their assignments. The conversion was completed in ample time for the inauguration on Monday morning.

Late Sunday afternoon, a representative of the Sprague organization by the name of Colonel Shepard who was in Boston to help with the changeover opined that "the people of Boston ought to feel proud of this road. There is nothing equal to it in the world. A train may be started and stopped at any grade with ease."[28] One comparison frequently stressed in discussion about the new el pointed out that a ninety-ton, three-car train could call on 900 horsepower for tractive effort, whereas the 1,000-ton consist of the New York Central Railroad's crack "Empire State Express" had but 1,000 horsepower at its disposal.

A massive change in surface-car operations coincided with the opening of the new line. Chiefly, this involved routing streetcars that had previously gone all the way downtown into the terminals and stations of the new el, where convenient transfers could be

managed between surface cars and the new el trains. At each of
the two terminals, Sullivan Square and Dudley, the trolley cars
rumbled up to elevated level on various kinds of ramps, and passengers were able to make an across-the-platform transfer from
streetcars to el trains. So complicated were the changes in schedules and routings that BERY suggested passengers pin copies of
the new timetables inside their hats.

At the Dudley Terminal in Roxbury, two sets of streetcar tracks
ran up a pair of ramps to el platform level. Each of these tracks
then looped and returned to the street, so that several car lines
could be accommodated on just two tracks. The streetcar loop
track to the west of the new el platform would be used by trolley
lines serving the growing residential areas of Forest Hills, Jamaica Plains, and Roxbury Crossing. A half-dozen or more lines
that fanned out into Roxbury and Dorchester would use the loop
track to the east.

Under the high vault of a train shed at Sullivan Square on the
Charleston end of the line, ten stub-end trolley tracks—five on
either side of the single elevated track—provided terminal facilities for the many feeder streetcar lines connecting with the new
el at this point. All of these tracks entered the terminal shed on
ramps located on the north side; only the el itself made an approach from the south.

(Convenient transferring between streetcars and rapid transit,
and more important, converting trolley lines that had previously
provided trunk-line service into downtown into feeder routes for
new rapid-transit service would be an important hallmark of
mass transport in Boston, one that, for a variety of reasons,
would not be extensively emulated in other U.S. cities that built
early rapid-transit lines. To this day, in fact, downtown Boston
has relatively little in the way of surface transit—that is, motor
buses—and the subway lines once operated by the West End
Street Railway and the Boston El continue to provide the principal public transit access into and out of the city's downtown
core.)

When the Main Line El opened for business in 1901, both
Sullivan Square and Dudley Street had but a single platform
where el trains both loaded and unloaded passengers. This often
lend to congestion and delay—not to mention unpleasant en-

counters between boarding and alighting passengers. In later years both terminals would be expanded and separate platforms provided for northbound and southbound trains.[29]

On that Monday morning when the new elevated line was ready to inaugurate service, more people than could be accommodated were on hand to ride the first revenue trains. At 5:00 A.M. there were over 500 people waiting to board at Dudley, for instance, and when ticket booths opened for business shortly after five o'clock, one Charles Cutter of Worcester Place, in Boston, purchased the first ticket. As a good-luck gesture, his nickel fare was returned.[30]

Precisely at 5:25 A.M., wooden el cars Nos. 065, 056, and 082 left Dudley on the line's first run, a motorman by the name of Dolan doing the head-end honors. But the train may have had a hex on it—near Boylston Station, inside the subway, the air brakes locked. BERY officials spent fifteen feverish minutes correcting the trouble, but the festive atmosphere in the train was not disrupted one bit by the mishap. One passenger cracked: "We're right under the [Hotel] Touraine; all out for breakfast."[31]

At Sullivan Square, on the north end of the line, there was confusion bordering on pandemonium. A crowd had gathered at street level there even earlier than at Dudley, and no record was made of who purchased the first ticket. Frustration, too, was felt when three streetcars rumbled up the ramp into the overhead train shed, giving their passengers a chance to bypass the crowd that had gathered below, and waited at street level in predawn darkness. For the record, the first trolley into the shed was from Medford, No. 2935; No. 2916 followed, also a Medford car; and No. 2949, out of Everett, was third.

Superintendent Neff had come to Boston after a successful stint on the elevated lines of Chicago. Described as a man who was fiercely proud of his adopted hometown, Neff had made a final test run over the entire line at 4:00 A.M. on Monday morning. At 5:20 he ordered the first train into the Sullivan Square Station from the adjacent storage yard; by 5:28 it was full of passengers, and at 5:30, five minutes after the first northbound train had departed Dudley at the south end of the line, the first revenue train left Sullivan Square, with Neff himself at the controls. Exactly twenty-three and a half minutes later, the train reached Dudley.

Over 200,000 fares were paid on that first day, an extraordinary count compared to a turnstile tally of 150,000 daily passengers who would ride a much-expanded Main Line El in the years after the Second World War. Speaking of turnstiles, incidentally, calls attention to the fact that in 1901 BERY did not use such hardware. The system then in force required passengers to purchase a small pasteboard ticket from what would today be the change booth and deposit it in a "chopper box" to gain entrance to the platform area. The chopper boxes were manned by vigilant uniformed guards to preclude the use of counterfeit tickets. It was not until 1915 that this ticket system was phased out and coin of the realm accepted as direct payment—coins that passengers were expected to deposit in new turnstiles.

The city celebrated its new transit line with enthusiasm. Like its predecessor, the original subway of 1897, the Roxbury-Charlestown Subway-Elevated Line was an immediate and large-scale success. True enough, persons living on the top floor of three-story apartments adjacent to the tracks had to be vigilant in keeping their window shades lowered, and some realtors sourly reported that "For Rent" signs were appearing along the el's route more frequently than elsewhere. But the advent of the new transit line served to solidify property values in territory far beyond the immediate range of the line's alleged disadvantageous effects. Cries would frequently be heard, though, that the "hideous structures which the Boston elevated company has been allowed to disfigure and darken our streets with" should be torn down and replaced with a subway.[32]

For the opening of the Main Line El, the Boston Elevated Railway supplemented older electric-generating stations that had earlier been built by the West End Street Railway with a large new power plant along the Atlantic Avenue waterfront at Lincoln Wharf. Three cross-compound reciprocating steam engines built by the Providence Engineering Company provided Lincoln Wharf with its initial power, with each engine linked to a 2,700-kilowatt electric generator. (In 1908, two additional generating engines were installed at Lincoln Wharf.) Current was then distributed to substations throughout the system before being fed into the third rail of the Main Line El and the overhead wires of the BERY streetcar system. Unlike the powerhouse built by the

Interborough Rapid Transit Company in New York, where electricity was generated as alternating current and later converted into direct current, at BERY's Lincoln Wharf facility—as well as the older stations originally built by the West End Street Railway—electricity was generated as direct current.[33]

The Main Line El was quickly expanded. On Thursday, August 22, 1901, an alternative and all-elevated routing was completed that allowed trains to operate from terminal to terminal without having to transit the Tremont Street Subway. This alternative line branched off the Main Line El just north of the Dover Street Station and rejoined the original route near North Station. Built largely over Atlantic Avenue, it linked the city's two major railroad stations, North Station and South Station, and provided access to numerous steamboat berths and ferry slips along the city's busy waterfront. Over the years a variety of routings would appear on head-end destination boards of trains using this line— through-service between Dudley and Sullivan via Atlantic Avenue, a special "Atlantic Circuit" train in loop service through the subway and over the waterfront el, a North Station–South Station shuttle. For a time, shortly after the Atlantic Avenue alternative opened, trains from both terminals, Sullivan and Dudley, ran over both subway and el and then looped back to their terminal of origin.[34]

By just about any standard, though, BERY's Atlantic Avenue El was never an out-and-out success. It was plagued by bad luck, particularly in January 1919, when a huge, iron, molasses tank belonging to the Purity Distilling Company on Commercial Street in the North End exploded. A 2-million-gallon wave of syrup surged into Atlantic Avenue, knocking out one support column for the el and weakening several others.[35] Patronage on the Atlantic Avenue el remained disappointing, and on September 30, 1938, BERY discontinued service along this line. The structure was later torn down and its steel contributed to the wartime scrap drive.

In 1909, the Main Line El was extended southward some 2½ miles from Dudley to an impressive terminal station in Forest Hills that used reinforced concrete, as opposed to steel girders, for its construction. BERY president William A. Bancroft unashamedly called it the "finest terminal station in the world."[36]

At Forest Hills, el-to-trolley transfers could be made to numerous points in the southwestern suburbs, and streetcar lines that had previously traveled all the way to Dudley to connect with the el were appropriately shortened. At 5:16 A.M. on Monday, November 22, a gong sounded in the new station, and five freshly painted el cars departed for Sullivan Square carrying forty-eight passengers and a bevy of BERY officials. "Running smooth as grease and every train on time," remarked trainmaster George Benjamin after the first day of operation.[37]

The el company's planning quickly raised prospects of a northward extension beyond Sullivan Square to destinations in Malden and Melrose, and even Lynn. Yet until the 1970s, the only northward extension ever to get beyond the discussion stage began service on March 15, 1919, when trains started running an additional elevated mile beyond Sullivan Square and across the Mystic River into a terminal at Everett. Believed at the time to be little more than a temporary terminal—the station itself was far from elaborate, and downright shoddy compared to Forest Hills—the terminal was to remain "temporary" for over fifty years.[38]

Steel cars were introduced to the Main Line El in 1907, and by 1928 all of the original wooden units had been retired. The reason why steel cars were not ordered in 1901, when the Main Line El inaugurated service, is simple enough—the all-steel passenger car was not invented until 1903, when George Gibbs designed car No. 3342 for August Belmont's Interborough Rapid Transit Company, as discussed in Chapter 1.

Over the years, the fleet of MU cars serving the Main Line El was upgraded to incorporate state-of-the-art advances in transit technology and design. For instance, original equipment featured open platforms and manual-gate entry, very like typical elevated cars in New York and Brooklyn. Cars with enclosed vestibules and sliding doors were first added to the roster in 1904, and eventually the open platforms of the 1901-era cars were enclosed and fitted with sliding doors.[39] BERY officials were quite pleased with their new sliding-door cars, and pointed out that between Sullivan and Dudley, while a train of open-gate cars had an average station dwell time of 21.1 seconds, a train equipped with sliding doors reduced this time to 17.9 seconds, thereby enabling more trains to carry more passengers over the line in a given period of time.[40]

Basic rolling stock acquired by BERY for the Main Line El, whether built of wood or steel, rather resembled equipment used in New York by the Interborough Rapid Transit Company— except that the Boston cars were just a bit smaller. Where Interborough cars were a small fraction over 51 feet long, BERY eventually settled on a car length of 46 feet, 7¼ inches, while at 8 feet, 7 inches in width, BERY el cars were 4 inches narrower than Interborough rolling stock. Looking beyond the few early units that were equipped with open platforms, BERY el cars featured end vestibules with passenger entry and exit doors, plus an additional center door. Like standard Interborough rolling stock, steel cars designed for Boston's Main Line El featured an under-floor "fish-belly" girder to ensure structural integrity. BERY el cars were also equipped with "trip" devices designed to bring a train to an immediate stop should a motorman happen to run past a red signal. During the early years, rolling stock on the el was painted maroon with gold trim. By the mid-1920s this aristocratic livery had been replaced by a typical railroad-coach green without trim, striping, or any sort of ornamentation.[41]

With respect to Boston's Main Line El, what was clearly more significant than any improvements in rolling stock design was a major alteration that took place in 1908, seven years after service was inaugurated. That was when el trains were removed from the original Tremont Street Subway and rerouted into a brand-new, $8 million, 1.23-mile tunnel under Washington Street for their passage through downtown Boston. "The beginning of operation of the new subway will witness the withdrawal of the elevated trains, which have been operated in the Tremont Street subway since the new service began in June, 1901, and the return of the surface cars to its through tracks. There can be no doubt that the [Tremont Street] subway is far more suited to the operation of single cars of the surface type than to large elevated trains,"[42] the *Street Railway Journal* commented.

Instead of running high-platform el trains along the outside tracks of the Tremont Street Subway, the 1897 facility would be reconfigured for trolley cars only, and el trains would have access to their own exclusive underground right-of-way, one that would permit more expeditious passage through downtown Boston since its tracks featured far less twisting and curving than the older trolley subway. On Monday morning, November 30, 1908, trains departing from Sullivan and Dudley at 5:24 A.M. became the first revenue runs through the new tunnel. The changeover from the Tremont Street routing had been accomplished, again in a single weekend, by frantic activity reminiscent of 1901.

In 1902, when the Massachusetts legislature enacted the measure that authorized the Boston Transit Commission to build the Washington Street Tunnel, it was assumed that a four-track subway would be built along the Washington Street corridor—two tracks for the Main Line El, and two additional tracks for a new trolley subway.[43] Only the two rapid tunnels were ever constructed, however.

THE EAST BOSTON TUNNEL

For its time, and for many decades afterward, the most ambitious transit project Boston ever undertook was a trolley tunnel under Boston Harbor. Subaqueous tunnels may be commonplace enough today; they surely were not in 1904.

The accepted method for tunneling through soft underwater silt relied on a device called the Greathead Shield. This circular device, named for its British inventor, Sir Henry Greathead, moves forward inside a pressurized air lock and allows a tunnel to be constructed in its wake from within. Early railway tunnels under the East River and the Hudson River in New York, for instance, were built this way. But the clay under Boston Harbor proved to be rather firmer than soft silt, and so a modified tunneling technique was used. The boring device was called a "roof shield," a semicircular steel vault also set up within a pressurized air lock. The construction procedure was this: Two small pilot tunnels were dug in advance of the shield and shored up with heavy timbers. Inside these bores, concrete footings for the final sidewalls of the tunnel were poured. Then, pushed forward by hydraulic jacks, the roof shield advanced, supported by rollers on top of the preconstructed footings. The vault of the shield shored up the cavity of the tunnel proper and, as soon as interior excavation was completed, the permanent structure was built, the roof shield doing double duty as a sort of mold.

At an average weekly advance of 32 feet, it took two-and-a-half years to complete the mile-long project under Boston Harbor, 2,700 feet of which were actually under water. Four unfortunate workmen lost their lives during the work, and the total cost of the project in 1904 was $3 million. To complete the tunnel, workers had to install 61,000 cubic yards of concrete and 1,450 tons of steel.

Howard Carsen, supervisor of the original Tremont Street Subway, was named chief engineer on the East Boston project, and when trolley cars began to run through the new tube in December 1904, it was only the second long-distance underwater vehicular tunnel in all of North America and stood as another splendid Boston transit accomplishment. (The first was an 1890 tunnel under the St. Clair River between Port Huron, Michigan, and Sarnia, Ontario, built by the Grand Trunk Railroad.)

East Boston marked the opening of the tunnel with uncommon gusto. The night before revenue service began, a formal dinner was held at Masonic Hall, and invited guests were treated by BERY president William A. Bancroft to a tour through East Boston neighborhoods aboard ten brand-new trolley cars. Streets came alive with celebratory activity despite the fact that it was winter, and fireworks lighted the night sky. Then the fleet of cars dipped down into the new tunnel for a preview look at the object of the celebration. Of those present, nobody had a grander time than Massachusetts governor John L. Bates. Ten years earlier, as a first-term state representative from East Boston, he had skillfully managed to have this district included in the 1894 legislation as both deserving of and requiring mass-transit service.[44]

The next morning, on December 30, 1904, motorman John Alexander left the Lexington Street car barn in East Boston at 5:20 A.M. on trolley car No. 581. Picking up passengers en route, the car wound its way to Maverick Square, entered the new tunnel, and at 5:37 A.M. was discharging the first customers to pay their way under Boston Harbor at the Court Street terminal station in downtown Boston. The fare they paid, incidentally, was a penny higher than BERY's regular five-cent tariff to help offset the cost of the new tunnel. Car No. 588 from Chelsea on the Broadway

Line came next, and the third trolley through the new tunnel was car No. 407 from Orient Heights.[45]

An immediate and noticeable effect of the opening of the new East Boston Tunnel was a serious drop-off in patronage on the municipally operated ferryboats that crossed the harbor. A reporter commented that only teams of horses and their drivers seemed to be using the old side-wheel steamers now that electric cars were running into Boston under the harbor.[46] Ironically, the eventual demise of ferryboat service in Boston would later be instrumental in the 1938 abandonment of BERY's own Atlantic Avenue El, since el trains provided connecting service for ferry passengers.[47]

From an operational perspective, the underground station at Court Street, where cars from East Boston terminated, proved to be cumbersome. It was a stub-end facility where cars had to change ends before returning to Maverick and East Boston, a time-consuming procedure that limited the number of trolleys that could operate through the tunnel. This shortcoming was rectified in 1916 by eliminating the original terminal and building instead a crosstown extension less than half a mile long to Bowdoin Square. Here there was sufficient room for both a more efficient loop turnaround and an incline up and out to surface tracks in the middle of Cambridge Street, hence making possible through trolley service, for example, between East Boston and Cambridge. The cost of the Bowdoin extension was $2.3 million.

Then, in the course of an April double-holiday weekend in 1924, the twenty-year-old East Boston Line underwent the strangest metamorphosis of any Boston transit operation before or since. Patrons on the line went home after work on Friday, April 18, the eve of Patriots' Day—a state holiday honoring the battles of Lexington and Concord—aboard their familiar trolley cars. But when they returned to work on Monday morning, the day after Easter, they rode aboard brand-new steel MU trains that they could board and alight from newly constructed high-level platforms. Three years of planning and preliminary construction preceded this dramatic weekend changeover.

As the final trolley rumbled clear of the tunnel in East Boston at 8:30 P.M. on Friday evening, a crew of 1,525 men were poised for work on a task so extensive that many observers doubted it could be done on time. Thousands of feet of trolley-style guard-rail had to be removed and replaced by rails that would allow the Master Car Builder–style wheel flanges of the new rapid-transit cars to negotiate the line. Old special work—340 feet of it—had to be ripped out, and 724 feet of new switches and crossovers installed. Nearly 4 miles of third rail had to be hoisted onto preset insulators, electrically connected, and tested. At the direction of Boston mayor James Michael Curley, many of the workers hired to handle the East Boston conversion were First World War veterans whose return home from the fields of Flanders in 1918 brought them face-to-face with a different kind of enemy: unemployment.

A new general manager was directing the Boston El in 1924, a man who would provide the transit system with more than thirty years of firm and knowledgeable leadership and who, many feel, directed BERY to its years of peak achievement. His name was Edward Dana, a Harvard graduate (class of 07) whose career with the company began after graduation, as a conductor. Dana not only saw the East Boston changeover through to completion on time, but he capped if off with verse appropriate to Patriots' Day:

> Listen good friends and you shall read
> Of an all night oil on an urgent need.
> On the eighteenth of April in twenty-four
> Hardly a soul heard the hammer's roar—
> Or thought of the men who accomplished the deed.

The first test train of steel MU cars was operating at 1:00 A.M. on Monday morning, April 21. At 5:05 A.M. that same day, General Manager Dana led a party of understandably sleepy dignitaries aboard the first revenue train to depart from Maverick Station in East Boston, a new underground facility where passengers traveling aboard the high-platform rapid-transit trains could make across-the-platform transfers to and from local streetcars at subway level.[48]

The cars themselves, series 0500 and built by Pullman, had already been tested on BERY's Cambridge Subway (see below) and thereafter through 1951 they were maintained and serviced at the Eliot Shops of this route in Harvard Square. Access be-

tween the two lines was via the former trolley-car incline at Bowdoin, a short haul over surface-level streetcar trackage, and then
into the Cambridge Subway at the midpoint of Longfellow
Bridge. This bizarre shunting operation, with the 0500-series
cars hauled by electric locomotives, was typically conducted in
the dark of night.

Designing the new rapid-transit cars presented many chal-
lenges to BERY's engineering staff. Because the East Boston
route had been designed for trolley cars, it had very sharp curves,
close clearances, and—in 1904, at least—no premonition of the
1924 conversion. The grade in the tunnel was 5 percent, severe
enough for trolley cars but even more so for MU subway trains.
The new cars each seated forty-four passengers, were short and
narrow—47 feet long and 8½ feet wide—and rode on small, 26-
inch-diameter wheels, thereby saving a few more precious inches
of height. The cars were permanently coupled into two-car sets,
each car sharing certain electrical equipment with its running
mate as a further weight-saving measure. A single 0500-series
subway car weighed by 44,400 pounds empty, while the final
series of trolley cars used in the East Boston Tunnel weighed
45,000 pounds each.[49]

Thus Boston's third rapid-transit line opened for business in
1904 and twenty years later was transformed into something its
original designers never imagined.[50] Still, the development of this
line was by no means complete. In the post–Second World War
era, it will be transformed once again, and in a manner that will
be almost as dramatic as were the changes that were effected in
1924.

REFLECTIONS ON THE BOSTON EL

The Boston Elevated Railway was a stockholder corporation
whose purpose, in classic economic parlance, was the earning of
dividends for its investors. Nevertheless, urban public transportation was—and continues to be—a public service not to be wholly
understood in a profit-and-loss context. This angle of the matter
explains, as much as anything else, the friction that developed in

Boston between citizen representatives and the overlords of the Elevated.

BERY would, of course, eventually surrender its status as a private corporation, an evolutionary process common to all U.S. cities where private interests had participated in the construction and operation of subways and elevated lines in the early years of the twentieth century. In 1947, the properties, liabilities, assets, and good name of the Boston Elevated Railway were transferred to a pubic agency, the Metropolitan Transit Authority (MTA), and the operation of mass transit in and around Boston became a public-sector responsibility. Yet between the halcyon days early in the twentieth century, when transit profits were both lucrative and automatic, and the advent of the MTA just before mid-century, the Boston El wrote some interesting chapters in the history of urban transport economics.

In 1918, BERY moved into a special status that was neither out-and-out laissez faire capitalism nor nonprofit municipal service. In Boston it was called "public control" and it was quite different from public-private transit partnerships in cities such as New York, Chicago, and Philadelphia.

"The transportation system of the Boston Elevated Railway is not meeting the public needs, for the property has not been kept in good, modern operating condition, the net earnings are shrinking, the service is poor and the credit is gone."[51] Such were the conclusions reached by the Massachusetts Public Service Commission (PSC) in a special report to the state legislature delivered in early 1918. Such a state of affairs had come to pass because BERY's income from transit fares had been fixed at five cents per passenger by the various lease agreements that permitted the company to operate its trains and trolley cars in publicly owned subway tunnels. As inflation continually drove the company's expenses higher, the requirement that transit fares remain at five cents eroded BERY's financial position to the brink of receivership.

To avoid this, the PSC, now the agency of jurisdiction, proposed that operating control of BERY be put in the hands of a new board of public trustees. There was to be a municipal guarantee of a specified rate of return for BERY securities, while the city of Boston would meet any deficits in day-to-day transit operating expenses. In addition, the notion of a permanent nickel fare was abandoned, and while municipal resources were available to meet short-term deficits, the public trustees were expected to set transit fares at whatever rate was required to meet anticipated expenses.[52]

The proposal was highly controversial, especially the idea of guaranteeing a specified rate of return to the investors of an otherwise private corporation. The notion of raising the fare was also unpopular, and whether public control of the company was, in retrospect, a good idea or a bad one, there was little doubt that the status quo was no longer tolerable. The PSC put it this way: "Unusual conditions demand unusual remedies. The commission believes that in the present emergency private credit and private enterprise are unequal to the task and that no fundamental improvement can be accomplished unless the whole community puts its shoulder to the wheel and pulls BERY out of the slough into which it is rapidly sinking."[53]

The *Electric Railway Journal* agreed with this diagnosis. In an editorial titled "Boston Relief Provisions Are Worthy of Enactment," the magazine said: "A bold move? Perhaps, but this is no time for halfway measures of relief. The Boston transit situation from a financial point of view demands potent measures, even if they are unprecedented."[54]

The public control bill became law in May of 1918. BERY president Matthew C. Brush characterized it as the "biggest, strongest, finest piece of legislation ever passed in the electric railway field."[55] Brokers quickly pointed out to their clients that the new law placed BERY "paper" on a plane only slightly less stable than United States treasury bonds. On August 1, 1918, the basic fare on BERY trolley cars and trains was raised to seven cents; the following year it became ten cents.

Economic difficulties aside, BERY accomplished some memorable things during its fifty-odd years of existence, earning high marks for equipment design, most notably a streetcar that excited the entire electric traction industry. This was the "center-entrance car," a piece of rolling stock that proved especially efficient in the specialized service environment of the Tremont Street trolley subway.

The first of these cars—seventy-five units built by the J. G.

Brill Company and twenty-five turned out by Laconia—appeared on the property in 1915 as motorless trailers that had to be hauled by a conventional trolley car; between 1915 and 1918 BERY acquired 225 such trailer cars. Then, beginning in 1917, the initial units of a fleet that eventually numbered 405 center-entrance motor cars were delivered by Brill, Laconia and Kuhlman. They were big—almost 49 feet long—and had an acceleration and braking rate of 1.95 miles per hour/per second. Two General Electric No. 247 motors powered each truck, and each car featured two motorized trucks. Streetcars of the era typically featured two motors mounted in a single motorized truck and one nonmotorized trailer truck. BERY, however, preferred the additional power that four motors supplied. Of the 405 motorized center-entrance cars, 300 were equipped with MU control to permit their operation as multicar trains, a style of service that quickly became critical for the successful operation of the original Boston trolley subway.[56]

Trolley poles atop the center-entrance cars were mounted in an unusual reversed fashion. The rope attached to the end of the trolley pole was worked from inside the car through an opening in the roof, a feature that was included because of the restricted confines of the subway. Of all the rail vehicles designed for service in Boston over the years, the bulky and awkward-looking center-entrance cars remain the favorite of many who knew them. "They got up heat real good on cold mornings," a former motorman once remarked, adding, "I'd say they were our best cars for getting through heavy snow."[57]

The center-entrance motor cars were initially assigned to the East Boston Tunnel service, but they are best remembered running outdoors in three-car MU trains on the Beacon Street and Commonwealth Avenue lines, from which they dived into the original subway complex. The wide center doors were ideal for the fast loading and unloading demanded of them at the Park and Boylston stations. Just prior to the acquisition of these new cars, the original Boston Subway was expanded in several directions.

In May 1912, a 1.8-mile elevated line was opened from the Haymarket incline of the original subway in Boston, across the Charles River on a concrete-arch viaduct, to Lechmere Square in East Cambridge. Here, streetcars using the Central Subway could reverse direction and return to Boston; here too, surface cars from various Cambridge neighborhoods could enter the right-of-way and operate into the Tremont Street Subway.[58] This extension cost $4 million to build, and service was inaugurated—with no public ceremonies or festivities, incidentally—early on the morning of June 1, 1912, when motorman Peter Marchand and conductor Thomas Finucane left the Bennett Street car barn in Cambridge aboard car No. 5287 at 4:51 A.M. and after entering the new line at Lechmere, reached North Station at 5:12.[59]

The year 1912 also saw the start of construction on a very important westward leg that was spliced onto the original Tremont Street Subway. Beyond the Public Garden incline, a two-track tunnel was built under Boylston Street and through the Back Bay to a new incline just east of Governor (now Kenmore) Square. Service to this quarter of the city had long been discussed, and a proposal that was called the Riverbank Subway at one time appeared to be on the verge of construction. It would have been a totally new trolley subway from Park Street beneath Beacon Hill to the bank of the Charles River and thence into the Back Bay area. The Riverbank Subway, though, was never built, and in 1914 an extension of the original trolley subway under Boylston Street became the initial westward expansion of rapid transit in Boston.[60]

In 1932, another extension was added to the trolley subway that took it beyond Kenmore Square and up to the surface on two different inclines—one at Blandford Street and Commonwealth Avenue, the other at Beacon and St. Mary's streets. An oddity of sorts is that the station at Kenmore was built with the thought of someday converting the entire trolley subway—or the Central Subway, as the Boston trolley subway came to be called—to high-platform operation, as had been done on the East Boston Tunnel in 1924. Consequently, the center pair of tracks in the four-track station was constructed on raised supports. The permanent floor beneath these supports was at a level that would be perfect for high-platform rapid-transit cars. Streetcars would always use the outside pair of tracks, or so it was reasoned, and thus a return loop was built so that trolleys on these tracks could transfer their passengers to the subway at Kenmore and then return from whence they came.[61]

The westward extension of the trolley subway has since become a very heavily trafficked line, but what was surely its most unusual operation took place on the night of December 13, 1917, when intervals between trains were somewhat relaxed. One Daniel Kinnally, of Chelsea, was making last-minute deliveries in the Kenmore Square area. He left his horse and wagon unattended while he quickly ran into an apartment building on Beacon Street. The horse—whose name, at this remove, is not known—took off on his or her own. Horse and wagon, the latter racketing along the cross-ties, headed down the incline at Kenmore Square and into the subway. The agent at the first station along the line, Massachusetts Avenue, was notified of the unscheduled operation. Timidly, he stepped onto the track to intercept the runaway. Out of the gloom of the tunnel galloped the strange consist, looking for all the world like a fugitive from the movie *Ben Hur*. Intrepid agent David Berry thus became the first—and likely the only—Boston transit employee who ever flagged down a horse in the Boylston Street Subway.[62]

ACROSS THE RIVER TO CAMBRIDGE

Talk of and plans for a rapid-transit line between Boston and Cambridge date back to the earliest era of subways in Boston. Indeed the metropolitan area's very street railway service, a horse-car line that inaugurated service in 1856, connected Boston with Cambridge, and the enabling legislation of 1894 that resulted in the original subway of 1897 also stipulated that the Boston Transit Commission should build a new bridge across the Charles River to Cambridge, a span to accommodate both street traffic and a new transit line. Such a bridge was begun in 1900, formally dedicated in 1907, and called the Longfellow Bridge. But the built-in transit right-of-way in the center of the $2.6-million span remained unused for another five years.

Initially, there was talk of an elevated line to Cambridge. It soon became clear, however, that a subway was a better idea. Work on the line did not begin until 1909, largely because a running and sometimes bitter feud had first to be resolved over the number of stations to be built along the line as it moved through

Cambridge. Local residents, championed by Cambridge mayor Wardell, wanted the new subway to serve primarily their needs, with at least four stations between Harvard Square and the Charles River. Opposed were suburbanites living beyond Harvard Square who wanted a more express service into Boston for their convenience and felt that a single intermediate station in Cambridge would suffice, obviously at Central Square, where transfers would be available to streetcars bound for Newton and Brookline.[63]

The conflict raged. Both sides retained outside consultants, and the issue was eventually settled by compromise—there would be two stations: one at Central Square, the other at Kendall Square. The Cambridge faction even marshaled a group of physicians who asserted that a long, station-free subway would become so charged with "mephetic exhalations" as to present a perilous health hazard for both riders and residents.[64]

The line was plotted to run from Harvard Square to a point beneath the Park Street Station of the Tremont Street Subway, after an earlier proposal to make Scollay Square the line's Boston terminal faltered. The project involved four separate construction phases. First and second, or vice versa, the Transit Commission would build a deep underground tunnel through Beacon Hill plus, as noted above, a rapid-transit right-of-way in the median of the new Longfellow Bridge. The third phase was to be the responsibility of the Boston Elevated Railway and it called for a short elevated link between the Longfellow Bridge and the tunnel under Beacon Hill. The fourth phase, also to be prosecuted by BERY, was the subway portion of the line in Cambridge. The new line was given two formal names: the segment in Boston proper was called the "Cambridge Connection," while across the river it was known as the "Cambridge Main Street Subway." Construction got underway in 1909—July 12, 1909, on the Cambridge Main Street Subway; September 29, 1909, on the Cambridge Connection segment in Boston.[65]

"Beacon Hill is presumably a glacial formation," ventured a 1911 issue of *Scientific American* in comment on the geology, not the politics, of the deep-tunnel route.[66] This section of the line required precision engineering. A 65-ton roof shield was used to push a 32-foot-diameter bore directly under what was both the city's top-drawer residential community and the seat of Massachusetts state government. At its deepest point, the floor of the tunnel rests a hundred feet below street level, and the tunnel cuts across numerous artesian wells dating from pre-Revolutionary days. Because the ground proved to be sufficiently firm—as engineers expected—the project was built without the complexity and additional cost of an air lock. Although a portion of the tunnel had to be negotiated through a 4,000-foot-radius arc, it "came out" within 6 inches of its calculated position. In early 1912, the Park Street–Harvard Square route was ready for service.[67]

On Monday, March 11, 1912, a party of 400 invited guests was treated to a special tour of the new route aboard one of the Boston El's new trains, with BERY president William A. Bancroft playing the role of proud host. Come Saturday morning, March 23, 1912, the new Boston-Cambridge Subway was ready for revenue service. The cost of its construction: $11,750,000.[68]

Mrs. Mary Collett of Revere Street, Cambridge, after standing on line at Harvard Square from 3:00 A.M., purchased the very first ticket to ride the new line, while a Cambridge physician by the name of William Dwyer was the first of his gender to purchase a similar ticket. Dr. Dwyer, wearing a fine black derby hat and an overcoat with an oversized collar, was on his way home after making an emergency night call and grew curious about all the people and noise at Harvard Square.

At 5:10 A.M., a three-car train moved into the departure track on the lower of the two levels in the Harvard Square Station, but when officials calculated the size of the waiting crowd, a fourth car was quickly dispatched from the nearby storage yard and coupled onto the rear of the train. At 5:20, passengers were let into the station, and on the dot of 5:24, the four-car train— composed of subway cars 0618, 0614, 0620, and 0623— accelerated away from Harvard Square on an eight-minute run to a new station called Park Street Under. William Miles was the train's motorman, and 286 passengers made the trip. Accounts of the inaugural spoke of the "varsity-like behavior" of the riders and suggested "perhaps the crimson trimmings of the Harvard station had a tendency to inspire the passengers upon the first train to give vent to this overflow of enthusiasm."[69]

(Two important Boston transit improvements were phased into service on the spring of 1912—the new Cambridge Subway in late March and the extension of trolley-subway service to Lechmere in May. In April, between these two inaugurals, another classic Boston venue opened for business for the very first time when the city's American League baseball team, the Red Sox, began playing ball in its newly built home, Fenway Park.)

Rolling stock for the new Cambridge Subway was a departure from earlier subway and el cars—in Boston, or anywhere else. Externally, the noticeable difference was that the cars had no vestibules at the ends for passenger entry and exit but, rather, three sets of doors spaced evenly along the sides of the cars. In addition, they were both longer and wider than the cars on BERY's older Main Line El. Their basic design was later adopted for subway service in New York by the Brooklyn Rapid Transit Company, the agency that joined August Belmont's Interborough in the construction and operation of the network of new subway lines called for in the Dual Contracts of 1913.

The Standard Steel Car Company built the first forty cars for the Cambridge Line. Each measured 69 feet, 2½ inches long and 9 feet, 6 inches wide at the door sills, in contrast to the typical Main Line car of 46-foot length and 8-foot, 7-inch width. An empty Cambridge car weighed 85,900 pounds and had seats for 72 passengers, versus 70,000 pounds and 44 passengers on the company's older elevated stock. The newcomers ran on Brill No. 27 M.C.B. trucks, one of which was a motor truck with 34-inch wheels, the other a nonpowered trailer with 31-inch wheels. Power for the motor trucks was delivered by two Westinghouse 200 horsepower No. 300B electric motors geared 20:63, with a free-running speed of 45 mile per hour.[70]

For all the advantages gained from the adoption of a different and larger set of specifications for the new line, there was a corresponding disadvantage. True enough, the almost 10-foot width of the Cambridge cars accommodated more passengers per car, and the line's wide radius curves meant that better speed could be maintained and passengers would reach their destinations with greater dispatch. But the new specifications also meant that equipment could never be interchanged routinely between the various high-platform rapid-transit lines in Boston. When cars from the Main Line El were at one time assigned to the Cambridge run during a temporary equipment shortage, they first had to be equipped with temporary steel extension plates at the door sills to bridge the gap resulting when cars 9 feet wide stopped at platforms built to handle larger rolling stock. Obviously 10-foot-wide cars could never be altered to run on a line built to operate nine-footers!

In short, the need to maintain separate car fleets would be a chronic bother for Boston transit managers over the years. Furthermore, when the East Boston Tunnel was converted to high-platform standards in 1924, as described above, its peculiar dimensions added yet a third set of specifications to BERY's rapid-transit fleet, a lack of standardization that continues into the twenty-first century. (When the Boston El began to evaluate converting the East Boston Line into a high-platform operation, a serious effort was made to see if the newer and larger Cambridge cars might be used there. Not only did that prove impractical, but tunnel dimensions were so restrictive that even Main Line El cars were too large and a specialized fleet had to be designed and acquired for East Boston service.)[71]

Harvard Square to Park Street was never intended to be the full extent of this new line. Within two months of its March 1912 opening, the Boston Transit Commission had executed the first contract for the new subway's continuation through downtown Boston and into residential communities to the south. Ground was broken on Winter Street just beyond the Park Street Under Station on May 30, 1912, and during subsequent years, service was extended southward.[72] By December 1917, a tunnel under Fort Point Channel—a surprisingly complex and difficult engineering task—brought the line to Broadway Station in South Boston. Here a massive underground transfer facility was built so that streetcars from various points could rumble down an incline and into the mezzanine level of the station.

In 1923, another bill cleared the state legislature, one that authorized still another extension of the Cambridge Connector, this time into Dorchester over the right-of-way of the Shawmut Branch of the New York, New Haven and Hartford Railroad. There were complaints from some residents of suburban Milton, who were irked at losing their direct steam-train service into

Boston's South Station, and many Dorchester residents would have preferred a subway under Dorchester Avenue, rather than further east along the less accessible Shawmut Branch. But the line was welcome nonetheless, and nobody was more pleased than one Charles Ufford when a ceremonial train arrived at Fields Corner in Dorchester on November 4, 1927.

For thirty years, Ufford had championed the cause of rapid transit in his native Dorchester. He spoke before civic groups, showed lantern slides to luncheon groups, wrote letters to legislators, and in general kept up pressure for a cause in which he believed. Ufford was neither special pleader nor professional lobbyist, just an ordinary citizen who had a transit dream and rode it through to actuality. "I stand today a happy man," said he during the inaugural ceremony at Fields Corner. Alas, it was a flawed happiness—because in adjusting various streetcar lines in the Dorchester area as part of the rapid-transit expansion, BERY decided that the Norfolk Street Line, which served Ufford's neighborhood, would be better routed into the Dudley Station on the Main Line El rather than any station along the new Dorchester Extension.[73]

The following year, 1928, saw the line extended by two additional stations to Ashmont. Here a high-speed trolley line was built along a private right-of-way to provide passengers with connecting service to Mattapan Square. In all, the Dorchester extension, including the Mattapan shuttle, marked the first time in Boston that an electric rapid-transit line was substituted for an older steam-railroad commuter line, a practice that would later become not at all uncommon in the planning of new transit services.

Between 1911 and 1928, BERY took delivery of 155 subway cars to serve what eventually came to be called the Cambridge-Dorchester Line—typically shortened to "CD Line," among BERY workers. There would be continual talk of further expansion—south to Braintree, perhaps, or north from Harvard Square to Arlington Heights.[74] But, save for the acquisition of new subway cars by the MTA in 1963 to replace all of the line's original rolling stock, the Cambridge-Dorchester Line would remain substantially unchanged once it reached Ashmont in 1928 until a new wave of transit expansion got under way in and around Boston in 1971.

A special seasonal service that the Cambridge-Dorchester Line provided early on involved the routing of passenger-carrying trains beyond the Harvard Square terminal through Eliot Yard and then up to a special outdoor station platform located adjacent to Boylston Street—Cambridge's Boylston Street, not Boston's. From here, football fans could meander across the Charles River on the Larz Anderson Bridge and into Harvard Stadium. The first such service operated on Saturday, October 26, 1912. Harvard beat Brown that day by a score of 30 to 10, but with the growing popularity of the private automobile in the years after the Second World War—and the impracticality of throwing "tailgate" parties adjacent to subway cars—this special service for Harvard football fans was discontinued.

THE FORTIES AND FIFTIES

Three transit extensions were built during the decades of the forties and fifties, one before the war, two shortly after it, with the prewar project providing a glimpse into the political maneuverings of a legendary Boston figure. Talk about a subway under Huntington Avenue had bubbled and simmered for many decades. But in 1933, when Mayor James Michael Curley advanced a proposal for a new subway that would link the Copley Square Station on the Tremont–Boylston Central Subway with the Museum of Fine Arts on Huntington Avenue in the Fenway area, he sparked an on-again, off-again debate that continued until 1941, when such a line actually opened for business.

Curley's proposal of 1933, though, was advanced in the very midst of the Great Depression, and BERY chairman Bernard J. Rothwell was aghast at the very thought of expanding operations, claiming it would add $375,000 to Boston El's annual operating deficit. Mayor Curley, though, saw construction of the Huntington Avenue Subway as something that would meet more than the city's transportation needs. He saw the project as an important source of new jobs at precisely a time when far too many Boston breadwinners found themselves out of work. Further, Curley was able to use political leverage to ensure that building the Huntington Avenue Subway would not become a drain on scarce local resources. Instead, it became the second-largest project to be funded by the U.S. Works Project Administration (WPA), second only to New York's LaGuardia Airport. Of the project's $7.1-million price tag, $5.2 million came from Washington, and $4.8 million of the project's total cost wound up in the pockets of over 2,000 Boston workers who labored to build the new transit line.[75]

Until final plans were drawn up, the precise length of the new subway was uncertain. The line should go all the way to the museum—no, it should end at West Newton Street—or how about Massachusetts Avenue? As built, the line veered off the Boylston Street Subway to the west of Copley Station by means of a rather unsatisfactory "flat junction" that to this day forces outbound Huntington Avenue cars to cross the inbound main at grade. The new subway then twisted under the Boston and Albany Railroad yards and beneath Huntington Avenue to an incline at Opera Place, adjacent to the campus of Northeastern University. Completion of the line permitted Boston to abandon the subway incline at Boylston Street and the Public Garden and thereby eliminate surface cars from an important section of Back Bay and Downtown.

On the evening of February 15, 1941, "Type 4" trolley car No. 5364 rumbled across temporary girders at the mouth of the new Opera Place incline. Once the car was clear, workers began to remove temporary steelwork and to open access to the newly built subway. Track crews worked through the night, and at 2:30 P.M. the following afternoon, Boston mayor Maurice J. Tobin drove home a golden spike linking the new subway with the older Huntington Avenue streetcar line, although His Honor's first swing of the mallet missed the spike by a rather wide margin. Following the "golden spike" ceremony, BERY motorman Thomas Carty manned the controls in the lead car of a three-car train of center-entrance cars and took the official party on a ceremonial ride into the new tunnel. At 3:25 P.M., the first revenue train departed from Opera Place, one of the very few times when a new Boston transit line did not begin regular service at the crack of dawn. In the world beyond Boston, attention was focused on less celebratory activity than inaugurating service over a new subway line. The lead story in the same *Boston Globe* that described the Huntington Avenue inaugural ceremony told of British fears of a possible surprise attack on Singapore by the Japanese.[76]

The early days of the new Huntington Avenue Subway proved to be the last hurrah for Boston's distinctive center-entrance cars. Through the early 1930s, a committee within the street-railway industry had been working on designs for new trolley cars that would supposedly be the industry's riposte to encroachments being made by the motor bus. The effort turned out to be one of the few times in urban rail-transit history when a reasonably common rail-car design did develop, one that could be used or adapted for service in different cities and systems. The motor bus would hardly vanish because of a new streetcar design, but this fact does not detract from the excellence of the new design that the Presidents' Conference Committee (PCC) of the American Transit Association developed. A single-ended streamlined body, a multinotch foot-operated controller, more rapid acceleration and braking rates than previous street-railway equipment, resilient wheels, and a variety of other improvements are the distinguishing characteristics of what came to be known as the "PCC car."[77]

The first production-model PCC cars were ordered by the Brooklyn and Queens Transit Corporation, the surface subsidiary of the Interborough Rapid Transit Company's Dual Contacts partner, the Brooklyn-Manhattan Transit Corporation.[78] A fleet of one hundred cars began running in Brooklyn in 1936, and in the following year, the Saint Louis Car Company delivered a single PCC car to the Boston El. Bearing the number 3001 and popularly called the "Queen Mary," it convinced BERY management that this was the car of the future—their future.[79] In 1941 BERY took delivery of twenty PCCs manufactured by Pullman-Standard. (Saint Louis Car Company and Pullman-Standard would be the only U.S. companies that built PCC cars.) Although not equipped for MU operation when acquired, they proved beyond doubt what had been suspected from experience with No. 3001—that the PCC was an appropriate replacement vehicle for BERY's aging fleet of center-entrance cars.

During the Second World War, the War Production Board authorized BERY to order PCC cars in substantial numbers, and the Boston fleet would eventually total 346 units. The wartime cars were rigged for MU train operation, and their arrival caused a quietus in the use of veteran center-entrance cars in heavy-duty subway service. The last of the center-entrance cars to carry passengers anywhere in Boston did so on various soon-to-be-motorized streetcar lines in 1953, some years after the breed had been replaced in heavy-duty service in the Central Subway by the new PCC cars.

An order for fifty unique "picture window" PCC cars that joined the MTA fleet in 1951 proved to be the last streetcars built for any U.S. transit system—at least for another quarter-century. In 1958 and 1959 Boston acquired twenty-five secondhand PCC cars of an unusual double-ended design from the Dallas Railway and Terminal Company, and by the end of the 1950s, streetcar service had been converted to motor-bus operation on all routes in Boston that did not feed into the Tremont-Boylston Subway—and even a few that did! The policy was to restrict the subway itself to heavy-patronage lines and let other routes become bus-feeder services. As none of the lines then entering the subway via the Broadway (originally Pleasant Street) incline carried heavy traffic, it was abandoned in 1962. (A slight qualification: One surviving Boston trolley line that was not tied into the Central Subway remained very much in business—the shuttle operation between Mattapan and Ashmont at the end of the Cambridge-Dorchester rapid-transit line.)

PCC cars performed well in Boston, if not ideally. The standard single-ended design with two sets of doors on the right side had to be modified, with a single set of left-side doors for loading and discharging passengers at several subway stations configured with left-side platforms, and the chief criticism leveled against the PCC in Boston service has to be that it did not perform flawlessly during rush-hour loading at busy stations when using these left-hand doors. (Another criticism emerged during the later years of PCC operation in Boston when maintenance had deteriorated, the aging fleet was in desperate need of replacement, and cars tended to arrive at busy rush-hour stations on warm summer days with the heat going full blast.) Eventually two classes of Boston PCC cars that were not delivered with MU control were retrofitted, leaving the ex-Dallas double-enders, as well as No. 3001 of 1937, as the only Boston PCC cars never so equipped.[80]

If the Huntington Avenue Subway was the first new Boston transit line built during the 1940s and the 1950s, the second—approved by the legislature in 1945—was an extension of the East Boston Tunnel service beyond Maverick Square over the right-of-way of an abandoned narrow-gauge railroad, the three-foot-gauge Boston, Revere Beach and Lynn Railroad, defunct since 1940.[81] The transit extension was opened in two phases—as far as Orient Heights in 1952, and on to Revere Beach in 1954. The project is unique on two counts.

First, the first station beyond Maverick Square serves Logan International Airport. Although it takes a short bus ride to get from subway station to airport terminal, it was the first U.S. rail transit line to serve a commercial airfield in any manner. The second distinction of the line involves its method of electric current collection, which changes beyond Maverick from third rail to overhead catenary. The line emerges from its belowground tunnel just beyond Maverick and continues on to Revere Beach at grade; the argument advanced to explain the dual systems of current collection is the danger of icing on a third rail so close to the ocean. And the line does indeed run close to the shore, giving passengers a wonderfully scenic view as they travel from one end to the other.

Forty new Saint Louis–built rapid-transit cars were ordered to expand the line's equipment roster for service over the extension. The new cars incorporated many of the same mechanical features as PCC streetcars and their construction required a royalty payment to the successor agency to the Electric Railway's Presidents Conference Committee, the Transit Development Corporation, for the use of such patented designs.[82] These forty new cars, together with the forty-eight Pullman-built cars that inaugurated high-platform service through the East Boston Tunnel in 1924, constituted the fleet that would serve the East Boston Line for the next twenty-five years. The latter cars had to be equipped with roof-mounted pantographs to permit their use over the catenary portions of the line.[83] As part of the extension, a new repair shop was built at Orient Heights, allowing the former practice of maintaining East Boston cars at the Eliot Shops of the Cambridge-Dorchester Line to be discontinued and the Cambridge Street incline beyond Bowdoin Station to be sealed.

Between the opening of the Huntington Avenue Subway in 1941 and the extension of the East Boston Tunnel to Revere in 1954, rapid transit in Boston saw yet another change in the form of its governance. The Public Control Act of 1918 was proving unworkable, and in early 1947 the Massachusetts legislature enacted a measure that saw the assets of the Boston Elevated Railway acquired by a newly created public agency, the Metropolitan Transit Authority (MTA). At the stroke of high noon on Friday, August 29, 1947, the formal transfer took effect and, in the words of General Manager Dana, "the residents of the fourteen cities and towns comprising the Metropolitan Transit Authority became owners of the Elevated."[84]

As for the third Boston transit extension of the 1940s and the 1950s, on July 1, 1959, yet another extension of the time-honored Tremont-Boylston Subway was dedicated. To make it possible, in May of 1958 the New York Central Railroad abandoned service along a 9.4-mile right-of-way through upscale neighborhoods of Brookline and Newton that the railroad called the Highland Branch and sold the line to the MTA for conversion into an electrified extension of the subway. It would be the first transit line in Boston to reach Route 128, a multilane roadway encircling the metropolitan area that was even then on its way to becoming the "main street" of the growing U.S. electronics industry. Construction began on July 10, 1958, and was finished in less than a year.

The Riverside Line, as it has generally been called since the conversion, marked the first time that PCC cars had operated over a lengthy, limited-stop line in Boston—but not without criticism, because they did not provide as fast or as comfortable a ride under such circumstances as more conventional rapid-transit equipment. One alteration that was made after gaining some experience with PCC cars on the Riverside Line was the replacement of their original resilient wheels with more conventional solid-steel wheels.[85]

The Riverside Line was built cheaply, though—the price tag was less than $10 million. And like the Revere Beach extension, it represented a new rail-transit investment at a time when few

U.S. cities were building any urban transport facilities other than highways. New York Central track was largely retained, and whether fact or legend, it was said that dating nails hammered into cross-ties by the railroad to indicate the year they were installed included some from the nineteenth century. The Riverside Line was able to open without the MTA's acquiring any new rail cars, even though it was the longest single transit line ever to be placed in service in Boston at one time. To free PCC cars for Riverside service, buses were assigned to the MTA's remaining streetcar lines in Cambridge, and it could also be argued that one benefit of the arrival of the ex-Dallas cars was to liberate other PCCs for the new service.[86]

The Riverside Line was a success from the very start, although not exactly in the way transit planners had expected. Forecasts had suggested that the bulk of its patronage would come from closer stations throughout Brookline, and it was expected that alternate rush-hour trains would terminate at a station called Reservoir at the new line's midpoint. In fact, the more distant station in Newton drew the larger crowds, the storage yard at Riverside had to be enlarged to four times its original size, and few trains terminated at Reservoir.

On the Fourth of July in 1959—three days after the line's official dedication—PCC car No. 3295 led a three-car train out of Riverside Terminal at 6:50 A.M. When it reached Park Street at 7:25, the line was in full operation. Most of the paying customers on that first trip were traction buffs delighted beyond words to participate in the opening of a new trolley line in an era when the more usual events in the industry were abandonments, cutbacks, and bus substitutions.

The year 1957 saw the arrival of the first of a hundred new Pullman-Standard cars for the Main Line El. Numbered in the 01100 series and resembling the Saint Louis–built cars that were acquired for the Revere Beach extension in 1952, they dispatched all but a handful of the older el cars to the scrap heap. Engineering assessments performed by the MTA determined that it was feasible to acquire slightly longer cars for Main Line El service, and the 01100 series cars were 55 feet long versus a shade over 46.5 feet for the equipment they replaced. A few veteran units were retained to help out during busy rush hours on into the early

1960s, but they were eventually scrapped as well. The 01100s would then soldier on alone until the mid-1970s.[87]

However satisfactory these postwar achievements of the MTA may have been, they certainly have a technical—one might even say prosaic—character about them. Yet it was during this same era that the MTA provided the inspiration for the first lyrics about the Boston Subway since—well, since General Manager Dana's poem of 1924. Composed and written by Jacqueline Steiner and Bess Hawes, the song describes the travails of a man who is identified only as "Charley." Caught broke on a subway train when the MTA implemented a five-cent surcharge for certain exiting passengers, Charley seems destined to ride forever beneath the streets of Boston, subsisting on nothing but a sandwich that his wife thrusts daily through the subway car window as his train goes rumbling though the Scollay Square Station. As recorded for Capitol Records by the Kingston Trio, *The MTA* was popular nationwide, and for the many weeks that it "made the charts," America became aware of mass transit in Boston as never before—and perhaps of the need for effective mass transit everywhere. Could Oliver Wendell Holmes have done more?

From MTA to MBTA

In 1963 the MTA took delivery of ninety-eight new, lightweight subway cars—once again built by Pullman-Standard—to replace all prewar rolling stock on the Cambridge-Dorchester Line.[88] Identified as the 01400 series, the cars were designed, like the 01100s on the Main Line El and the 0500s used in East Boston service, to operate in "married-pair" configuration, a weight-saving arrangement where two cars are semipermanently coupled together and share components such as batteries, air compressors, and motor controllers. In the following year, an idea that had germinated during a series of "Citizen Seminars" at Boston College took root: the MTA service district of fourteen cities and towns that had been established in 1947 was enlarged to seventy-nine, and the older authority, the MTA, was succeeded by a new agency, the Massachusetts Bay Transportation Authority—the MBTA, or just plain T, as it is more commonly known. One can only wonder if any of the civic leaders who attended the Boston College Citizen Seminars that produced the MBTA traveled to the sessions at the Chestnut Hill campus from Downtown aboard PCC cars whose destination signs read: "BOSTON COLLEGE–COMMONWEALTH."

Soon after it was created, the new authority adopted a color code to identify its various transit services: red became the designation of the Cambridge-Dorchester Line, orange the color of the Maine Line El, blue was reserved for East Boston, and the Tremont–Boylston Central Subway was designated green. People in and around Boston took to the new codes, and the colors were capitalized to become the proper names of the various transit services—Red Line, Orange Line, Blue Line, and Green Line.[89]

As part of a its more colorful approach, the T began to repaint its rolling stock—including the previously traction-orange PCC cars—in neutral shades of gray, but this proved to be less than an aesthetic triumph. Eventually—and sensibly—the T refurbished its vehicles in colors corresponding to the code of the line on which they operated. As long as unique equipment was required for each of the system's four transit lines, there was no danger that cars painted in a given color would ever wind up operating on a different line. To make the color-coding of rolling stock complete, the MBTA's bus fleet inherited the color yellow, and when the region's commuter-rail system passed from the corporate hands of the Penn Central and the Boston and Maine railroads in the 1970s to become an integral part of the MBTA itself, commuter cars and locomotives used in suburban service were identified by a distinctive shade of purple.[90]

The MBTA did much more than paint its rolling stock in distinctive colors. During 1964, the year the MBTA was founded, a small program of capital assistance for urban mass transportation was established by the federal government in Washington that quickly grew into a major resource for new investment. More details about this federal program will be discussed in Chapter 5, but just as Mayor James Michael Curley was quick to understand that federal dollars would enable him to build a Huntington Avenue Subway and create Depression-era jobs at the same time, so the executives who were running the MBTA in the 1960s and the 1970s understood that capital assistance from Washington was the key to turning Boston's mass-transit dreams into hard reality.[91]

The federal program of mass-transit assistance will help cities from San Juan to Seattle build major new mass-transit projects. But no city in any state has leveraged the federal program more completely—or more creatively—than Boston has. It began with a six-mile extension of the Red Line across the Neponsit River to Quincy, which opened in 1972. The new extension branched off the older Cambridge-Dorchester Line just beyond Andrew Station in South Boston and then headed south over a right-of-way that was once the Old Colony Line of the New York, New Haven and Hartford Railroad.[92]

Following the successful extension of Red Line service to Quincy in 1971, over the next decade or so, the MBTA went on to:

- Tear down the Orange Line (i.e., Main Line El) elevated structure north of Downtown to Sullivan Square and Everett, build a new tunnel under the Charles River and extend the line at grade into Malden and Melrose;
- Replace the elevated portion of the Orange Line southward to Forest Hills with a new at-grade line that shares a right-of-way with the onetime New Haven Railroad main line to Providence and New York;
- Continue the South Shore extension of the Red Line from Quincy to Braintree;
- Extend the Red Line beyond Harvard Square to Alewife Brook Parkway on the Cambridge-Arlington Line;
- Replace rolling stock on all four lines with new air-conditioned cars, including a major upgrade of the Green Line with new generations of what are now called light rail transit vehicles;
- Build new and up-to-date maintenance and repair shops for the Red Line, the Orange Line, and the Green Line;
- Upgrade important elements of transit infrastructure such as signal and communication systems, electrical distribution networks, and the passenger amenities of stations.[93]

And this does not even begin to address the way the MBTA first stabilized, then upgraded, and eventually expanded the area's commuter-rail service. Between the opening of the Tremont Street Subway in 1897 and the completion of the Cambridge-

Dorchester Line in 1928—call it a span of three decades—Boston's transit system went from essentially nothing to one that could boast 21.9 route miles of high-platform rapid-transit service and 2.6 miles of downtown trolley subway. From the opening of the South Shore Line to Quincy in 1972 through the completion of an at-grade replacement for the Orange Line to Forest Hills in 1987, the MBTA expanded or upgraded its system by the construction of 23.9 route miles of new rapid-transit service.

Boston opened North America's first subway on September 1, 1897, and began its incremental expansion immediately afterward. As New York celebrates the centenary of its first subway in 2004, the expansion of the Boston Subway is still very much a work in progress. Shortly after the IRT begins its second century of service, the MBTA will shift Green Line service between Haymarket Square and Science Park from the elevated/viaduct line that opened in 1912 into a newly built subway tunnel, and on the very day New York celebrates the centenary of the Interborough, Boston residents from Roxbury and the South End will be riding aboard the MBTA's newest rapid-transit service—the Silver Line, a hybrid operation using dual-powered buses that operate along an at-grade right-of-way as well as through underground subway tunnels. And to bring the Boston transit story full circle, the new Silver Line will soon be running its diesel-electric buses into the original Tremont Street Subway via the long-unused Pleasant Street incline.[94]

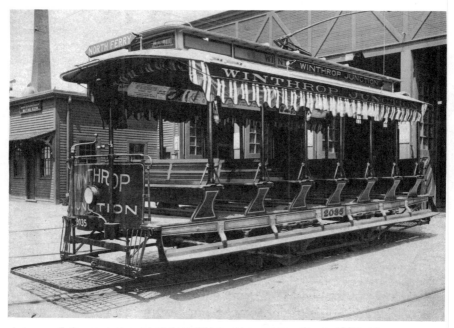

A turn-of-the-century open-bench electric trolley car in Boston. Similar cars originated service into the 1897 subway.

Trolley cars head in and out of the Central Subway in Boston in this view from the 1920s.

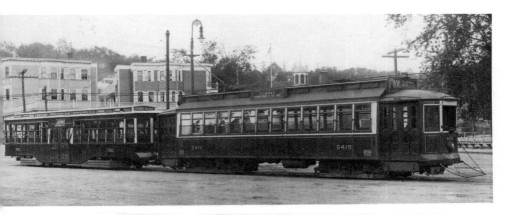

A two-car train bound for the Tremont Street Subway operates along Commonwealth Avenue. Lead car No. 5419 is a Type 4A3 motorized unit that was built by Jewett in 1914, while car No. 7001 is a motorless center-entrance trailer that was turned out by the J. G. Brill Company in 1915.

Boston's Main Line El was extended south to this handsome terminal station at Forest Hills in 1909.

A train on the Main Line El heads for Sullivan Square in Charleston in this 1945 photo.

When the Metropolitan Transit Authority was created in 1947, Boston trains and trolleys began to sport a new logo that included a map of the system.

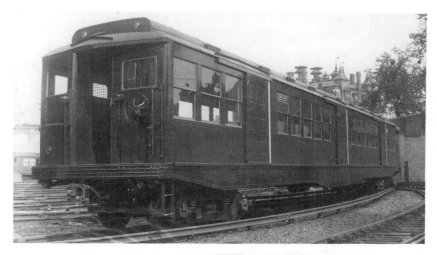

Car No. 0699 was one of the steel subway cars that the Boston El acquired for service on the Cambridge-Dorchester Line.

Front-end view of PCC Car No 3312.

The MBTA's Watertown Line no longer operates rail service, but this incline is still used by the Commonwealth Avenue Line. The Cities Service sign in the background, later updated when the company renamed itself Citgo, has itself become a veritable landmark in Boston.

A train of Pullman-built 01500-series cars that were acquired to inaugurate service over the new Red Line extension to Quincy in 1971.

A Blue Line train leaves Orient Heights bound for Revere Beach.

New articulated light rail cars provide service in Boston's Central Subway, now known as the Green Line.

3

The World's First Subway

As DESCRIBED in Chapter 2, Boston opened the first subway in North America on September 1, 1897, seven years before the Interborough Rapid Transit Company welcomed passengers aboard New York's first underground railway in 1904. But Boston's Tremont Street operation was not the first subway on the face of the earth—or *under* the face of the earth, to be a bit more precise about it. The world's very first subway opened in London, England, on the Saturday afternoon of January 10, 1863, thirty-three years before the Boston inaugural—and ten days after President Abraham Lincoln issued the Emancipation Proclamation. To provide a further sense of context for the inauguration of subway service on the Interborough in 1904—and the first century of subway service in the City of New York in the years between 1904 and 2004—a brief and necessarily general review of subway developments in London in particular, and Europe more generally, will be helpful.

LONDON

(Before discussing rapid transit in London, an advisory word is in order about the quantity of written material that is available on the subject. It may well be the case that there have been more books, articles, and pamphlets written about the London Underground than about any other electric railway in the world. As just one example, in the year 2001 alone, two comprehensive books have appeared that treat the general development of the railway. In addition, there are multiple volumes about every single underground line in London, not to mention specialized studies dealing with stations, rolling stock, tunnel construction, and so forth.

Many of these works are cited in the notes or listed in the bibliography.)

When intercity railroads were built in Great Britain in the early years of the nineteenth century, the narrow, twisting streets and extraordinarily dense concentration of buildings in the center of London precluded any of the new railways from extending their rights-of-way into the heart of the British capital. And so the first railways to reach London necessarily terminated on the city's outskirts. Euston Station, opened in 1837, and King's Cross, built in 1852, were two important railway terminals along London's northern perimeter, while to the south one could find Victoria Station (1860), Waterloo (1848), and Charing Cross (1864), among others.[1] This exclusion of mainline railways from the central portion of London was a matter of formal public policy, since "a Royal Commission of 1846 had recommended that no railway should penetrate the inner London area between the River Thames and the New Road (now Marylebone, Euston and Pentonville roads), and Parliament seemed reluctant to go against this."[2] London's first subway evolved, then, as an effort to link these various railway terminals with the city's central core.

The enterprise that opened in January 1863 as the Metropolitan Underground Railway took the better part of a decade to develop, plan, finance, and build. A principal mover behind the venture was the City Solicitor of London, Charles Pearson, who began pressing for an underground urban railway after a pedestrian tunnel was successfully built beneath the River Thames in 1853 under the direction of Marc Isambard Brunel. Brunel, whose son, Isambard Kingdom Brunel, would bring even more engineering acclaim to the family name, took eighteen years to complete his Thames Tunnel. It was an extraordinary achievement from an engineering perspective. Perhaps more important, it served to dispel a variety of popular fears about traveling belowground, a style of transport many people associated with unsavory journeys in dark realms of ancient mythology.[3]

Pearson secured authorization from Parliament to begin work on London's first subway in 1854, but construction did not get under way until 1859. The initial segment, almost 4 miles long, ran from Bishop's Road, Paddington, to Farringdon Street along London's northern rim, connecting Euston Station with King's

Cross along the way. On the afternoon before the Metropolitan formally opened—that is to say, on Friday, January 9, 1863—between 600 and 700 invited guests assembled at Bishop's Road for a ceremonial trip over the new line. Two special trains, each hauled by a pair of hand-polished steam locomotives, traveled the length of the line, pausing at several intermediate stations so guests could inspect the design of the new road. When the trains reached Farringdon, passengers disembarked and were treated to a formal dinner in the station. Appropriate toasts were raised to everything from the health of Her Britannic Majesty, Queen Victoria—who was not in attendance, incidentally—to the engineering wonders wrought by the Metropolitan's engineers and designers.[4] With more than an ample dose of civic pride, *The Times* noted: "Indeed the line may be regarded as the great engineering triumph of the day."[5]

When revenue passengers were permitted to ride the Metropolitan the day after the inaugural ceremony, large crowds materialized, and "many thousands were enabled to indulge their curiosity in reference to this mode of traveling under the streets of the metropolis." Indeed, the crowds were so large that "neither the locomotive power nor the rolling-stock—was at all in proportion to the requirements of opening day."[6]

Over the next several years, the Metropolitan would expand until its route eventually became part of a 13-mile circumferential transit line, the Inner Circle, as it was called, that created a transit perimeter around London. In addition, branch lines were built that extended Metropolitan service outward from this Inner Circle into suburban territory further removed from the city's core. At one time, the Metropolitan company envisioned itself as becoming a major intercity railroad in England, with lines to points as far away as Birmingham, over 100 miles away. There was even talk of extending the Metropolitan to Paris through, of all things, a railway tunnel under the English Channel! This was not, however, the way the company would develop and evolve.[7]

The Metropolitan might have opened many months earlier than it actually did. At one point a July 1862 inaugural was being planned, and a trial trip was run over the line on May 14, 1862. But on June 18, mere weeks before the intended opening, a wall in the newly built tunnel collapsed. The Fleet Ditch Sewer burst into the unfinished subway and flooded the right-of-way from Farringdon Street all the way to King's Cross Station to a depth of 10 feet, a mishap that pushed the opening back another six months.[8]

Promoters of the Metropolitan subcontracted the actual operation of their new undertaking to one of Britain's intercity carriers, the Great Western Railway (GWR), a company whose principal main line connected London with Bristol, to the west. Of a stock offering of a million pounds sterling that was issued to underwrite the construction costs of the Metropolitan, the Great Western subscribed 175,000 pounds, and when the Metropolitan opened in 1862, it was GWR equipment—operated by GWR personnel—that provided the service.[9] The GWR was, at the time, a broad-gauge railroad whose tracks were laid down with 7 feet and a fraction of an inch between the rails. To accommodate GWR rolling stock, the new Metropolitan was built as a dual-gauge undertaking, with broad-gauge tracks for the GWR straddling, after a fashion, more conventional standard-gauge "iron" that was 4 feet, 8½ inches between the rails for any other railways that might use the new tunnel facilities. (Broad-gauge and standard-gauge trains used a common rail adjacent to station platforms, with dual rails on the opposite side.)

Trains on the Metropolitan were, of course, steam-powered, but two design features attempted to mitigate the adverse effects of locomotive exhaust on the line's passengers. The first involved the line itself, which was not built entirely in a belowground tunnel. Instead there were frequent points along the route where trains emerged from their tunnels and traveled through open cuts, a feature that helped dissipate locomotive exhaust. When the Metropolitan was being extended under Leinster Gardens, in Bayswater, toward the end of the 1860s, the company acquired—and tore down—two five-story dwellings for the construction of its right-of-way. When the subway was completed, the fronts of the buildings at No. 22 and No. 24 Leinster Gardens were restored, but they were only false fronts to disguise the fact that exhaust from Metropolitan steam locomotives wafted into the atmosphere in an open area behind the new fronts.[10]

A second feature designed to mitigate the effects of smoke and exhaust was the fact that locomotives used on the new line included onboard condensers to capture and recycle exhaust steam; GWR acquired a fleet of twenty-two tank engines with a 2-4-0 wheel arrangement that were equipped with these condensers. But the crowds that made the Metropolitan such a success had a negative impact on the ability of the locomotives to operate as they were designed. "The engines were built to work well and condense all their steam with ordinary trains of three or four carriages," noted *The Times;* with additional cars added to handle crowds that were "one-third greater than were anticipated," engines were forced to labor beyond the ability of the condensers, and "this has resulted sometimes in the annoyance of steam in the tunnel, sometimes in the sulphureous gas being drawn from the fires and let into the tunnel in sufficient quantities to make it most unpleasant."[11]

Another interesting feature of the new locomotives was that engine crews were not afforded the protection of a typical cab but worked, rather, on an open platform. The semi-enclosed nature of the belowground right-of-way lessened the disadvantages of such a feature to some extent, but the principal reason it was selected was to avoid condensation on the glass in cab windows that could obscure visibility. Rolling stock used on the Metropolitan—also supplied by GWR—was a fleet of forty-five conventional passenger cars, 42 feet in length, which featured passenger accommodations in first, second, and third class. Illumination inside the cars was supplied by a system of coal-gas lighting, the fuel for which was carried in collapsible bags carried on the roof of each car. Since the steel passenger car was not invented until George Gibbs designed No. 3342 for the Interborough Rapid Transit Company in 1903 (as discussed in Chapter 1), cars used on the Metropolitan in 1863 were necessarily made of wood.

Despite valiant efforts to minimize its impact, locomotive exhaust in the tunnels proved to be a major drawback of the new Metropolitan. An observer of no less acuity than Arthur Conan Doyle's famous crime fighter, Sherlock Holmes, commented about the dreadful conditions encountered along the smoky and sooty Metropolitan Railway.[12] Holmes would undoubtedly have boarded the world's first subway at the Baker Street station, one of the seven stops along the original 1863 route.

The evolution of the Metropolitan over the following 140 years is colorful and interesting and provides a perspective on the general development of urban railway technology and operations, albeit with a few unique twists all its own. Before the line was a year old, the Great Western Railway served notice that it was withdrawing as the line's contract operator, and the Metropolitan was forced to take over such tasks itself. At first the Metropolitan had to lease motive power and rolling stock from other railways. It soon designed and acquired its own locomotives and passenger cars, though, and rather than the 2-4-0 type locomotives that GWR used to inaugurate subway service in London, the Metropolitan developed a tank engine with a 4-4-0 wheel arrangement that became "the basic design for practically all the locomotives used on the Underground operations until electrification."[13] With the departure of GWR, broad-gauge trains would no longer routinely operate on the Metropolitan.

One bothersome issue that the Metropolitan had to face early on was a popular demand that smoking be allowed aboard its trains, even while the company sought its prevention. In 1868 an amendment to the Railway Regulation Bill was proposed in Parliament that would require all British railroads to provide accommodations for smokers. The amendment passed, in part because of the spirited advocacy of philosopher-statesman John Stuart Mill, whose speech on behalf of onboard smoking was the last he would make as a member of the House of Commons. While the amendment that Mill favored exempted the Metropolitan from the new legal requirement, in 1874 the company bowed to popular pressure and agreed to let its passengers "light up."[14]

In late 1863—again before the world's first subway celebrated its first anniversary—a separate corporate undertaking called the Metropolitan District Railway Company was organized to build a subway that would complement and connect with the older Metropolitan and together with it establish the Inner Circle. The first leg of a railway that came to be called over the years simply the District Line opened for business on Christmas Eve in 1868.[15] Just as the original Metropolitan subcontracted its operations to the Great Western, so did the new District Line contract with the Metropolitan to supply its equipment and operate its trains.

Originally, the Metropolitan and the District were allied undertakings; several individuals served on the board of directors of both companies, and the two retained many of the same engineers and contractors. Indeed so closely were the two companies allied in 1868 that historian Charles Lee comments that "at first it was little realized outside financial circles that [the District Line] was constituted as a separate railway company."[16]

But the District Line soon elected to chart a more independent course. In 1871, three years after it began service, the District Line took over operational control of its own railway from the Metropolitan. It was not until October 6, 1884, though, that the final links of the Inner Circle were completed and circumferential service around London over the rails of both companies was inaugurated. Metropolitan trains operated clockwise on the outer track of the Circle loop, while District Line trains operated counterclockwise on the inside loop.[17]

Over the years both companies built various branch lines outward from this circular trunk line into London's nearby suburbs, with the Metropolitan being more aggressive in such expansion than the District Line. In other instances, service was operated from points along the Inner Circle to places as far as 100 miles from London over the lines of other railway companies, although the rights-of-way of neither the District nor the Metropolitan were ever extended this far.[18]

In the early years of the twentieth century, both the District and the Metropolitan were electrified, but not without a measure of contretemps. The District Line preferred a conventional system that would use 600 volts of direct current distributed by trackside third rail, while the Metropolitan had in mind a more novel concept that called for 3,000 volts of three-phase alternating current distributed through overhead wire. Such a dispute between alternating current and direct current for railway electrification was emerging in the United States at the very same time, pitting two principal suppliers of electrical equipment, Westinghouse and General Electric, as competitive adversaries. In Britain, the rivals were the British-Thomson-Houston Company, a corporate ally of General Electric (GE), as the supplier of the DC gear favored by the District, while the Metropolitan was pressing for an AC installation known as the Ganz system, which was similar to one recently deployed in Budapest. Because the District and the Metropolitan were unable to resolve their disagreement on this important technical matter and neither was willing to back down, the issue was resolved through arbitration by the Board of Trade, a process that resulted in a decision on behalf of the District—and direct current.[19]

J. Graeme Bruce has characterized yet another difference the two companies faced as they sought to electrify their operations: "The District Railway determined to eliminate steam working altogether, while on the other hand the Metropolitan, with its country services, had a programme which limited electric traction to the more congested inner areas, leaving the extension services to be worked by steam."[20] What this led to was a fleet of electric locomotives on the Metropolitan that were used to haul what still more resembled conventional intercity rolling stock than city subway equipment, while the District acquired a fleet of third-rail multiple-unit (MU) cars. The advent of electrification saw the Metropolitan acquire MU cars for its local services; but more so than the District, the Metropolitan required electric locomotives in addition, to haul trains that were destined for points beyond the electrified zone. Trains bound for the suburbs on the Metropolitan would, at the end of the electrified zone, exchange the electric locomotive that had hauled it outward from London for a steam engine and complete its trip over a nonelectrified outer branch. The Metropolitan was acquiring new steam locomotives for such services as late as 1920.

The first MU cars on the District Line entered service in 1904, and they would have been perfectly at home on August Belmont's Interborough Subway—or General Bancroft's Main Line El in Boston. Measuring a few inches less than 50 feet in length, the wooden-bodied cars were equipped with passenger entry and exit doors in the end vestibules, plus a mid-car center door. The railway acquired both motorized units as well as trailer cars, motor cars being powered by two GE model 69 motors supplied by the British-Thomson-Houston Company, a GE licensee.[21]

By late September of 1905, steam-powered trains were no longer hauling passengers on the Inner Circle, and with their departure, the District and the Metropolitan undertook a vigorous program to clean and scrub their various underground stations and remove four decades-worth of soot and grime that the steam locomotives had left behind. It was during the electrification of the District and the Metropolitan that what later became the London standard for urban railway electrification was developed. It called for a conventional outside third rail for current distribution but also required a separate "fourth rail" between the running rails for current return. This is quite different from standard practice in the United States, where the regular running rails of a railway are used to complete the electrical circuit.

While some locomotive-hauled trains continued to work for the Metropolitan until the mid-1960s—as late as 1959 London Transport's roster included fifteen electric locomotives and seventy-one locomotive-hauled passenger cars—the combined system that was originally the Metropolitan and the Metropolitan District Railway eventually came to be served by third-rail MU cars exclusively. More important, in a complex series of mergers and consolidations, what were originally two independent railway companies operating trains on the Inner Circle and out into nearby (and not-so-nearby) suburban areas eventually evolved into four separate rail transit services under the unified management of an agency known as London Underground.

More on the emergence of London Underground below. The four contemporary London rapid-transit lines that have developed from the original Metropolitan and the original District are: 1) the Metropolitan Line, serving suburbs to the northwest of London and also operating along the northern rim of the Inner Circle; 2) the District Line, serving suburbs to the east and the southwest and operating along the southern rim of the Inner Circle; 3) all stations on the 13-mile Inner Circle itself, served by a separate operation called the Circle Line; and, 4) a line known as the Hammersmith and City, once a part of the Metropolitan, which travels along the northern rim of the Inner Circle, branches off near Paddington to serve neighborhoods west of central London, and also continues beyond the Inner Circle to neighborhoods east of London. There is also a short and now almost shuttlelike service called the East London Line that can be regarded as part of the overall rapid-transit network that developed from the Metropolitan and the District.[22]

(When a sightseeing company was established in New York in 1945 that offered 35-mile lecture cruises around Manhattan Island, one of the principals, who had been stationed in England during the Second World War, recalled his travels around London and suggested that the sightseeing service be named the Circle Line.)

An important dynamic involving all of the rapid-transit services that evolved from the Metropolitan and the District of the 1860s is the fact that responsibility for the operation of a number of branch lines in areas around London was rationalized over the years between the joint Metropolitan-District rapid-transit system and the suburban network operated by Britain's intercity railways, a process that was fostered when large elements of the railways were electrified. Interestingly, though, it is no longer possible to ride a train of today's Metropolitan Line between Farringdon and Paddington, where the Metropolitan Underground Railway inaugurated subway service in 1863. Trains of the Hammersmith and City Line do operate between the two stations, however, and thus enable any Londoners who are of such a mind to retrace the route followed by the world's first subway train on a January Saturday afternoon in 1863.

Today, London Underground calls the rapid-transit operation composed of the Metropolitan, the District Line, the Circle Line, the Hammersmith and City Line, and East London its *surface* lines, a usage that in North America generally refers to buses or trolley cars operating at grade. In calling the London quintet surface lines, London Underground is mindful of the fact that the tunnels in which such trains travel are built immediately below the surface and wishes to draw a distinction between these lines and a different style of underground railway that we shall examine below. (Some authors have attempted to clarify matters by referring to the five as London Underground's *subsurface* lines.)

Whatever they are called, these transit lines can be seen as a unified system that operates compatible rolling stock of a rather conventional sort. The five must be understood as separate and distinct from a very different style of underground urban railway that is popular in London: deep-bored tunnels, 50 to 150 feet belowground, that are known as tube lines and require the use of as specialized a fleet of transit cars as exists anywhere in the known universe. Indeed far more than the surface lines, the deep-tunnel tubes enjoy a special identity with London itself, an identity that was surely enhanced when stations along many of the lines were converted into makeshift—but quite effective—air-raid shelters during the awful nights when the Luftwaffe was conducting bombing raids against London during the Second World War. Writing some years after the war of the way Highgate Station so functioned, one author said: "It was an unforgettable sight when traveling non-stop through this station, to see it brightly lit and crowded with sleeping people."[23] In addition, completed tunnels through which trains had not yet begun to operate in the early 1940s were converted into factories of various sorts to supply equipment for the British war effort, and during the height of the Blitz in 1940 and 1941, Prime Minister Winston Churchill's war cabinet regularly met in the recently closed Down Street station on the Piccadilly Line.

In the foreword of a wonderful 1968 book called *Tube Trains under London,* A. W. Manser, then the chief mechanical engineer for London Transport's railways, explained London's two styles of underground rapid transit this way:

> Too often in referring to the London Underground System the word "tube" is applied quite indiscriminately. The tubes are, in fact, the bored circular tunnels, not to be confused with the "cut and cover" tunnels of the District and Metropolitan lines. These latter have their counterparts today in a great many other cities throughout the world. Nowhere else, however, is there to be found such an extensive systems of bored tunnels as exists in London.[24]

London's first underground tube line opened for revenue service on December 18, 1890—fourteen years before the Interborough, seven years before the Tremont Street Subway in Boston—but twenty-seven years after the Metropolitan. The line had been dedicated a month earlier, on November 4, when His Royal Highness the Prince of Wales—the eldest son of Queen Victoria and a man who would rule as Edward VII between 1901 and 1910—presided at a formal ceremony.[25]

The venture was called the City and South London Railway; its initial route ran slightly over 3 miles from Stockwell, south of the River Thames, to King William Street, in the heart of the City of London. Most tellingly, though, the venture featured the style of deep-bore construction that would soon come to typify underground urban railways in and around London. In common with London's other early rapid-transit ventures, the City and South London was built entirely with private capital.[26]

The City and South London ran through a pair of tunnels that were bored below the streets of London at an average depth of 60 feet and were lined from the inside with cast-iron rings that were bolted together to form a secure cylindrical-tube structure. Such an effort required minimal surface excavation for its construction. Access to each of the new line's five underground stations was by a pair of fifty-passenger hydraulic elevators, and it was only by burrowing deep below the congestion of London in this manner that rapid transit was able to reach into the heart of the city. In addition, the geology of London cooperated immensely by providing a subterranean environment of soft blue clay that made such deep-bored tunnels eminently practical.

Writing about the London Underground, H. F. Howson explained matters this way: "Had there been rock such as New York is partly built on, instead of the stodgy but amenable clay, it is certain that London's tube railways would not have been so extensive as they are."[27] More colorful language was used by *The Times* to describe the milieu in which the new underground railway was built: "The new subway might be described with sufficient accuracy as a gigantic iron drain pipe, or rather two drain pipes side by side, thrust by main force into the solid London clay, much in the fashion in which the cheesemonger thrusts a scoop into his Cheddar or Gloucester."[28]

More often than not, this layer of clay was sufficiently firm that deep-bored tunnels under the streets of London were built with a Greathead Shield at the business end of the effort, but no pressurized air lock behind the shield, as would be required when tunnels were driven through, for example, soft underwater silt.[29] Tube lines in London feature tunnels of a much smaller size than most other subways around the world, so consequently the trains that run through them are smaller than rolling stock used on more conventional subways elsewhere—or even on the Metropolitan and the District lines in London, for that matter. Eventually the tube lines of London were standardized by Act of Parliament, with an inside tunnel diameter of 11½ feet.[30] Specifications used on the City and South London were a bit narrower than this, though, and London's first tube underground in 1890 was built with tunnels that were a few inches over 10 feet in diameter. (In later years, the City and South London would become part of

London Transport's Northern Line, and its 10-foot tunnels would be expanded to make them compatible with the rest of the tube system.)

Returning to 1890, on the altogether reasonable assumption that there was very little to see while riding through a dark tunnel far belowground, the first tube cars built for the City and South London Railway—a thirty-car fleet turned out by the Ashbury Railway Carriage and Iron Company, a predecessor of today's Metro-Cammell, Ltd.—were built without any kind of real windows. They did feature small ventilating windows just below the roof line, but the bulk of the inside walls of the cars were covered with the upholstered backs of the thirty-two longitudinal seats that were provided for the line's passengers, a feature that quickly prompted Londoners to refer to the new cars as "padded cells." Railway executives in London soon learned that tube passengers preferred rolling stock with windows, even for travel below ground in deep-bored tunnels, and these original thirty cars would be the only windowless rolling stock built for the London Underground. Indeed, the original thirty cars were later rebuilt with more conventional windows.[31]

There were many design features pioneered on the City and South London that remain standard for London tube stock even today. To conform with the circular profile of the tube tunnels, the cars featured a sharply arched roof. Maximum headroom is only available at the very center of the car, and on the 1890 fleet acquired for the City and South London this measured a mere 6 feet from floor to ceiling. (On today's tube stock, the comparable measurement at the center of a car is a shade over 7 feet.)

In common with all subsequent London tube lines, the City and South London was a standard-gauge railway. Its cars rode on a pair of four-wheeled trucks the wheels of which were 24 inches in diameter. Because the floor of each car was only 1½ feet above the top of the rails, a cutout was provided in the floor over each truck to allow the use of 24-inch wheels. These cutouts did not reduce passenger-carrying space inside the cars since they were located under cars' seats. In later years, when the standard diameter of tube tunnels in London became 11½ feet, the floor of tube rolling stock was standardized at 3 feet above the rail. Cutouts above the wheels remain a standard feature of tube rolling stock, however, although at one time certain cars featured a step-up raised floor over the car's trucks to achieve necessary clearance.

The City and South London was equipped with a 500-volt DC third rail for current distribution. Although London practice would eventually standardize with an outside third rail for current distribution and a center "fourth rail" for current return, the City and South London used a third rail positioned between the running rails for current distribution, much in the manner associated with Lionel toy trains, with the running rails serving as a ground. The third rail on the City and South London was between the rails but off center to remain clear of the coupling apparatus on the low-profile rolling stock. In 1890, the City and South London did not believe that self-powered electric cars were practical in the limited confines of its underground railway. Consequently, after rejecting a proposal to use cable traction for the new subway, London's first tube line ordered a fleet of specially designed electric locomotives to power its trains.

They were small units by all standards—14 feet long, riding on four 27-inch diameter wheels mounted in a rigid frame, and powered by a pair of electric motors. H. F. Howson claims that the tiny locomotives "resembled two upright pianos, in iron, placed back to back on wheels."[32] Like the electric locomotives that would later used by the New York Central Railroad to inaugurate electric service into New York's Grand Central—which we shall learn about in Chapter 4—the London locomotives employed a gearless drive for power transmission. "The two traction motor armatures were wound directly on the two axles—the first time in electric traction that the arrangement not using either gearwheels or a chain drive has been tried."[33] The locomotives were equipped with Westinghouse air brakes, but because the subway route was so short, instead of using onboard air compressors, they recharged their air reservoirs from a fixed pump at the Stockwell end of the line after each round-trip. As would be the case with virtually all early electric railways, the City and South London built its own powerhouse to generate electricity, an installation that featured three vertical-compound reciprocating steam engines, each linked to its own electric generator.

The City and South London was expanded in several stages in

the early years of the twentieth century. Before any of this happened, a special visitor arrived in London in 1894 to inspect the new undertaking. He was William Barclay Parsons, then in the process of developing technical parameters for a proposed new subway in New York, and it has been said that Parsons's favorable impressions upon seeing the City and South London helped shape his final recommendations for improving mass transport in New York.

While the City and South London was a technical success, it was, unfortunately, a financial disaster. And so as proposals to build additional tube lines emerged in London in the years after 1890, financing was not forthcoming for such ventures, and it would not be until a totally improbable individual arrived in London at the turn of the century that the construction of tube lines moved into high gear and the basic system that is now so closely identified with the city was built.

Two additional tube lines were constructed in the waning years of the nineteenth century even before that improbable individual came on the scene and accelerated construction of the city's underground system. The first of these was called the Waterloo and City Railway. It opened in 1898 and connected Waterloo Station, on the south bank of the Thames, with the heart of the city at a station called Bank, a little over 1½ miles away. The Waterloo and City, while an important tube line, had no intermediate stations at all between its two terminals; its primary purpose was to allow passengers getting off railway trains at Waterloo Station to reach the heart of London on the other side of the Thames. Rolling stock was built in the United States by Jackson and Sharp, and unlike the City and South London's locomotives, the Waterloo and City began service using four-car trains, the front and rear cars of which were motorized, the center cars being motorless trailers. The motor cars were not equipped with MU control; instead, a series of high-voltage cables ran the length of the train to permit operation of both cars from either end, a practice the government later banned for other tube lines because of the fire risk that such cables represented. (One of the advantages of Frank Sprague's MU control is that car-to-car control circuits can use low-voltage current, while each motor car draws high-voltage current directly from the third rail.) Waterloo and City used a center third rail with direct current at a potential of 500 volts, and running rails were used for current return.

As transport matters evolved in the British capital during the twentieth century, Waterloo and City would remain an independent operation and did not become part of various efforts to unify London's underground railways. Waterloo and City eventually came under the control of British Railways (BR), and was regarded as a shuttle service to and from BR's Waterloo Station. But when British Railways itself was devolved into various privatized entities, London's second-oldest tube line was absorbed by London Underground in 1994, 106 years after it carried its first passengers.

London's third tube line opened on July 30, 1900, and ran on an east-west course across central London between Shepherd's Bush and Bank, the latter being the same in-city location where the Waterloo and City terminated. The new line was called the Central London Railway—and would later become the Central Line of London Transport. Because of the uniform rate of fare the line initially charged, it was also known as the "two-penny tube" for many years—long after the uniform fare was replaced by a zone system with fares based on distance traveled. (The City and South London also charged a uniform "two-penny" fare, but only the Central London earned the nickname.)

The line's inaugural was presided over by the same Prince of Wales who had performed similar honors for the City and South London a decade earlier in 1890. The company specified a broader tube diameter than had been used on the City and South London, namely 11½ feet, and it soon became the London standard. Like London's earlier tube undertaking, the Central hauled its trains with electric locomotives. These were of a larger, twin-truck design that was 30 feet long, not the small rigid-frame locomotives used on the earlier City and South London Railway, and were built in Schenectady, New York, by General Electric.[34]

The Central London Railway was no small operation. It required 168 wooden trailer cars and thirty locomotives to inaugurate service in 1900. When a locomotive arrived at either terminal, it was uncoupled from the front of the train, and a different locomotive was coupled to the rear for the return trip. The incoming locomotive then positioned itself for a return assignment on a following train. (When steam locomotives powered elevated trains in Brooklyn and New York in preelectrification days, a similar relay arrangement was used to shift locomotives from inbound to outbound trains.) But the operators of the Central London Railway were keeping abreast of developments in the United States, where Frank Sprague had perfected the system known as multiple-unit control, and a mere three years after the line began service, a fleet of sixty-four motorized cars was ordered to replace the electric locomotives. There had also been complaints that the heavy, 44-ton electric locomotives were inducing vibrations in buildings along the route. April 14, 1903, was the final day the Central London operated exclusively with electric locomotives. A gradual phase-in of the new electric motor cars was then begun, and on June 8 of the same year all service on the "two-penny tube" was being provided by the new motorized cars.[35]

As was the case when motorized cars were built for the Waterloo and City, the motor controller, the air compressor, and other devices associated with the operation of an electric-powered train were located in a compartment over the power truck and behind the motorman's station at one end of the car. On typical U.S. subway cars—and on the District Line's MU cars, as well—this equipment is mounted under the floor and out of sight. Given the close clearances underneath tube cars, this was not an option; a windowless compartment 14 feet long within the car body itself was reserved for control equipment. It would not be until the onset of smaller control apparatus before and after the Second World War that tube cars in London could eschew control compartments inside the car and place such equipment under the floor or the seats.

Britain's Board of Trade, the regulatory agency for the country's railways, decided that as a safety measure, tube passengers must be able to move freely from car to car. Consequently, motorized cars—with their large control compartments immediately behind the motorman's cab—could be positioned only at the front or the rear of a train, since placing one at midtrain would preclude passengers' moving from car to car. Another mandate issued by the Board of Trade was that these control compartments be constructed of steel as a fire-prevention measure, even though the rest of the car body was wood-sheathed.[36]

Another interesting feature of London's early tube rolling stock involved passenger entry into the cars. In a manner somewhat reminiscent of elevated railways in cities like Brooklyn, New York, and Chicago, each tube car featured an open platform at one end that was enclosed by a trellislike gate. (*The Times* called such gates *grilles*.) Passengers stepped onto the car via this platform and then moved inside through a bulkhead door that led into the car's center aisle. Each gate—or grille—was operated manually by a crew member assigned to that position.

Because of the unusual profile demanded by the tube environment, London's tube cars retained open-platform entry long after sliding side doors had become standard on other subway cars— even on cars operated by the District and the Metropolitan. Sliding side doors did not become standard until after the First World War, and when they were developed they involved not merely an opening in the side of the car, but one that intruded up into the roof, as well. The sidewalls of a typical tube car measure only 5 feet from top to bottom, so additional headroom had to be found elsewhere so passengers could use the doors without ducking—or at least without excessive ducking.[37]

Frank Sprague made an important contribution to the Central London Railway even before the company eliminated its electric locomotives and adopted MU control. Like the City and South London, the Central initially planned to use hydraulic elevators for passengers to reach its underground stations—and in fact several were installed. In 1897, Sprague was awarded a contract to install forty-nine electric elevators at various locations on the line, and electric-powered elevators soon became standard.

There were other interesting American connections with the early underground railways of London. Car builders such as Jackson and Sharp and American Car and Foundry turned out considerable numbers of new subway cars for London, but the most interesting link of all involves a man who had earlier earned a rather unsettling reputation as a ruthless traction financier during the construction of elevated railway lines in Chicago.[38]

His name was Charles Tyson Yerkes, Jr. Born in Philadelphia in 1837 to Quaker parents, he went to work as a brokerage clerk at the age of seventeen. Four years later he established his own brokerage firm and three years after that he had his own bank. Ruined in the Panic of 1871 and then imprisoned for the way he handled an account of the City of Philadelphia during the collapse, he was pardoned by the governor of Pennsylvania after seven months in jail and, ever resourceful, soon had his ventures up and running again. In 1882 Yerkes headed west to Chicago, and over the next eighteen years would put as singular an imprint on that city's developing system of elevated railways as any individual possibly could.[39]

By the turn of the century, though, Yerkes's welcome had worn thin in Chicago. In 1899, for instance, he attempted to secure a no-cost extension for one of his street railway franchises from the City Council that would be run for the modest term of 100 years. During council debate, an angry mob surrounded City Hall demanding that Yerkes be repudiated. The council rejected his proposal, even though Yerkes later claimed he had handed out over a million dollars in bribes to secure favorable action on the measure. Soon afterward Yerkes sold his Chicago traction interests, moved to New York, acquired a magnificent home at 68th Street and Fifth Avenue, and was seemingly intent on spending the rest of his days tending to his extensive art collections.

On October 1, 1900, though, acting as the point man for a U.S. syndicate, Yerkes acquired franchise rights in London for something that was then known as the Hampstead Tube, an underground railway that had been authorized but on which construction had yet to begin. The transaction involved an investment of 100,000 pounds sterling.[40]

Several months later, in March of 1901, Yerkes secured effective control of the Metropolitan District Railway and announced plans to electrify its operations. It was Yerkes, for instance, who insisted on using a DC system for the District. Looking ahead to the construction of the Hampstead Tube and perhaps additional lines as well, Yerkes had a large electric-generating plant built on the banks of the Thames in Chelsea that came to be called Lots Road. Its initial complement included seven 7,500 horsepower steam turbines, each coupled to an electric generator that produced 11,000 volts of alternating current which was stepped down and converted to 600 volts of direct current in separate substations located strategically throughout the city.[41] At the time it was built, Lots Road was the largest electric-generating station in all of Europe.

Building this massive generating station brought Yerkes into conflict with another American expatriate, James McNeill Whistler. Whistler felt the large smokestacks of the proposed generating plant would destroy the peaceful vista along the riverfront, but soon enough local artists—although not Whistler himself, because he passed away in 1903 before the structure was completed—were incorporating the reflections of the new smokestacks on the water's surface in their renditions of the Thames.[42] Next, the Yerkes syndicate acquired a variety of separate authorizations that had been awarded to various entities to construct new tube lines through London, and these were eventually combined under the umbrella of a holding company called the Underground Electric Railways of London, Ltd. Yerkes was not merely investing his own money in these multiple railway ventures in London. As Charles Lee notes: "The principal parties to the new company were Yerkes himself, and the financial houses of Speyer Brothers of London, Speyer and Co, of New York, and the Old Colony Trust Company of Boston, U.S.A. A little later, the Amsterdam house of Teixeira de Mattos Bros. participated."[43]

Mergers and consolidations, long a defining characteristic of Yerkes's approach to urban transport, brought the amalgamation of a number of earlier proposals, and out of these transactions would emerge three important London tube lines: the Northern, the Bakerloo, and the Piccadilly lines, the heart of London's system.[44] The Northern Line proved to be the most complex of the three; it involved two separate north-south lines through central London, multiple branches north of the city, and even the eventual takeover of the original City and South London operation of 1890 and its upgrading to specifications compatible with the newer lines. An important section of what came to be called the Northern Line was originally the Hampstead Tube, the first London route that Yerkes acquired in 1900.

The Bakerloo Line was rather straightforward, a north-south tube line with, eventually, two branches on its northern end.[45] Three features of the original Bakerloo Line are worth noting. For technical reasons, it was necessary to reverse the polarity on this line, and the central rail carried positive current, while the outside rails were used for current return. (By the time the Bakerloo Line was extended in 1917, the problem had been solved, and the line was converted to the standard London arrangement of positive rail outside, return rail between the running rails.)

A second feature of the Bakerloo Line that merits attention was the coining of its unusual name. It was originally called the Baker Street and Waterloo Railway Company; some construction had begun when financial difficulties brought work to a halt and made the property an attractive acquisition for Charles Tyson Yerkes. He took over the company in 1902, construction was resumed, and the line carried its first passengers in 1906. As to the name, today "Bakerloo" is as common a piece of nomenclature in London as Big Ben and Hyde Park. But when a newspaper writer coined the Bakerloo name as a foreshortening of Baker Street and Waterloo after Yerkes acquired the company, it met severe resistance from "some of the more sedate British railway officers."[46] The journal *Railway Magazine* felt that for a tube line "to adopt its gutter title, is not what we expect from a railway company."[47] But Bakerloo it was and Bakerloo it remains.

A third interesting feature of the Bakerloo Line is that when the American Car and Foundry Company (ACF) built thirty-six motorized cars and seventy-two trailers for the line, they were London's first all-steel subway cars. (As discussed in Chapter 1, ACF also built the first production-model steel cars for the Interborough.) Designed and built in Berwick, Pennsylvania, but then "knocked down" and shipped to Manchester, England, for reassembly at an ACF facility in Trafford Park, the cars followed what had become typical tube design of the era—an enclosed control compartment immediately behind the motorman's cab, and motorized units capable of hauling several trailer cars.[48]

Yerkes's reputation followed him across the North Atlantic. In their *History of London Transport,* Barker and Robbins said of Yerkes that he "specialized in . . . spreading false rumors about his competitors' businesses and depressing the value of their stock, so making them more vulnerable to a take over bid; and in manipulating the financial affairs of his own companies in such a way that accounting specialists who went later through his books found amazing revelations of buccaneering methods."[49]

Yerkes himself did not enjoy a lengthy tenure in London. In June of 1905 he was diagnosed as having an incurable kidney disease; after attending a board meeting of his underground company in London on November 7, 1905, he sailed for New York. And there, in a suite of rooms in the Waldorf-Astoria Hotel, Charles Tyson Yerkes passed away on December 29, 1905, at the age of sixty-eight.[50] While he did live to see the onset of electrified operation over the District, Yerkes died before any of the new tube lines he had promoted and financed operated their first trains.

Charles Tyson Yerkes remains one of those individuals in transport history whose achievements, while significant, generally took place below the radar of popular history and awareness. Students of American literature, for example, are not likely to be familiar with the historical Yerkes. But they are surely aware of Frank Algernon Cowperwood, the principal figure in three famous Theodore Dreiser novels: *The Financier, The Titan*, and *The Stoic*. Cowperwood is modeled after Yerkes so closely that in the absence of a true biography about the man, *The Dictionary of American Biography* recommends the Dreiser trilogy for those who would like to learn more about him.

Yerkes, though, was not the only American investor who had designs on creating a financial empire by building new tube lines in London during the first decade of the twentieth century. Another was J. Pierpont Morgan, who attempted to form a consortium in conjunction with a London streetcar company, London United Tramways, Ltd., and deny Yerkes the authorizations he was seeking to build an underground empire. At the time, Morgan was well along in the establishment of a combine, an entity known as the International Mercantile Marine, the purpose of which was to dominate North Atlantic shipping. Morgan was also heavily involved in the New York, New Haven and Hartford Railroad, and one may certainly speculate whether he gave the London underground business anything like his undivided attention. Speyer Brothers, one of Yerkes's investment partners, quietly secured financial control of London United Tramways, and that spelled the end of Morgan's efforts.[51]

The development of underground railways in and around London would continue, but never again with the kind of energy and enthusiasm that was the hallmark of the first decade of the twentieth century, when Charles Tyson Yerkes emerged on the London scene. Indeed, after the final leg of the Northern Line was opened through London on June 22, 1907, there would not be another new tube line built through the heart of the city until Queen Elizabeth II presided at the formal opening of the new Victoria Line on March 7, 1969, fifty-two years later.[52]

There was new and steady mass-transit investment in and around London between 1907 and 1969, but it was largely confined to expanding existing lines further into the suburbs, acquiring new rolling stock, building connections of various sorts between the several lines, and rationalizing services between the tubes, the surface lines, and various intercity railways that provided service in the London suburbs.[53] Because both tube and surface lines utilize the same track gauge and the same system for current distribution, rolling stock of both styles can operate over common trackage and use the same maintenance facilities, although surface equipment will not fit into tube tunnels. There are even a few stations on the outskirts of the system where tube and surface trains serve the same platform. Such platforms are built at a compromise level midway between those of typical tube and typical surface stations, with tube passengers having to step up and surface passengers having to step down to reach the platform.

There was also continual evolution in the governance structure of the London tubes and surface lines. The Bakerloo, Piccadilly, and Northern lines were amalgamated as London Electric Railway in 1910. In 1933 a new public corporation called London Passenger Transport Board acquired London Electric, the Metropolitan, the District, the Central London Railway, and the City and South London; from that time on, the unified entity was popularly known as London Transport. But London Transport of 1933 was still regarded as a commercial enterprise. As noted in a 1970 discussion paper prepared for the Greater London Council: "When London Transport was formed in 1933 by the amalgamation of a number of independent transport undertakings, the possibility of its not paying its way was not envisioned."[54] Because of this perspective, as the 1970 discussion paper notes, it seemed "reasonable to give London Transport in return for its monopoly two equal statutory obligations: to provide an adequate service and to pay its way (including interest charges)."[55] Such a policy, of course, effectively closed the door on any recourse to government financial resources to underwrite the cost of new underground construction.

In 1948, coincident with the nationalization of all British intercity railways, the London Passenger Transport Board was superseded by the London Transport Executive, and London's urban railways were transformed into a fully public-sector operation.[56] Even so, the fiscal assumptions with respect to investment capital for transit did not change at all. Unless the London Transport Executive could secure resources for their construction, new underground lines in London would remain nothing but unfulfilled dreams.

The Victoria Line that opened in 1969 was authorized by Parliament in 1962, but not until a sea change of extraordinary proportion had transformed British urban transport policy. A Committee of Inquiry was appointed by the Minister of Transport in 1953 to explore the future of London Transport, and a report issued in early 1955 specifically addressed a new rail line in the corridor where the Victoria Line now operates: "Although the proposed railway may not in the near future pay its way directly we are of the opinion that the indirect advantage to London Transport and to London's economy as a whole [is] so important that this project should not be abandoned or postponed because on the basis of direct revenue or direct expenditure it appears to be unprofitable."[57]

It was the acceptance of this principal by the British government that led to the construction of the Victoria Line, the first new underground railway to be opened in the heart of the British capital since David Lloyd-George, the man who would lead Britain as Prime Minister during the First World War, presided at the inauguration of what is now known as the Northern Line on June 22, 1907. Public-sector financing for the construction of new underground lines—something without which the subways of Boston and New York would might never have been built at all—did not come to pass in London until a full century after that city inaugurated service along its first such railway.

The Victoria Line was built in conformity with more generous tunnel dimensions that had been adopted in the 1930s. Whereas the earlier standard had been 11½ feet, tubes on the Victoria Line feature a 12-foot inside diameter, even though for the foreseeable future the line will continue to operate rolling stock built to the same loading gauge as older tube equipment. The Victoria did include the very latest in automatic train control and automatic train operation, similar to equipment used on such new transit lines as the Bay Area Rapid Transit (BART) in the San Francisco Bay Area and other newly built rapid-transit lines.[58] Given the restricted dimensions of tube rolling stock, it took some engineering skill to find locations for all the gear that automated operation requires. As a result, one will find "equipment of some sort under every seat on these trains—not an inch of space is wasted."[59]

While there was a sixty-two-year interval between the opening of the Northern Line and the Victoria Line, London began to plan its next tube undertaking even before the Victoria Line was completed. It was to be called the Fleet Line, and its first element opened for service northwest of central London in 1979. Initial plans called for the new line to proceed through London on a south-by-southeast heading, cross under the River Thames near the Tower of London, and terminate in Lewisham, south of Greenwich. On its opposite or western end, the new Fleet Line would take over one of the Bakerloo Line's two northern branch lines.

Building the Fleet Line proved to be a protracted exercise. For one thing, in 1977, before any trains entered service, the project was renamed the Jubilee Line to commemorate the twenty-fifth anniversary of the coronation of Queen Elizabeth II. And when the new line was eventually built through central London in the late 1990s, it followed a more southerly course than originally intended. The Jubilee Line tunnels under the Thames farther east than originally planned to serve Waterloo Station, where intercity trains that operate through the new tunnel under the English Channel now terminate. Then, instead of continuing southward to Lewisham, the new line tunnels back under the Thames to the East End of London and connects there with a host of other Underground and railway lines.

In anticipation, perhaps, of fully automated trains in future years with no onboard operators at all, stations on the newest segment of the Jubilee Line, from Westminster to Stratford, include permanent glass walls between platform and track, with sliding doors positioned opposite the point where a train's doors will stop. In this respect, the Jubilee Line is not unlike an elevator, in that routine stops require two sets of doors to open and close—one aboard the vehicle, one at the station (or floor) the vehicle is servicing.[60]

Between the construction of the Victoria and the Jubilee lines, London Transport built an interesting extension of the older Piccadilly Line, one of the three tubes that were part of the Yerkes's consortium in the early years of the twentieth century. It was not a new line into central London; instead, in the mid-1970s the Piccadilly Line was extended 3½ miles westward from its previous terminal at Hounslow West all the way to Heathrow Airport, with an underground loop eventually providing service to all four of the airport terminals.[61] Given the worldwide destinations that can be reached from Heathrow, it is perfectly correct to say that one can now depart from Leicester Square in central London and travel to Hong Kong, Tokyo, Johannesburg, or Los Angeles aboard London Underground's Piccadilly Line—with but a single change of vehicles en route.[62]

The foregoing has been a very concise treatment of the development of subway service in and around London; much material has necessarily been condensed, much more has been omitted. One seemingly modest development of London Transport, though, deserves a brief mention. It happened almost by accident in 1933.

A man by the name of Harry Beck was an electrical draftsman who worked for the Underground drawing up circuits for signal systems and electric power distribution networks. Something that had long resisted easy and clear graphic rendition was a map of the Underground's various routes and services. Beck went to work on his own time and tried to simplify London's rail system in the same way that an electrical diagram presents a schematic rendition of otherwise complex networks of wiring and cabling. His effort, completed in 1933, has become a world transit classic. Rather than show every twist and turn of every route, Beck's map emphasizes the relationship of one line to another and enables passengers to understand the Underground system as a whole while still appreciating at which station one must get off the Hammersmith and City Line and change to the Bakerloo tube if one's destination is, say, Oxford Circus.

In addition, Beck used color codes to distinguish one line from another, and so successful did his map and concept become that not only is an updated edition of it still used by London Underground today, but maps of a similar style have been developed by rail-transit systems the world over. The identification of transit lines by their color code has never achieved popular usage in Britain apart from the map, and the various lines continue to be identified by their names. In London one still rides the Piccadilly Line, not the Dark Blue Line, for instance. But in U.S. cities such as Washington and Boston not only are transit systems depicted on "Beck-style" schematic maps on station walls and in subway cars, but various lines and services are almost universally identified in these cities by the color code used on the map—and by the color code alone. The Red Line in Washington, for instance, has never been called anything but the Red Line, while in Boston, the subway-elevated line we read about in Chapter 2 as the Main Line El is today universally identified as the Orange Line.

Speaking of color, the livery of London Underground's rolling stock has seen an interesting evolution. By the late 1930s, the standard exterior color for surface and tube cars had become a very rich shade of dark red accented by gold-leaf lettering. After the Second World War, London Transport began to specify exterior sheathing of unpainted aluminum for newly acquired fleets of cars, and in time such rolling stock outnumbered the solid red cars. Many older vehicles were even repainted to mimic the new aluminum stock.

In the 1980s, though, an unwelcome import from the New York subways—spray-painted graffiti—caused London Underground to revise its policy. Because it was difficult to remove graffiti from unpainted aluminum, a painted livery of red, white, and blue was adopted instead.

Moving from the outside of underground rolling stock to the inside, and to emphasize further a difference between equipment of the London Underground and the subway cars that serve New York, there is the matter of how standing passengers have restrained themselves from falling down as trains speed around sharp curves along their routes.

Both New York and London originally outfitted their cars with flexible leather straps suspended from an overhead bar, a piece of equipment that survives to this day in popular nomenclature, since subway riders in New York are often referred to as "strap-hangers." (The usage actually predates the subway in New York and was initially coined during the horse car era.) The leather straps themselves, of course, have long since been superseded by newer mechanical hardware, but New York and London have gone in slightly different directions.

New York continues to prefer spring-loaded handles suspended from the ceiling that standing passengers latch onto for support, while on the London Underground, the handgrip for standing passengers was for a long time a spherical device about the size of a golf ball hanging from the ceiling at the end of a flexible cable. London Underground recently abandoned these handgrips, and standing passengers now avoid falling by holding on to strategically located poles and bars.

Finally, to gain some understanding of the relative size of the two different styles of rolling stock used on the London Underground—and to compare such equipment with subway cars used on New York's IRT—Table 3.1 displays a number of relevant data elements.

DOCKLANDS

While London has continued to expand its rail transit system by building new tube lines under and through the heart of the city, more recently a different style of rail transit was deployed to serve a newly redeveloped section of the metropolitan area. A district to the east of central London called the Isle of Dogs was long a center of commerce and industry because it was here, beginning in the early days of sailing ships, that oceangoing vessels loaded and unloaded cargo. (The massive oceangoing steamship *Great Eastern,* designed by Isambard Kingdom Brunel, was built on the Isle of Dogs in 1858.) The onset of containerization as the principal form of ocean shipping shifted much of this sea

TABLE 3.1
ROLLING STOCK STATISTICS

	IRT R-62A[a]	London Tube Stock[b]	London Surface Stock (C69)[b]
Builder (date)	Bombardier (1985)	Metro-Cammell (1967)	Metro-Cammell (1967)
Length	51'	52' 9"	52' 7"
Maximum Width	8' 10"	8' 8"	9' 7"
Height (rail to top)	11' 10"	9' 5"	12' 1"
Weight	75,550 lbs.	n/a	71,000 lbs.
No. of Seats	44	40	32
Doors per Side	3 sets	2 sets	4 sets
Propulsion	4 GE 1257E1 or 4 Westinghouse 1447J motors	4 L.T. 115 motors	4 Brush 33 v L.T. 117 motors

a. All cars of all trains composed of R-62A units are motorized.
b. Motorized and nonmotorized trailer cars typically assigned to trains; data shown are for motorized units.

traffic to Britain's larger coastal ports, leaving London with an expanse of underutilized land adjacent to the center of the city.

In 1982 the government began an effort that led to large-scale redevelopment of London's docks, with new commercial and residential construction throughout the area of the Docklands. Instead of providing rail transport into and around this redeveloped area solely by expanding the city's basic underground system, London elected to deploy a new style of transit here—an automated rail network that connects with several Underground and commuter railroad stations and serves important points in the redevelopment area.

The system is called the Docklands Light Railway (DLR). Construction began in 1984, and on July 31, 1987, Queen Elizabeth II presided at a ceremony to mark the line's opening.[63] While the system clearly identifies itself as "light rail," it bears little similarity to the new kinds of light rail lines being built in many world cities. While smaller (and lighter) than London's tube or surface rolling stock, DLR trains draw current from a trackside third rail and certainly cannot operate at grade along city streets, an operational characteristic typically associated with light rail transit. Indeed London itself recently inaugurated such a new light rail service, a three-route system in the south

London suburb of Croydon, with active plans for additional lines elsewhere. Transport for London identifies this new service as a tramway, with the service name Tramlink, thus reserving the "light rail" designation for DLR. (Just in passing: with respect to more traditional British tram cars, London converted the last of the distinctive double-decker trolley cars that were once so common on its streets to motor bus operation in the summer of 1952.)

Likely the most distinctive characteristic of the new DLR operation is the fact that its trains operate in fully automated fashion with no onboard operators. The heart of the system is a transfer station called Canary Wharf, a facility that includes a large train shed not unlike those associated with classic nineteenth-century railway terminals. DLR's Canary Wharf transfer station is built aboveground; directly below is a station served by trains operating on London Underground's new Jubilee Line. This is the only landfall that any conventional tube line makes in the Docklands area.

The initial element of the Docklands system that opened in 1987 was 4½ miles long and included fifteen stations. In more recent years, DLR has expanded to 16.8 miles in length with twenty-seven stations and a tunnel under the River Thames to Greenwich, with service continuing beyond to Lewisham.

DLR operates as a subsidiary of Transport for London but is separate from London Underground, the agency that operates the tube and surface rapid-transit lines. Plans are moving along for additional expansion of DLR, including an extension to London City Airport. After its first five years of operation, in 1992 DLR was carrying 23,000 passengers a day. By 2002 the count on this new and different rail system in London was in excess of 130,000 daily passengers.

GLASGOW

Although new light rail transit systems are starting to be built in a number of cities in the United Kingdom, including a 37-mile system in and around Newcastle called the Tyne and Wear Metro that includes several miles of underground operation, there is only one other city in the British Isles besides London that can boast a traditional subway system. That is Glasgow, the onetime shipbuilding center on the banks of the River Clyde and the largest city in Scotland. "Subway," and not "underground," was originally the proper descriptor for Glasgow's belowground urban railway. In 1936, though, the term "subway" was banished and "underground" formally adopted. As a result, both terms enjoy popular usage among contemporary Glaswegians.

The Glasgow underground includes a number of features that mark it as different from any other in the world. It is an old system, for one thing, dating to 1896. In fact, in all the world only London and Budapest have subways that are older than Glasgow's. But age is hardly this system's most defining characteristic. The Glasgow Subway is a totally self-contained bidirectional underground loop 6½ miles in length.[64] (By comparison, the Inner Circle in London is 13 miles around.) The line crosses under the Clyde twice and serves important residential neighborhoods as well as the principal elements of the city's core. Many of the outlying stations on the subway system are places where passengers can make convenient transfers to motor buses and commuter railroads for continuing service into the farther suburbs, with the loop underground serving as a distributor through the heart of the city's business and commercial districts.

The Glasgow Subway features tube construction reminiscent of London's, although its tunnels are smaller in diameter than those in the British capital. While some sections of the line were built through unstable sand and required the use of a pressurized air lock for their construction, in certain places south of the river the line was built using cut-and-cover construction. The interior diameter of a classic tube line in London is 11½ feet, while the tubes in Glasgow measure a shade less than 10 feet across. Consequently, rolling stock in Glasgow is smaller than the cars that operate on the tube lines in London, and while the London tubes run on standard-gauge track that is 4 feet, 8½ inches between the running rails, Glasgow uses a distinctive track gauge that measures an even 4 feet across; station platforms are a shade over 2 feet above the top of the running rails. Also by way of comparison, the Glasgow tubes are generally much closer to the surface than are the tubes in London. The latter often require rides aboard multiple escalators to travel from street to platform level. To reach underground stations in Glasgow usually requires nothing but a short walk down a flight or two of stairs.

What is surely the most unique feature of the Glasgow Subway, though, is the fact that when the system opened in 1896—and for almost forty years afterward—it was served not by conventional electric-powered rail cars but, rather, by trains whose propulsion was effected by latching onto an endless cable that was in constant motion between the running rails. Authority to build the line was awarded by Parliament in 1890, the same year the City and South London inaugurated electric-powered tube service in the British capital. But electricity was hardly a tried-and-true transport technology during the years the Glasgow Subway was under design, and the choice of cable traction was an understandably cautious decision.

When it opened in 1896, the Glasgow Subway operated either single cars or two-car trains, with only one car of a train being equipped with a cable grip. Because a different style of cable grip was required on each of the two loops, grip cars were restricted as to which of the two tracks they could transit. (Even-numbered grip cars worked the outer, or clockwise, loop, while odd-numbered cars were restricted to the inner loop.) Some Glasgow Subway cars were of double-truck design and measured 40 feet, 9 inches in length; others were single-truck cars that were a mere 25 feet long, although many of these were rebuilt into forty-footers over the years.

The 1896 subway was owned, financed, and operated by a private firm, the Glasgow District Subway Company, and initially it proved to be quite popular. Once local streetcars were converted from animal power to electric propulsion at the turn of the century, though, patronage on the subway reached a plateau and leveled off. To keep expenses under control, the company reduced levels of service, but this hardly enhanced the line's popularity. Eventually, in 1923, the subway left the private sector and became part of a public agency known as Glasgow Corporation Transport, the same agency responsible for the city's streetcar system. Shortly afterward, in 1935, the system was electrified and cable operations discontinued.

No new rolling stock was acquired in 1935; the line's older cable-powered cars were refurbished and retrofitted for electric propulsion, and thanks to the substitution of sliding doors for the original open-gate entry, by 1935 Glasgow Subway cars bore little resemblance to the fleet that had inaugurated service back in 1896. An outside third rail was used for current distribution, and the running rails completed the return circuit, unlike London system of separate third and fourth rails.

During the Second World War, the Glasgow Subway proved invaluable, and patronage levels soared to new heights. Because the tunnels are not that far belowground, underground stations were not the obvious air-raid shelters they proved to be in London. In fact, in September of 1940, a Luftwaffe bomb caused serious damage near the Merkland Street Station, and the system had to be closed for over four months while repairs were made.

After the war, plans and proposals for expanding the Glasgow Subway were discussed. What eventually came to pass in 1978 and 1979 was not an expansion but a thorough rebuilding of the original system.[65] The line was closed for two full years, stations were rebuilt, new traction power and signal systems were installed, and a fleet of thirty-three new motorized cars was acquired from Metro-Cammel. Thanks to their vivid paint scheme, the new cars were quickly nicknamed "clockwork oranges" by Glasgow Subway riders. Her Royal Majesty Queen Elizabeth presided at a formal dedication ceremony for the newly modernized Glasgow system on November 1, 1979. Not all work had yet been completed on the day of the official ceremony, and passenger service was not restored until April 16, 1980. In the early 1990s, the Metro-Cammel cars were supplemented by eight new cabless trailer cars built by Hunslet TPL to allow additional three-car trains to be operated.

Another betterment that was incorporated into the system during the 1978-to-1979 rehabilitation was the construction of a two-track ramp from the underground right-of-way up to the system's ground-level maintenance and storage facility, the Broomloan Depot in Govan, south of the River Clyde. Previously, cars had to be lifted out of the tunnel by a crane for maintenance at

Broomloan. The line's tunnel right-of-way passed through the basement, so to speak, of the maintenance facility, and a pair of cable slings placed under a subway car would enable the crane to hoist cars into and out of the tunnels. Prior to the 1978-to-1979 rehabilitation, cars were typically lifted out of the tunnels for routine maintenance every ten days. Now entire trains move back and forth between the tunnels and the surface-level maintenance and storage facility under their own power.

Originally all station platforms were located between the two tracks. Because these platforms are only 10 feet wide, during the rehabilitation platforms at many key stations were supplemented with additional side platforms so trains operating in each direction could use a separate platform. An additional station was added to the loop line during the 1978-to-1979 effort, and it is the only station on the system that features a pair of outside platforms. This is Partick, located at the westernmost point on the loop line north of the river and a key transfer point to regional commuter rail services. The Glasgow underground continues to feature fifteen stations as it did in 1896, since the new Partick replaced a nearby older station that was phased out during the rehabilitation work.

When the Glasgow Subway opened in 1896, cable-powered trains required forty minutes to make a full circuit around the 6-mile loop. Since the 1978-to-1979 rebuilding, the same trip now takes only twenty-four minutes—assuming no untoward delays in loading or unloading passengers.

The Glasgow Subway is now under the governance of Strathclyde Passenger Transport, a regional agency established under the provisions of the 1968 British Transport Act that also coordinates the area's transit bus service and elements of an extensive commuter rail network. As the Glasgow Subway enters the twenty-first century, this nineteenth-century transport facility is enjoying robust years. Immediately prior to the 1978-to-1979 rebuilding, annual patronage on the line had dropped to 7.34 million riders. It has since doubled, and almost 15 million passengers now ride the line each year. And if anyone would like to get a sense of what service must have been like on the Glasgow Subway back in the days of cable operation, one of the system's original cars, trailer car No. 41—or at least half of it, split down the middle—is on permanent display on the mezzanine level of the Buchanan Street station in central Glasgow.[66]

PARIS AND OTHER RUBBER-TIRED SUBWAYS

Like other major world cities, Paris was facing terrible problems of crowding and congestion in the final years of the nineteenth century. And because "an elevated structure would be quite out of the question in a city which prides itself on the beauty of its streets, the only alternative was an underground railway."[67] Two days after France celebrated Bastille Day in July of 1900, the city of Paris opened its first subway. It was an east-west line that ran along the north bank of the River Seine and was built with public funds but leased to a private company for operation, the operator being required to supply rolling stock, signals, and other equipment. Unlike London and Glasgow, where early subways were built entirely with capital that was privately raised, Paris was more akin to New York and Boston in that its subway involved public investment for basic infrastructure but private operation of day-to-day service. Like New York and Boston, it was assumed that rental payments for the use of the subway would eventually repay the municipal government for its investment.

The company that contracted with the city to operate the new Paris Subway and whose name was boldly proclaimed across the letter boards of its new subway cars was Chemin de Fer Metropolitain. This was a title that was quickly foreshortened in Paris to a crisp Le Metro, a term that would eventually became a popular designation for subway systems the world over. According to the provisions of the operating contract, the company had to offer both first- and second-class service on the new line. A first-class ticket was initially priced at the equivalent of five cents, while a second-class ticket was three cents, with second-class passengers also having the ability to purchase a round-trip for five cents. The company was required to pay the city government one cent for each three-cent ticket it sold, two cents for every five-cent ticket, and in addition, a specified per-passenger tax for all passengers carried in excess of 140 million per year. (The Paris Metro continued to offer first- and second-class tickets until the 1980s.)

The initial rolling stock acquired by Chemin de Fer Metropolitain was quite unusual. The cars were short—a few inches less
than 30 feet from end to end. The company's initial order for
motorized units was placed with Ateliers de Construction du
Nord de la France and was for forty-six cars. As many as 100
nonpowered trailers were also acquired, and on opening day
twelve three-car trains were in service, each consisting of a motorized unit on the head end that featured second-class accommodations, one trailer that was also for second-class passengers
only, and another trailer that offered both first- and second-class
service. Motorized cars were placed at the head end of each train,
and trains reversed directions at each terminal by passing around
a small loop. Because of these loops, most motorized units featured a control station at only one end of the car, although the
company did acquire some motorized cars with operating stations at both ends to handle any unusual short-turn assignments
that might develop. As additional new cars were delivered during
the early months of operation, longer trains with two motorized
units became common. The cars were not equipped with
Sprague-style MU control, though, and high-voltage cables had
to be run from one motorized unit to another in such cases.[68]

Another interesting feature of the initial cars that provided subway service in Paris is that they were of solid-frame, single-truck
design. The frame of each car was made out of steel, and the
upper portion of the frame was painted in a color that told subway workers—and interested passengers, too—whether a given
car was a motorized unit or a trailer. The upper frame was
painted black on trailer cars and red on motorized units, and the
bodies of the cars were built of smartly varnished wood. By
1903, Paris recognized the need for larger Metro cars, and a fleet
of double-truck thirty-six-footers was acquired. These still featured wooden car bodies; the first steel cars arrived in 1906, and
by this time car length had increased to 44 feet.

The man who supervised construction of the first Paris Subway, and who would later be referred to as *le pere du Metro,* was
named engineer-in-chief of the project in 1896 and remained
with the system for many decades afterward.[69] He was Fulgence
Bienvenue, and French transit historians have noted that it was
his energy and ingenuity that resolved the many obstacles the

project faced as it moved forward. One interesting touch that made the subway's construction far less intrusive than it might otherwise have been was the digging of four small tunnels perpendicular to the route of the subway between the construction site and the River Seine, so that debris could be removed from the project by barge without having to be hauled through the streets of Paris. Under Bienvenue, work was begun on the city's second subway line even before the first one was completed; its initial leg opened for revenue service in mid-December of 1900, less than six months after the first line began the subway era in Paris. This second Metro Line was expanded into a crescent-like circumferential service across the northern rim of the city.[70]

Sad to say, the Paris Metro would become the scene of a horrible transit disaster shortly after it celebrated its third anniversary. It happened on the evening of August 10, 1903, on the system's second line, the one that opened in December 1900. Train No. 43, with eight cars, had departed from Porte Dauphine and had almost completed its circumferential journey across the city's northern rim to Nation. When it reached Les Couronnes station, an electric motor failed; the train's passengers were off-loaded and the following train, with passengers still aboard, coupled onto the rear of No. 43 and began to push the empty train toward the maintenance yard.

The failed motor was not merely inoperative, though; it was also on fire. Barely 200 yards beyond Les Couronnes, flames burst through into the wooden car and quickly spread. Passengers began to flee, but conditions were so restricted and the smoke so acrid and severe that many passengers were overcome. And then a third train smashed into the two stalled trains, adding still more passengers to the underground panic. The fire burned for many hours, and rescue workers were unable to enter the tunnel until the next morning. When they did, they discovered that eighty-four people had perished in the disaster. Reported the *New York Times:* "The names and occupations of the victims give pathetic evidence of their humble condition. The names are characteristic of the French working class, and occupations are given as painter, mason, plumber, tailor, seamstress, locksmith, &c."[71]

A factor that contributed substantially to the death toll was the difficulty passengers faced in trying to flee the tunnel; bodies of many victims were found behind locked gates that would have led to safety. On the day after the disaster, August 11, yet another train on the same line of the Paris Metro caught fire. It was but a minor blaze, and the only casualties were minor injuries to two passengers. But it touched off a rather severe panic, given the tragedy of the previous day. A municipal committee that investigated the disaster quickly recommended that the practice of using motorized cars on both ends of a train be eliminated immediately and that lighting circuits for station platforms be separated from traction power circuits.[72]

Paris identified its subway routes that opened in 1900 sequentially as *ligne A* and *ligne B,* since from the outset a multiline system was envisioned. In later years a number system was adopted to replace the original letters, but what are now called *ligne 1* and *ligne 2* remain important elements of the contemporary Paris Metro system. Expanded over the years and now served by more conventional subway equipment than the 30-foot wooden cars that inaugurated service at the turn of the century, *ligne 1* continues to run along the north bank of the Seine—the Right Bank—and now links La Defense at its western terminal with an eastern terminal at Chateau de Vincennes, while *ligne 2,* the route that saw the terrible fire in 1903, remains a twenty-five-station semicircumferential service that features transfers to more Paris Subway lines than any other.

All subway lines that have been built in Paris continue the letter/number sequence that was begun in 1900, and by the early years of the twenty-first century, the newest subway in Paris was *ligne 14,* a route that closely parallels *ligne 1* across the Right Bank for much of its length but incorporates the very latest in automated transit technology. Indeed, because this new *ligne 14* is so different, it is identified in Paris as part of a new generation of rapid transit that will be known as Meteor service.

Unlike London's underground rail—and certainly unlike New York's Subway—the Paris Metro consists of a series of fourteen underground lines that are totally separate from one another. There are no junctions, no branch lines funneling trains onto other routes, no trunk lines through the city's central core that are used by trains from various feeder routes. Each of the system's fourteen lines is a separate and independent two-track operation, and while passengers may freely transfer from one line to another at many central points, trains remain on their designated lines. Two of the Paris lines—*ligne 7* and *ligne 13*—do feature branch-line services. But these are operated independently of the trunk line, and passengers must typically change trains if they wish to travel between main-line and branch-line stations.

This was not always the case. During its early years Paris did feature some interline operations. But as the system was expanded and upgraded in the years after the Second World War, officials elected to realign various routes and create a system in which all trains operate on their own two-track lines and no switching of trains from one track to another is required during routine operations. Building a large urban rail-transit system with many lines but no junctions and no interline service is not uncommon in contemporary mass transit. An extensive Metro system that was built in Mexico City in the years after 1969, for example, includes eleven separate lines, but with all trains remaining on their own designated two-track routes. Likewise, the Metro in Barcelona, Spain—briefly discussed below—is of a similar configuration.

Shortly after control of the Paris Metro was placed in the hands of a new public agency in 1949, Regie Autonome des Transports Parisiens (RATP), the city adopted—one might even say invented—a most unusual style of rapid transit: subway trains that run on rubber tires. Only one totally new line in Paris has ever been built as a rubber-tired operation from the outset, and that is RATP's new *ligne 14*, which began service in 1998. After a successful demonstration of its new technology on an abandoned portion of *ligne 7* in 1952, the new rubber-tired concept was retrofitted to four other Metro lines—including the city's pioneer subway, *ligne 1*—in the years following 1952. If low-profile tube trains running through deep-bored tunnels are the defining characteristic of the London Underground, and if busy four-track lines featuring local and express service are the hallmark of the New York subways, then rapid-transit trains rolling on rubber tires represent the feature that is most identified with the Paris Metro—even though conventional, steel-wheel subway lines outnumber rubber-tired ones in Paris by a ratio of nine to five, and no additional conversions are planned.[73]

The rubber-tired subway trains of Paris are more correctly described as a combined technology that uses both rubber tires and steel wheels. Looking down at such a right-of-way from a subway platform, for example, one sees what appears to be a conventional railroad right-of-way built with ordinary steel running rails. (Individuals with an engineering eye might note that the cross-ties are spaced a little further apart than on a conventional rapid-transit line.) Outboard from the twin rails and seemingly at the same height as the top of the rails are a parallel set of concrete or steel guideways over which the rubber tires roll. Finally, outboard from these flat guideways is something that looks not unlike an outside third rail, except that there will be such a device on each side of the right-of-way.

Here is how it all works. Axles of the subway cars are fitted with both steel wheels and rubber tires. The steel wheels are positioned over the steel rails, and the rubber tires are outboard from these so they can roll along the flat guideways and provide basic support and traction for the car. Each truck of each car also contains a set of smaller tires positioned horizontally which roll against the side structure that looks like a third rail. These side structures do double duty; they keep the train on the guideway and they also distribute current to the train as it moves along, although it takes a separate shoelike device maintaining contact with the outside rails for current collection, since the small rubber tires do not conduct electricity.

The return circuit is through the running rails, but here is where matters get a little complicated, not to say counterintuitive. Because a car's steel wheels do not normally touch the steel rails but are suspended above them, separate shoes are included to maintain contact with the running rail and complete the electrical circuit. So why are steel wheels required at all?

Should any of the pneumatic tires suffer a loss of pressure, the steel wheel is there as a backup safety feature to maintain a car's equilibrium. More important, when a rubber-tired subway train has to negotiate its way through a set of switch tracks, the guideway on which the rubber tires roll dips down several inches, and the steel wheels descend to engage the track and guide the train through the switch. The steel wheels also play an important operational role when a train is brought to a stop, since brake shoes are brought to bear against them. Finally, what are called "steel wheels" on rubber-tired subway trains are not like the cast-steel wheels used on more conventional railway rolling stock. They have much deeper flanges, for one thing, to help engage switch tracks, but they are also hollow in the middle—and look not unlike a tinfoil pie plate or a shallow bowl. The steel wheels are fully capable of supporting the weight of a subway car should the pneumatic tires fail. But if that were to happen, the steel wheel would not substitute for the rubber tire and allow the train to continue in service. The steel wheel would prevent a disaster from happening, electronic sensors would warn the train's operator that a tire had failed, and the train would be taken out of service and removed to a maintenance facility—where its flat tire would be repaired!

What are the advantages of rubber-tired subway trains? One can generate a controversy that is virtually geopolitical in its dimensions in trying to argue any advantage—or disadvantage—inherent to rubber-tired subway trains. Proponents stoutly claim they offer a smoother ride; opponents argue the opposite just as forcefully. They are surely able to negotiate steeper grades than conventional steel-wheel equipment, but their ability to operate outdoors under snowy and icy conditions remains at least an open question. In Paris, *ligne 6* includes a section of outdoor operation in the vicinity of the Eiffel Tower, and *ligne 1* emerges from belowground for a short distance near Bastille Station, but when the city of Montreal opted to copy Paris and build its entire transit system with Paris-style rubber-tired subway trains, every inch of the system was built in underground tunnels to avoid the perils of winter.

At the dawn of the twenty-first century, six world cities were operating rubber-tired subway systems similar to that which Paris pioneered, and there certainly appears to be a strong Gallic connection in the choice of this unusual technology. In addition to Paris, the city of Lyon, France, operates a three-line rubber-tired system whose initial segment opened in 1983, while a Metro system in Marseilles that inaugurated service in 1977 is a two-line network with rubber-tired trains similar to those of Paris. (Before its current transit system was built, Marseilles operated an extensive system of streetcars that included some belowground operations. A single such line has been retained and functions as a feeder to the new Metro system.) Two additional cities in France, Lille and Toulouse, also operate rubber-tired transit lines, but these are more akin to various styles of automated people-mover systems found in many airports and are not of the same technological kind as the rubber-tired trains of the Paris Metro. (A three-line transit system in Sapporo, Japan, employs rubber-tired trains, but it uses yet another technology that is also rather different from that of Paris.)

Three transit systems in the Western Hemisphere have opted for Paris-style rubber-tired trains. A three-line system opened in Montreal in 1966; it has since added a fourth line, although its more significant post-1966 expansion has been in the extension of two of the original three lines into residential sections further removed from Downtown. The Montreal Metro, interestingly enough, operates more rubber-tired mileage than does Paris.[74] What is clearly the largest rubber-tired transit system in the world—and the first deployment in a city where French is not the native language—is that of Mexico City.

Mexico City's rubber-tired rapid-transit mileage is three times larger than that of Paris and almost equals all other world cities combined. As was the case in Montreal, there was considerable reliance on French consultants in designing the system, and at the start of the twenty-first century, Mexico City was operating ten rubber-tired lines with a combined length of 114.8 miles. Given Mexico City's climate, snow and ice were not matters of concern for the system's designers. Still, a robust 60 percent of the system operates in underground subway tunnels.

The cars used on the Mexico City Metro feature a very different and distinctive sharply angular design and are painted in a fiery shade of bold Aztec red. What may well be the most impressive aspect of the system is that while it is today among the larger rapid-transit operations in the world, Mexico City's first subway did not carry its initial passengers until 1969—107 years after the Metropolitan welcomed its first passengers in London and almost seven decades after the Interborough Rapid Transit Company began running subway trains in New York.

Mexico City boasts one rapid-transit line that uses steel-wheel technology and overhead catenary for current distribution. Cars that operate on this line are painted white, not the distinctive red used on the rubber-tired network, and Line A, as this service is called, operates from a marvelously diverse terminal called Pantitlan, where three important rubber-tired Metro lines from Downtown terminate. The steel-wheel line provides connecting service to La Paz in suburbs to the southeast. Another steel-wheel rapid-transit adjunct of the Mexico City Metro is a light-rail line at the southern terminal of the No. 2 Line which provides connecting service to a place called Xochimilco. In all, the Mexico City transit system owns and operates over 2,500 subway cars and carries a 1½ billion passengers each year.[75]

The final city in which one can find rubber-tired subway trains in daily operation is Santiago de Chile, whose system's service was inaugurated in 1975 and quickly grew to three separate lines that operate 394 Althom-built rapid-transit cars.

Table 3.2 displays the extent of "Paris-style" rubber-tired rapid transit that was in operation at the start of the twenty-first century. Conventional steel-wheel service which also operates in any of the noted cities is not included in this tabulation.

ELSEWHERE IN EUROPE

There is considerable variety in the way of subway service throughout Europe. Full statistical information is provided in Table 3.3, but certain characteristics of one city or another are worth dwelling on, even if but briefly.

The oldest subway on the continent—and only the second elec-

TABLE 3.2
PARIS-STYLE RAPID TRANSIT

City	Number of Lines	Total Mileage
Paris	5	33.5
Marseilles	2	11.9
Lyon	3	17.4
Montreal	4	39.8
Mexico City	10	114.8
Santiago de Chile	3	23.4

trified subway in the world—opened in Budapest in 1896, in the same year that cable-powered service was inaugurated in Glasgow. It was a 2.5-mile line that ran inland from the east bank of the Danube River through tunnels that were built immediately below the surface. Trains drew electric current from overhead trolley wires, and the service has long been known as the Millennium Line. This was not an early reference to the dawn of the twenty-first century 104 years in the future, but rather a commemoration of the fact that when the Budapest Subway's service was inaugurated in 1896, Hungry—kingdom, state, or nation—was a modest 1,000 years old.

Budapest's Millennium Subway of 1896 saw little in the way of system expansion until quite recently. Some new construction was begun in 1949, but work had to be suspended shortly afterward, and it was not until 1970 that Budapest inaugurated service on the first of two new metro lines and even added a modest northward expansion to the original 1896 line. All Budapest subways, new as well as old, operate on standard-gauge track, but the original line features a much narrower loading gauge than the newer lines, as well as a different form of electrification. Consequently, the 1896 route in Budapest is referred to today as a "small-profile" metro operation. Its current rolling stock is a fleet of twenty-three three-car articulated units built in Hungry between 1973 and 1987 by Ganz, while the two newer lines operate a fleet of 371 cars built by Mytischy of Moscow to standard designs once used in all Warsaw Pact countries.

The German capital city of Berlin boasts an extensive rapid-transit system. Its original line, some 8½ miles in length, began service in 1902 and incorporated both underground and elevated construction. Like New York—and like Budapest, too—the Berlin system operates on standard-gauge track but includes two separate networks, each with rolling stock of a unique width. One fleet includes 866 cars that are a trifle over 8½ feet wide, while the other network operates 516 cars that measure 7½ feet across. These latter may well be the narrowest subway cars currently in use in any major world metro system. Major portions of the Berlin Subway also utilize a form of electric current distribution that we shall see more of in Chapter 4—namely, a trackside third rail that trains contact on its underside with a spring-loaded third-rail shoe rather than the more common arrangement of shoes running along the top of a third rail.

An unusual aspect of the Stockholm Subway is that it features "left-hand" running, similar to the railways and underground lines of Great Britain. Such a practice stands in contrast to ordinary street traffic in Sweden, which operates in a more conventional "right-hand" fashion.

Streets in Sweden were not always so aligned, however. Alone among Scandinavian countries, Sweden had long observed "British-style" left-hand traffic patterns. In 1967, following a public referendum in 1963 and years of planning and preparation, the entire country switched over to the same system used by its neighbors. There was no need to convert the country's railways, including the Stockholm Subway, to the new standard, and so trains in Sweden continue to operate on the "wrong" track.

New York Subway riders will find familiar touches here and there in the Stockholm Tunnelbana. The system features overriding third rails with cover-boards that look very much like those used on the Lexington Avenue Line in New York, and much of the system's rolling stock is equipped with the same style of coupler that was long the standard in New York. What may well be the single feature of the Stockholm system that most resembles New York—and clearly differentiates the system from one like the Paris Metro—is the fact that a number of branch lines both north and south of the city's center funnel into a four-track trunk line that runs through the heart of Downtown—which is located on a small island. There are five branch lines to the north, six to the south; and the overall system includes 68 route miles, over half of which are underground.

An interesting side feature of the Stockholm Subway was the adoption of a distinctive logo for the system, a black capital T on a circular white background. To find a subway station in the Swedish capital city, even if one lacks familiarity with the local language, one simply looks for the logo. When the MBTA in Boston tried to establish a new identity for that venerable system in the late 1960s, its consultants decided to import the Swedish T and make it the symbol of the new authority.

On the Iberian Peninsula, the capital cities of Lisbon, Portugal, and Madrid, Spain, are served by important subway systems. In

Madrid all trains on a ten-line system draw 600 volts of direct current from overhead catenary, and, similar to both London and Glasgow, Madrid also boasts a circumferential rapid-transit line that encircles the city's central core. Lisbon, which has long operated some of the world's oldest streetcars on a thirteen-line tramway system, inaugurated service on a new Metro in 1959 that has since grown to almost 12 miles in length.

The Catalonian city of Barcelona, Spain, also features an interesting subway system. The most senior of its five lines opened in 1924, and the system has been steadily expanded over the years. Although Barcelona's Mediterranean climate is certainly mild, the city's subway system is built almost entirely belowground, with only two short sections where trains emerge into the light of day. The Barcelona Metro has recently completed the conversion of all its lines to overhead catenary for current distribution, and like those in many European cities, the subway operates in close coordination with various electrified commuter-rail services that provide additional service to both urban and suburban sections.[76]

Table 3.3 presents data and information about thirty-four major subway systems in Europe. There are instances in several other European cities where streetcars operate in subway tunnels as they make their way through congested downtown business districts, much in the manner of the original Tremont Street Subway of 1897 in Boston. Such light-rail deployments—or "pre-metro" systems, as they are sometimes called; Stuttgart, Germany, is an example—are not included in the table.[77]

TABLE 3.3
MAJOR EUROPEAN SUBWAY SYSTEMS

	Amsterdam	Athens	Barcelona	Berlin	Brussels	Bucharest	Budapest	Frankfurt am Main[f]
Route Miles	31.7	20 (approx.)	50.3	89.0	21.1	39.1	19.1	31.6
Underground Miles	3.4	13.4	49.6	74.7	7.5	n/a	n/a	n/a
Number of Stations	49	18	112	172	52	45	41	73
Number of Cars	n/a	168	488	1,382	217	610	380	190
Gauge	broad (5')	standard (4' 8½")	c	standard[d]	standard	standard	standard	standard
Electrification	a	750-volt DC third rail	1,200-volt DC catenary	780-volt DC third rail	900-volt DC third rail	750-volt DC third rail	e	600-volt DC catenary
First Line Opened	1977	2000[b]	1924	1902	1976	1979	1896	1968
Annual Patronage	56.4 million	270,000 (daily)	280 million	400.7 million	85.9 million	143.3 million	314.7 million	90.9 million

	Glasgow	Hamburg	Helsinki	Kiev	Lille	Lisbon	London[h]	Lyons	Madrid
Route Miles	6.5	60.8	13.1	30.4	17.8	11.8	243.6	17.1	75.1
Underground Miles	6.5	25.8	3.0	25.9	n/a	10.6	106.3	16.9	n/a
Number of Stations	15	89	16	39	39	25	267	39	164
Number of Cars	41	794	84	537	166	197	4,912	180	1,142
Gauge	narrow (4')	standard	broad	broad	g	standard	standard	standard	standard
Electrification	600-volt DC third rail	750-volt DC third rail	750-volt DC third rail	825-volt DC third rail	750-volt DC guide rails	750-volt DC third rail	630-volt DC third & fourth rails	750-volt DC guide rails[i]	600-volt DC catenary
First Line Opened	1896	1912	1982	1960	1983	1959	1863	1978	1919
Annual Patronage	13.7 million	160 million	35 million	205.0 million	50.0 million	117 million	832.0 million	125.4 million	397.0 million

	Marseilles	Milan	Minsk	Moscow	Munich	Newcastle	Nuremberg	Oslo	Paris[j]
Route Miles	12.1	43.0	11.5	162.8	48.4	37.6	18.6	49.8	125.2
Underground Miles	9.7	29.8	11.5	152.2	40.4	4.0	11.4	10.3	n/a
Number of Stations	24	84	18	160	89	46	39	101	297
Number of Cars	144	714	132	4,192	508	90	150	207	3,453
Gauge	2000	standard[k]	broad	broad	standard	standard	standard	standard	standard
Electrification	750-volt DC guide rails[i]		825-volt DC third rail	825-volt DC third rail	770-volt DC third rail	1,500-volt DC catenary	750-volt DC third rail	750-volt DC third rail	750-volt DC third rail
First Line Opened	1978	1964	1984	1935	1971	1980	1972	1966	1900
Annual Patronage	53.8 million	339.1 million	139.0 million	3,208.0 million	40.1 million	35.3 million	6.0 million	59.0 million	1,157.0 million

	Prague	Rome	Rotterdam	Stockholm	St. Petersburg	Vienna	Warsaw
Route Miles	31.0	20.8	47.2	67.1	68.4	18.7	6.7
Underground Miles	31.0	17.1	7.2	39.8	68.4	11.6	6.7
Number of Stations	43	43	42	100	60	40	14
Number of Cars	504	377	171	896	1,343	175	168
Gauge	standard	standard	standard	standard	broad	standard	standard
Electrification	750-volt DC third rail	1,500-volt DC catenary	750-volt DC third rail[f]	650–750 volt DC third rail	825-volt DC third rail	750-volt DC third rail	750-volt DC third rail
First Line Opened	1974	1955	1968	1950	1955	1976	1995
Annual Patronage	407.0 million	217.0 million	77.7 million	263.0 million	721.0 million	202.8 million	48.8 million

a. Combination metro and light rail system. Electrification includes both 750-volt DC third rail and 600-volt DC catenary.

b. Date shown is for the opening of new full metro system. An older nineteenth-century suburban rail line has been incorporated into the metro network and has been providing electrified subway service since 1957.

c. Line built in 1924 is broad-gauge; others are standard-gauge.

d. All lines standard-gauge, but some operate narrow-profile cars.

e. Line built in 1896 uses 825-volt DC third rail and operates narrow profile cars; other lines operate conventional rolling stock and use 600-volt DC catenary.

f. Combination light rail and metro system.

g. Fully-automated rubber-tired system, but using a different technology from "Paris-style" rubber-tired rolling stock.

h. Operates both low-profile tube trains and more conventional rapid-transit equipment; see text.

i. Operates "Paris-style" rubber-tired equipment.

j. Four of the system's fourteen lines operate rubber-tired rolling stock.

k. Of three lines, two use 1,500-volt DC catenary, while the third, which originally used 750-volt DC third rail, has recently been or soon will be converted to 1,500-volt catenary.

A soot-spewing steam locomotive brings a Metropolitan train into the Baker Street Station. Might Sherlock Holmes be waiting to board?

The classic look of the London Underground is exemplified by this tube train operating on the Bakerloo Line.

Charles Tyson Yerkes, the man who built many important underground tube lines in London. (Chicago Historical Society.)

Bound for Whitechapel, a Hammersmith and City train drifts into the Farringdon Station.

An automated train on the Docklands Light Railway heads into the Canary Wharf Station.

Passengers in London use the Underground's classic map to plan their travels. (John B. Cudahy.)

Small trains and narrow platforms are characteristics of the loop subway that has served Glasgow for over a hundred years.

Rubber-tired subway trains were developed in Paris and later adopted by other world cities, such as Montreal.

The right-of-way used by Paris-style rubber-tired subway trains features conventional running rails plus a raised guideway outboard of each track for the pneumatic tires. This installation is in use in Mexico City.

An eight-car subway train heads into downtown Stockholm.

Subway trains in Berlin feature a distinctive bright-yellow livery.

Surface-running trolley cars provide underground connections with the Metro subway system in Marseilles.

Barcelona's five-line Metro system has recently been converted to overhead catenary for current distribution.

A new rapid transit line provides service in Helsinki.

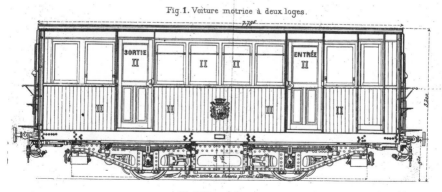

Subway cars that instituted service in Paris in 1900 were short and featured wooden bodies.

Subway trains have long provided mobility for the residents of Hamburg, Germany.

Entrance sign leads passengers to a station of the Paris Metro.

Rubber-tired trains serve four important lines in Paris, France.

4

New York's Electrified Railroads

IN MANY CITIES throughout the world, local mass transport involves multiple styles of railway services. There are, of course, urban-oriented electric railways, commonly operating in below-ground tunnels and known as subways—or metro systems, or the underground. These services are often complimented by trains operating between a central city and its outlying suburbs using electric-powered equipment along the routes of railroad companies whose principal markets are longer and intercity in nature.

Many cities in Europe feature such diverse styles of electric-powered local transport. In the United States, though, the electrification of intercity railroads has achieved relatively modest proportions, and while there are important suburban-oriented commuter passenger services in cities such as Boston, Los Angeles, and San Francisco, these trains are hauled entirely by diesel locomotives and are for the most part restricted in their operation to outdoor rights-of-way.

Electric-powered railroad trains, on the other hand, are able to operate through subterranean tunnels into, under, and around downtown business districts much in the manner of city subway systems. Five metropolitan areas in North America feature electric-powered suburban railways in addition to city subway services. North of the border in Canada, Montreal has long included such an operation, while in the United States, Philadelphia, Chicago, and Baltimore-Washington are members of this somewhat exclusive club.[1] The most extensive network of electrified commuter railroad lines in North America, however, is in New York. Important tunnels constructed under the Hudson and East Rivers in 1910 by the Pennsylvania Railroad—six years after the city's first subway train carried its first passengers—today funnel commuter trains of both the Long Island Rail Road and New Jersey

Transit into a midtown facility at Seventh Avenue and 32nd Street that is still known as Penn Station, while ten blocks north and four blocks to the east will be found the magnificent structure known as Grand Central Terminal, where a contemporary agency called the Metro North Railroad dispatches electrified trains into the city's northern and northeastern suburbs over rails that some years ago were part of the New York Central Railroad and the New York, New Haven and Hartford.

The stories of the two magnificent Manhattan terminals, Penn Station and Grand Central, have been told often, but typically with an emphasis on their famous long-distance trains, such as Pennsy's "Broadway Limited" and New York Central's "Empire State Express."[2] One aspect of the New York operation of the railroads that built these two terminals has been overlooked; to continue our centenary tribute to the Interborough Rapid Transit Company, let us explore the specialized electric railway services these railroads developed for suburban operations when they electrified their Manhattan operations in the first decade of the twentieth century.

The New York Central Railroad

It was shortly after six o'clock on a raw and cold winter morning, before the first hint of dawn began to show in the eastern sky, when train No. 223 of the New York, New Haven and Hartford Railroad (NYNH&H) pulled away from the depot in Danbury, Connecticut. It was a seven-car accommodation train—one baggage car, six coaches—under the supervision of conductor John Dyas. In the cab of the steam locomotive at the head end of the train, engineer Thomas Sweeney let out the throttle and fireman Elmer Purdy shoveled coal into the firebox as No. 223 began its trip southward down the Saugatuck Valley to Norwalk. Here it would turn to the west, join the railroad's Boston-New York main line, and continue on to Grand Central Depot in the City of New York, where it was scheduled to arrive at 8:17 A.M. It was Wednesday, January 8, 1902.

An hour or so later, at 7:30 A.M., with light snow flurries swirling through a steel-gray winter sky, engineer John Wiskar and fireman E. W. Fyler swung aboard a New York Central and Hudson River Railroad (NYC&HR) locomotive at White Plains, New York. Their train—No. 118, a seven-car accommodation running on what was then called the railroad's Harlem Division—was also bound for Grand Central Depot, with arrival scheduled for 8:14 A.M., three minutes ahead of the New Haven train from Danbury.

Neither train would reach its destination on this bleak and snowy January morning. At twenty minutes after eight o'clock, with both trains running out of sequence and a few minutes behind schedule, NYC&HR No. 118 plowed into the rear of NYNH&H No. 223 while the latter was stopped near 56th Street in the tunnel approach to Grand Central under New York's Park Avenue. Seventeen passengers lost their lives in the disaster.[3]

The last two cars on the train from Danbury were routinely kept empty until the train reached New Rochelle, New York. Here commuters bound for Grand Central streamed aboard, and that unfortunate Westchester County community felt the awful brunt of the Park Avenue tragedy. The agent on duty that morning in the New Rochelle station, a man by the name of Waterbury, first suspected something was wrong when he began to receive a series of strange telegraph messages from people in Manhattan shortly before nine o'clock. Their common theme was one of reassuring family members back home that the senders were not among the dead or injured. One such telegram read: "Am safe and sound. Don't worry."[4] An official announcement moved over the company wire soon afterward, and telegrapher Waterbury spent the rest of the day posting the names of passengers who were killed or injured in the window of the New Rochelle station.

Engineer Wiskar would later maintain, and on January 24 a corner's jury agreed, that obscured visibility in the four-track Park Avenue Tunnel leading to Grand Central caused by smoke, steam, and fog prevented his seeing any block signal indications. Here is what happened.

New Haven train No. 223 cleared Mott Haven Junction, just to the north of the Harlem River, at 8:07 A.M. New Haven trains bound for Grand Central left their own rails at a place called Woodlawn, 7 miles north of Mott Haven and just below the Westchester county line, and continued southward to their destination over New York Central trackage. Grand Central itself was owned and operated by NYC, with the New Haven's use of the facility being much in the manner of a tenant.

A few minutes later, when No. 118 reached 96th Street in Manhattan at the northern end of the Park Avenue Tunnel, the train was switched onto track two, the easternmost of the two center tracks in the four-track tunnel. New York Central No. 118 from White Plains passed Mott Haven at 8:08:30, a minute-and-a-half behind the New Haven train. It too was making its way to Grand Central along track number two as the inbound rush of morning trains from the suburbs was at its peak.

The Park Avenue Tunnel was an unusual railroad structure. With four tracks in overall width, the tunnel had two center tracks that featured frequent open-air skylights in the center median of the thoroughfare above, allowing exhaust from steam locomotives below to escape into the atmosphere. Because of this feature, dispatchers preferred to route trains along these center tracks whenever possible. Each of the two outside tracks— popularly known as the rapid-transit tunnels—were fully enclosed, with ventilation of steam locomotive exhaust possible only through horizontal vents that led into the center tunnels. The name "rapid-transit tunnel" was a reference to the fact there were passenger stations at 60th Street, 73rd Street, and 86th Street that trains using these outside tracks could serve with a rapid-transit style of service. (The 86th Street station could also be served by trains using the center tunnels.) Remnants of these platforms are still visible from contemporary commuter trains using these same tunnels, although information is scarce about how extensively the three were ever used as scheduled passenger stops. They function today as emergency exits from the belowground tunnel.

Interestingly enough, New York Mayor Abram S. Hewitt saw these rapid-transit tunnels as an underutilized transportation resource. When Hewitt proposed a major municipal investment in new rapid-transit lines in 1888—a development that was discussed in Chapter 1—he suggested converting these tunnels to true rapid-transit use, building a set of connecting tunnels under

Grand Central, and linking them into a major new subway line that would continue southward to the City Hall area.[5]

In any event, construction of the Park Avenue Tunnel, jointly financed by the railroad and the New York City municipal government, began in 1872 and was completed two years later. It ran from 98th Street at its northern extreme to 56th Street at the south. Here trains emerged from the sheltered confines of the tunnel and moved into a vast open expanse that extended south to 42nd Street. It was in this at-grade and open area where storage tracks, passenger platforms, turntables, and other facilities associated with Grand Central were located. While there were some viaducts for pedestrians and other traffic to cross these sprawling railroad yards, their multiacre expanse represented a barrier of serious proportion to the orderly growth of New York City in the area immediately north of Grand Central. Even the thoroughfare that was Park Avenue and that was built atop the railroad tunnel to the north of 56th Street came to an abrupt end at the southern end of the tunnel. Park Avenue—one block to the east of Fifth Avenue and parallel with it—was originally called Fourth Avenue.

Another unusual feature of the Park Avenue Tunnel in the year 1902 was operational in nature. While both the New York Central and the New Haven railroads otherwise operated their trains in the conventional "right-hand" fashion that was common in North America, because departure platforms at Grand Central were on the west side of the depot and arrival tracks were on the east side, trains using the Park Avenue Tunnel operated in a British-style "left-hand" manner to avoid conflicting moves in the terminal area.

New Haven train No. 223 stopped at 56th Street at the southern end of the Park Avenue Tunnel, awaiting a signal that would give it the authority to proceed into the terminal and discharge its passengers. An earlier train that had proceeded south through the easternmost rapid-transit tunnel was moving into the terminal ahead of No. 223. Signalman Charles Flynn, on duty in a tower located at 56th Street, checked to make certain that a "distance signal" behind train No. 223 at 63rd Street was displaying the proper aspect to tell approaching trains that they must "proceed with caution expecting to find the home signal at danger."

On the New York Central Railroad's approach to Grand Central in 1902, the color used to indicate such a restricted signal was green, not the yellow that would become almost universal on both railroads and highways in later years. The signal aspect used by the NYC in 1902 to indicate clear—or "proceed at maximum allowable speed"—was white. The railroad switched over to green-means-proceed and yellow-means-restricted signal aspects in 1907 at the same time that the unusual practice of left-hand running was eliminated on the approach to Grand Central.[6]

On January 8, 1902, the home signal was located at 58th Street, immediately behind train No. 223. It displayed the color red, and its 8-inch semaphore arm was set in a horizontal manner, an indication to any approaching train that the block ahead was occupied and that it should proceed no further. Flagman Fred Barnum, in accordance with prevailing railroad rules, swung down from the rear car of No. 223 and took up a protective position 200 feet behind the stopped train with a pair of red signal lanterns in hand.

The next point remains a little unclear a century or more after the fact, but neither alternative is inconsistent with known facts nor substantially alters the story. New Haven No. 223 had either been cleared to proceed into the station and had just begun to move, or else it was still stopped at 56th Street.

In either case, New York Central No. 118 passed a white "clear" signal at 72nd Street doing an allowable 20 miles per hour. When fireman Flyer realized that Wiskar was making no speed reduction as they approached the "restricted" distance signal at 63rd Street, he tried to shout a warning across the cab to his engineer. When Flyer then saw the red home signal at 58th Street and realized an accident was both immanent and unavoidable, he jumped onto the tender behind the locomotive cab.

Down at track level, flagman Barnum also quickly knew that a disaster was about to happen. He hurled his two red lanterns against the locomotive cab of train No. 118 as it continued past his position, but it was a futile gesture. (The fact that flagman Barnum was still on the ground behind his train is consistent with the New Haven train's being stopped and not with its having begun to move into the terminal.)

Wiskar later claimed that he made an emergency brake application as soon as he realized he was not picking up signal indications, but even if he did, it was both too little and too late. The New York Central locomotive plowed into the rear car of the New Haven train. This wooden-bodied car then telescoped forward into the car ahead of it, and when the NYC train finally came to rest, the pilot, or nose, of its locomotive was close to the end of the next-to-last car of the helpless New Haven train. The sheer force of the collision killed some passengers instantly, while others became victims of the scalding steam that soon began to escape from the damaged New York Central locomotive.

A policeman walking the beat on Park Avenue above the site heard the crash and quickly summoned Fire Department units. At Police Headquarters in downtown Manhattan, the dreaded "four-four-four" call was soon sounded, a summons for all available ambulances in the city. Pending their arrival, wagons of the Adams Express Company from Grand Central Depot were pressed into emergency service as makeshift ambulances. Rescue operations were hampered by escaping steam from the ruptured locomotive boiler as well as the confined nature of the below-ground tunnel, an environment the *New York Times* described as "Stygian blackness."[7] Many injured passengers could not be removed and taken to hospitals for treatment until dead bodies pinning them down were carried away. One piece of timely action that may well have prevented further catastrophe can be credited to Conductor Dyas of train No. 223. He had the presence of mind to jump from his train immediately after the accident and run southward in the center tunnel to ensure that no trains approached the derailment scene on the parallel northbound track, since debris from the accident had fouled that track.

A temporary morgue was established in a police department station house on 51st Street, and one soul-crushing scene took place in the afternoon when a man arrived to inquire about his missing brother. Before he had a chance to speak to the desk sergeant on duty, he noticed a familiar piece of clothing amid a pile of tattered effects and broke into uncontrollable sobs.[8]

As railroad accidents go, the 1902 Park Avenue crash was not a major tragedy, if that may be said without disrespect to those who lost their lives. It was a relatively low-speed collision and had it occurred anywhere else in the country, it would have been consigned to railroad history as little more than a totally unremarkable footnote. Because it happened precisely where it did happen, though, it managed to turn public attention to something that had long been considered a serious civic liability—the positively awful conditions that continually prevailed in the thirty-five-year-old tunnel approach to Grand Central, a project that was called, ironically enough, "the Fourth Avenue improvement" when it was designed and built in 1872.

A year before the tragic accident, in 1901, a grand jury had investigated conditions in the Park Avenue Tunnel and outlined the extent of the problem. The tunnel was "declared by many passengers and residents along the road to be a nuisance and a menace to health."[9] One Cyrus Edson, MD, a former president of the New York City Board of Health, testified that the 600-plus steam locomotives using the tunnel each day raised the temperature inside coaches using the tunnel—whose windows necessarily had to remain closed to keep out smoke and soot—to as much as 118 degrees during the summertime, and described the Park Avenue Tunnel as "worse than the black hole of Calcutta."[10] Editorial writers, not to mention real-estate developers in suburban Westchester County, were convinced that the growth of New York's northern suburbs was being seriously hampered by the awful conditions in the tunnel that trains had to use to reach Grand Central Depot.

At a hearing held by the New York State Board of Railroad Commissioners in the Fifth Avenue Hotel shortly after the January 8 accident, William Barclay Parsons, the chief engineer on the ongoing construction of New York's Interborough Subway, testified that there were only two practical solutions to the problem of the Park Avenue Tunnel: either to daylight (take the "roof" off) the whole 2-mile tunnel, a clearly unacceptable alternative, or else to replace both New York Central and New Haven steam locomotives with clean-running electric locomotives and multiple-unit (MU) cars.[11]

In fact, the New York Central and Hudson River Railroad had been interested in an electrified approach to Grand Central even before the 1902 accident—but not with the same sense of urgency that would prevail after January 1902, since mainline railroad electrification involved new and virtually experimental technology at the time. On the day of the Park Avenue accident, for instance, while there was much talk in the railroad industry of electrification projects and several small-scale installations of a clearly experimental nature here and there, there was only one heavy-duty railroad main line in all of North America where trains were being hauled by electric locomotives. This was a 1½–mile tunnel under Howard Street in downtown Baltimore, Maryland, where the Baltimore and Ohio Railroad had deployed the county's very first electric-powered locomotives seven years earlier, in 1895.[12]

In 1898, a man by the name of William J. Wilgus, then an engineer in the New York Central and Hudson River Railroad's maintenance-of-way section, was paid a visit by Frank Sprague. Wilgus—born in Buffalo in 1865 and educated at Cornell—worked at various mid-Western railroads from 1885 until 1893. He then returned east and began a career with the New York Central that would see him rise to the position of vice president and chief engineer.[13] Sprague suggested to Wilgus that a branch line into Yonkers off the New York Central's Putnam Division would be a perfect site for an experimental electric traction project. Following this meeting—and thanks, no doubt, to Sprague's unbridled enthusiasm for railway electrification—Wilgus decided that electric power could be deployed on a more extensive scale than a mere experiment on the Yonkers branch, and that "suburban trains . . . might be operated southerly through the side tunnels to 56th Street and thence by means of additional tracks in a widened open cut in Park Avenue to a loop station to be built beneath the old depot."[14]

Wilgus prepared a formal plan for such an electrification project in 1899, and it was adopted by the railroad's board of directors, although neither was it made public nor was construction authorized. In August of 1901, the railroad retained Bion J. Arnold, a man whose work for the Interborough Rapid Transit Company was touched upon briefly in Chapter 1, "to study the feasibility of handling heavy through trains by electricity between Mott Haven and the terminal."[15]

Matters were still in the discussion stage, and no decisions had been reached, but in three short years the stakes had been raised—from Sprague's suggestion of an experimental electrification on a branch line in Yonkers, to Wilgus and the idea of electrifying all suburban service operating into Grand Central, and finally to Arnold's evaluation of electrifying the railroad's long-distance trains as well.

Arnold's report was in the affirmative, but it was not delivered to the railroad until February, 1902, several weeks after the Park Avenue disaster.[16] By this time, pressure to replace steam locomotives on trains using Grand Central had substantially increased, and whatever reluctance the railroad may have earlier had about moving ahead on so large a scale soon evaporated.

Articles in the popular press quickly began to discuss the advantages of electrified motive power. Said the editors of the *New York Times:* "The substitution of a comparatively noiseless and positively odorless system of propulsion will do away with one of the most grievous of our municipal nuisances."[17] One curious letter to the editor of the *Times,* however, sounded a strangely cautionary note, and stranger still was the signature at the bottom of the letter: George Westinghouse, one of the genuine pioneers of railway electrification.

Westinghouse raised many problems that electrification would entail and spoke of positively awful potential for utter disaster that the New York Central was likely to experience. "As a matter of fact, with an electrically operated train the risk of accident will, judging by experience, be increased rather than diminished because of the presence of the heavy electrical machinery which it is proposed to attach to several cars of each train," Westinghouse wrote.[18] Only a follow-up letter from Frank Sprague two days later gave some hint about Westinghouse's curious appraisal. For what was happening behind the scenes—and Sprague was in a position to know—was that the New York Central was leaning more and more toward signing a contract with General Electric (GE) for a system of direct current railway electrification distributed by trackside third rail and giving less thought to a once-discussed test of both GE's direct current system and an alternating current system that was then under development by Westinghouse.[19]

(The Westinghouse and GE firms worked cooperatively on many projects, and each company often manufactured electrical components under license that had been designed by the other. But George Westinghouse himself was a very intense partisan in what has often been called the "AC-DC debate," and he and Sprague frequently squared off over the relative merits of the two rival systems, with their disputes often becoming quite personal.)[20]

Toward the end of 1902, the New York Central announced preliminary details of a massive multi-million-dollar New York terminal redevelopment plan. Many aspects of the project were still fluid at this time and would take additional years to firm up. For example, while it was certain from the outset that the project would include a double-deck passenger terminal, it was not immediately clear if this would entail building a new lower level under Grand Central Depot, a structure that was built in 1871, or tearing it down and starting afresh. As the railroad began to think about building a subterranean level under Grand Central Depot, a bolder alternative emerged: Build a totally new, double-deck terminal, depress *both* levels below grade, and make arrangements to sell "air rights" over station platforms and railroad yards that would effectively create valuable real estate in the very heart of uptown Manhattan.

This proved to be an extremely important aspect of the overall program. The open acreage that the railroad owned for requisite terminal facilities and that was denied to New York for other commercial development could become a stream of significant income for the railroad if the entire terminal area were to be depressed below grade and air-rights development allowed to take place over the tracks. And this is exactly how the railroad eventually did proceed. The superlative structure called Grand Central Terminal would be completed on the site of Grand Central Depot in 1913, and the previously open-air expanse of railroad yards beyond the older terminal was converted into upscale urban real estate of the highest imaginable order. Before the railroad could proceed with its terminal plans, though, it had to be certain that electrification of its trains was both possible and feasible.

In late November of 1903, GE stock started to fluctuate on Wall Street and then quickly rose six points. On Thursday, November 28, the New York Central Railroad released the following statement, confirming what many Wall Street analysts had begun to suspect:

> The New York Central and Hudson River Railroad Company have [*sic*] placed an order with the General Electric Company for eight turbo-generators of a capacity of 7500 horsepower each. The turbines are of the four stage vertical Curtis type. The generators are twenty-five cycle, triphase, generating a current as a pressure of 11,000 volts. This is by far the largest order for steam turbines ever placed in this country or abroad.
>
> The New York Central Company has also placed with the General Electric Company in cooperation with the Schenectady works of the American Locomotive Company, an order for thirty-five electric locomotives. These locomotives are of an entirely new design, will weigh eighty-five tons each, with an adhesive weight in the vicinity of sixty-seven tons. Each locomotive will have a capacity of 2200 horsepower, and will be capable of hauling a train of 500 tons at a speed of sixty miles per hour. This is by far the largest order for electric locomotives ever placed in any country.[21]

Most observers were taken by surprise to learn of the American Locomotive Company's role in the arrangements, and an option written into the contract for more locomotives at a later date was also an unexpected part of the negotiations. An additional piece of news made public in November of 1903 was that while the new electric locomotives would replace steam locomotives and haul long-distance trains in and out of Grand Central, local suburban service within the electrified zone would be assigned to a new fleet of "self-propelling" MU electric cars, not locomotive-drawn trains.

The New York state legislature eventually enacted a law outlawing steam engines south of the Harlem River, and many popular accounts repeat the contention that the railroad electrified its Manhattan operations as a result of this legislation and in reaction to it. It is clear, however, that the New York Central was committed to the concept of electrified service through the Park Avenue Tunnel into Grand Central even without this action. In fact, the legal prohibition against the operation of steam locomotives onto Manhattan Island was enacted as part of permissive legislation the railroad both required and sought in order to undertake various aspects of its New York terminal improvement program. There was, certainly, pertinent state legislation that outlawed the operation of steam locomotives through the Park Avenue Tunnel. But it should not be regarded as anything that was forced upon an unwilling and uncooperative railroad.[22]

The New York Central established a special team of experts to supervise the electrification project. Formally called the Electric Traction Commission, it was commonly known throughout the company as "the staff." Headed by William Wilgus, by then a vice president with the railroad, its members included such important figures from the early days of railway electrification as Bion Arnold, Frank Sprague, and George Gibbs. Also a member of the staff was Arthur M. Waitt, the NYC's superintendent of motive power. Waitt would soon be replaced by John F. Deems, while Edwin B. Katte of the New York Central acted as the group's secretary.

In the fall of 1904, about a year after the New York Central contracted with GE for the design and construction of its first electric locomotives—and at the same time that the Interborough Rapid Transit Company was instituting subway service in New York—a series of road tests were begun between mileposts 162 and 168 west of Schenectady, New York, on the NYC main line. The eastbound freight track on the four-track right-of-way there was equipped with a third rail—in fact, with various styles of third rail. Trolley wire was strung at a few strategic spots, and cables were strung to bring high-voltage electric current to the site from the GE plant 5 miles away. A small engine house was built on a stub siding adjacent to the newly electrified test track, where adjustments and repairs could be conducted.

The star of the show was the New York Central's very first electric locomotive, L-class motor No. 6000, which spent over six months at the test site proving that her design predictions were either correct or understated, and doing it through sleet, snow, and sunshine. A provision of the 1903 contract between GE and the New York Central called for the prototype locomotive to undergo an exhaustive 50,000-mile test regimen before production could begin on the rest of the order.

On April 29, 1905, a final series of evaluations were run, pitting the new L-motor against an example of the NYC's best and newest steam power, K-class Pacific No. 2797. Table 4.1 displays

TABLE 4.1
STEAM VERSUS ELECTRIC (APRIL 1905)

	L-Class Electric No. 6000	K-Class Pacific No. 2797
Loco Length	36 feet, 11.25 inches	67 feet, 7.75 inches[a]
Loco Weight	200,500 pounds	342,000 pounds[a]
Driving Axles	4	3
Driving Wheel Diameter	44 inches	75 inches
Weight on Driving Axles	142,000 pounds	141,000 pounds
Weight per Driving Axle	35,500	47,000
Revenue Load	307.25 tons	256 tons[b]
Rate of Acceleration to 50 mph	0.394 mph/ps	0.246 mph/ps
Time Required to Reach 50 mph	127 seconds	203 seconds

a. Including tender.
b. Excluding tender.
Source: Railroad Gazette, 38 (May 26, 1905), 584.

the results of "run D" on that spring morning many decades ago. Both trains were started simultaneously and on adjacent tracks with similar six-car trains in tow.

Fifteen hundred feet from the start of the run, the electric locomotive was leading the steam engine by a full train-length. No. 6000 accelerated to 50 miles per hour almost twice as rapidly as did the Pacific, an operational characteristic that foretold of an important additional benefit the railroad would realize with a new fleet of electric locomotives: Not only would the Park Avenue Tunnel be free of smoke and soot with the advent of electric traction, but the enhanced acceleration of the new motive power would permit more trains to move in and out of the terminal during a given period of time, thereby increasing capacity and performance.

The Schenectady tests were declared a success; GE and the American Locomotive Company were instructed to move into high gear and build the thirty-four additional locomotives that NYC had ordered. The original electric locomotive, No. 6000, was reclassified as a T-1 motor, while the remaining thirty-four production models, differing but slightly from the prototype, became the T-2 class, and the whole fleet was numbered—or in the case of No. 6000, renumbered—in the 3400 series.[23]

New locomotives were not the only electric rolling stock the railroad planned to acquire. An order had also been placed with American Car and Foundry (ACF) for 125 electric MU cars that would be used in suburban service, and the first of these were delivered from ACF's Berwick, Pennsylvania, works in early 1906. On July 20, 1906, the first testing of electric-powered equipment was conducted along newly electrified trackage in the New York area.

Two of the new electric locomotives, together with a single MU car, were put through their paces on a third-rail-equipped track along the Harlem River at Kingsbridge in the Bronx. A steam locomotive hauled the new electric equipment to the test area and then sat by as the newcomers demonstrated their stuff.

The design that GE's Asa Batchelder had developed for the new electric locomotives offered little in the way of external aesthetics. One observer felt that the new T motors resembled "two steam locomotive tenders coupled back to back," while others thought they were "too clumsy to be of any practical value," and even "too ugly to be of any use."[24]

But the noiseless and relatively heat-free electric locomotives were very impressive when they began to do what they were built to do, and that was not to be an object of visual appreciation. The tests prompted this observation: "It was easily seen that the electric machine was far ahead in every respect of the steam locomotive."[25] And just to drive the point home with added emphasis, NYC officials proceeded to couple one of the new T motors, plus the steam locomotive that had brought the electric equipment to the test site, behind the single electric MU car. On signal, it moved off in effortless fashion with both locomotives in tow.

Two months later, on Sunday afternoon, September 30, 1906, T-2 locomotive No. 3406, with a pair of white flags mounted on her pilot beam and electric marker lights hanging from her superstructure, stood poised at the New York Central's Highbridge Station in the Bronx with seven passenger cars coupled to her drawbar. Aboard the train was a collection of railroad and GE officials and at precisely 2:40 P.M., the T-2's four electric motors were fed 650 volts of direct current with Vice President Wilgus himself sitting in the engineer's position and doing the honors. At 2:58 P.M. the train arrived at Grand Central—7 miles in eighteen minutes, including speeds as high as 45 miles per hour on the Park Avenue Viaduct north of the tunnel. It was the first operation of an electric-powered train into the famous depot and prompted "engineman" Wilgus to remark: "The trip was thoroughly successful. I am sure that we shall have the engines running by November 10. It has been a big piece of work, but it is well done."[26]

Wilgus's prediction fell a little short of the mark, as the new electrified zone was fine tuned by engineers and technicians through the months of October and November. Finally, with little in the way of festivities to celebrate the event, a local train bound for Yonkers left Grand Central at 12:11 P.M. on Tuesday, December 11, 1906. The afternoon train included three electric MU cars and it was the first revenue service out of Grand Central over the New York Central and Hudson River Railroad using electric power. The 3400-series electric locomotives would quickly become a hallmark of the New York Central's newly electrified service. But the very first electric train to carry revenue passengers out of Grand Central was not hauled by one of the new T motors; it was a three-car train of MU cars.[27]

At Highbridge, in the Bronx, a steam engine was coupled to the train for the remainder of its trip to Yonkers. An additional three MU trains operated on that initial day of electric service, and it was not until late January of 1907 when the first electric locomotives were placed in service. Six months, later on July 1, ten daily trains on the New York Central that were still being hauled into and out of Grand Central by steam engines switched to electricity, and the conversion was complete.

(It was complete as far as the New York Central was concerned. In July of 1907, the New York, New Haven and Hartford Railroad was only beginning its switch to electric traction, and 80 percent or more of its daily schedules were still protected by steam. It would be several more months before all New Haven service into and out of Grand Central was converted to electric propulsion. More on the New Haven's electrification efforts below.)

One immediate effect of the advent of electricity was that despite the continued presence of steam locomotives on most New Haven trains, summer passengers in 1907 dared to ride on the open platforms of observation cars through the Park Avenue Tunnel. Another change was a marked reduction in the number of light-engine movements in the terminal area with the introduction of bidirectional equipment. NYC's new electric locomotives operated equally well in either direction, although they did have to be coupled onto the head end of whatever train they were hauling. The electric MU cars, on then other hand, were even more flexible in this regard. All that was required to operate in the opposite direction was for the motorman to walk the length of the train and set up his control station on the end platform of what had been the train's rear car.

With respect to the MU cars, the initial order was for a fleet of 125 all-steel passenger motor cars. These were quickly supplemented by six combination coach-baggage motorized cars, and fifty-five unmotorized trailer units. (The trailers were later converted to motorized status.) All of the New York Central's MU cars were 60 feet long and they included such then-novel features as electric lighting and heating. The new cars were also fitted with temporary Pintsch gas lights and included provision for locomotive-supplied steam heat, since until the third rail was extended to the full limits of the proposed electrified zone, they would be hauled by steam locomotives for a portion of most trips. The new MU cars were also equipped with electric fans to cool passengers during warm weather months and featured "walk-over" seating that was finished in "hygienic woven cane." Cars that were all-passenger in their configuration had seats for sixty-four patrons, and in a throwback to an older era of passenger-car design, each pair of side windows was topped off with a small arch window of green cathedral glass that filtered sunlight into the interior of the car. (In later years, NYC eliminated this feature by welding steel plate over these upper windows and in doing so created a passenger car that many felt had a decidedly "top-heavy" appearance.)

The all-steel bodies of the new MU cars were built at the Berwick, Pennsylvania, plant of the ACF, while the trucks on which they rode were products of American Locomotive. Each car featured a motorless trailer truck that rode on 33-inch wheels and a power truck whose 36-inch wheels were driven by a pair of GE 250-horsepower model 69C motors with 2:1 gearing. The cars could accelerate at a rate that was unheard of in the railroad industry at the time: 1.25 miles per hour per second, a rate that was in excess of the performance that NYC's new electric locomotives had recently recorded. A train of MU cars had a relatively modest maximum speed of 52 miles per hour, but this was all that the railroad felt was needed, given the short distances between stations in the suburban area. Empty motor cars weighed 102,600 pounds; trailer cars weighed 78,600 pounds.

The NYC's new MU cars were equipped with four-position Sprague-GE type M master controllers, and the ordinary forward operating sequence was switching or lap position; full series; parallel lap; and full parallel. Each of these positions in the operating sequence of a piece of electric railway motive power is analogous to various gear arrangements in the operation of a typical automobile. Feeding current to the motors of an MU car—or an electric locomotive—in "full series" is the equivalent of "first gear" with an automobile and is appropriate when getting under way. "Full parallel," on the other hand, might be compared with "high gear" or "overdrive," and is employed at high speed.[28]

During early planning, Wilgus and "the staff" entertained a hope that the New York Central's new fleet of electric MU cars could connect with New York's Interborough Subway and provide through-service from the suburbs north of New York all the way south to the Battery. Plans were drawn up to run a short connecting tunnel from the lower-level loop of the new Grand Central Terminal into the Interborough Subway line that was being built under Fourth Avenue south of the terminal, and the plans that William Barclay Parsons executed for the subway included a provision for such a connection between the two express tracks just to the south of Grand Central. As mentioned earlier, New York mayor Abram Hewitt had even suggested such a connection in his landmark message to the Board of Aldermen in 1888. But as the trade journal the *Railroad Gazette* noted in late 1905, "this plan was later abandoned for a number of reasons, the principal one being the limited clearance of the Subway which would prevent running cars of the railroad company's standard dimensions."[29]

The New York Central's T-class electric locomotives went on to achieve unexpected popularity when various toy-train manufacturers used the design as the prototype for several lines of tinplate locomotives. A reasonably significant alteration in their appearance was made shortly after they entered service, when it emerged that the two-wheel leading trucks of the 1-D-1 locomotives represented a serious design flaw.[30] On February 16, 1907, less than a month after the new locomotives had begun revenue, an especially tragic accident took place near Woodlawn on the Harlem Division that resulted in twenty-two deaths—more than the Park Avenue collision of 1902. A five-car northbound train with two of the new electric locomotives on the head end—motor No. 3421 was in the lead, with No. 3407 as the trail unit—departed Grand Central during the height of the evening rush hour and was scheduled to run nonstop to Wakefield, where a steam locomotive would take over and continue the trip northward. The train had been added to the NYC's timetable on only the previous day, and its schedule was tailored to take maximum advantage of the operational capabilities of the new electrification system.

The derailment occurred at 6:40 P.M., just after the train rounded a curve near 205th Street and just below the engine-change point at Wakefield. For rescue forces from the New York City Fire Department (FDNY), the Woodlawn derailment was their first major disaster along a third-rail-equipped railway line, and the FDNY learned many important lessons on that February evening that would prove beneficial during later incidents along railway and subway lines.[31] On March 4, 1907, a coroner's jury brought in a finding that the New York Central was "culpably negligent" for failure to take "all the necessary possible and proper precaution to safeguard its passengers," and indictments were later handed down.[32] No prosecutions ensued, and all charges were eventually dropped.

For William Wilgus and his people, the Woodlawn derailment forced a thorough reevaluation of the design of their new electric locomotive. After extensive engineering analysis, they concluded that the substitution of a four-wheel pilot truck for the original two-wheel design would correct the stability problem that likely was the cause of the derailment.[33] The newly rigged (and now slightly longer) 2-D-2 locomotives were redesignated the S-1 and S-2 motors, classifications they would retain for the rest of their service lives.

New York Central's electric locomotives were powered by four bipolar GE model 84A motors, each rated at 550 horsepower, and propulsion was by means of a gearless drive. What this means is that the motor armature was mounted on the driving axle, while the field magnets surrounded the axle and were attached to the locomotive frame. The axle itself, in other words, served as the shaft of the motor, and hence no gears were required. (In Chapter 3 we learned that electric locomotives used on certain early London tube railways featured similar gearless drives.)

An S-class electric locomotive was capable of maintaining a steady 60 miles per hour on level track with 600 tons in tow, and a single locomotive would regularly handle trains with as many as fourteen cars out of Grand Central, despite a short stretch of 1.02 percent grade that had to be negotiated in the tunnel shortly after departure. One early accomplishment that demonstrated the capability of the new locomotives happened on the afternoon of April 26, 1907, when a few NYC trains were still being hauled out of Grand Central by steam locomotives. Train No. 19, "The Lake Shore Limited," departed Grand Central behind an Atlantic-type steam locomotive that afternoon with nine Pullman cars in tow. Shortly after it entered the Park Avenue Tunnel, the locomotive hauling the Chicago-bound limited experienced problems and came to a halt on a stretch of 0.5 percent upgrade. As reported in the *Railroad Gazette:*

> Following this train was a local train of seven standard day coaches hauled by one of the new electric locomotives. The electric locomotive, coupled on behind No. 19 and pulling its own train, started the entire load on the grade without assistance from the steam locomotive, which was dead. The 16 cars and two locomotives weighed approximately 1,000 tons. The electric locomotive started with good acceleration and pushed No. 19 north to 125th street up the 1.02 per cent grade one-half mile long from 72d street to 83d street, without any difficulty and at good speed.[34]

Like the NYC's MU cars, the new S motors were equipped with Sprague-GE MU controls, the very first railroad locomotives to feature such hardware. Exceptionally heavy trains could be assigned two S motors, in other words, and both could be controlled by the engineer in the lead engine. The master controller was a good deal more complex than that required on the suburban cars. Twenty-four operating positions were provided, the first ten for series, the next seven for series parallel, and the final seven for full parallel operation of the motors. NYC's fleet of electric locomotives was expanded in 1908 and 1909, when a dozen slightly larger but otherwise look-alike locomotives were delivered by GE and Alco. Designated the T-3 class, these newcomers weighed 120 tons, compared to the 95-ton weight of the original fleet.

An interesting feature of the NYC's Manhattan electrification is that while the locomotive normally draws current from trackside third rail, at long gaps in the third rail—say, at special work in terminal areas such as slip switches—an overhead "fourth rail" was provided for supplementary current collection. Each locomotive was equipped with a pair of small, pneumatically controlled pantographs which the engineer could raise as needed to ensure contact with the overhead fourth rail. Much of the overhead power system at Grand Central in the early years of electric operation was built on a temporary basis with wooden supports, since the full Grand Central improvement project was in no way complete when the electrification was ready for service in 1906. MU cars lacked but did not need this feature, since a train of several cars would itself serve to bridge any gaps in the third rail.

The third rail itself was also unusual in that the pickup shoes—four per MU car and eight per S-class locomotive—made contact with the underside of the power rail, not the top as was more common practice among early twentieth-century electric railways such as New York's Interborough Subway. This under-running third rail was designed specifically for Grand Central and was called the Wilgus-Sprague system, since both William Wilgus and Frank Sprague were instrumental in its development. During the Schenectady tests, a variety of third-rail designs were deployed and evaluated, and it was the under-running third rail that was felt to provide greater protection from accidental electrocution for people working around trains in the electric district than was possible with a more conventional system. The under-running third rail was also found to be less prone to disruption from the winter torments of snow and ice.[35] Third-rail shoes were spring-loaded to press against the contact surface, and since shoes had to be adjusted to somewhat closer tolerances with an under-running third rail than a more conventional one, a monitoring system at 110th Street was able to detect "out of gauge" shoes on passing trains and signal a railroad supervisor by sounding bell tones of different pitches for various defects.

The third rail was mounted $\frac{1}{16}$ inch less than 27 inches outside the running rail, and the underside of the power rail was $2\frac{3}{4}$ inches higher than the track surface. The third rail used special 70-pound-per-yard bullhead rail suspended from cast-iron brackets. These in turn were bolted to extra-long cross-ties on 11-foot centers.[36]

(Under-running third rails would never became terribly popular in North America. They were subsequently used by the New York Central for a small electrified zone under the Detroit River between Detroit and Windsor, Ontario, as well as on the Central-controlled West Shore Line—an interurban railway, really— between Utica and Syracuse in upstate New York. Both of these installations were later "de-electrified," but an important subway-elevated operation in Philadelphia, the Market-Frankfort Line, continues to use an under-running third rail. Several European subway systems—Berlin is one example—use similar under-running third rails.)

The third rail was fed electric current from two virtually identical New York Central generating stations, one located at Port Morris, in the Bronx, the other in Yonkers. Like the Interborough Rapid Transit System, the NYC did not believe that commercial utilities of the era could supply reliable current for its purposes, and so it built its own powerhouses. Each building was 237 feet long, 167 feet wide, 105 feet high, and capped off with a pair of 250-foot smokestacks. Each station generated 25-cycle triphase alternating current at 11,000 volts for transmission to eight track-side substations, where it was converted into direct current by three rotary converters after first being stepped down in voltage by transformers. When Port Morris went on-line in May of 1906 just prior to the first locomotive testing, it generated its electricity using a semi-bituminous grade of coal that was mined exclusively for the railroad in Clearfield County, Pennsylvania. Initial equipment in each power station included sixteen boilers to generate steam and four Curtis-GE steam turbines engines, each linked to its own 5,000-kilowatt electric generator. Each of the two NYC powerhouses was designed so it could eventually house twenty-five boilers and six turbo-generators.

An interesting contrast between NYC's generating stations and that designed just a few years earlier by the Interborough Rapid Transit Company is the fact the latter primarily relied on reciprocating steam engines, although it did include some newer steam turbine engines. Just a few years later, though, the NYC was sufficiently comfortable with steam turbine technology that it did not specify any reciprocating engines for its powerhouses and generated its electricity solely with the newer style of engine.[37]

Between 1906 and 1913, the New York Central Railroad completed its planned electrification project. The third-rail district extended 24 miles from Grand Central to North White Plains on the Harlem Division and 34 miles to Croton on the Hudson Division. Croton is a river town a mile north of a place that came to be called Harmon, the site of the railroad's electric shops and destined to be the changeover point between electric and steam locomotives for many decades.[38] North White Plains and Croton were intended to be the northern limits of the electrified zone from the outset, but until extensive grade-separation projects were completed along both lines between 1906 and 1913, Highbridge, on the Hudson Division, and Wakefield, just south of Mount Vernon on the Harlem Division, served as the initial northern limits of the electrified zone; temporary facilities were established at both points for the servicing of locomotives.

The railroad's principal maintenance facility for its new electric equipment was built at Harmon, complimented by a smaller facility at North White Plains.[39] Because the Harmon shops came on-line before the third rail had been extended that far, both electric locomotives and MU cars were towed there for servicing for a number of years. Table 4.2 displays the dates when electrified service was extended to various points. Until the third rail reached Croton in 1913, though, the change in motive power from electric to steam on through trains operating over the Hudson Division continued to take place at Highbridge, in the Bronx. The electrified service that reached Yonkers in early 1907, in

TABLE 4.2
EXTENSION OF NEW YORK CENTRAL ELECTRIFIED SERVICE

Date	Route Segment	Division (or branch)
12/1906	Grand Central to Highbridge (via Mott Haven)	Hudson
1/1907	Mott Haven to Wakefield	Harlem
2/1907	Wakefield to Mount Vernon	Harlem
4/1908	Highbridge to Yonkers	Hudson
3/1910	Mount Vernon to North White Plains	Harlem
12/1910	Yonkers to Glenwood	Hudson
2/1911	Glenwood to Tarrytown	Hudson
2/1913	Tarrytown to Croton-on-Hudson	Hudson
8/1926	Mott Haven to Port Morris[a]	Port Morris Branch
1926	Sedgwick Avenue to Getty Square (Yonkers)[b]	Yonkers Branch; Putnam Division
6/1931	Spuyten Duyvil to West 23rd Street, Manhattan[c]	West Side Freight Line

a. Electrification discontinued in 1965.
b. Electrification discontinued in 1942.
c. Electrification discontinued in 1959.

other words, involved only that provided by MU cars operating in suburban service.

Save for the West Side freight line into midtown Manhattan south from Spuyten Duyvil, a short freight-only connection in the lower Bronx between Mott Haven and Port Morris, and a branch line off the Putnam Division into central Yonkers, Grand Central to Croton and North White Plains would remain the extent of the railroad's electrification efforts out of New York for many years. Rumors were rife in the early years of the twentieth century that the third rail was to be extended, possibly even as far as Buffalo, 435 miles from Grand Central. On the day of the Kingsbridge tests, July 20, 1906, a representative of one of the electrical suppliers told a reporter in very knowing terms that an announcement about extending electric service to Buffalo was only a few days away. "At present," the man said, "the intention is to keep the plans a secret."[40] Such an announcement would never come, and the rumors were quickly denied by the railroad. "It is not true that we are going to use the third rail for through trains all the way to Buffalo," a company engineer responded when told of the reports that were circulating.[41] Indeed, it was only when suburban passenger service into and out of Grand Central Terminal became a public-sector responsibility in the late 1960s under the aegis of an agency called the Metropolitan Transportation Authority (MTA) that the northern limits of the Grand Central electrified zone were expanded to any significant extent.

(It was not on the onetime New York Central main line along the Hudson River that MTA decided to expand the electrified zone. Rather it was on the former Harlem Division to North White Plains through central Westchester County—now called the Harlem Line—that the third rail was pushed north to Brewster, in New York's Putnam County, 29 miles beyond North White Plains and 53 miles from Grand Central. The MTA inaugurated electrified service over this extension in 1984.)

The expansion of electrified service to Yonkers over the Putnam Division in 1926 is interesting on several counts. The NYC had long served Yonkers with an important station along the Hudson Division that was served by the company's electric trains en route to Croton—and even by some mainline trains bound for points beyond the electrified zone. The first electrified train to carry passengers out of Grand Central in 1906, for instance, was bound for this Yonkers station. The NYC's Hudson Division served Yonkers on that city's west side, while the Putnam Division extended into Yonkers from the east and terminated at a place called Getty Square.

(There was yet another NYC station whose name boards proudly proclaimed it to be Yonkers—even if just for a short time. When the musical *Hello Dolly!* was turned into a major Hollywood film, the NYC station at Garrison, New York, was renamed Yonkers and used as a set for the movie.)

The Putnam Division was a rather unusual operation, more reminiscent of a modest short-line railroad than a division of the mighty New York Central. Formerly the independent New York and Northern Railroad and once a link in a through-route to Boston, in a complicated financial maneuver in 1894 the New York and Northern became the New York and Putnam Railroad Company and was leased by the New York Central, a lease that was converted into an outright purchase in 1913.[42]

But Putnam Division trains never operated into Grand Central.

The southern terminal of the New York and Northern was a transfer facility at the northern end of the Sixth Avenue and Ninth Avenue elevated lines of Manhattan Railways on the west bank of the Harlem River at 155th Street in Upper Manhattan, immediately behind the Polo Grounds where the New York Giants played baseball. (In baseball parlance, the transfer terminal between railroad and el trains was located behind the "power alley" in right-center field.)[43]

In 1916, what was then the Putnam Division of the New York Central Railroad abandoned the 155th Street facility, retreated across the Harlem River, and established a new southern terminal at Sedgwick Avenue in the Bronx. The railroad's bridge across the Harlem River was then acquired by the Interborough Rapid Transit Company and used to extend its Ninth Avenue and Sixth Avenue elevated lines into the Bronx and to a connection with the new Dual Contracts–built Jerome Avenue Line at 167th Street, with a stop along the way at the Sedgwick Avenue Terminal of the Putnam Division. Putnam passengers typically transferred to the el to continue into midtown Manhattan—at 155th Street before 1916, at Sedgwick Avenue afterward. Passengers from Putnam Division points could also reach midtown Manhattan by transferring to Hudson Division NYC trains at Highbridge, one station north of Sedgwick Avenue.

When the Yonkers Branch of the Putnam Division was electrified in 1926—and along with it, the Putnam main line between Sedgwick Avenue and a point north of Van Cortlandt where the Yonkers Branch veered westward—MU trains using this branch did not operate in and out of Grand Central but terminated at Sedgwick Avenue, just like other Putnam schedules. But this Putnam-Yonkers electrification project would prove to be short-lived. As discussed in Chapter 1, the Ninth Avenue el was abandoned south of 155th Street in June 1940 just prior to the municipal acquisition of the Interborough itself, and absent this important connection, patronage on the Putnam Division declined so significantly that the New York Central was compelled to eliminate electric-powered service over the Yonkers Branch in 1942, a mere sixteen years after it began. Curiously, in 1898 Frank Sprague visited William Wilgus and recommended that this same Yonkers branch would be an appropriate place for the deployment of the railroad's very first experiment in electric traction.

On Saturday, February 1, 1913, the new Grand Central Terminal was formally and officially opened for business, its design and construction having taken almost a full decade. The project involved a monumental task of building the new under and around the old and keeping the trains running through it all. Over 3 million cubic yards of earth and rock were removed for the excavation and used chiefly for right-of-way improvements along the Hudson Division. An especially tricky construction maneuver involved the removal of the old 600-foot by 200-foot train shed, a project that yielded the following salvage: 1,350 tons of wrought iron, 350 tons of cast iron, 90,000 square feet of corrugated iron, and 60,000 square feet of glass.[44]

Some suburban service began using the lower level of the new terminal in late October of 1912, but Grand Central could not really be said to be in service until the main, or upper, level was ready for business. New Haven train No. 2, "The Boston Express," slipped out of the new terminal at 12:01 A.M. on February 3, 1913, the very first revenue departure. Less than a half-hour later, at 12:25 A.M., New York Central's "Buffalo Express" became the host railroad's inaugural service.[45] Many observers, though, felt that the opening of Grand Central was not really official until 2:45 P.M. that day, when "The 20th Century Limited" departed for Chicagoland, a daily ritual that would help define Grand Central for the next half century.

Grand Central Terminal would become identified with an age—a gilded age of railway travel—when such things as all-Pullman consists, multiple sections of "The Wolverine" departing nightly for Detroit, and "The Merchants Limited" speeding north to Boston at the end of every business day were conventional elements of intercity mobility. But as a reporter noted in 1913 in describing the new terminal's Botticino marble concourse, constellation-studded ceiling, two levels of tracks, and other wonderments: "The rock-bottom fact of the entire enterprise is the electric motor—powerful, swift, silent and clean."[46]

In the same year that the new Grand Central Terminal opened, 1913, the NYC took delivery of the first ten units of a new fleet of high-performance electric locomotives, the T-1 motors, and these would quickly become the standard motive power used to haul passenger trains into and out of Grand Central for the next four decades. As the fleet of new T-motors increased in numbers over the years—by 1926 there were thirty-six of them on the property—the older S motors that had inaugurated electrified service were largely assigned to shifter service and other lesser roles, tasks they took to with ease and facility.[47]

As for the NYC's MU fleet, it was steadily expanded from 1906 through 1929 as the suburban territory between Grand Central and the northern limits of the electrified zone increased in population. Various car builders turned out new MU cars for the NYC—Saint Louis Car Company, Pressed Steel, Standard Steel, and American Car and Foundry—and eventually the fleet numbered 351 units.[48] The great majority were all-coach in their configuration, but the fleet also included twelve baggage-coach combination cars, four baggage-mail units, and five all-baggage cars. Only the very first MU cars were equipped with cathedral-glass decorative windows; later units had more conventional windows, and while there were minor changes in specifications from one order to another, the basic design of the original MU cars continued to govern.[49] Five MU cars were de-motored and rigged to serve as trailers that would be hauled by self-powered gas-electric cars at various points in the NYC system, and all cars that were initially acquired as motorless trailers were eventually equipped with electric motors and converted into powered units. Otherwise, consistency and steadiness are the principal characteristics that the New York Central MU fleet exhibited for many decades.

It was not until 1950 that an MU car of a totally new and different design appeared in the NYC electric zone. Built by the Saint Louis Car Company, a fleet of 100 new cars in the 4500-series expanded the suburban fleet to accommodate the many new commuters who had moved to Westchester County following the Second World War. Unlike the 60-foot length of the original specifications and the 69-foot length of later MU cars, the new equipment measured 85 feet in length and featured 130 seats per car. The new rolling stock made use of what was becoming a popular technique to provide additional seats, namely the use of "3-2 seating." (A seat on one side of the aisle was conventional and provided space for two passengers, but the opposite seat was a bit longer and was expected to accommodate three seated patrons.) The NYC had begun to reconfigure some of its older MU cars to 3-2 seating, but even so equipped, a new 85-foot car had a seating capacity that was 30 percent greater than an older 60-foot one. On May 31, 1950, the 10:32 A.M. departure from North White Plains of a six-car train bound for Grand Central was the first revenue run using the new equipment.[50]

The New York Central Railroad purchased these 100 cars in 1950 with its own resources, and they cost $13 million, or $130,000 per car.[51] Subsequent rolling stock acquired for service in the NYC electric zone over the next decade and a half would involve public-sector financial assistance of one sort or another, and eighty-seven cars similar to the St. Louis–built cars of 1950 joined the fleet and permitted the retirement of the least reliable of the railroad's older MU cars. A New York State program was established in 1959 that enabled railroads to acquire new commuter cars under lease arrangements managed by the Port Authority but backed by the state's credit.[52] Eventually, though, the entire suburban operation into and out of Grand Central would become a publicly operated service under the management of the MTA, the same agency that took over control of the Long Island Rail Road (LIRR) in 1966 and the city subway system in 1968. (We shall learn more about the origins of the MTA when we discuss the Long Island below.)

With respect to New York Central suburban territory, at first the MTA was merely a funding partner, while the trains were operated by the corporate successors of the NYC—Penn Central after 1968 and Conrail beginning in 1976. In 1983, the MTA's role significantly expanded, and it took over day-to-day operations of both the onetime NYC commuter network as well as commuter services formerly operated out of Grand Central by the New York, New Haven and Hartford Railroad. MTA called the combined operation the Metro North Commuter Railroad, a name that was shortened to Metro North Railroad in 1994.

(In an urban-transit world where far too many agencies from coast to coast are identified by like-sounding sets of initials, a compliment is in order for those who coined the Metro North name. It is distinctive, it is different—and it works. In 2002, an

MTA reorganization merged the LIRR and Metro North into a new subsidiary called MTA Rail Road. How functional this merger will prove to be, and whether the name MTA Rail Road will achieve common usage among Long Island and Metro North commuters, remains to be seen.)

Under MTA auspices, a major equipment acquisition program was undertaken that saw the development of a common specification for new high-performance MU cars that would be used on both the former New York Central lines out of Grand Central as well as the LIRR—with a look-alike companion car of slightly different specifications developed for use on the electrified lines of the former New Haven Railroad.

Designated the M-series cars and originally dubbed Metropolitans by the MTA's image-makers—a name that would never achieve any measure of popular usage—the early cars were built by the Budd Company and later units by GE. Specifications were developed by a team of consultants retained by the MTA that included the industrial design firm of Sundberg-Ferrar, plus an engineering joint venture that was composed of three firms—Parsons, Brinkerhoff, Quade and Douglas; Gibbs and Hill; and Louis T. Klauder and Associates. (The "Parsons" of Parsons, Brinkerhoff is William Barclay Parsons, the chief engineer for the original Interborough Subway, while the "Gibbs" of Gibbs and Hill is none other than George Gibbs, the man who designed the Interborough's first all-steel passenger car in 1903. Both George Gibbs and William Barclay Parsons were founding principals of the engineering firms that today memorialize their names.)

The very first of the 85-foot stainless-steel M-class cars were ordered for Long Island service in August of 1967. Three years later, in 1970, the MTA contracted for eighty units—at $288,750 per car—to begin the systematic replacement of older MU cars serving the former New York Central lines. Each M-series car has a control cab at one end and is semipermanently coupled with a similar unit to form a two-car set known as a "married pair." In a married-pair set, the two cars share certain mechanical equipment and neither car is capable of operating without its partner. With the M-series, even-numbered A cars carry batteries and other electrical equipment, while odd-numbered B cars contain the air compressor and communications gear.

While the M-series cars set new standards for electric MU equipment in a variety of important technical areas, from a passenger's perspective a feature that represented a marked difference from earlier commuter rolling stock was the fact that the new cars featured transit-style sliding doors, not the more traditional arrangement of entry and exit via end vestibules that are still common on most other commuter railroads. In fact, M cars have no end vestibules at all, and since there are no steps, or traps, at the "quarter-point" positions where the sliding doors are located, all stations served by the new fleet must include high platforms for passenger entry and exit. The MTA had to execute a crash program to build such high-level platforms throughout its electrified territory, since prior to the advent of the new M-class, the only station in the former New York Central commuter district that included high platforms was Grand Central.

There was some speculation at the time that the M-class entered service that the new cars were but the first phase of an MTA plan to convert major elements of the region's commuter services into full rapid-transit-style operations, with prepaid fare collection and more frequent levels of service. But despite the M-class cars' similarities with subway trains and other upgrades the MTA subsequently made in various commuter services, fare collection continues to rely on crew members passing through each car and calling out the classic phrase: "Tickets, please!"

A century after the Interborough Rapid Transit Company inaugurated serviced on the city's first subway in 1904, electrified commuter trains operating into and out of Grand Central Terminal remain an important element within the overall mass-transit infrastructure of the New York metropolitan area. The newest rolling stock on the former NYC network will be a fleet of 180 new 4000-series cars known as the M-7 class, which will represent the first major alteration in basic external appearance since the initial M-1 units arrived on the Long Island Rail Road in the late 1960s. When the first M-7 units begin to enter Metro North service in mid-2004, they will allow the last of the pre-MTA MU cars that were built in the 1960s and that survived into the twenty-first century to be fittingly retired. One factor that helped these veteran cars enjoy such a lengthy service life is the fact the MTA upgraded them in the early 1990s. In their final years, they featured newly developed styles of AC motors, coupled with on-board equipment to convert DC current from the third rail into AC.

Interestingly, though, intercity passenger trains no longer serve Grand Central; all arrivals and departures at the famous terminal are now commuter in nature.[53] Perhaps there was more symbolism than William Wilgus and his associates could possibly have realized on December 11, 1906, when the very first electric-powered train that carried revenue passengers on the New York Central Railroad was not an overnight limited bound for St. Louis or Chicago, but an unassuming MU local whose destination was nearby Yonkers.

THE NEW YORK, NEW HAVEN AND HARTFORD RAILROAD

The New York, New Haven and Hartford Railroad had to electrify its trains if it wished to continue using Grand Central as its Manhattan terminal in the years after the 1902 accident in the Park Avenue tunnel. A relatively simple course of action would have been to adopt the same style of direct-current, third-rail electrification that the New York Central had pioneered and to establish an electric-to-steam transfer point at, perhaps, New Rochelle, 17 miles from Grand Central and 5 miles from Woodlawn, where New Haven trains left NYC trackage and entered their own right-of-way.

The New Haven, though, had far more grandiose electrification plans in mind. In 1891, financier J. P. Morgan had acquired control of the railroad and pursued an aggressive policy of acquisition and merger that expanded what had previously been a largely suburban-oriented railway out of New York City into a New England–wide transportation consortium—many would say monopoly—that included steam railroads, street railways, and even steamboat services. Because of these expansionist policies, by the turn of the century the railroad was commonly referred to as the Consolidated Lines. (Morgan's heyday on the New Haven preceded his unsuccessful effort to best Charles Tyson Yerkes,

Jr., for control of tube railways in London, an effort that was touched upon in Chapter 3.)

Under Morgan, the New Haven began to experiment with various styles of direct current electrification on several of its branch lines in Massachusetts, Rhode Island, and Connecticut as early as 1895.[54] And so when the New York terminal issue made mainline electrification necessary early in the twentieth century, the railroad was prepared to take a bold step. In 1903 a man by the name of Charles S. Mellen had advanced to the position of president of the New York, New Haven and Hartford, and under the joint leadership of Morgan and Mellen, the railroad would not merely copy the New York Central and use DC locomotives to move its trains into and out of New York's Grand Central. Instead, the New Haven would adopt a Westinghouse system of alternating current for powering its trains and extend electric traction much further along its main line than the New York terminal zone. If this was successful, Morgan and company envisioned a day when New Haven trains would travel all the way from New York to Boston behind electric locomotives.

Matters grew considerably more complicated, though, because for their entry into Grand Central, New Haven trains would have to draw direct current from the New York Central's third rail. In cooperation with Westinghouse, New Haven engineers were thus forced to develop a dual-function electric locomotive, one that could use high-voltage AC distributed by overhead wires along its own rails and then switch over to (relatively) low-voltage DC at Woodlawn once NYC trackage was reached. This was a serious engineering challenge. Not only was the New Haven Railroad developing and deploying the very first main-line example of railway electrification in the United States using high-voltage alternating current technology for traction power, but it was adding an almost impossibly complicating factor to the mix with the need to design locomotives that could also operate over NYC's direct current system. In commenting editorially on the New Haven project in 1907, the trade journal the *Railroad Gazette* said: "It is an experiment in the sense that it is new and untried in actual service of this kind, but it has been carried out on such a tremendous scale that it must succeed, because the railroad and the builders of the apparatus simply will not let it fail."[55]

The New Haven selected a system that used 11,000 volts of single-phase, 25-cycle alternating current for traction power over its own lines. Onboard transformers in a locomotive or MU car would step this current down before feeding it to the motors, which were also designed to function when the locomotive was drawing direct current south of Woodlawn. In practice, the system worked like this: as a Grand Central–bound New Haven train approached the New York Central junction at Woodlawn operating under the AC catenary, the engine crew first pressed a button to lower the third-rail shoes to engage the under-running third rail. Then, as the train continued to roll along, another button was pushed to lower and lock down the pantographs, switches in the cab were thrown to set up the proper circuits for the transition, and as the train coasted onto third-rail trackage, the locomotive was ready to power its motors with direct current. Outbound from Grand Central, the procedure was reversed, and the charm of this system was the fact that it could be accomplished without stopping.

The first phase of the New Haven's electrification was completed in 1907; it involved building an overhead catenary system from the junction with the New York Central at Woodlawn to Stamford, Connecticut, a distance of slightly over 21 miles. Here trains would change locomotives much as the New York Central did at Harmon—steam-for-electric on schedules bound for New York, electric-for-steam in the opposite direction. Stamford, though, was no further from Grand Central than was Croton—each was 33 miles out—and electrification to that distance need not have entailed the complexity that an AC system involved. But AC, although untested in North America at the time, was thought to be superior for railway electrification over longer distances, and the New Haven clearly had its eye on a much more extensive system of electrification.

Limiting main-line electrification to Woodlawn-Stamford in 1907 was dictated by two factors, one technical, and the other, financial. On the one hand, Woodlawn-Stamford would allow the New Haven to gain some practical experience with AC traction before making a larger investment and extending the wires further. But economic conditions in the years immediately following 1907 were such that funding a more extensive electrification investment was not feasible at that time.

A railroad-owned generating station was built along the banks of the Mianus River in Cos Cob, Connecticut. Its external architecture was described as Spanish Mission, and the facility was strategically located so it could receive coal either by rail or from barges. Like the New York Central Railroad—but unlike the Interborough Rapid Transit Company—Cos Cob generated its electricity exclusively with steam turbine engines. Cos Cob produced AC current at 11,000 volts, the same potential that the New Haven used for traction power, and it was fed directly into the catenary system. Because the New York Central also generated its electricity as 11,000-volts of single-phase AC that was later stepped down and converted to direct current at substations located throughout its electrified zone, the New Haven was able to feed current to the NYC system via the latter's Port Morris generating station in compensation—or at least partial compensation—for the electricity that New Haven trains used while operating on NYC trackage. There had been some earlier disagreement between the two railroads over charges the NYC planned to levy for New Haven trains to draw current from its third rail. But matters were quickly resolved, and the connection between Port Morris and Cos Cob was part of the arrangement.[56]

The executive committee of the New Haven's board of directors met in New York at Grand Central on Thursday, July 11, 1907, to review final plans for inaugurating electrified service. After their meeting, the committee traveled to North River Pier 19 at the foot of Warren Street and boarded a Fall River Line side-wheel steamer for an overnight journey to Fall River. Here they transferred to a boat-train of the Old Colony Railroad for the final leg of a trip to Boston, where the committee had further railroad business to conduct. In 1907, both Fall River and Old Colony were part of the New Haven's empire.[57]

Although the initial electric zone extended from Woodlawn to Stamford, revenue service was inaugurated in phases. On July 24, 1907, a train bound for New York that departed New Rochelle at 7:50 A.M. became the first electric train to carry revenue passengers under the New Haven's new AC wires. It reached Grand Central 38 minutes later at 8:28 A.M. On August 5, electrified service was extended to Port Chester, and the full Wood-lawn-Stamford section was placed into service on October 6, 1907.[58]

Initially, the New Haven experienced a number of technical problems with its new AC electrification system. These were hardly unexpected, given the radical nature of the technology the railroad had deployed, and they were promptly addressed and corrected. For instance, on July 14, 1908, a severe thunderstorm hit the suburbs north of New York, and a lightening strike at the Cos Cob generating station just before the evening rush hour knocked out the entire AC system. Although the New York Central's DC system remained in operation, New Haven trains were held at Grand Central, since they would not be able to operate at all once they reached Woodlawn Junction. An emergency call was put out for operable steam locomotives and the roundhouse at Stamford dispatched engines to Woodlawn. By early evening, the problem had been diagnosed, power was restored, and corrective measures designed to avoid similar outages during future thunderstorms.[59]

Another serious problem the railroad encountered was the utterly unforgiving and quite lethal danger that the 11,000-volt catenary represented. New Haven brakemen were accustomed to climbing to the top of freight cars during routine switching maneuvers, and in the early days of the AC system there were several instances of brakemen being electrocuted.[60]

In 1914, seven years after the railroad inaugurated electric service between Stamford and New York, the New Haven extended its AC catenary an additional 39 miles along the main line from Stamford to New Haven—which was 60 miles from Woodlawn, 72 miles from Grand Central, and, for its day, by far the largest and longest railway electrification in the world. The New Haven's main line was also four tracks wide, so 60 route-miles from Woodland to New Haven entailed 360 main-line track-miles, plus all manner of secondary tracks, yards, and so forth. In addition, it seemed clear throughout the railroad industry that the New Haven had every intention of extending wires all the way to Boston in the not-too-distant future. A plan to install an AC catenary system between Boston and Providence was under active discussion in 1912, for instance, and it would have been a logical next step in eventually stringing wires all the way from Boston to New York.[61]

But J. P. Morgan would soon lose his grip on the New Haven, and the railroad would fall on difficult days. In late 1915, eleven past and present directors of the New Haven had to face federal charges of "having conspired to violate the Sherman law by seeking to monopolize all the transportation facilities of New England."[62] In 1935, the once-robust railroad was forced to seek the protection of receivership, and extending the AC wires to Boston was delayed, postponed, and seemingly forgotten about, while the proposal to electrify Boston to Providence was never realized. New Haven, 72 miles from Grand Central, seemed destined to be the permanent end of the railroad's electrified zone.

(The idea of electrified service to Boston would not die, though. It was eventually achieved under Amtrak auspices on January 28, 2000, eighty-six years after the Stamford–New Haven link was electrified, and ninety-three years after the first New Haven electric locomotives hauled trains under the AC wires.)

In 1912, two years before completing the Stamford–New Haven electrification, the New Haven installed AC catenary over an important branch line that left its own main line in New Rochelle and proceeded due south to Port Morris on the Harlem River, eleven miles away. This Port Morris branch was used largely by freight trains, although there was some limited passenger service into a small depot on the Harlem River, a facility that would never rival Grand Central in the number of trains it dispatched but was an alternative where passengers could transfer to elevated trains of the Interborough's Manhattan Division and continue into the city that way.[63] The New Haven's Oak Point yard, where freight cars were interchanged with other railroads in the metropolitan area aboard barges known as car floats, was also at the southern end of the Port Morris branch, and there was also a freight interchange at Port Morris between the New Haven and the New York Central.[64]

The New Haven's Port Morris branch would soon achieve additional importance. The railroad had earlier joined forces with the Pennsylvania Railroad to acquire the charter of something called the New York Connecting Railroad, and together the two companies would use New York Connecting as a corporate vehicle for building the massive Hell Gate Bridge across the East River between the Bronx and Long Island in 1917. Thanks to connections in Long Island City, Hell Gate Bridge allowed New Haven passenger trains from Boston to recross the East River into Manhattan via the Pennsy's tunnels, pause in Midtown at Penn Station, and then continue south of New York to Philadelphia and Washington.[65]

There was even speculation in the railroad industry that the New Haven was harboring serious intentions of severing its ties with the New York Central, moving out of Grand Central entirely, and operating all of its passenger trains down the branch to an expanded Port Morris depot on the Harlem River, to Penn Station via Hell Gate Bridge, or perhaps to both.[66] The improvements that the New Haven installed along this line—expansion to six tracks in width and elimination of all grade crossings in 1910, electrification in 1912—certainly fueled such speculation. But the New Haven did not abandon Grand Central, and the Port Morris branch simply gave the railroad additional operational flexibility. (The Port Morris branch of the New Haven Railroad remains an active electrified railway in the twenty-first century and provides a critical link in Amtrak's important Northeast Corridor between Washington and Boston.)

The New Haven also extended its AC catenary over two suburban branch lines in southern Connecticut, one between Stamford and New Canaan, the other between South Norwalk and Danbury. The Danbury branch was where the New Haven's ill-fated train No. 223 began its journey on the morning of January 8, 1902, while the New Canaan Line was the site of one of the railroad's early experiments with a direct current system of electrification.[67]

Another initiative that bears on our story happened in 1912, at the height of the Morgan-Mellen expansion, when the New Haven inaugurated service over a totally separate suburban railway subsidiary that ran from the banks of the Harlem River in the lower Bronx northward over two separate lines, one to White Plains, the other to Port Chester. Called the New York, Westchester and Boston Railway, this was a suburban-oriented and primarily passenger railway—it owned but a single freight

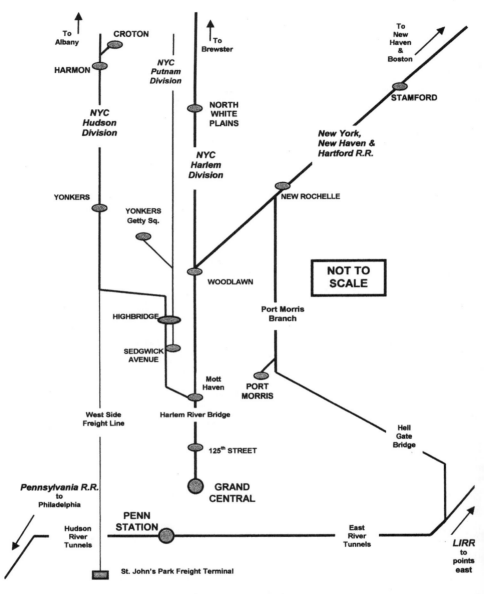

Principal New York commuter railroad lines and facilities.

locomotive—and was powered by high-voltage alternating current, identical to the parent railroad's own main line. L. B. Stillwell, who assisted in the design of the electrification system for the 1904 New York Subway, developed a distinctive MU car for the railway, and ninety-five units were built to Stillwell's specifications.[68]

The Westchester, as the new line was commonly called, labored under a tragic shortcoming. Despite the extraordinary capital investment it represented and the high engineering standards to which it was built, and despite, too, the fact that the central Westchester County territory it served would soon experience unprecedented population growth, the line failed to offer its passengers a "one-seat" ride into the business districts of midtown Manhattan and forced them to rely, instead, on el connections in the south Bronx from the same terminal at the southern end of the Port Morris branch at which certain New Haven trains also terminated. (The Westchester leased two of the six tracks along the Port Morris branch from its parent road between the Harlem River and a point in the central Bronx at West Farms, where it veered westward and continued northward along its own right-of-way.) From early 1917, Westchester passengers could also transfer to Interborough Subway trains at the East 180th Street station on the Dual Contracts–built White Plains Road Line. But this still required Westchester passengers to change trains before they could reach midtown Manhattan.

The New York, Westchester and Boston failed to survive the Great Depression and on December 31, 1937, it operated its last scheduled passenger train. (The New Haven itself had eliminated operation of its own passenger trains out of the Harlem River terminal in 1931.) As described in Chapter 1, 4 miles of the Westchester main line within the City of New York still remain in service as the Dyre Avenue Line of the IRT Division, but otherwise the Westchester is today little more than a memory.

A technical innovation that the New Haven adopted when the Port Morris branch was electrified is worth mentioning, as it would eventually become standard practice for electric railways—and subways, too. Because commercial sources of electric power had reached new levels of dependability, in 1915 the railroad was able to develop contractual arrangements with both the New York Edison Company and the United Electric Light and Power Company to supplement current from its own Cos Cob generating plant with commercial power. Such purchased power was used for both the New Haven's own trains as well as those of its Westchester subsidiary after being fed into the railroad's electrical grid at a special substation in West Farms that was owned by United but built on railroad land.[69]

The New Haven made yet another technical change to its electrification system coincident with the extension of AC wires to New Haven in 1914. The capacity of Cos Cob was expanded with additional turbo-generators, and the facility continued to produce current at a potential of 11,000 volts. When Cos Cob first came on line in 1907, this 11,000-volt current was fed directly into the catenary system for traction power. Because higher voltages facilitate transmission over distance, in 1914 the railroad installed step-up transformers at Cos Cob and began to transmit current to substations along the right-of-way at a potential of 22,000 volts. It was stepped back down to 11,000 volts at the substations and then fed into the catenary.

At first, locomotives hauled all New Haven trains operating into and out of Grand Central—local or long-distance—and the railroad's initial electric equipment included no MU cars. Given all the complexities associated with the main-line electrification program, adding another dimension in the way of MU cars that would also have to draw current from both AC and DC electrification systems was thought to be unwise. The New Haven had conducted earlier tests of self-propelled electric cars along several of its direct current experimental installations, but the first MU equipment for Grand Central service was not acquired until 1909, and it was a rather modest fleet at that—four motorized cars and six trailers. (Recall that New York Central's initial MU fleet of 1907 totaled 125 units.)

When the New Haven's first MU cars for Grand Central service were delivered—bodies by the Standard Steel Car Company, electrical gear from Westinghouse—it was their ability to operate from both high-voltage AC and low-voltage DC power systems that drew the most attention from the trade press.[70] Far more elaborate equipment had to be installed aboard the cars than was required for more conventional direct-current MU cars—a transformer and its associated cooling apparatus were required, for instance—and it was quite an engineering challenge to find room for all this hardware beneath the car floor. From the perspective of external appearance, though, what was surely the most unusual feature of the New Haven's initial MU fleet was the fact that while the cars were all-steel in their construction, they included no enclosed vestibules but, rather, featured end platforms that were fully open, a design feature generally identified with wooden passenger cars built in the nineteenth century. At first, MU cars were used only in a relatively short-haul service between Grand Central and Port Chester, a one-way distance of slightly more than 16 miles. Revenue passengers first rode aboard New Haven MU trains out of Grand Central on February 28, 1910.

The New Haven would expand its fleet of open-platform MU cars in 1912 with four additional motorized coaches, ten trailer coaches, and two additional trailer cars that were configured as combination baggage-coaches. Something common to all New Haven MU cars was that powered units as well as trailers were all equipped with operating cabs on both ends for maximum flexibility. Another constant specification on the New Haven was that all powered MU cars were equipped with four motors each. The New Haven relied on a larger proportion of unpowered trailer cars than most other electric railways of the time, so its motorized units had to have sufficient muscle to haul such trailer cars. Each powered car was equipped with two pantographs for drawing current from the overhead catenary, although only one was normally raised during routine operations.

One change in propulsion between the New Haven's very first MU cars and subsequent orders was that the initial motor cars were equipped with a system called a "geared-quill" drive. In such a system, the motor is geared to a hollow shaft that surrounds the driving axle, and power is transmitted to the wheels from this shaft by a series of driving pins that engage depressions in the rear surface of the wheel. Various styles of quill drive would prove to be practical on heavy-duty electric locomotives, but the New Haven quickly decided that it was not appropriate for MU cars. Following the initial order, a more conventional gear-drive arrangement was specified on the railroad's subsequent MU cars, and the original fleet was converted to a similar system.

During the first decade that the New Haven Railroad operated electric-powered trains into Grand Central, MU equipment was not the dominant style of service the railroad provided, and electric locomotives powered most New Haven schedules, suburban as well as long-distance. The railroad had updated its specifications for MU cars, though, and with the arrival of some new equipment in 1914, open end platforms were eliminated in favor or more conventional enclosed vestibules. The New Haven's MU fleet remained relatively modest through the years of the First World War and did not break the 100-unit mark until the early 1920s. The railroad's thinking about MU equipment was evolving, though, and between 1920 and 1930, the MU fleet would more than double and assume a larger role in suburban operations.

The New Haven also had a handful of AC-only MU cars on its roster. The first of these were two wooden cars that were acquired for shuttle service on the New Canaan branch in 1908—they actually predated the first AC-DC cars—and in subsequent years AC-only cars would continue to operate on this line as well as the Port Morris branch down to the Harlem River, where the capability to switch to direct current was not a requirement.[71]

By the time the Second World War began to loom, the MU fleet of the New York, New Haven and Hartford Railroad had grown to almost 200 cars—78 motorized units and 121 trailers. The original open-platform MU cars remained in service and were not retired until the mid-1950s, thus providing a curiously anachronistic touch to an electric railway operation that was an otherwise forward-looking installation which pioneered many important technical innovations.

(A personal aside: I first rode open-platform MU cars on the New Haven in the 1940s when my parents took me to visit relatives in Greenwich, Connecticut. When we boarded our train in the darkened caverns of Grand Central, I was so taken by the overall experience that I failed to notice the open-platform feature. When we collected our belongings and headed for the exit as the train approached Greenwich, I was flabbergasted to discover that the end vestibule was really an open platform.)

The MU cars acquired by the New Haven in the years before the Second World War ranged in length from 71 feet to 79 feet and were turned out primarily by Osgood-Bradley and Standard Steel Car. Most were of an all-coach configuration, although there were some baggage-coach combines, as well as six cars that were rigged as special commuter club cars. (Three of these six, Nos. 5001, 5002, and 5005, were later equipped with an "ice-powered" air-conditioning system.) Like the New York Central—and also like August Belmont's Interborough Rapid Transit Company—the New Haven Railroad reconfigured many of its MU cars from trailer units to powered cars as conditions warranted. The railroad's suburban territory, of course, continued to grow in population, and efficient service into and out of Manhattan became a staple of the company's operations. While there were some short-turns that operated merely between Grand Central and New Rochelle, the two principal destinations for MU-equipped trains out of New York were Port Chester and Stamford. Inspection, maintenance, and storage facilities were located at Stamford, while Port Chester included a small yard just beyond the station where MU cars could lay over between runs. Table 4.3 indicates the number of revenue trains that operated in these various MU-oriented services on a typical weekday during the winter of 1946 and 1947.

TABLE 4.3
NEW HAVEN SUBURBAN SERVICE (1946–1947)

Service	Number of Weekday Trains
Grand Central to New Rochelle	4
New Rochelle to Grand Central	5
Grand Central to Port Chester	16[a]
Port Chester to Grand Central	15[b]
Grand Central to Stamford	29
Stamford to Grand Central	29
Total MU trains scheduled	98

a. Includes one Grand-Central-to-Rye schedule.
b. Includes one Rye-to-Grand-Central schedule.
Source: New Haven Public Timetable (Form 200), effective September 29, 1946.

By the end of the Second World War, the New Haven's MU fleet was starting to show its age. But in an era when large-scale public financing was yet to be available for commuter railroads, the New Haven itself could afford only relatively modest improvements. In 1954 the same Worcester plant that was once the Osgood Bradley works and that had turned out many MU cars for the New Haven over the years—but was then owned by Chicago-based Pullman-Standard—delivered a fleet of 100 new high-performance MU cars to the railroad for its electrified suburban service. Operationally, they were equipped with something called ignitron rectifiers, devices that convert the alternating current delivered through the overhead catenary into direct current, and the cars were hence able to be equipped with DC motors, which were then regarded as heftier and more dependable than AC equivalents. (The New Haven also acquired a small fleet of new electric locomotives for its long-distance trains at roughly the same time that also featured ignitron rectifiers and DC motors.)

Externally, the new MU cars looked very different from the railroad's older fleet because their sides were sheathed in shiny and corrugated stainless steel, a feature that caused the new units to be unofficially dubbed "washboards."[72] At 87 feet in length, the new cars were a bit longer than earlier suburban rolling stock on the railroad, and they were also the first New Haven MU cars to be equipped with true mechanical air-conditioning, a form of passenger comfort that quickly underscored their improvement over the road's prewar rolling stock. (As noted above, three older MU club cars had been equipped with an ice-actuated system of air-conditioning.)

Arrival of these new cars in 1954 allowed the New Haven to retire many of its older MU fleet, including the last of the open-platform cars. Curiously enough, in the postwar era, both the New Haven and the New York Central were each able to secure corporate resources for the purchase of exactly 100 new MU cars for Grand Central service—NYC's 4500-series cars of 1950 and the New Haven's 4400-series "washboards" of 1954. Additional new suburban rolling stock for either railroad would have to wait for the availability of public-sector financing for such projects, something that was looming on the horizon.

The New Haven was hardly a robust corporation in the postwar era. Its intercity passenger service was relatively short-haul in nature—Boston's South Station is only 229.1 miles from Grand Central—rendering it vulnerable to competition from newly built freeways and turnpikes, not to mention innovations like the no-reservations air shuttle service developed by Eastern Airlines. In 1946, the New Haven was dispatching twenty-two daily trains out of New York for Boston; by 1968, this number had fallen to thirteen. In 1961, the railroad entered receivership for the second time in its history, and in January 1969, the New York, New Haven and Hartford Railroad surrendered its independent identity and was merged into the Penn Central.

The New Haven's inclusion in the Penn Central was forced on all parties by the Interstate Commerce Commission (ICC) as a necessary condition for its approval of the merger of the Pennsylvania and the New York Central. The ICC was firm in ruling that all of the New Haven's New York–area commuter service had to be continued, but not indefinitely. "In recent months . . . the states have demonstrated a willingness to provide an increased level of public support for essential passenger services. We will give close scrutiny to the good faith and the efficacy of all of the parties in any future passenger train discontinuance case with this commission," the ICC said.[73]

Once the New Haven was absorbed into the Penn Central, New York–Boston departures were quickly reduced to eight per day, and two years later, in 1971, Penn Central was relieved of any obligation to provide intercity passenger service at all as a new organization called Amtrak came on the scene and took over such responsibilities. (Under Amtrak auspices, Boston–New York passenger service has been substantially upgraded. As the New York Subway celebrates its centennial, eighteen weekday trains are scheduled each way between the two cities.)

Public officials in New Haven's service area had almost worked out an arrangement in 1964 that would have allowed the bankrupt carrier to acquire eighty new electric MU cars under New York State's program which authorized the Port of New York Authority to lease commuter rolling stock to area railroads. Both the New York Central and the Long Island had acquired new MU cars under this program, and the trustees of the bankrupt railroad were in agreement on details of such an arrangement, as was the federal judge who was overseeing the railroad's receivership. But the court's approval was contingent on the payment of $450,000 in subsidies from the state of Connecticut and $400,000 from Westchester County. Connecticut agreed, but Westchester did not, and on the strength of its refusal the deal collapsed; new rolling stock for commuters who rode into Grand Central on the New Haven every morning would have to await fundamental structural change in the way the railroad was governed—and financed.[74]

Public control would come to the commuter services operated over the former New Haven lines in a multistage process. Eventually New York's MTA would acquire former New Haven trackage within its borders—essentially Grand Central to Port Chester—while the State of Connecticut would do likewise within its jurisdiction. Operation of the former New Haven services then became a responsibility of MTA's Metro North Commuter Railroad, with each of the two states providing a proportional share of requisite operating and capital financial assistance. The initial units in a fleet of 144 new M-class cars that were acquired by the MTA and the state of Connecticut to replace the line's older equipment began to roll off a new General Electric assembly line in Erie, Pennsylvania, in 1972, even prior to Metro North's taking over the system's operations.

M-class equipment for the New Haven service, while generally similar in appearance to cars used in New York Central and LIRR services, incorporated important differences. For one thing, the New Haven fleet was jointly owned by the MTA and the State of Connecticut, with each entity holding full title to individual cars. Some cars were hence delivered with the MTA logo on their end bulkhead, while others displayed the seal of the State of Connecticut. In addition, because they require the capability to operate from both low-voltage DC third rail and high-voltage AC catenary, M-class cars for the New Haven service—initial units were designated the M-2 fleet—feature an array of roof-mounted hardware, including a pantograph, that gives them a slightly different profile from their strictly DC running mates. The M-2 cars measure 14 feet 9 inches in height, while the DC-only M-class cars are 13 feet from rail to roof. The M-2 units weigh 130,000 pounds versus 91,600 pounds for the DC-only cars.[75]

Twenty units in the original order of 144 were rigged as café cars, so commuters could enjoy a bracing cup of hot coffee on the way to work in the morning and perhaps a relaxing vintage beverage as they traveled home—a betterment denied passengers traveling aboard DC-only M-class equipment—and in a purely decorated touch, while M-class cars operating on both NYC and LIRR services were delivered with stainless-steel bodies accented by a broad stripe of royal blue, M-2s on the New Haven Line service featured a bright red stripe.

Eventually, as additional M-class cars were acquired for the New Haven service, the MTA incorporated a revision in its specifications. As a result, the fleet now includes a number of cabless cars that are semipermanently coupled between two cab-equipped cars to create a three-car set. (While a two-car set of semipermanently coupled cars is commonly referred to as a "married pair," one hesitates to use the term "married trio" to describe a three-car unit.)

The difference between an M-1 unit acquired for service over the former New York Central lines and an M-2 designed for use on the New Haven was reflected in the price tags the cars bore. In 1970, the MTA ordered 144 new M-2 cars for the New Haven service and 80 M-1A cars for use over the former New York Central lines. Each of the eighty M-1A cars cost the MTA $288,750, while the M-2s each carried a price tag of $423,611. Just about every dime of the differential was attributable to the need of the M-2 cars to include AC-DC capability.[76] In any event, the M-2 era on the New Haven formally began at 8:20 A.M. on April 16, 1973, when a revenue train composed of the new rolling stock left Stamford for Grand Central.

Like the former New York Central electrified network, the New Haven Line has been equipped with high platforms all the way from Grand Central to New Haven, since M-class cars lack steps and traps and cannot board passengers from track-level platforms. During the dark days of the New Haven's receivership in the early 1960s, the catenary was removed from the Danbury branch, and Metro North commuter service along this line now features trains hauled by diesel locomotives. But the single-track

New Canaan branch remains electrified, and as it meanders through the rural Connecticut countryside, it bears more resemblance to an electric interurban railway than a heavy-duty mainline railroad.

Both the MTA and the State of Connecticut have invested significant sums in upgrading the suburban right-of-way along the former New Haven Railroad. In recent years, major sections of the catenary system have been replaced along the main line, and plans call for the entire catenary, from Pelham to New Haven, to be replaced by the year 2005. The aging Cos Cod generating station has been closed, because Metro North now purchases all of its electricity from commercial utility companies. In fact, when Cos Cob was taken off-line, the New Haven electrification system was converted from its original 25-cycle frequency to a more common 60-cycle specification. (Contemporary electrified rolling stock is able to switch from one frequency to another with little more than the flip of a switch in the cab.)

Another change involves the place where trains shift from third rail to overhead catenary. From 1907, this transition had taken place just beyond Woodlawn Junction, at the very start of the New Haven's own right-of-way. As part of the catenary replacement program, the under-running third rail was extended another 2 miles or so along the former New Haven main line, and trains now shift from one power source to another just to the west of the Pelham station, between milepost 15 and 16. (By making this shift, Metro North was able to eliminate high-voltage catenary under a number of highway overpasses.) And in what was really just a minor operational change—but symbolic of the fact that the Harlem Line and the New Haven Line are now part of the same railroad—where New Haven trains were previously not permitted to make passenger stops between Woodlawn and Grand Central, save at 125th Street, now certain New Haven Line trains also stop at Fordham Road.

PENNSYLVANIA RAILROAD'S MP-54 AND ITS SUCCESSORS

The Pennsylvania Railroad (PRR) was in a class apart in the development of new railway technology. A frequently heard characterization of any important technical improvement in the railroad industry onward from, say, 1890, is that if it was any good, the PRR either invented it or owned more of it than anybody else.

For example, one simply may not talk about electric locomotives without extensive discussion of Pennsylvania engines known as the DD-1 and the GG-1; no treatment of the American railroad passenger car could possibly be complete without ample reference to Pennsy's famous P-70 day coach; and the history of the steam locomotive cannot be told adequately without talking about such classic PRR engines as the E-6s Atlantic and the K-4s Pacific.

What may well be the PRR's most unremarked and underrated success story in the way of specialized railway equipment is a fleet of electric MU cars that bore the unassuming designation MP-54. Developed and designed in the early years of the twentieth century, the MP-54 provides a fascinating link between the style of electric railway technology that was used on New York's original Interborough Subway and that William Wilgus adopted for Grand Central, and the high-performance world of contemporary electrified railways such as the high-speed TGV service in France and the swift Acela Express that Amtrak now operates up and down the Northeast Corridor.

The story of Pennsy's MP-54 electric MU car begins in 1907, when the railroad was orchestrating a wholesale acquisition of new steel passenger cars. With the prospect of having to use none but steel cars for revenue service through the new Hudson River tunnels that PPR was building to bring its trains into Manhattan, a variety of standardized designs were developed to replace the road's older fleet of wooden-bodied cars.[77] In 1903, Pennsy's Altoona Shops had built the world's very first all-steel passenger car, a subway car for New York's Interborough Rapid Transit Company that we learned something about in Chapter 1. In subsequent years, PRR turned out additional steel cars of an experimental nature, and it was from these various efforts that the 1907 standards were developed.[78] In August of 1906, on the condition that he be identified only as a "high official in the motive power department," an anonymous official of the PRR told a reporter: "All future passenger equipment of the Pennsylvania Railroad will be made of steel. The necessity of providing non-collapsible, absolutely fireproof passenger cars for the New York tunnel has simply hastened the day when this transformation must take place."[79]

The full spectrum of designs included a variety of cars for various passenger services—long-distance coaches, baggage and express cars, diners, and so forth. Among the several styles of new steel cars the PRR felt it required was a specialized coach that would be ideal for short-haul suburban work, a car that would measure 64 feet, 5¾ inches from the face of one coupler to the other. On the Pennsylvania Railroad, though, length was typically expressed as the distance between a car's interior bulkheads, not overall exterior length. Thus measured, the new all-steel suburban coaches were closer to 54 feet in length, and they were hence identified with the classification P-54—*P,* for passenger; *54,* for the distance in feet between the inside bulkheads. (The PRR's new standard for long-distance passenger coaches was a car that was 70 feet between interior bulkheads—although 80 feet long overall. It was hence designated the P-70, arguably the most famous railroad day coach of all time.) In addition to an all-coach configuration, the P-54 fleet included various styles of baggage cars, baggage-mail cars, and baggage-coach combination cars.

Other than various experimental steel cars that the Pennsylvania Railroad acquired between 1903 and 1907, the railroad's initial acquisition of production-model steel cars was an order for 200 units that was placed in mid-1907. Other U.S. railroads were then on the verge of specifying all-steel construction for new passenger stock, and some had acquired various one-of-a-kind experimental cars or even small fleets of all-steel cars. The New York Central's initial MU cars of 1906, for instance, were notable for their all-steel design. But the Pennsy's order in 1907 stands alone in world railway history as a major carrier's deciding that henceforth it would acquire none but steel cars for passenger service. Commented the trade journal the *Railroad Gazette:* "The Pennsylvania's recent order for 200 steel passenger cars of various types . . . marks the beginning of a period of standardization in the evolution of passenger car construction for regular road service from wood to steel."[80]

There was something special about the technical specifications the railroad developed for its P-54 suburban coach. From the outset, this car was designed to facilitate later conversion into an electric-powered MU car. End vestibules could easily be converted into operating stations for such a train's engineer, for instance, and duct work and other provisions were incorporated that would permit the later installation of control apparatus, wiring, and so forth. Even the car's frame was modified: "to provide sufficient space for motors the center sill is made more shallow."[81]

The Pennsylvania's initial acquisition of 200 steel passenger cars was quickly followed by additional orders, and PRR also worked with the Pullman Company to ensure that all-steel sleeping cars would be available to operate with its own coaches and dining cars.[82] By early 1910, PRR had over 300 steel passenger cars on its active roster, with more under construction, and this total would increase almost tenfold to 2,800 before the end of 1912.[83]

In 1907, when PRR ordered its first production-model steel cars, electrification of any of the railroad's main lines was still a few years away. Tunnels under the Hudson River into New York were then under construction—they would be completed in late 1910—and a system of electrification using a DC third rail would be installed between Penn Station and an unusual spot out in the Jersey Meadows called Manhattan Transfer, where trains to and from New York would change locomotives—steam to electric on eastbound trains, electric to steam on trains heading west.[84] When Penn Station opened in 1910, in other words, the Pennsylvania's electrified terminal district was relatively modest in length—considerably shorter, for instance, than the New York Central's Grand-Central-to-Croton installation. Tunneling under the Hudson River in 1910, of course, was an engineering achievement that could hardly be described as modest, but the fact remains that Manhattan Transfer was a mere 8 miles from Penn Station. The railroad's new fleet of electric locomotives—designated as class DD-1—would also haul trains under the East River between Penn Station and a major storage and servicing yard in Long Island City, in addition to working schedules between Penn Station and Manhattan Transfer, but the railroad opted for a DC electrification system, among other reasons because it was intended to be a short-haul installation.

With the opening of Penn Station in 1910, the railroad shifted most of its long-distance trains out of its former waterside terminal at Exchange Place in Jersey City, where ferryboats had long provided connections across the Hudson River to New York. Exchange Place would remain active in the years after 1910, but more as a commuter-oriented facility catering primarily to short-haul suburban passengers. In addition to being the place where trains bound for Penn Station swapped their steam locomotives for electric engines, Manhattan Transfer was also the junction where the new line to Penn Station diverged from the old main line to and from Exchange Place.

Once its trans-Hudson electrification was in operation, the Pennsylvania rigged its first P-54 units for electric operation, a small fleet of six cars that the railroad used in shuttle service over the direct current line between Manhattan Transfer and Penn Station. When so equipped for electric service, a Pennsy P-54 car was reclassified as an MP-54—*M* for motor.

(PRR's six DC electric cars were not the only MP-54s to operate into Penn Station during its early years. As will be discussed in more detail presently, the Pennsy-owned Long Island Rail Road began acquiring a fleet of MP-54 cars for its own electrified operations in 1910, and since LIRR trains entered Penn Station from the east, its MP-54s also carried passengers into the new terminal. In fact, LIRR revenue service into Penn Station was inaugurated on September 8, 1910—over two full months before PRR trains began using the Hudson River tunnels on November 27—and so the first passenger trains to serve Penn Station consisted of LIRR MP-54 MU cars.)

With respect to the development of PRR electrification in general and the MP-54 in particular, what happened next takes us somewhat afield from New York. In any event, with its new Penn Station in midtown Manhattan a magnificent showpiece of a big city railway terminal, the Pennsylvania was understandably dissatisfied with the principal station its trains used in Philadelphia, a city the railroad long regarded as its "hometown." Pennsy trains terminating in Philadelphia arrived and departed from a terribly outmoded facility called Broad Street Station. Located in the heart of the city's downtown, close to the intersection of Broad and Market streets, Broad Street Station was a sixteen-track, stub-end terminal that trains approached from the west at second-story level atop a massive masonry structure that eventually spread out to accommodate the entire terminal facility. If the New York Central and Hudson River Railroad long prevented real-estate development in important sections of midtown Manhattan because of the vast expanse of at-grade railway facilities it required immediately north of Grand Central Depot, the Pennsylvania had an equally negative impact on central Philadelphia by virtue of what many called a "Chinese wall" that its elevated right-of-way represented through the very heart of the city.[85]

Aside from its civic liabilities, Broad Street was also a problem from the perspective of railway operations. Its limited size was a serious impediment to the railroad's operating additional service, and there was not the slightest possibility that the station itself could be expanded. Furthermore, to the extent that important long-distance PRR trains did not terminate in Philadelphia at all but stopped there as part of a longer journey—New York to Washington, Chicago to New York—stub-end Broad Street was not a facility they could serve swiftly and efficiently, if at all.

Ultimately, PRR would address its overall Philadelphia terminal problem with a comprehensive strategy that included a variety of separate investment projects, including the eventual abandonment of its Broad Street Terminal in 1952 and the tearing down of the infamous Chinese wall.[86] Not unlike the New York Central's efforts in New York, the electrification of Pennsy trains was a crucial part of the solution—not quite as crucial, perhaps, as was the case with New York Central, but certainly important.

On March 12, 1913—less than three years after DD-1 electric locomotives had made Penn Station a reality in Manhattan—the board of directors of the Pennsylvania Railroad authorized the expenditure of $4 million to design and install a system of electrification along its main line between Broad Street Terminal and the Philadelphia suburb of Paoli, 20 miles to the west.[87] (As a matter of railroad fact, Paoli was located on the PRR's main line to the west. In a somewhat different sense, however, the upscale suburban territory that the PRR served along the way to Paoli has long been known as the Main Line.)

For Philadelphia-Paoli service, the railroad would use a 25-cycle, single-phase system of alternating current distributed through overhead catenary at a potential of 11,000 volts, similar in many important respects to the New York, New Haven and Hartford Railroad's installation between Woodland and New Haven. As was the case with the New Haven, Westinghouse would be the principal supplier of electrical equipment for the project. Unlike the New Haven, however, by 1913 commercial sources of electric power had reached a sufficient level of dependability that the PRR felt no need to build any generating stations of its own, and for its Philadelphia-area electrification, the railroad would purchase current from the Philadelphia Electric Company. Philadelphia Electric had a major generating station on the east bank of the Schuylkill River, and current was delivered to the railroad's Arsenal Bridge substation on the opposite bank through underwater cables.[88]

No electric locomotives were to be acquired, though—at least not initially—for use in the railroad's new AC electrified zone. Instead, the only rolling stock the railroad needed for the first phase of its project was a fleet of MU passenger cars. The introduction of bidirectional MU cars into Philadelphia-Paoli service would greatly decrease the quantity of terminal switching necessary at Broad Street Station. As was earlier the case at Grand Central, with steam power the arrival of an inbound train and its subsequent departure on an outbound schedule involved eight separate maneuvers through the interlocking plant at the throat of the terminal, not to mention the turning of the locomotive on a turntable. With MU cars this was reduced to two maneuvers, and an inbound train could be re-dispatched as an outbound one in a matter of minutes. And so if expanding the facility itself could not increase the capacity of Broad Street Terminal, reducing the number of movements Philadelphia-Paoli trains had to make when they used the terminal could certainly enhance the terminal's functional capacity.

George Gibbs, the man who designed the world's first all-steel passenger car for the Interborough Rapid Transit Company in 1903 and who also played an important consulting role in the design of the New York terminal electrification projects for both the PRR and the New York Central, put matters this way just after electrified service was inaugurated between Broad Street and Paoli: "The suburban passenger train electrification of the Pennsylvania at Philadelphia is an application under complicated terminal conditions of an electric system which is designed to be adapted for future extension over long distance main lines and to then handle all classes of service."[89]

Gibbs had earlier suggested that electric MU cars, with their higher acceleration and braking rates, had the ability to annex additional territory to a metropolitan area's commutation zone. Using sixty minutes as a maximum tolerable one-way commuting time, Gibbs argued that a steam-powered train could be expected to cover only 24 start-and-stop miles in an hour, while electric MUs could easily manage 30.[90]

The mere improvement of Philadelphia suburban service could have been more than adequately handled by a conventional system of direct current electrification. The choice of alternating current by Gibbs and Company was a clear tip-off that, like the New Haven in 1907, the Pennsylvania Railroad had its eye on a much larger prize. Speculation in the railway trade press suggested that the PRR had designs on extending the new electrification westward in the years ahead so that powerful electric locomotives could replace steam on the company's busy main line across the Allegheny Mountains.[91]

The initial phase of the AC electrification effort was far more modest, though, and for its newly electrified Philadelphia-Paoli segment, the Pennsylvania sent eighty-two of its P-54 passenger coaches, along with eight baggage-coach combination cars and two baggage-mail cars, to its own Altoona Shops, where they were equipped for MU service. The eighty-two coaches were identified as the MP-54-E1 class, the baggage-coach combines were designated the MPB-54-E1 class, and the baggage-mail cars became the MBM-62-E1. (Baggage-mail cars had a different interior design, and hence their interior measurement was 62 feet.)

Each car was equipped with one power truck and one trailer, two 168-KW Westinghouse single-phase repulsion-starting motors provided tractive effort, and a single pantograph was mounted on the motor end of the car to draw current from the catenary. Catenary voltage was stepped down to an 850-volt maximum by an on-board transformer, the cooling vents for which were visible on one side of the car, and Pennsy technicians were convinced that the use of 25-cycle, single-phase alternating current in conjunction with series-wound alternating current motors was an effective substitute for the muscle and reliability of DC motors in the kind of service the new MU cars would operate.[92] Horsepower was listed as 400 per car, acceleration was 1.6 feet per second/per second up to 30 miles per hour, top speed was 60 miles per hour, and MP-54 cars were equipped with electropneumatic brakes. Basic brake action continued to be effected by air pressure, but "brake pipe reduction is made on each car by means of electric control instead of being made entirely with the engineer's brake valve," as reported in the *Electric Railway Journal.*[93] Adding electric control to an otherwise pneumatic system of braking hastens braking action, a desirable feature in start-and-stop suburban service.

The basic body design of the P-54 was simplicity itself, although two distinctive touches gave the MP-54 a jaunty look all its own. One was the fact that the cars were fitted with round, porthole-like windows in their end bulkheads to give engineers a view of the upcoming right-of-way, a feature that has encouraged some to describe the cars as "owl-like." The second distinctive feature was a large, boxy headlight enclosure that was set into the end slope of the roof monitor as cars were rigged for electrified service. Initially, this headlight was small and undistinctive, but within a decade or so of the first cars' entering service, a larger design was developed and retrofitted to older cars.

The engineer's operating station for a train of MP-54 cars was located on the front vestibule of the lead car, as was the case on all railroad MU cars of the era save the New Haven's open-platform cars, where the operating cab was built inside the car body. The controller handle pivoted at the bottom and operated through a vertical arc. It was notched to the right to go forward, left to go backward, with off being at dead center. At first, PRR operated its MP-54 cars in trains of three to seven cars, but this was soon increased to ten. Company technicians felt that longer trains were possible, but voltage drop in the 32-volt DC control circuits made a ten-car maximum a prudent practice. In later years this was revised upward—or possibly just ignored—and twelve-car trains were not uncommon.[94]

At 5:55 A.M. on the morning of September 11, 1915, a train of new MP-54 cars, with engineer W. J. McClintock in the cab of the lead car, departed Paoli for Broad Street Station in downtown Philadelphia, and before the day was over, the same train had made four round-trips over the newly electrified line.[95] Additional trains of MP-54 cars were added to the timetable in the weeks and months following the inaugural, and so successful was this initial deployment that the railroad soon expanded its AC electrification to other suburban points in metropolitan Philadelphia—and increased the size of its MP-54 fleet accordingly. The first post-Paoli expansion was put in service in early 1918, when electric service was inaugurated over a branch line to the important Philadelphia suburb of Chestnut Hill.[96] Over the next decade, AC wires were extended outward from Philadelphia to Whitemarsh in 1924, to both West Chester and to Wilmington, Delaware, in 1924, to Norristown and to Trenton, New Jersey, in 1933.

One interesting betterment that PRR developed as part of its AC electrification project was an entirely new and different form of railway block and interlocking signals, the all-important wayside indications that inform engineers about the conditions on the right-of-way up ahead. Because the rails would be used as the return, or "ground," for the high-voltage AC electrification, and because low-voltage signal circuits are also transmitted through the rails, a new signal system that would be compatible with the electrification was required. In typical Pennsy fashion, the railroad first tested and then deployed on a large scale a unique signal system whose aspects were displayed not by old-fashioned semaphores and not even by green-yellow-red signal lights; PRR designed a new system that used rows of amber-colored lights to advise approaching trains of track conditions ahead. In imitation of older semaphore signals, lights displayed in a vertical fashion were the equivalent of a "green" signal, lights displayed horizontally were the same as a "red" signal, and lights displayed on a 45-degree angle became the PRR version of a "yellow" or "approach" indication.

The new signals were originally called "beam lights," and

early deployments featured four lights in a row. They would later be known as position-light signals, three lights in a row would prove to be adequate, and they quickly became yet another PRR signature design as they guarded the railroad's main lines from New York to Washington, Chicago, and Saint Louis. The interesting historical relationship is that PRR initially deployed such position-light signals on the Philadelphia-Paoli Line coincident with the introduction of MP-54 MU cars into revenue service.[97]

As the railroad's AC electrification expanded outward from Philadelphia, it began to assume a much larger dimension than a source of traction power for purely suburban trains. Somewhat surprisingly, though, as the catenary expanded to become a source of traction power for intercity trains, the principal direction of its growth was not westward toward and over the mountains, but north and south along what would later be called the Northeast Corridor. The AC electrification was eventually extended as far west as Harrisburg, slightly over 100 miles from Broad Street Terminal, but the rugged mountain grades where electrification might have proved useful were further west than Harrisburg.

The Pennsylvania Railroad made this policy change in late 1928 because it recognized that electrification was the proper solution to the steadily increasing traffic levels it was experiencing on its north-south line between New York and Washington.[98] On January 16, 1933, PRR train No. 207 eased away from its assigned platform at New York's Penn Station, slipped into the Hudson River Tunnel, and continued all the way to Broad Street Terminal in Philadelphia—without a change of engines at Manhattan Transfer. The AC catenary now linked New York and Philadelphia, and while new electric locomotives would handle the railroad's intercity trains, the PRR's expanding fleet of MP-54 cars could now be deployed in suburban service out of New York as well as Philadelphia. In fact, in stringing catenary along its main line, PRR spared no expense and electrified seemingly minor branch lines and sidings. The old Pennsylvania riverside terminal at Exchange Place in Jersey City, for instance, was included in the electrified network, and until it was abandoned outright around 1960, a common sight along its platforms during the day were long lines of MP-54 cars awaiting the evening rush hour and assignments to South Amboy, to Trenton, and to other intermediate points, taking commuters home from work.

The MP-54s worked virtually everywhere Pennsy's AC catenary went. They served the railroad's many electrified branch lines in Philadelphia; they provided service between Philadelphia and Harrisburg; they operated commuter service into Washington, D.C., from points as far away as Baltimore; and they served points in Northern New Jersey from both Penn Station and Exchange Place. Indeed to keep its main line fluid during the extraordinary press of wartime traffic, the Pennsylvania often used trains of MP-54 cars to supplement locomotive-hauled trains in intercity service between Philadelphia and New York.

But the MP-54 was most at home in short-haul suburban work. A common experience aboard a fast-moving PRR train bound from New York to Philadelphia was to notice increasingly larger groups of passengers waiting on the New York–bound platform of successive suburban stations. Eventually one would pass a train of MP-54s out of Trenton bound for Penn Station and ready to take the waiting passengers onboard. And no sooner would one's Philadelphia-bound train pass the local than the sequence of waiting passengers would begin again on the various New York–bound platforms.

Following the Second World War, the MP-54s kept rolling along, although their age was beginning to show. Pennsy was hardly the robust corporation of days gone by and could not afford major fleet replacement in the days before governmental subsidies became available for commuter services. On the other hand, the company did not remain static. Between 1950 and 1952, forty-nine unpowered P-54 coaches and fifty-one older MP-54 MU cars were given an extensive rebuilding, emerged as the final class of "new" cars to join the MP-54 fleet, and were designated the E5 and E6 subclasses. These postwar cars were equipped with four motors rather than two, while on some of the rebuilds, liquid-cooled transformers replaced the air-blast originals. Such betterments as air-conditioning, roller-bearing trucks, leather upholstery, and aluminum sash in lieu of deteriorating wooden frames were added to the fleet on a more or less random basis and as finances permitted.

In the 1930s, a subclass of semipermanently coupled motor-trailer sets had been added to the fleet. Heftier motors on the power car of such a combination raised the horsepower from the original 400 to 725, and since two-car sets shared certain components, they were another example of the "married-pair" concept that would later become popular in transit circles. Despite such betterments and changes, it is correct to say that the basic appearance of the MP-54 changed but little over a span of sixty years. Their paint scheme was simple, but classic PRR: car bodies in basic Tuscan red, "PENNSYLVANIA" in gold leaf along the letter board, but no gold striping or other frills such as the railroad typically applied to its long-distance passenger cars. In their final PRR years, MP-54s featured a more austere livery—solid Tuscan red decorated only with a red-and-white PRR "keystone" emblem adjacent to each door. Following the creation of Penn Central in 1968, some cars were repainted Penn Central green and decorated with that road's rather unfortunate logo, but that is a phase of the MP-54s aesthetic history that is best passed over lightly.[99]

Pennsy workers liked the MP-54, although not without qualification. The drafty vestibule cabs were not the last word in comfort, especially on cold days, and some felt the motor-trailer sets could have used heftier air compressors. A veteran PRR engineer, who would later hold down an assignment on a fast Metroliner schedule between Washington and New York, remembered the MP-54 this way: "If you had a two-car train of red cars, the four-motor jobs, and a light, mid-day load, you could get it up to 90 with no trouble."[100]

While it lacked postwar cash for wholesale car replacement, PRR did acquire six Budd-built Pioneer III MU cars in 1958 for experimental suburban service in the Philadelphia area. These 85-footers weighted 89,000 pounds empty, a good 20 tons less than an average 64-foot MP-54.[101] They could accelerate at 2 feet per second/per second, had a nominal top speed of 90 miles per hour, and their success paved the way for a thirty-eight-car order with Budd in 1963, placed not by the railroad but by the city of Philadelphia through something called the Passenger Service Improvement Corporation (PSIC). It was one of the first instances of public money being used to improve a U.S. commuter railroad service, and PSIC actually acquired fifty-five new MU cars from Budd at a total cost of $13.7 million—or $249,000 per car. The other seventeen cars were assigned to the Reading Company's electrified lines out of Philadelphia. The new Silver-liners, as they were called, were about 5 tons a car heavier than the experimental Pioneer IIIs, had a 600-to-400 horsepower edge on the six experimental units, and featured an automatic coupler with integral air and electrical connections.[102]

Both the Pioneer IIIs and the Silverliners were subclasses of what the Pennsylvania designated its MP-85 fleet.[103] Like the New Haven's postwar MU cars of 1954, which were popularly called "washboards," Pennsy's MP-85s were equipped with DC traction motors and onboard equipment to convert AC current into DC.

In 1967, Philadelphia bought twenty additional Silverliners to increase the PRR fleet of MP-85s to sixty-four. GSI–Saint Louis, and not Budd, was awarded this contract and the cars are distinctive in that the engineer's control station is located on the left side of the car to enable an additional door to be used by commuters when boarding or alighting from conventional "right-hand" platforms. Then, in August of 1968, the first two cars of a $9.9-million, twenty-five-unit order were delivered for service into Penn Station from points in northern New Jersey. The firm of Louis T. Klauder and Associates developed specifications, and the cars were owned by the state of New Jersey and leased to the railroad. Much understandable hoopla surrounded the delivery of the initial cars, including a $500 prize for naming the new design the Jersey Arrow. On a press run out of Trenton on September 11, 1968, a train of the new cars effortlessly hit 100 miles per hour. Two Jersey Arrows were hauled around the state by a locomotive to barnstorm for voter support in an upcoming transit bonds referendum. Jersey Arrow No. 107 ventured even further afield. On January 11, 1969, it raised its pantograph on a new industrial railroad in southeastern Ohio called the Muskingum Electric Railway and ran a series of tests on that line's 25,000-volt, 60-cycle, single-phase AC system.

The 85-foot Jersey Arrows were also classified as MP-85 units; their most unusual visible feature was a sliding door in the very center of each car. Unlike the MTA's M-class equipment, the Jersey Arrows featured conventional end vestibules with traps and steps, and these were the ordinary means of passenger entry and exit. The sliding center doors were included to speed boarding at especially busy stations, such as Penn Station and Newark. Since the center doors lacked steps and a trap, they could be used only at high-level platforms.[104]

The year 1971 saw additional contracts executed for new MU cars. Philadelphia and the state of New Jersey joined forces and signed a contract for 214 new MUs from General Electric. Of the total, 130 cars were assigned to ex-PRR lines around Philadelphia, and these included both single-unit cars as well as semipermanently coupled two-car sets. Fourteen single units went into Reading's Philadelphia service, while the remaining seventy cars joined the Jersey Arrows running out of Penn Station—and were eventually dubbed the Jersey Arrow II fleet. The seventy New York cars included a center sliding door, while the Philadelphia cars did not, although the design of the Philadelphia car, both inside and out, is such that one can easily discern where such a door would have been positioned—and presumably could be retrofitted. The Jersey Arrow II fleet was delivered during 1974 and 1975.[105]

Even before GE had completed this order, the state of New Jersey contracted for an additional 230 cars. These were eventually dubbed the Jersey Arrow III fleet; they were delivered in 1978. Taken together, all three classes of Jersey Arrow cars totaled 335 units, far more than would ever have been required to replaced all the ex-PRR MP-54s needed to meet suburban assignments out of New York's Penn Station.

Something else was happening to require such an expanded fleet. Just as the MTA initially subsidized and provided new equipment for commuter services originally operated by the New York Central and the New Haven and eventually assumed combined operational responsibility for these lines, a similar story of public takeover and consolidation was playing itself out in New Jersey.

The Delaware, Lackawanna and Western Railroad (DL&W) had electrified a 70-mile network of suburban lines on its Morris and Essex Division in northern New Jersey in the early 1930s. Unlike the New York Central or the Pennsylvania, though, the Lackawanna did not operate into the City of New York. It terminated its trains across the Hudson River from Manhattan, in Hoboken, New Jersey, where passengers completed their journey into the city either by the rapid-transit trains of the Hudson Tubes or by ferryboat. DL&W selected neither low-voltage direct current like the New York Central nor high-voltage alternating current like the New Haven and the Pennsylvania for its electrification system. Its MU trains were powered instead by direct current at a potential of 3,000 volts delivered through overhead catenary.[106]

The Lackawanna merged with the Erie to form Erie-Lackawanna in 1960, Erie-Lackawanna was absorbed by Conrail in 1976, and as the state of New Jersey began to play a more active role in the governance of the area's commuter railroad services, some kind of unification of its various components seemed sensible. The ex-DL&W electrification network was in need of serious repair, but rather than rebuild it to its original specifications, the New Jersey Department of Transportation decided to convert the Lackawanna network into one that was compatible with the high-voltage AC electrification system used on the ex-PRR network, and the reason why New Jersey ordered such a large fleet of electric MU cars in 1978 was to have equipment available to operate over the ex-DL&W network once its conversion to alternating current was complete.[107]

Because DL&W's electrified Morris and Essex Division runs parallel to the ex-PRR main line for a mile or so in the Jersey Meadows adjacent to the site of Manhattan Transfer, New Jersey Transit (NJT)—the public agency that eventually emerged to operate the area's unified mass-transport services, including the commuter railroads—designed and built a set of ramps and connecting tracks so that electric trains from the ex-DL&W system can now operate into and out of Penn Station in Manhattan via the ex-PRR Hudson River tunnels. NJT coined the service name Midtown Direct for trains that use the new connection, and then, in September 2002, the formerly stub-end Montclair Branch of what was once the DL&W's Morris and Essex Division was connected to a nearby ex-Erie line, and electrified service now operates an additional 5 miles into bedroom communities of Northern New Jersey.

It was the Jersey Arrow II fleet—ordered in 1971 and delivered in 1974 and 1975—that permitted the final MP-54s still operating in the New York area to be retired. Some MP-54s continued to operate in the Philadelphia area after 1975, and a small contingent of cars ran in commuter service between Washington and Baltimore until 1980, perhaps later. Documentation is a bit weak as to when the final MP-54 operated in revenue service—it was undoubtedly sometime during the early 1980s—but eventually all of the old cars were retired. The Pennsylvania State Railroad Museum in Strasburg acquired car No. 607 for preservation. It was one of the PRR's earliest MU cars from the MP-54-E1 class. Its onboard transformer was liquid-cooled, however, and this has proven to be an environmental hazard. Until specialists in "moon suits" can remove all the contaminants and scrub the car clean, its restoration has been put on hold, and the car rests in isolation on the museum grounds.

As a technical matter, the MP-54 designation was formally dropped several years before the last MP-54 car was retired from active service. In the early 1970s, Penn Central reclassified its MU equipment, and the ex-PRR sixty-five-footers were placed into various subclasses of the MA-9 grouping. The MP-85 designation was dropped as well, and the newer MU cars were known as the MA-1 fleet.

A final point is that in the early years of the twenty-first century, NJ Transit is placing less reliance on MU cars for its suburban electrified service than PRR and DL&W once did. NJT's newest rolling stock under the wires involves conventional passenger cars hauled by electric locomotives but capable of operating in either direction. In a technique called "push-pull" service, the locomotive remains coupled to one end of the train, but the engineer is able to operate the train from either end—in the locomotive when traveling in one direction, in an MU-like cab in the end vestibule of the rear car when traveling in the opposite direction. NJT has even converted many of its Jersey Arrow I cars into such control cars for push-pull service. The Jersey Arrow II fleet has been retired, leaving the 270 Jersey Arrow III units as the sole electric MU cars carrying on the MP-54 tradition.

MUs on the LIRR

Although the MP-54 electric MU car was designed by the Pennsylvania Railroad and became a long-term fixture in suburban service throughout Pennsy's electrified territory, there was another railroad whose fleet of MP-54 cars included almost three times as many units as the PRR's. This was the Long Island Rail Road, a sometime subsidiary of the Pennsylvania that adopted—and adapted—the parent railroad's P-54 suburban coach design for use in its own third-rail electrified zone.[108]

The Pennsylvania Railroad acquired a controlling interest in the LIRR in 1900, a transaction that took the railroad industry rather by surprise. "The railroad sensation of the week has been the acquisition by the Pennsylvania of the control of the Long Island," the *Railroad Gazette* reported.[109] There was immediate speculation about the reasons for Pennsy's action, although it was quickly realized that it must have something to do with PRR's plans for bringing its trains into the City of New York.[110] And indeed so it was; the Pennsylvania was completing plans for a major new Manhattan terminal that would include tunnels under both the Hudson River and the East River, with a large storage and servicing yard for its passenger equipment in Long Island City, adjacent to the Long Island's right-of-way. Bringing LIRR under the Pennsylvania's control facilitated the latter's design of its New York terminal, and also looked to the future, when PRR and the New Haven would coordinate in the construction of the Hell Gate Bridge to establish a through-route between New England and points beyond New York along the Pennsy. In addition, apart from practical issues associated with the development of its New York terminal, the Pennsylvania was still in an expansionist mode in 1900, and the Long Island Rail Road seemed like a useful addition to its overall rail empire.

Prior to the advent of Penn Station and the river tunnels, the Long Island's principal western terminal was on the bank of the East River, in Long Island City. Here LIRR passengers boarded ferryboats and continued across the East River to Manhattan. Once acquired by the PRR in 1900, LIRR would be afforded access to the new Penn Station in Manhattan when it opened in 1910—we shall learn more about such developments below.

LIRR had an alternative western terminal to its principal facility in Long Island City. Its trains also served central Brooklyn on a right-of-way along Atlantic Avenue with a depot at Flatbush and Atlantic Avenues. (Recall from Chapter 1 that in 1908 the Interborough Rapid Transit Company's initial subway into

Brooklyn also terminated at Flatbush and Atlantic and provided connections into Manhattan for LIRR passengers.)

Plans and proposals had been moving forward in Brooklyn since at least 1896 to improve the LIRR's line into Brooklyn by replacing its at-grade Atlantic Avenue right-of-way with a subway; both the railroad and the municipal government intended to invest money in the project.[111] Such planning predated the Pennsylvania's acquisition of a controlling interest in the Long Island in 1900 and even included the prospect of LIRR trains continuing into Lower Manhattan through a proposed East River tunnel. On October 8, 1897, for instance, LIRR president William H. Baldwin returned to New York from Europe aboard the steamship *Saint Louis* where he had "inspected tunnels and underground railways with a view to the proposed building of the Atlantic Avenue subway and the East River tunnel."[112]

Just prior to the formal announcement of the Pennsylvania's acquisition of the Long Island, the LIRR declared that it was backing away from any idea of building its own East River tunnel.[113] Negotiations continued on the Atlantic Avenue portion of the project, and because of all the political pulling and hauling that was necessary for multiple parties to reach agreement on so complex a piece of business, construction did not begin until late 1901, shortly after the PRR entered the picture. While the PRR agreed that the Atlantic Avenue betterment was important and should move forward, the fact remains that momentum for building an Atlantic Avenue Subway predates the Pennsylvania Railroad's acquisition of the Long Island Rail Road.

The project that began in 1901 called for a two-track tunnel for LIRR trains from Flatbush Avenue to Bedford Avenue, a distance of 1.3 miles, and a new underground terminal at Flatbush and Atlantic. Between Bedford Avenue and Ralph Avenue, a distance of 1.5 miles, the previous at-grade line would be replaced by an elevated structure, while another tunnel, this one a little over ½ mile in length, extended from Ralph Avenue to, roughly, East New York. Another elevated section continued a mile or so beyond East New York to Atkins Avenue, while the LIRR right-of-way remained at-grade between here and Jamaica, Queens. (In 1939 construction began on a grade-separation project that built a further subway under Atlantic Avenue between East New York and a point just west of Lefferts Boulevard, replacing the East-New-York-to-Atkins-Avenue elevated segment and ending all at-grade operation on the Brooklyn-Jamaica Line. The original elevated segment between Bedford Avenue and Ralph Avenue remains very much in active service in the early years of the twenty-first century.)

As plans were perfected for placing LIRR trains in a tunnel beneath Brooklyn's Atlantic Avenue, electrification was necessarily part of the project. Because most Long Island trains operated a relatively short-haul suburban service, it was thought wise to electrify entire branch lines and use MU electric cars from one terminal to another. As the *Street Railway Journal* pointed out in 1905: "it was obviously impossible to adopt an electrification plan which contemplated electric haulage for part of the journey and steam haulage for the remainder."[114]

The Atlantic Avenue project included the electrification of a defined network of LIRR branch lines that essentially extended south of the Atlantic Avenue corridor. Looming on the horizon as work on the LIRR's first electrified district began, of course, was the matter of Penn Station and a substantial expansion of the railroad's electrified operations. But the initial phase of the railroad's electrification has a discreet identity and includes some interesting and distinctive features, even though it led seamlessly into a much larger electrification effort.

Because of a cordial working relationship between the LIRR and the Interborough, it was planned to incorporate track connections between the railroad and the subway at Flatbush and Atlantic Avenues, and this would require, among other things, a compatible system of electrification. So LIRR adopted a system of 650-volt DC distributed by trackside third rail that would facilitate such through-service. Some elements of a track connection between the two lines were in fact put in place at Flatbush and Atlantic, and those who enjoy industrial archeology can even detect, almost a century after it was built, the alignment the connection would have followed.[115] But no revenue passenger service ever operated between the LIRR and the Interborough, although legends continue to persist that the Interborough's president, August Belmont, Jr., traveled from one system to the other in the company's private subway car, a unique piece of rolling stock that bore the name *Mineola.*

In 1898, the LIRR had begun operating joint service over certain elevated lines of the Brooklyn Rapid Transit Company (BRT) using steam-powered trains. Its choice of low-voltage DC third rail for its electrification permitted these joint LIRR-BRT services to continue during the early years of the electric era.[116]

To supply current for the new LIRR electrification network, a generating station was built on the banks of the East River in Long Island City, a facility whose location was largely dictated by the fact that it would later be used to supply current for Penn Station and the Pennsylvania's new line out to Manhattan Transfer. (In this one respect, the LIRR's initial electrified network was not a discreet and stand-alone effort and has to be seen in conjunction with later developments involving the Pennsylvania.) Indeed, one may correctly call the Long Island City powerhouse a PRR, and not an LIRR, facility. Curiously, though, it would prove to be the only railroad-owned generating station to supply traction power to the Pennsy. As discussed above, when the PRR began to expand its electrification with an AC system out of Philadelphia some years later, it relied on commercially produced electric power. In any event, because "the Long Island electrification forms a part of the general scheme for the operation of the Pennsylvania Railroad terminal," the generating station that supplied current for the LIRR's initial electrified network was not located at the "center of gravity" of the initial system but in a spot that looked ahead to future developments.[117]

The generating station was initially equipped with three steam turbine engines and it generated three-phase alternating current at a potential of 11,000 volts. This was transmitted throughout the LIRR electric zone and both stepped down and converted into direct current at five substations, then fed into the third rail. The largest of the substations was equipped with three 1,500-killowatt rotary converters, the smallest with two 1,000-killowatt units. In addition to the five permanent substations—one at Grand and Atlantic Avenues in Brooklyn, others at East New York, Woodhaven Junction, Hammel and Rockaway Junction—LIRR had two portable substations in rail cars, each equipped with a single 1,000-killowatt rotary converter, which could be moved to any point where additional current capacity was required.[118] Various Long Island racetracks, with their seasonal services, were places where the portable units were frequently deployed.

The LIRR's initial third-rail district extended eastward from Brooklyn along Atlantic Avenue, through the road's critical transfer station in Jamaica where passengers could change to and from Long Island City trains, and all the way to a terminal station just off the main line on the grounds of Belmont Park Racetrack in suburban Nassau County, 14.5 miles from Flatbush and Atlantic.[119] In addition, a line was also electrified that veered southward from the Brooklyn-Jamaica Line along Atlantic Avenue in western Queens county at a place called Woodhaven Junction and crossed Jamaica Bay to Rockaway Beach on a long wooden trestle. Likewise included in the LIRR's first phase of electrification were two separate lines between Jamaica and Valley Stream— one via Laurelton that was known as the Atlantic Branch, another via Saint Albans that was called the Montauk Branch—as well a line that doubled back from Valley Stream, served the Rockaway peninsula from the east, and joined up with the Woodhaven-Rockaway Line in Rockaway Beach. This first phase of LIRR electrification included 35 one-way route miles, but because of the multitrack nature of the LIRR, the effort involved installing a third rail along 95 miles of track. It was by all standards the largest railway electrification effort in the United States.

The first trial trip over the new electric network took place on July 18, 1905, and it was a modest enough achievement—two round-trips along Atlantic Avenue between Woodhaven Junction and Flatbush Avenue. There were some untoward incidents when the railroad first energized the third rail along its ground-level right-of-way. The *New York Times* reported that when "the current was turned on there were leaks at several crossings," and a horse that was hauling a wagon across the tracks at Shaw Avenue was electrocuted, while another received such a jolt that it bolted and ran away. "Sparks shot from the rails on which the trains run, which are not supposed to be charged," the *Times* also reported.[120] Because the running rails serve as a ground to complete an electrical circuit back to the powerhouse, it is quite normal for a few sparks to jump between wheels and rails until usage develops smooth contact between the two. In no sense, though, does this mean that the running rails are "charged," as the *Times* suggested.

The matter of grade crossings in an electrified zone equipped with a ground-level third rail was rather novel in the New York area. The Interborough Subway had no grade crossings at all, while electrified elevated trains of the BRT switched from third-rail current collection to overhead trolley wire when they descended from elevated rights-of-way and operated at ground level. To this very day, though, LIRR lines that operate electric-powered trains feature scores of grade crossings throughout Nassau and Suffolk counties, where a live third rail is mere feet away from sidewalks that people use to cross the tracks.

There was one segment of the LIRR that was intended to be included in the 1905 electrification effort but ultimately was not—although stories in the trade press at the time made it sound as if it had been. This was a cutoff between Laurelton and Cedarhurst that had been removed from service some years earlier as the LIRR absorbed previously separate railroads into a unified system and eliminated redundant mileage.[121] Restoring and electrifying this line might have shortened the running time to places like Far Rockaway, but for a variety of reasons, service along the cutoff was never restored.

If anything serves as a distinctive characteristic of this first phase of electrification on the Long Island Rail Road, it is the fleet of MU cars that the railroad purchased to inaugurate electrified service. LIRR's electrification would later be identified with its extensive fleet of PRR-designed MP-54 cars, including some variations on the Pennsy design that were unique to the Long Island. But when the first LIRR electric train to carry revenue passengers left Rockaway Park for Flatbush and Atlantic Avenues at 7:55 A.M. on Wednesday, July 26, 1905—a week and a day after the first trial trip between Woodhaven Junction and Flatbush Avenue—save for its Tuscan red paint, the seven-car train bore no visual similarity whatsoever to any Pennsylvania passenger equipment. It was composed of cars, though, that many New Yorkers would quickly have recognized.

The first MU electric cars to run on the Long Island Rail Road were look-alike copies of the all-steel Gibbs Cars that began carrying passengers on the Interborough Subway ten months earlier on September 27, 1904. LIRR acquired a fleet of 134 such steel cars from American Car and Foundry—the same company that had turned out the Interborough's own Gibbs Cars—although a few adaptations were necessary for the unique demands of suburban railroad service. Roof-mounted headlights were added to each end of each car, as one instance, and a makeshift set of steps and traps were fitted at the entry doors, since most LIRR stations featured track-level platforms. Another piece of equipment the LIRR cars required, but the Interborough felt comfortable without, was a metal pilot below the coupler to ensure that no debris along the right-of-way would damage the electrical equipment mounted under the car. One article in the trade press claimed the LIRR cars also differed from Interborough specifications in their use of railroad couplers, rather than transit-style Van Dorn couplers like the Interborough cars. Indeed the article even included a photograph of LIRR car No. 1001 clearly sporting a railroad-style MCB coupler.

The photograph is misleading, though, and for all of their LIRR days the Gibbs Cars used transit-style couplers—or drawbars, as they are more often called in transit circles. The railroad coupler on Car No. 1001 in the 1905 photograph was undoubtedly a temporary arrangement to facilitate the car's delivery by rail from ACF's Berwick plant to Long Island.[122]

Otherwise, though, LIRR and Interborough cars were quite similar, and well they might be, since the railroad and the transit company were thinking seriously about joint operations from one system to the other. Seating arrangements were identical, as was electrical equipment. (The Interborough divided its order for electrical gear between General Electric and Westinghouse, though, while LIRR specified Westinghouse equipment exclusively.) George Gibbs, who designed the original Interborough cars, was also retained by the LIRR so his design could be adapted. Because the 50-foot Gibbs Cars measured 41 feet between their interior bulkheads, they were identified on the Pennsy-owned LIRR as MP-41 units.

LIRR signed a contract with ACF on January 20, 1905. ACF completed all aspects of the cars, except the installation of their electrical equipment, at its Berwick, Pennsylvania, factory and then shipped the cars to a temporary LIRR facility just beyond Jamaica and adjacent to what was then called the Metropolitan Racetrack for the installation of motors and control apparatus. (The Metropolitan track no longer exists, but in later years it would be known as the Jamaica Racetrack.) The first new steel car body arrived on LIRR property in early April of 1905, a fully outfitted car was exhibited in Washington, D.C., in May of that year at the International Railway Congress, and all cars were delivered by mid-August.[123]

LIRR was even able to expand the fleet of passenger cars it could use in electrified service beyond the 134 MP-41s by rigging 100 older open-platform cars to run as trailers between a pair of the new, steel, motorized units. LIRR owned a number of essentially el cars that were used in joint service over the BRT elevated system behind small steam locomotives, and it was these wooden cars that were converted into MU trailers. LIRR abandoned the practice of operating steel Gibbs Cars in trains with wooden open-platform el cars in 1915, but the MP-41s themselves enjoyed a lengthy service life, albeit in rather restricted services.[124] The Gibbs Cars were never regularly assigned to Penn Station-bound schedules, for instance, and they more or less spent their days serving the network of lines that constituted the railroad's original electrified district—eastward out of the Flatbush and Atlantic terminal in Brooklyn and then onto various branch lines that headed south of the Atlantic Avenue corridor.

Once the larger MP-54s became common on the LIRR, the narrower Gibbs Cars were fitted with new traps that effectively bridged the gap between the cars and high-level platforms built to accommodate wider rolling stock. What was likely the final regular assignment worked by MP-41 cars was a shuttle service between Mitchell Field and Country Life Press that was operated as a branch of the Hempstead Line, and the last units of the LIRR's Gibbs Car fleet were not retired until the mid-1950s—at just about the same time as the last of the Interborough's Gibbs Cars were retired from IRT service.

The first MP-54s that saw electric service on the LIRR joined the roster in 1910, just prior to the inauguration of service through the new East River tunnels into Penn Station, and the railroad would never acquire any additional Gibbs Cars beyond its initial order of 134 units. On the outside, LIRR's MP-54 cars looked rather like the cars that would later run to Paoli, Chestnut Hill, and Trenton for the Pennsylvania, save for the absence of both a roof-mounted pantograph and cooling vents along the side. LIRR MP-54s were also delivered with a much smaller headlight than the cars used on the parent road, but over the years LIRR retrofitted its fleet with the distinctive large boxy headlight housing that became such an important aspect of the car's profile. (Even LIRR's MP-41s were eventually equipped with large, MP-54-style headlights.) Like the earlier MP-41s, the Long Island's first MP-54 units were built by ACF.

And so MP-54 MU cars became a fixture in the Long Island's third-rail zone six years before the first PRR MU cars began running out of Broad Street Station in Philadelphia.[125] The LIRR would put a distinctive imprint on the basic MP-54 design by the development of an arch-roof variation on the P-54s railroad-roof profile.

This arch-roof variation on the MP-54 design, with five unusual box-style ventilators mounted along the centerline of the roof, became a distinctive characteristic of the LIRR's third-rail service for almost half a century. What is not generally known, however, is why the Long Island ever made such a change in the PRR's original design standard, especially since the Long Island was a subsidiary of the Pennsylvania when this variation was developed, and the parent railroad's engineering standards were not something a subsidiary would change without compelling justification.

In the early days of electric operation, LIRR saw much heavier traffic on many of its important branch lines during the warm weather months of summer than at other times of the year, as passengers flocked to beaches and racetracks. Consists of MU trains had to be expanded to meet such seasonal demand, but the railroad had no desire to invest in conventional MP-54 cars that would only see service carrying beachgoers to the Rockaways during June, July, and August. The compromise was to design a more economical car that could operate as a trailer unit between conventional MP-54 motorized cars, would be the equivalent of

an MP-54 in external dimensions, and yet, because it would operate only during warm weather, could forego the expense of such
things as insulation and heating apparatus. Additional cost and
weight savings could also be achieved by substituting a simple
arch roof fabricated out of sheet metal for the more complex
railroad-style roof specified in the design of the basic P-54 suburban coach.[126]

And so the first arch-roof cars were twenty motorless trailer
units that the LIRR acquired from the Standard Steel Car Company in 1915 for service during warm-weather months only. In
something of a variation on basic PRR notation, the LIRR classified the new cars as T-54 units. (A motorless trailer car used in
MU service on the PRR was designated an MP-54T.) A typical
MP-54 motor car on the Long Island weighed 110,000 pounds,
while the motorless T-54 arch-roof trailers tipped the scales at a
mere 63,000 pounds, a trifle over half the weight of the heavier
units. By 1917 the T-54 fleet totaled ninety units, with both Standard Steel and Pressed Steel producing such cars.

As the LIRR MU fleet continued to expand during the 1920s,
the railroad acquired arch-roof cars that were motorized units
equipped with heating apparatus and insulation for year-round
service.[127] Interestingly, until the very last MP-54 joined the roster in 1930, LIRR was ordering both arch-roof and monitor-roof
versions of the famous car, and the very last MP-54 the road
acquired was a monitor-roof car.

The principal visual difference between a motorized arch-roof
unit and a more conventional monitor-roof car was most apparent
when the car was viewed head-on. With a monitor-roof car, the
roof itself curved gently down at the end of the car and the headlight was (eventually) a large, boxy unit that extended out from
the slope of the roof, just as it did on PRR MP-54 units. The roof
on an LIRR arch-roof MP-54 had no slope at all and was dead
level from one end of the car to the other, and the headlight was
completely recessed into the bulkhead immediately above the
end door.

Arch-roof cars were intermixed with their monitor-roof running mates quite indiscriminately by the LIRR in day-to-day operations, but the railroad understood that the arch-roof variation
was a distinctive piece of equipment on a railroad that was other-

wise dominated by PRR standards, designs, and even colors. When a civic ceremony was held on May 20, 1925, in Babylon to mark the extension of electrified service to that South Shore community—it was the only expansion of third-rail service into Suffolk County until the MTA era almost a half-century later— the railroad took pains to ensure that the first ceremonial MU train to reach Babylon was composed of none but its distinctive arch-roof cars.[128]

The LIRR roster also included an extensive fleet of P-54 passenger cars for service behind steam locomotives on its several nonelectrified lines. Like the MU fleet, these included both monitor-roof and arch-roof versions. In a usage whose origin resists explanation, rail buffs commonly refer to LIRR's distinctive arch-roof fleet—trailers as well as MUs—as "ping-pong" cars. Like the New York Central, the New Haven, and the Interborough Rapid Transit Company, the Long Island was prone to converting cars from one configuration to another—from motorized MU car to MU trailer and then, perhaps, to non-MU car for use outside the electrified district.

In 1932—a mere two years after the LIRR took delivery of what turned out to be its final MP-54—the pilot model of a new and improved MU car design was developed for LIRR service. Designed and built in Altoona by the Pennsylvania Railroad, the new design was popularly referred to as a double-deck car, al-though this was a bit of a misnomer. The new car was in fact a single-deck car that featured overlapping sets of passenger seats on either side of a center aisle, with some seats two steps up from the aisle, others one step down. Seated passengers rode on two different levels, but the new LIRR car was more "split-level" than "double-decker." The first such car, No. 200, was a motor-less MU trailer 72 feet in length which could accommodate 120 seated passengers—compared to seventy-five on the average MP-54. Because passengers faced each other on permanently fixed seats, the New York Times reported that the "seating arrangement is similar to that of a Pullman car."[129] LIRR revenue passengers had a chance to ride aboard No. 200 for the first time on Saturday, August 13, 1932, when the new car was coupled into a train that made two round-trips between Penn Station and Port Washington and one between Penn Station and Babylon.

A second trailer unit, No. 201, arrived on the property from Altoona in 1937, along with a motorized companion car, No. 1347. Both of these were 80 feet long—8 feet longer than No. 200—and this would become the new standard for future LIRR "double-deckers." No. 200 and No. 1347 each had room for 136 seated passengers; the pair entered service in late December of 1937. The three prewar experimental cars were also distinctive in the extensive use of aluminum used in their construction, but wartime shortages and priorities postponed the construction of any additional cars until after VJ Day, when a fleet of sixty additional "double-deck" cars were built for Long Island service by the PRR. Classified as MP-70 units and delivered between 1947 and 1949, they were never terribly popular with either passengers or crews. True, they were LIRR's first MU cars to feature air-conditioning, but women passengers were said to feel uncomfortable using the upper-level seats for reasons of modesty, conductors disliked having to stick their heads into all sorts of nooks and crannies to collect tickets, car cleaners were supposedly the most dissatisfied, and many passengers disliked the forced companionship that face-to-face—and knee-to-knee—seating demanded. In addition, the requirement that all passengers had to navigate steps to move between seats and aisle made for delays in loading and unloading. Whether parent Pennsy ever thought about acquiring similar MP-70s for its own AC electrified lines is something of an unknown, but the fact remains that no such cars were ever built.[130]

The Long Island's "double-deckers" were designed to operate in multiple unit with the road's older MP-54 cars, and that made life a bit easier for LIRR personnel in charge of assembling train consists. But the MP-70s were not able to operate into Brooklyn because of tight clearances along this line, and this is something that offset other flexibilities. (One can only wonder what might have happened if, in the press of schedule disruptions on some unusually hectic day, an LIRR dispatcher had sent a train with MP-70 cars in its consist into the Atlantic Avenue Subway.)[131]

PRR delivered the final "double-deck" MP-70 to the LIRR in 1949. But placing a new MU car in service was hardly the most dramatic development the Long Island Rail Road would experience that year. In late February of 1949, Walter S. Franklin, a man who held the position of executive vice president with both the LIRR and the PRR, announced that the parent road would no longer honor drafts drawn by the Long Island to other railroads in payment of bills for hauling interline passenger and freight traffic. What this technical change meant, in Franklin's own words, was that the PRR's wholly owned subsidiary would have to "stand on its own feet for everything from now on." [132] Stated differently, the economic and fiscal foundation on which the Long Island Rail Road had rested since 1900 had been suddenly removed, since it was credit advanced by the Pennsylvania Railroad that had long been keeping the LIRR afloat. LIRR was said to have a total indebtedness in excess of $53 million in 1949, assets worth little more than $11 million, and a mere $60,000 in cash to pay its bills. Unlike other PRR subsidiaries that had been fully absorbed into the operations of the parent system, the LIRR's insular character gave it a decidedly separate—and separable—status.

The PRR took its action on Friday, February 25, 1949. Five days later, on Wednesday, March 2, Richard R. Bongartz, an attorney acting on behalf of the LIRR, filed a document in federal court in Brooklyn petitioning for a reorganization of the company under Section 77 of the bankruptcy laws. [133] Absent continued support from the Pennsylvania, the Long Island had no practical alternative but to seek protection from the courts. It was the third time the railroad had filed for bankruptcy, the previous instances being in 1850 and 1875.

Once receivership was granted, the LIRR attempted to establish a visual identity for itself that no longer emphasized its traditional ties with the PRR—even though the Pennsylvania was still very much the "owner" of the Long Island Rail Road and certainly held considerable amounts of LIRR debt. Furthermore, PRR cooperation would be singularly instrumental in the Long Island's eventual stabilization and survival. But appearances can be important, and on October 30, 1949, the trustees unveiled a new color scheme for the road, one that was about as far from Tuscan red as the visible spectrum allowed. Passenger cars would be painted in several shades of gray, with a dark-green underbody and dashes of bright red here and there. The first unit to be shown to the press in the new livery was, appropriately enough, an arch-roof MP-54 car, photographs of which ran in New York newspapers on October 31, 1949—Halloween.[134] LIRR gray would undergo a series of iterations over the next decade and a half, and light gray would morph into dark gray, but it would remain the railroad's basic livery during the interval between full PRR control and the advent of the MTA in the 1960s.

If 1949 was a year of fiscal crisis for the LIRR, the following year, 1950, was one of unspeakable tragedy. On February 17, LIRR train No. 192 left Penn Station bound for Babylon at 10:03 P.M. A half-hour later, train No. 175 left Babylon on a trip headed for Penn Station. Normally, the two trains would pass each other going in opposite directions—and on separate tracks—in the vicinity of Rockville Center. But LIRR operations in the Rockville Center area were not at all normal in February 1950. A major grade-separation project was under construction there, and a temporary gauntlet track had been installed which trains traveling in both direction had to transit. (A gauntlet means that tracks in two different directions share the same right-of-way and overlap. In terms of train dispatching, a gauntlet must be treated as if it were a single-track railroad.)

It was later determined that engineer Jacob Kiefer aboard the Babylon-bound train failed to observe a stop signal at the western end of the Rockville Center gauntlet. Because it had been given signal authorization to do so, westbound train No. 175 entered the gauntlet unaware of the danger it would soon encounter. At 10:43 P.M. the two trains collided head-on, and thirty-one people lost their lives in a disaster that the *New York Times* called the "worst in the history of the road."[135]

The Rockville Center disaster would be eclipsed in horror before the year was over. On Wednesday evening, November 22, 1950—the day before Thanksgiving—LIRR train No. 780 left Penn Station for Hempstead at 6:09 P.M., with a rush-hour crowd of 1,000 passengers aboard. Four minutes later, at 6:13 P.M., train No. 174 eased out of Penn Station bound for Babylon and carrying 1,200 passengers, including many standing. Both trains had ten-car consists, and both were scheduled to run nonstop to Jamaica; neither would ever get there.

Between 6:20 and 6:25, train No. 780 rolled up to a stop signal in Richmond Hill just east of the point where the right-of-way crosses Metropolitan Avenue. Delays were not uncommon at this point on the railroad—and they remain frequent to this day—since the busy complex of Jamaica Station is just ahead and the rush hour was at its height. Engineer William J. Murphy was working No. 780 that evening, and he was soon given a signal that authorized his continuing toward Jamaica. No sooner had he begun to notch out the controller and his train began to move, than a mechanical malfunction brought it to a sudden and unexpected stop. Moments later, at 6:26 P.M., train No. 174, with engineer B. J. Pokorny in the cab, plowed into the rear of No. 780. The lead car of No. 175, MP-54 No. 1523, telescoped into and under the rear car on train No. 780, MP-54 No. 1516, and the death toll that Thanksgiving evening was seventy-eight unfortunate souls, including engineer Pokorny. The *Times* had to find new language to characterize the LIRR's second tragedy of 1950 and called it the "grimmest disaster of its ill-starred career."[136] Taken together, the Rockville Center and the Richmond Hill collisions of 1950 claimed 109 lives.

If the notion of "hitting bottom" before serious recovery can ever begin has applicability in the world of commuter railroading, surely the LIRR "hit bottom" in 1949 and 1950, when a serious but probably manageable financial crisis was compounded by two horrible and altogether avoidable fatal accidents. There would be a "road back" for the railroad, though, one that involved a number of unusual twists and turns as the LIRR moved from Pennsy subsidiary to independent company and eventually became the nation's first publicly owned and publicly operated railroad under MTA auspices in 1966.

The state of New York would play an important role in stabilizing the LIRR. A special-purpose state agency called the Railroad Redevelopment Corporation was established, and in 1954 successful negotiations were completed with the Pennsylvania Railroad to end the LIRR's receivership and begin a twelve-year program of reinvestment in the line. During this period, the LIRR would be given generous exemption from various state and local taxes, and the PRR not only agreed to forego any payments from the Long Island on its older debt, it even advanced the LIRR an additional $5.5 million in capital to get the program started.[137] Under this redevelopment program, some new equipment was acquired, the worst of the old was sent to the scrap heap, and an extensive rehabilitation effort was undertaken for the rest, including, with memories of the two 1950 accidents still vivid, the installation of automatic devices that would prevent LIRR engineers from running through stop signals.[138]

In 1953, Pullman-Standard delivered a small fleet of twenty new single-deck MU cars for LIRR service. They were in excess of 80 feet long and, thanks to the same style of 3-2 seating that was becoming the standard for new commuter equipment, the MP-70T units, as they were designated, could accommodate 128 seated passengers per car, only four fewer than the earlier "double-deckers." Unlike the "double-deckers," however, the new cars were not air-conditioned and, in reliance on preferences indicated in a passenger poll, the MP-70T units featured fixed seats arranged in face-to-face fashion. While this small order may have been statistically insignificant—twenty new cars in a fleet that was then in excess of 1,000 units—they were the first new cars to be delivered in the LIRR's recently adopted two-tone gray color scheme. Each of the twenty newcomers was a motorized unit, but all were cabless cars that could be operated only in a train that included an older car—an MP-54 or an MP-70 "double-decker"—equipped with an engineer's cab.[139]

An additional 140 MU cars were acquired in 1955 and 1956 and identified as MP-72 units. By this time the LIRR was able to take advantage of a new program that the State of New York had enacted in 1959 to improve commuter transportation. Under this effort, the Port Authority acquired fleets of new commuter cars that were then leased to various commuter railroads, with the full faith and credit of the State of New York securing the bonds the Port Authority sold to pay for the cars.[140] The 140 new cars were mechanically similar in many respect to the twenty Pullman-Standard cars that were added to the roster in 1953, except that they included three types of cars—motorized cab cars, motorized cars without cabs, and motorless trailers. In addition, they were all fully air-conditioned. The newcomers could operate in trains with similar MP-72 units or in MU with any of the railroad's older equipment—the twenty MP-70s, the MP-70 "double-deckers," and the entire fleet of MP-54s.

The final new MU cars to be acquired for LIRR service before the onset of the MTA era in 1966 was a fleet of thirty cars that were built by Pullman-Standard in the early 1960s and were especially decorated for service along the Port Washington branch to the site of the 1964-to-1965 New York World's Fair. The LIRR livery had by this time evolved to a darker shade of gray with bright-orange trim, and the new cars acquired for World's Fair service had this slogan along their sides below the windows in orange letters: "Your Steel Thruway to the Fair Gateway."[141] Like the "double-deckers," none of these new MP-70 or MP-72 units were permitted to operate on the Jamaica-Brooklyn Line because of restricted clearances on the approach to the terminal at Flatbush and Atlantic. So just as the LIRR's Brooklyn terminal became the stomping ground of MP-41 units long after MP-54s were the standard elsewhere in the electrified zone, when newer MU cars began to operate in and out of Penn Station in the 1950s and 1960s, service into Flatbush Avenue was provided exclusively by veteran MP-54s.

The legislation that established the Railroad Redevelopment Corporation was firm in specifying that the railroad's preferential status would last only twelve years. Some may have supported the legislation in the hope that a redeveloped LIRR would be restored to profitability as a bona fide private corporation at the end of the twelve-year period. But what became eminently clear as the term of the redevelopment program was drawing to a close was that full public ownership with public operation was the only way the LIRR could survive.

Through the instrumentality of a newly created state agency called the Metropolitan Commuter Transportation Authority (MCTA), on December 22, 1965, a down payment of $10 million was made against the negotiated price of $65 million which would transfer the LIRR to the MCTA. William J. Ronan handed a check for the additional $55 million to the railroad's outgoing board of directors on behalf of the MCTA on January 20, 1966. The *New York Times* used a rather unusual metaphor to describe the event: "In yesterday's transaction at the railroad's Jamaica offices, the 131-year-old Long Island made the switch to an untried track as smoothly as an express rolling over a punched-out commutation ticket."[142]

Ronan, a close confident of New York governor Nelson Rockefeller, was the chairman of the new MCTA and would oversee the subsequent rebuilding of the LIRR under state auspices. As for the proceeds of the $65 million sale, they were conveyed to the Pennsylvania Railroad to end, formally and officially, a relationship that had begun in 1900 and that gray paint had been attempting to mask since Halloween of 1949.

In subsequent years, the MCTA also became the governing instrumentality for subways and buses operated by the New York City Transit Authority as well as such other transport agencies as the Triborough Bridge and Tunnel Authority. The agency's name was changed by statute to reflect better its new responsibilities, and the MCTA became the MTA. With William Ronan now the man in charge of a vastly expanded transport enterprise, yet another transformation was about to begin for the electrified suburban service on Long Island.[143]

We learned earlier in this chapter of the MTA's later role in preserving commuter rail services out of New York over the former NYC and the New York, New Haven and Hartford railroads. The new agency cut its teeth, so to speak, on the LIRR, and it was initially for LIRR service that specifications were developed in late 1966 for a dramatically new style of electric MU car that the MTA would try to call the Metropolitan—but would be more commonly known as the M-1.

Ronan announced the MCTA's plans for acquiring a fleet of 500 new LIRR MU cars on August 19, 1966. A 200-page book of specifications was prepared and circulated to companies throughout the world that were known to have the technical capability to produce such a car. While interior and exterior styling was not yet complete, basic technical and performance specifications were, and the aspect of the new cars that caught the eye of the editors of the *New York Times* was the matter of speed capability; "100 M.P.H. Trains Due on the L.I.R.R." headlined the newspaper in reporting Ronan's announcement.[144]

When the MCTA eventually sought formal bids for the new cars, only domestic manufacturers were solicited. The first contract for new M-1 cars was awarded to the Budd Company, of Philadelphia, in August of 1967. It called for the construction of 270 units at $212,000 per car, with an option that would permit the MTA to order additional cars at a later date.[145] In August of

1968—before the first of the new cars were in service—Ronan announced that the MTA would exercise the option and purchase 350 additional cars at $214,000 each, an order the *New York Times* characterized as the "largest single rail passenger car purchase in American history."[146] The final unit in the 620-car order was placed in service on May 14, 1971, and in 1973 an additional 150 cars were ordered to expand the LIRR's M-1 fleet to 770 units.

By this time the Budd Company had withdrawn from the passenger rail car manufacturing business, and General Electric became the prime contractor for MTA orders. Some years later, a company called Transit America—a successor to the Budd Company—was awarded a contract for 174 additional cars built to slightly revised specifications and designated the M-3 units.[147] In all, the MCTA and the MTA acquired 944 new electric MU cars for LIRR service. Unlike the former NYC lines out of Grand Central, where some pre-MTA MU cars remained in electrified service after the new M-class was acquired, all older cars were withdrawn on the LIRR, and the new units became LIRR's sole MU fleet. The LIRR converted most of the MP-72 units into motorless trailer cars to be used behind diesel locomotives in nonelectrified territory, thus obviating the need to acquire new rolling stock for such service.

Phasing the M-class into service was not entirely painless, and for a short time it almost seemed as though the design of the new cars was fatally flawed. But persistence on the part of MTA management coupled with cooperation on the part of the Budd Company soon overcame all difficulties.[148] Budd established a facility adjacent to the LIRR right-of-way in Flushing where modifications were made to in-service cars, and as the fleet's dependability improved, the M-1s began to be appreciated as providing a new level of quality service for LIRR commuters.

The exterior design of the M-1 cars helped create a "family-look" among the MTA's expanding transport responsibilities. The same Sunberg-Ferar firm, which developed the exterior design for the new commuter cars, also produced a visually similar treatment for new subway cars that were being acquired by the MTA's mass-transit subsidiary, and subway cars identified as R-42, R-44, and R-46 units, when viewed head-on, bear a strong resemblance to the M-1. On December 22, 1968, MTA Chairman William Ronan appeared on a Sunday morning news interview program and told any and all who were interested that the first revenue operation of the new M-1 cars would take place on the Monday after Christmas, December 30, 1968.[149]

In terms of the LIRR's "corporate culture," what may have been the most dramatic aspect of the new M-1 units was the fact the newcomers could not operate in MU with any of the railroad's older cars. While this certainly seemed a radical departure from earlier LIRR policy, in which such flexibility was regarded as important, Ronan and the MTA intended to acquire sufficient numbers of new M-1s to replace all of the line's older MU cars, so compatibility was simply no longer an issue. Why constrain the specifications for new equipment by a requirement that they be able to operate in the same train as older equipment when there were not going to be any older cars on the roster for them to operate with?

New cars were only one aspect of the MTA's investment plans for the LIRR. The time-honored ritual of so many passengers having to "change at Jamaica" was in no sense a desirable arrangement, and the MTA sought to provide a "one-seat" ride for a greater proportion of its patrons by expanding the electrified district.

Prior to the MTA, the third rail ended at Mineola on the main line. Shortly after the new agency assumed control, the third rail was extended 6.3 miles eastward to Hicksville and then further into the suburbs along the busy Port Jefferson branch as far as Huntington, 9.8 miles beyond Hicksville. (The LIRR station is called Huntington, but the name of the community where the station is located is Huntington Station. The village of Huntington itself is a mile to the north of both the station called Huntington and the village called Huntington Station.)

The second important expansion of electrified service was completed in 1987 and pushed the third rail further east along the main line from Hicksville to Ronkonkoma, a distance of 23.5 miles. Coupled with the Huntington electrification—between them, the two projects bore a price tag of $300 million—the Ronkonkoma electrification vastly expanded the territory served by LIRR's MU fleet and gave many more passengers an opportunity to travel all the way to Penn Station or Flatbush Avenue without the bother of changing trains. For that matter, many LIRR commuters whose journey from home begins aboard a diesel-powered train had long been able to avoid changing at Jamaica by riding their train to a railroad-to-subway transfer station called Hunters Point Avenue in Long Island City which many nonelectrified trains have long used during peak hours. The LIRR's Hunters Point Avenue station is located adjacent to the portals where Penn Station–bound trains enter the East River tunnels and is just a short walk from the Hunters Point Avenue station on the IRT Flushing Line.

Another betterment in LIRR MU operations that was completed by the MTA was the construction of a 20-acre storage yard in Manhattan to the west of Penn Station, where out-of-service equipment can lay over between rush hours. Named in honor of the late John D. Caemmerer—a state senator from Long Island who was instrumental in securing the passage of important transportation legislation—the yard can accommodate thirty-two ten-car trains, and when it was completed in 1987, it enabled the LIRR to discontinue an extensive—and expensive—pattern of dead-heading trains back to Long Island for midday storage after the morning rush hour and then returning them to Manhattan in late afternoon.

A new state-of-the-art maintenance facility was also built in the Hillside section of Queens just to the east of Jamaica, since adequate repair shops for its MU fleet was never an especially strong suit on the LIRR in the pre-MTA era. All stations inside the electrified zone had to be equipped with high-level platforms before the new M-class cars could operate there, and in later years, the MTA even extended high platforms to its nonelectrified territory when new double-deck cars—true double-deckers, this time—that were acquired to replace older rolling stock beyond the electrified zone featured, like the M-1 fleet, quarter-point doors and no steps or traps.

With the arrival of these new cars and a new fleet of diesel locomotives to haul them the LIRR even revived a practice that was common in the 1930s and the 1940s. In those years, a number of former PRR DD-1 electric locomotives that were rendered surplus when the parent road switched its New York electrification from DC to AC in 1933 were transferred to the Long Island. With such DC locomotives on its roster, the LIRR was able to change motive power from steam to electric at Jamaica and operate select trains from beyond the electrified zone into Penn Station. (There was never a large quantity of such trains, though, because shifting an inbound DD-1 to the opposite end of a train after it arrived at Penn Station was a complicated maneuver that tied up valuable platform space that MU trains could serve more efficiently.)[150]

In any event, since many of the new diesel locomotives that LIRR acquired in the late 1990s are able to draw direct current from the third rail as well as operate independently, they too are able to operate all the way to Penn Station from places such as Port Jefferson and Montauk. Because these trains feature push-pull operation and do not require the locomotive to be shifted from one end to the other at Penn Station, their operation through the East River tunnels into Manhattan is no more complicated than an MU train—at least theoretically.

In late 2002, the LIRR put the first of a new generation of MU cars into service. Built by Bombardier of Canada, these new M-7 units, as they have been designated, will permit the retirement of the oldest of the line's M-1 cars. The initial contract was for 326 M-7 units—at $2.1 million per car—with an option for as many as 372 additional cars. Thanks to the development in recent years of more efficient AC traction motors, the new M-7s draw direct current from LIRR's third rail but convert this DC into alternating current for propulsion.[151] The M-7s differ in appearance from the cars they will replace and feature a front-end treatment that is sharp and angular, in contrast to the rounded and even sculpted look of the original MTA era.

The LIRR's M-1 cars have themselves seen a variety of changes over the years. Originally, the MTA equipped the cars with subway-style roll signs on both front and sides—but these never proved popular on the LIRR and quickly fell into disuse. LIRR also eliminated the blue band that was such an important visual characteristic along the sides of the M-class, while for visibility purposes, a bright-yellow band has replaced blue on the head end of each car. Curiously, Metro North has followed a separate course with respect to the decoration of its M-class cars, retaining the original blue (or red) band along the side of each car. More recently, Metro North has begun to decorate the head end of its cars in either blue or red, with white diagonal stripes to enhance visibility.

(Another personal aside: It is surely a matter of perspective, not to mention age, but I find it exceedingly difficult to appreciate that many M-1 cars have reached the end of their useful service life and are ready for routine replacement. I still tend to regard the M-1s as the "new cars" on an LIRR whose perennial roster surely consists of endless numbers of MP-54s. The fact remains, though, that many Long Island residents who are approaching retirement age have spent their entire working careers commuting to Manhattan jobs aboard M-class cars.)

The most dramatic external change in the M-class cars was the result of safety regulations promulgated by the Federal Railroad Administration (FRA). The FRA mandated that all railroad locomotives—and in the FRA's world, a MU car is treated as if it were a locomotive—must be equipped with something called "ditch lights," in addition to a conventional headlight.[152] Ditch lights aimed at oblique angles were first deployed by Canadian railroads so that engineers could manage a faster look around curves in Rocky Mountain territory and get an early warning of rock slides, washouts, and other dangers. The FRA mandated forward-facing ditch lights to enhance general visibility.

The M-class was designed with unusual dual headlights located just above floor level. Faced with the FRA mandate, LIRR rigged these original headlights as the FRA-mandated ditch lights and mounted a new sealed beam unit on the end of the roof over the end door. Metro North, of course, had to do the same with its M-class cars.

Finally, as the LIRR looks to the future, something that would have seemed altogether improbable not that many years ago is on the verge of becoming a reality; namely, the routine operation of LIRR trains into and out of Grand Central Terminal.

The most difficult part of the project—building a new tunnel under the East River—was accomplished some years ago when the MTA completed work on the 63rd Street Tunnel, a two-level structure designed to accommodate subway trains on the upper level and LIRR commuter trains on the lower level. Subway trains have been using the upper level since 1989, and it will be no small task to link the Manhattan end of the 63rd Street Tunnel with Grand Central and the Long Island City end of the tunnel with the LIRR main line. But a consensus appears to be building that the project is needed, and it is entirely reasonable to predict that one of these days commuters will be able to board Babylon-bound trains of LIRR M-7 units in the terminal whose basic design was supervised by William R. Wilgus.[153]

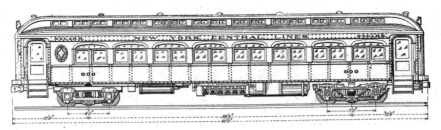

The first electrified operation out of Grand Central was provided by a fleet of all-steel MU cars.

A preproduction rendition of the initial electric locomotives that the New York Central ordered from General Electric.

Production-model locomotives featured sharper lines than those shown
in the preproduction drawing.

Trains await the evening rush hour in Grand Central Terminal in the
Spring of 2003.

A train of 1954-built MU cars speeds along under the catenary on the
New Haven Railroad.

M-3 cars used on the New Haven Line are similar-looking to equipment that operates on other MTA-controlled commuter rail lines.

The end treatment executed on the Pennsylvania's MP-54 electric MU car has often been called "owl-like."

PRR MP-54 car No. 607 awaits restoration at the Pennsylvania State Railroad Museum in Strasburg. The car behind No. 607 once ran in Philadelphia commuter service for the Reading Company.

Contemporary electric MU cars operated by New Jersey Transit continue the tradition pioneered by PRR's MP-54.

The original electric MU cars acquired by the Long Island Rail Road were based on a design that had been developed earlier by the Interborough Rapid Transit Company.

The LIRR developed a variation of the basic MP-54 design by specifying an arch roof rather than the more traditional railroad roof.

LIRR multiple-unit trains lay over between runs at the terminal in Hempstead. Train at left is composed of the road's distinctive "double-decker" cars.

A train of M-1 units approaches Huntington on the Long Island Rail Road.

Classic MU electric cars of the New Haven Railroad that long provided suburban service out of Grand Central.

The Legacy of the IRT

FOR THE FIRST QUARTER-CENTURY or so that the New York Subway was in operation, the general popularity of urban mass transit remained on the upswing, and more passengers rode America's subways, els, and streetcars year after year.[1] The extraordinary expense of building underground subway lines, though, meant that this unique and effective form of high-volume transport saw relatively little replication in the United States, even while public transportation itself was experiencing years of steady growth. As discussed in Chapter 2, Boston built a network of diverse subway lines that connected its downtown core with various residential neighborhoods on the city's periphery. But it was Chicago that for many decades could claim the title of being the home of America's second-largest rail rapid-transit network.

CHICAGO

While there was continuous talk during the early years of the twentieth century of building downtown subways in Chicago—Bion Arnold delivered a comprehensive subway plan for the city as early as 1902, for instance—in point of fact rapid transit, Chicago style, took the form of an extensive system of elevated railways, including a unique downtown delivery system for such trains that was known as the Union Loop.[2] To this day, downtown Chicago itself is referred to as "the Loop," although this usage predates the construction of the elevated loop in 1898 and was coined in reference to various surface loops that the city's extensive network of street-running cable railways used to reverse direction and head back to their outlying terminals.

When the Union Elevated Railway inaugurated revenue service around the Union Loop on October 3, 1897—a month and some days after Boston opened its Tremont Street Subway—it was a unique undertaking. For one thing, the Union elevated company itself owned no rolling stock and operated no trains. Instead, it leased trackage rights over its 2-mile right-of-way around the city's downtown business district to three other elevated railway companies, and trains of these lines provided service over Union's facility.[3] To the south of downtown Chicago, one found the right-of-way of the city's oldest elevated company—the Chicago and South Side Rapid Transit Railroad Company, whose steam-powered trains carried their first revenue passengers in 1892.[4]

Due west of Downtown ran the right-of-way of the Lake Street Elevated, opened in 1893, while the Metropolitan West Side Elevated Railroad operated multiple lines that served neighborhoods both west and northwest of downtown Chicago. The Metropolitan operated its first train in 1895 and, unlike those of the two earlier L companies, its trains were electrified from the outset. These, then, were the three elevated companies that inaugurated L service around the Union Loop in the fall of 1897. A fourth company, the Northwestern Elevated Railway, whose lines extended northward from the loop, joined the older trio in the spring of 1900.[5]

The principal figure behind three of Chicago's five L companies—Lake Street, the Northwestern, and Union Elevated—was Charles Tyson Yerkes, Jr., a man introduced in Chapter 3 as an important force in the construction of tube railways in London. Yerkes's tenure in Chicago was a stormy one, and his role in the development of mass transportation there was not warmly regarded. Nevertheless, prior to his rapid-transit ventures in London, Charles Tyson Yerkes was heavily involved in the development of Chicago's network of elevated railways.[6]

In 1924 Chicago's four L companies—four, not five, because Union had been absorbed by the Northwestern in 1904—were unified as the Chicago Rapid Transit Company. Plans to tear down the Union Loop and replace it with a system of subways continued to be discussed in Chicago, but no action was forthcoming until 1938, when the availability of public works money from Washington prompted the city of Chicago to begin construction of two downtown delivery subways that would allow some but not all of the L trains using the Union Loop to be routed through the new tunnels. Initial estimates suggested that when both subways were complete, the sixty-eight peak-hour trains previously using the Union Loop would be reduced to thirty-eight.

Both of the new subways were constructed with a north-south orientation, one under State Street, the other a block to the west under Dearborn Street. Unlike the "cut-and-cover" construction techniques used for most other U.S. subway lines, Chicago elected to build its downtown subways as deep-bore tunnels, much like the tube lines in London, although not nearly as far belowground. The State Street Tunnel was completed and opened for revenue service in October of 1943, linking elevated lines to the north that were once part of the Northwestern L with lines south of the city that were originally the Chicago and South Side Rapid Transit Company. Work on the Dearborn project was suspended during the Second World War, and its first trains did not operate until 1951. When it was completed, it allowed lines that were once part of the Metropolitan West Side Elevated to forsake the Union Loop and use the new tunnel for their passage through downtown Chicago.

Both the State Street and the Dearborn Street subways include a rather unusual construction feature, a single long platform in the heart of downtown Chicago along which trains make three separate stops. The State Street platform, at 3,300-feet long, merits a mention in *The Guinness Book of World Records* as the longest subway platform in the world. As a practical matter of passenger information, the separate stops along these lengthy platforms are identified as discreet stations.[7]

Chicago rapid transit shifted from the private sector to the public in 1947—in the same year that a similar transformation took place in Boston—and lines that had previously been known as the Chicago Rapid Transit Company became the Chicago Transit Authority (CTA).[8] While there continued to be talk about tearing down the Union Loop and putting all downtown rapid transit underground, as transport matters developed in Chicago during the last quarter of the twentieth century, the old Union Loop developed a venerable and unique status and is now seen as a defining civic asset in Chicago, not as an outmoded transport facility that must be replaced. Millions of dollars have been spent upgrading operational aspects of the Union Loop while retaining its distinctive nineteenth-century architectural character. In all of twenty-first century North America, Chicago is the only city whose central downtown area is still served by elevated trains.

Under CTA auspices, rapid transit expansion in Chicago has focused on extending and expanding lines in outlying districts. In the years immediately after the Second World War, some lightly trafficked branch lines were "pruned" from the system, but more recently an aggressive program of expansion has seen new lines built in several outward directions, including service to the city's two major airports, O'Hare (to the northwest) and Midway (to the southwest). The construction of such rights-of-way, at grade, in the median strips of major area expressways has become a virtual trademark of rapid transit expansion in Chicago.

Despite the fact that today's CTA has roots in multiple private companies, all of the system's rapid-transit rolling stock is built to compatible specifications; trains run on standard-gauge track and draw current from a trackside third rail.[9] CTA cars are much smaller than typical North American rapid-transit rolling stock, measuring 48 feet in overall length and a shade over 9 feet in width.[10]

For most of the twentieth century, the elevated and subway network of Chicago ranked as the second-largest rail rapid-transit system in the United States. While Chicago's system has grown in recent years, it has been forced to surrender its "number two" ranking to a totally new system that was built in and around Washington, D.C., during the final quarter of the twentieth century.[11]

PHILADELPHIA

Another U.S. city that undertook a program of subway and rapid-transit construction in the years immediately following the opening of New York's Interborough Rapid Transit in 1904 was Philadelphia. Philadelphia is unique in that its initial downtown subway was constructed entirely with private capital and involved no public funds at all.[12] The subway in question was an east-west line that bisected Philadelphia along Market Street, and while primarily an elevated service, it dropped belowground as it entered the city's central business district and served six subway stations in the city's downtown core.[13]

A distinctive feature of Philadelphia's geography is the fact that City Hall is located at the very center of the city, the place where the east-west Market Street intersects the north-south Broad Street. Westward from Broad Street, the Market Street Subway that opened in 1907 included four tracks—a center pair for the exclusive use of high-platform subway-elevated trains, plus an outside pair that was used by streetcars that emerged from the tunnel once away from Downtown and continued their outbound journey into various residential neighborhoods over city streets.[14]

Philadelphia enjoyed its new form of urban mobility, and plans for expansion and extension quickly emerged. The Philadelphia Rapid Transit Company (PRT), however, was not in a position to finance any further construction with corporate resources, and following the opening of the original Market Street Subway-El in 1907, all subsequent subway and elevated expansion required public funding. At its eastern end, the original Market Street Line emerged from its tunnel just beyond Downtown and terminated at an elevated station adjacent to ferry slips along the city's Delaware River waterfront. An elevated extension that was completed in 1922 left the original line just before it reached the waterfront and continued into the northeast portion of the city and a terminal in the Frankfort neighborhood. Because a new bridge across the Delaware opened in 1926 and the ferries had little future, service to the original waterfront terminal was discontinued in 1939.[15] Something of a unique feature of the Market-Frankfort Line was its use of an under-running third rail for current distribution, much like the Wilgus-Sprague system developed by the New York Central Railroad for its Grand Central electrification in 1906, which was described in Chapter 4.

Over the years, there would be only two additional changes in the alignment of the Market-Frankfort Subway Elevated. The first was a westward extension of the tunnel portion of the line that opened in late 1955. Instead of emerging from underground at 23rd Street on the east side of the Schuylkill River, as had been the case since 1905, Market-Frankfort trains now serve three additional underground stations and do not ascend onto the elevated structure until they reach 44th Street. Subway-surface streetcars using the trolley portion of the Market Street Subway also benefited from the 1955 project and instead of emerging from the subway along with the el trains at 23rd Street, they too tunnel under the Schuylkill and continue underground to 40th Street and Woodlawn Avenue through a trolley subway tunnel whose route diverges from that of the Market-Frankfort Line at 36th Street. The second change was just beyond downtown Philadelphia on the Frankfort leg of the line, where in 1977 a 1.2-mile portion of the original elevated structure was replaced by a new right-of-way in the median strip of Interstate Highway I-95, a transit betterment that was paid for with federal highway funds since the original el structure had to be removed before the highway could be constructed.

In 1914, Philadelphia began work on a companion subway to the east-west-oriented Market Street Line: a north-south route under Broad Street. Since Broad and Market effectively divide the city into quadrants, they represent obvious corridors for rapid-transit service.

When the city built the Broad Street Line, it adopted a different set of specifications from those that PRT had used for the older Market Street service. The Market Street Line had been built with a track gauge of 5 feet, 2½ inches, unusual by most standards but common among Pennsylvania streetcar companies. The new Broad Street Subway, on the other hand, used standard track gauge of 4 feet, 8½ inches, and as a result of this disparity, an old saw that one sometimes hears among Philadelphia transit buffs is: "Market is broad, while Broad is standard."

Despite the fact that its track gauge is ½ foot wider than the Broad Street Line, tunnel dimensions specified for the Market Street route require the use of slightly shorter and narrower cars.[16] This has created a rolling stock situation not unlike those seen earlier in Boston and New York—different subway lines requiring rolling stock built to different specifications. In addition, when designing the Broad Street Line, the City of Philadelphia saw no need to adopt Market Street's under-running third rail, and used a more conventional over-running third rail instead, thus creating yet another technical contrast between the two lines.

Service was inaugurated along the northern portion of the Broad Street Line between City Hall and Olney Avenue in 1928.[17] As additional segments were completed, service was expanded, until the line eventually extended 9.4 miles from Fern Rock at its northern end to Pattison in South Philadelphia. With the sole exception of the Fern Rock terminal, the entire line is underground; unlike any other subway in the world—save those of New York—for a good portion of its length, Philadelphia's Broad Street Subway is four tracks wide, with two outside tracks for local service and two inside tracks for express service.[18] In 1932, service was inaugurated along a short spur that left the Broad Street Line just to the north of Downtown and that was to have become part of a larger, looplike distributor line around the city's central business district. Plans for such a loop subway foundered, though, and the Ridge Avenue Spur, as it has generally been known, has remained a branch line.

A third subway line opened in Philadelphia in 1936. Built to the same general dimensions as the Broad Street Subway and connecting with that line's Ridge Avenue Spur at 8th and Market Streets, it was not part of the basic PRT transit system. Rather, the new line was managed by the Delaware River Joint Commission (DRJC) and provided service between Philadelphia and Camden across the Ben Franklin Bridge, which had been built in 1926 and was also a DRJC responsibility. DRJC contracted with PRT for the actual operation of the line, and a fleet of twenty-six new cars were acquired for the transbridge line that were operationally compatible with PRT's Broad Street equipment but differed in external styling, as well as having four motors per car rather than two in deference to 5 percent grades on the bridge. DRJC rolling stock was maintained by PRT at the Fern Rock maintenance base at the north end of the Broad Street Subway.[19]

The Bridge Line was never an outstanding mass-transit success in its original configuration. It would become the nucleus of an important transit success story in 1969, though, after a new agency with the acronym PATCO—Port Authority Transit Corporation—assumed control of the Bridge Line and extended it eastward from its original terminal in downtown Camden to the suburban community of Lindenwold over a rebuilt right-of-way that was formerly the Pennsylvania-Reading Seashore Lines.[20] When service was inaugurated over what had become a 14.2-mile line on February 15, 1969, it was the very first deployment in the United States of fully automated rapid-transit service under a system known as Automatic Train Operation (ATO).

A single onboard attendant opens and closes a train's doors at each station, but otherwise all aspects of operation—acceleration, braking, observing proper spacing between trains, and coming to a stop at the next station—are handled in a fully automated fashion, including the transmission of signals between the train and central computers to line up proper routes, throw switch tracks, and so forth.

With the arrival of a fleet of seventy-five new, high-performance, Budd-built cars for PATCO service, the original bridge cars of 1936 were sold to the city of Philadelphia and ran for a number of years on the Broad Street Subway. The original seventy-five-car fleet soon proved insufficient to handle PATCO's growing patronage, and it was supplemented by forty-six additional units, cars built not by the Budd Company, but by Canadian Vickers.[21]

PRT itself would undergo a two-phase corporate transformation, the full complexity of which is beyond the scope of this brief review. On January 1, 1940, PRT was succeeded as the principal mass-transit provider in the City of Brotherly Love by a new company, the Philadelphia Transportation Company (PTC), after earlier efforts to engineer a takeover of PRT were unsuccessful. PTC proved to be a transitional entity, and in late 1968 its assets were conveyed to a new public agency, the Southeastern Pennsylvania Transportation Authority (SEPTA). Philadelphia thus became the final American city with an old and venerable rapid-transit system to shift operational responsibility for such service from the private to the public sector. In the years since it was created, SEPTA has upgraded both the Market Street and the Broad Street lines by acquiring new rolling stock and installing new signal and communications systems as well.[22]

Philadelphia's most important transit investment project of the last quarter-century involved commuter rail service, not rapid transit. As discussed in Chapter 4, both the Reading Company and the Pennsylvania Railroad had long operated electrified commuter service into Philadelphia. Under SEPTA, a new downtown tunnel was constructed to link these previously separate networks, and Philadelphia now boasts a unique commuter rail system where most trains originate their runs at an outlying terminal, operate through downtown Philadelphia via the new Central City Connector, as it is called, and terminate at an outlying terminal on the other side of town.[23]

Elsewhere

When the United States entered the Second World War in 1941, the only genuine rapid-transit-style subways in America were those of Boston, New York, and Philadelphia, although active construction was underway in Chicago that would open for revenue service in 1943, and that city could also boast a truly extensive system of elevated railways. There were a few modest subways here and there that were served by trolley cars—Rochester, New York, Newark, New Jersey, and even a mile-long subway into downtown Los Angeles that was part of the Pacific Electric Railway there.[24] Another important older subway system was one that opened in 1908 and linked Manhattan with several railroad stations located across the Hudson River in New Jersey and then continued across the Jersey Meadows to the nearby city of Newark. This was the Hudson and Manhattan Railroad, a unique and extraordinarily interesting underground railway that is all too often overlooked because it is so totally overshadowed by the overwhelming size and proportion of the subway system in New York.[25]

There were plans for subways in a variety of other North American cities—Cleveland and Cincinnati come to mind, as does Toronto—but as the world directed its attention to the war effort, such plans were obviously put on hold.[26]

The Postwar Scene

After VJ Day, there was little immediate expansion of rapid transit in America. In both Chicago and New York, many older elevated lines were abandoned as unnecessary, including the 1955 abandonment of the Manhattan portion of the Third Avenue El, an action that effectively reduced the IRT Division to subway lines and elevated feeders that were built under the provisions of Contracts One, Two, and Three.

A few subway projects that had been initiated before Pearl Harbor were seen through to completion after VJ Day, and an essentially new rapid-transit system in Cleveland was completed in 1955.[27] The U.S. city that swam against the tide most vigorously in the immediate postwar era was surely Boston, where the East Boston Tunnel was upgraded and expanded, and the New York Central Railroad's Highland Branch was converted into a feeder line for Boston's Boylston-Tremont Central Subway, as discussed in Chapter 2.

Several benchmarks must be identified as North America came to grips with the new transport realities of the postwar era. One was the opening of a totally new subway in Toronto in 1954, a twelve-station line under and adjacent to Yonge Street that ran from Union Station in downtown Toronto to Eglinton, 4½ miles due north and that was steadily expanded into a citywide system in subsequent years and decades.[28]

As important as the service the new Toronto Subway offered to the denizens of that city was the way it also served as an important case in point for transit advocates throughout the United States who were attempting to convince policy-makers that there was an efficient and attractive alternative to building more and more freeways as a source of urban mobility. Equally important was an electoral decision that was made by voters in the Bay Area of San Francisco and Oakland on November 6, 1962. That was the day when voters elected to create a new regional mass-transit district and to impose a tax on themselves for the construction of an entirely new rapid-transit system. Out of the 1962 vote would emerge the Bay Area Rapid Transit District, an agency popularly identified by the acronym BART; after an exhaustive evaluation of the appropriate technology to use for the intended new transit system, BART engineers determined that conventional rail rapid transit, supplemented with all the latest in automated controls, was the proper hardware to deploy. (It was an era when many thought that conventional rail transit was much too old-fashioned and that something futuristic—like a rubber-tired monorail, perhaps—was the wave of the future.)

As BART moved from planning to construction, a 71-mile system emerged that included three branch lines into residential communities in the East Bay area: one to Richmond, one to Concord, and one to Fremont. The three lines came together in Oakland and then proceed through a tunnel under San Francisco Bay and into a trunk-line subway under Market Street in downtown San Francisco, before continuing on to Daly City. In addition, for most of its length the Market Street Tunnel would include two levels: one for BART trains, and another for streetcars of the San Francisco Municipal Railway.

The first BART trains carried revenue passengers in the East Bay on September 11, 1972—a decade after the 1962 referendum—and two years later, on September 16, 1974, revenue service was inaugurated through the trans-Bay tube. More recently, three extensions have been added to the original 71-mile BART system: two in the East Bay, plus a major addition beyond Daly City that will eventually provide service to San Francisco International Airport.

BART certainly experienced more than its share of early glitches. Car reliability was one problem, and the entire automated control system eventually had to be effectively redesigned and replaced. The basic geometry of BART's original rolling stock also proved inefficient. All cars were powered, but they included two different body styles: The A cars were 75 feet long and featured a cab at one end, while the 70-foot B cars had no cabs at all. Operational flexibility was severely curtailed, however, because the A cars included a futuristic-looking slanted nose made of molded fiberglass that precluded their being coupled anywhere but on the end of a train. In the late 1980s when increasing patronage required BART to order additional cars, a third body style was developed—a cab-equipped "C" car that features a flat end so that it may also be used at midtrain positions.

Despite early setbacks, BART was able to work its way through its problems, and as Joseph Strapac noted in a book published in 1972 to commemorate the system's opening: "Every rail transit system built in the United States from now on will owe much to BART pioneering."[29] More important, "BART pioneering" inaugurated an era that saw dozens of North American cities elect to address their mobility needs with the construction of new and expanded subway systems.

JFK AND UMTA

One of the key factors that helped foster such transit development was a 1962 proposal that President John F. Kennedy sent to Congress calling for a new program of federal financial assistance to provide investment resources for the construction of new urban mass-transit systems. At first the proposal languished in Congress, and only a few, small, demonstration projects were authorized. Following Kennedy's assassination in 1963, such a program became part of President Lyndon Johnson's "Great Society" initiative, and Congress enacted the Urban Mass Transportation Assistance Act of 1964.

At first the new program was modestly funded; its annual appropriation barely rose above $100 million during the years of the Johnson administration, although two important new transit lines were built with early program resources: the extension of existing rapid-transit lines in both Boston and Cleveland.[30] The federal transit assistance program saw its first billion-dollar budget year under President Richard M. Nixon in 1973; budget levels continued to increase in the years following, and by the end of the twentieth century, federal funding for mass-transit investment was in excess of $5 billion a year, the cumulative total since 1964 was over $100 billion, and the resources made available under this new program have been instrumental in making the final quarter of the twentieth century the most active era of new rapid-transit construction in the United States since—well, since the Dual Subway Contracts were signed in New York in 1913.[31] An important symbolic development in the program's history was legislative action to establish an independent source of revenue for transit investment from a portion of the federal tax on motor fuel.

Relying on federal funds made available from an agency in the U.S. Department of Transportation that was known as UMTA—

the Urban Mass Transportation Administration—major new rail rapid-transit systems were constructed in Baltimore, Atlanta, Miami, and Los Angeles, important transit extensions were added to existing systems in Boston, Cleveland, and Chicago, and new light rail transit systems were built in many additional cities, involving substantial subway mileage.[32]

Buffalo, New York, for example, opened a light rail system in 1985 that operates through the city's downtown business district along an at-grade mall but descends into a 5.2-mile subway tunnel away from Downtown as the line taps important residential areas to the north.

Pittsburgh converted an older streetcar network that included some at-grade operation along private right-of-way in residential areas into a modern light rail system that now includes two separate terminals in downtown Pittsburgh and important subway mileage away from Downtown as well.

In San Francisco, construction of the new BART system under Market Street included a separate level so that local streetcars could also operate with all the efficiency of true rapid transit. (San Francisco has even retained the surface-running portion of its streetcar system—with an interesting touch: rebuilt PCC and other heritage equipment serve what is now called the F Line, with individual cars decorated in the color schemes of various North American cities. One can hence board a cream-and-orange PCC car lettered "BOSTON ELEVATED RAILWAY," as well as cars in the liveries of Chicago, Philadelphia, Brooklyn, and other cities.)

New light rail systems in Saint Louis, Dallas, and Los Angeles also include subway mileage in their systems.[33]

By far the largest new rail rapid-transit system built in the United States during the final quarter of the twentieth century was substantially funded by the federal government, but its dollars were largely derived from appropriations separate from the UMTA transit assistance program. This was a 103-mile rail rapid-transit system built to serve Washington, D.C., and its surrounding suburbs, a rail system operated by the Washington Metropolitan Area Transit Authority (WMATA) and known as Metrorail—or more crisply, just plain Metro. The first leg of the 103-mile system opened for revenue service in 1976, the final link was completed in early 2001, and Metro has lately turned to expansion beyond the original 103-mile network. As the New York Subway celebrates its centenary in 2004, the new Metrorail system in Washington has surpassed Chicago's CTA as the second-largest rail-transit system in North America.[34]

And yet for all the billions of dollars in both federal assistance and local matching funds that have been invested in building dramatic new transit lines throughout the country in the years following 1964, a much larger proportion of federal dollars has been invested in the rehabilitation and modernization of the nation's older rail-transit systems—new rolling stock, rebuilt stations, upgraded electrical distribution networks, improved rights-of-way, and the very latest in "high-tech" signal and communication systems.[35]

North of the border in Canada, the 4.5-mile Toronto Subway of 1954 has been steadily expanded into a citywide system of multiple lines and routes that total 35 miles in length, while Montreal has constructed a four-line subway system using "Paris-style" rubber-tired trains. (Details about the Montreal Subway were presented in Chapter 3.) Both Calgary and Edmonton now feature new light rail systems, while Vancouver has built a largely elevated rapid-transit system called SkyTrain. SkyTrain certainly seems an appropriate name for a contemporary rapid-transit system whose right-of-way is largely built along a modern elevated structure. But what should one make of the fact that for its passage through downtown Vancouver, a rapid-transit system called SkyTrain descends from its elevated structure and operates through underground subway tunnels?[36]

If people living in the United States or Canada in August of 1945 wished to head downtown and participate in civic celebrations being held to mark VJ Day, only those in Boston, New York, Philadelphia, and Chicago could have traveled by subway. (Los Angeles, Rochester in New York State, and Newark in New Jersey could be added to the list if one chose to include their modest trolley subways in the tally.) Move the calendar ahead another fifty-five years, make the civic celebration the dawn of the new millennium on January 1, 2000, and people were able to head downtown aboard a subway train of one sort or another in all of those cities save Rochester—plus Baltimore, Washington, Atlanta, Pittsburgh, Buffalo, Toronto, Montreal, Cleveland, Saint

Louis, Dallas, San Francisco, Oakland, Vancouver, Edmonton, and Calgary.

Where there were but seven in 1945, there were twenty-two in 2000, and that does not include new rail rapid-transit of one sort or another that operates either at grade or along elevated structures. Were such municipalities to be included, the list would also include Miami, Denver, Salt Lake City, San Diego, San Jose, Sacramento, and Portland, Oregon.[37] Also worthy of note is a downtown subway in Seattle, Washington, that is currently served by electric-powered buses but includes rails for the eventual addition of a light rail transit component; a new rail transit system will also soon open in San Juan, Puerto Rico. Nor has any mention been made of the many cities that have deployed tourist-oriented trolley services of one sort or another in localities as diverse as Memphis, New Orleans, and Vancouver, British Columbia, among others.

This explosive growth of rail rapid transit in the final quarter of the twentieth century must be declared an extraordinarily important social trend. It is also a trend that surely owes much to something equally extraordinary that happened under the sidewalks of New York on a brisk autumn afternoon in the year 1904.

Tables 5.1 and 5.2 provide general statistical information about subway operations in North America at the centenary of the Interborough Rapid Transit Company.

TABLE 5.1
U.S. SUBWAYS

	Atlanta	Baltimore[c]	Boston	Boston
Agency	MARTA	MTA	MBTA	MBTA
Style of Rail Transit	rail rapid	rail rapid	rail rapid	light rail
Total Route Miles	49.2	15.3	37.6	25.5
Underground Route Miles	8.7	5.9	12.7	3.2
Number of Stations	38	14	53	34[a]
Number of Cars	340	100	408	194[b]
Gauge	standard	standard	standard	standard
Electrification	750-volt DC third rail	700-volt DC third rail	600-volt DC third rail & catenary	600-volt DC catenary
First Line Opened	1979	1983	1900	1897
Annual Patronage	78.4 million	12.8 million	107.6 million	65.0 million

	Buffalo	Chicago	Cleveland	Cleveland
Agency	NFTA	CTA	GCRTA	GCRTA
Style of Rail Transit	light rail	rail rapid	rail rapid	light rail
Total Route Miles	6.4	107.5	19.1	13.4
Underground Route Miles	5.2	11.2	0.5	0.5
Number of Stations	14	140	18	33
Number of Cars	27[b]	1,192	60	48[b]
Gauge	standard	standard	standard	standard
Electrification	650-volt DC catenary	600-volt DC third rail[d]	600-volt DC catenary	600-volt DC catenary
First Line Opened	1985	1892	1955	1920
Annual Patronage	6.9 million	84 million	6 million	5.4 million

	Dallas	Los Angeles	Los Angeles	Newark[e]
Agency	DART	MTA	MTA	NJ Transit
Style of Rail Transit	light rail	rail rapid	light rail	light rail
Total Route Miles	19.9	17.4	41.2	5.1
Underground Route Miles	3.5	17.4	1.0	1.7
Number of Stations	21	15	38	13
Number of Cars	95[b]	60	121[b]	16[b]
Gauge	standard	standard	standard	standard
Electrification	750-volt DC catenary	750-volt DC third rail	750-volt DC catenary	600-volt DC catenary
First Line Opened	1996	1993	1990	1935
Annual Patronage	11.5 million	12 million	22.3 million	4.4 million

	New York	New York[f]	Philadelphia	Philadelphia
Agency	NYCT	PATH	SEPTA	SEPTA
Style of Rail Transit	rail rapid	rail rapid	rail rapid	light rail
Total Route Miles	247.3	13.8	24.0	37.9
Underground Route Miles	138.6	7.4	14.6	2.5
Number of Stations	468	13	53	8[a]
Number of Cars	5,799	342	345	284
Gauge	standard	standard	I	broad[i]
Electrification	625-volt DC third rail	650-volt DC third rail	625-volt DC third rail[i]	600-volt DC catenary
First Line Opened	1904	1908	1906	1905
Annual Patronage	1.2 billion	56 million	48.2 million	11.7 million

	Philadelphia	Pittsburgh	St. Louis	San Francisco
Agency	PATCO	PAT	Bi-State	BART
Style of Rail Transit	rail rapid	light rail	light rail	rail rapid
Total Route Miles	14.5	10.7	34.2	95.1
Underground Route Miles	2.6	2.4	1.1	19.3
Number of Stations	14	15	27	39
Number of Cars	121	55[b]	37[b]	669
Gauge	standard	broad	standard	1676
Electrification	685-volt DC third rail	650-volt DC catenary	650-volt DC catenary	1,000-volt DC third rail
First Line Opened	1936	[g]	1993	1972
Annual Patronage	10.7 million	7.5 million	14.5 million	76.0 million

	San Francisco	Washington
Agency	SF Muni	WMATA
Style of Rail Transit	light rail	rail rapid
Total Route Miles	26.1	103.1
Underground Route Miles	6.2	32.8
Number of Stations	9[a]	83
Number of Cars	244[b]	764
Gauge	standard	standard
Electrification	600-volt DC catenary	750-volt DC third rail
First Line Opened	[h]	1976
Annual Patronage	36.7 million	194.0 million

a. "Stations" refer only to defined facilities belowground or along private right-of-way, not to every stop made by street-running light rail service.

b. Articulated cars consisting of two or more units.

c. Baltimore also features a companion light rail transit system that operates fully at grade.

d. One branch line features 600-volt DC catenary electrification.

e. In addition to the Newark City Subway operation identified here, NJ Transit also operates an elevated and at-grade light transit rail between Jersey City and Hoboken.

f. Statistics include PATH service between Jersey City and the World Trade Center in Lower Manhattan, which was suspended on September 11, 2001.

g. Older streetcar service upgraded to light rail standards; downtown subway opened for revenue service in 1985. Track gauge is 5 feet, 2½ inches.

h. Older streetcar service upgraded to light rail standards, including downtown subway under Market Street built as part of the BART project; see text.

i. SEPTA's Market-Frankfort Subway-Elevated Line and its subway-surface light rail network operate on broad-gauge trackage that is 5 feet, 2½ inches between running rails, while the Broad Street Subway is standard-gauge. Broad Street uses a conventional over-running third rail, while Market-Frankfort features an under-running third rail.

Agency Abbreviations

BART: San Francisco Bay Area Rapid Transit District
Bi-State: Bi-State Development Agency
CTA: Chicago Transit Authority
DART: Dallas Area Rapid Transit
GCRTA: Greater Cleveland Regional Transit Authority
MARTA: Metropolitan Atlanta Rapid Transit Authority
MBTA: Massachusetts Bay Transportation Authority
MTA: Mass Transit Administration (of Maryland)
MTA: Los Angeles County Metropolitan Transportation Authority
NFTA: Niagara Frontier Transportation Authority
NJ Transit: New Jersey Transit Corporation
NYCT: New York City Transit
PATH: Port Authority–Transit Hudson
PAT: Port Authority of Allegheny County
PATCO: Port Authority Transit Corporation
SEPTA: Southeastern Pennsylvania Transportation Authority

MEANWHILE, BACK IN NEW YORK . . .

Interestingly enough, one U.S. city that did not manage to expand its subway system during this era of extraordinary rapid-transit growth was New York. In fact, thanks to the elimination of significant portions of its older elevated lines, New York's total rapid-transit route mileage was actually reduced in the final decades of the twentieth century.[38] Elevated lines in Brooklyn along Myrtle and Lexington Avenues and the Third Avenue Line that served both Manhattan and the Bronx were torn down in the post–Second World War era. Subway route mileage saw one important increase in 1956, though, when the Rockaway Line of the Long Island Rail Road was conveyed to the City of New York and converted into a branch of the IND Division, thereby adding 12.1 route miles to the overall subway system.[39] But even this substantial increase failed to offset the elimination of elevated mileage.

While New York has not been as aggressive as, say, Boston or Chicago in building major new extensions of its subway system during the era of federal assistance for urban mass transit, there

TABLE 5.2
CANADIAN SUBWAYS

	Calgary	*Edmonton*	*Montreal*	*Toronto*
Agency	Calgary Transit	Edmonton Transit	STM	TTC
Style of Rail Transit	light rail	light rail	rubber-tired rail rapid[b]	rail rapid
Total Route Miles	18.2	7.6	40.4	43.5
Underground Route Miles	1.2	2.9	40.4	32.3
Number of Stations	31	10	65	61
Number of Cars	85[a]	37[a]	750	806
Gauge	standard	standard	standard	1495
Electrification	600-volt DC catenary	600-volt DC catenary	750-volt DC third rail	570-volt DC third rail
First Line Opened	1981	1978	1966	1954
Annual Patronage	28.3 million	2.7 million	197 million	142.1 million

	Toronto	*Vancouver*
Agency	TTC	BC Transit
Styles of Rail Transit	automated rail rapid[c]	automated rail rapid[c]
Total Route Miles	3.7	17.9
Underground Route Miles	0.2	1.0
Number of Stations	6	19
Number of Cars	28	130
Gauge	standard	standard
Electrification	600-volt DC third rail	600-volt DC third rail
First Line Opened	1985	1986
Annual Patronage	7.5 million	33.8 million

a. Articulated cars consisting of two or more units.
b. "Paris-style" rubber-tired system.
c. Fully automated transit system that utilizes no onboard operators.

Agency Abbreviations

STM: La Societé de Transport de Montréal
TTC: Toronto Transit Commission

has been steady and strategic capital investment in the New York subways—quite a bit of it, in fact. A new tunnel under the East River between Long Island City and the foot of East 63rd Street in Manhattan allows IND trains from central Queens to reach mid-Manhattan more efficiently, but the primary investment goal for mass transit in New York has been to stabilize and upgrade the existing system, not to expand it into new markets.

Important elements of infrastructure such as automatic signals, power distribution networks, and communication and control systems have been thoroughly upgraded to ensure dependable operation. The mere fact that New York Subway trains are now entirely air-conditioned means that the demand for electric current is, perhaps, 20 percent higher on a hot and humid summer day than it would be otherwise. The design and acquisition of new rolling stock for a system whose roster includes almost 6,000 subway cars is a virtually never-ending process.

What may well stand out as the single most dramatic betterment for New York Subway passengers since October of 1904 was the development of a new electronic system for fare collection that was designed and installed in phases in the final years of the twentieth century. Instead of putting tokens—or in days gone by, nickels—into subway turnstiles, passengers now purchase plastic cards and pay to have monetary value encoded onto the cards. Contemporary turnstiles subtract the cost of a single ride as a passenger enters the system, but far more dramatic than the new hardware is a new policy that allows passengers to transfer onto a continuing bus ride without paying an additional fare. There is always agitation in New York whenever the question of increasing the subway fare is under discussion. With the introduction of the new electronic fare-collection system in the late 1990s, passengers whose trip required both a bus and a subway ride saw their regular fare cut in half!

That element of New York City Transit called the IRT Division has seen virtually no expansion of its service at all. Indeed, since the completion of the new routes and lines that the Interborough built under the terms of the 1913 Dual Subway Contracts, there have been only two instances when the onetime Interborough Rapid Transit Company has been expanded at all. In 1940, portions of the abandoned New York, Westchester and Boston Railroad that were within the Borough of the Bronx were acquired by the City of New York and, after several seasons of operation as an off-line adjunct of the IND Division, became an element of the IRT. The second IRT expansion came in 1968, when revenue service was instituted over trackage beyond the 137th Street terminal of the Lenox Avenue route that had previously led merely into a maintenance and storage facility. It was not, in other words, a major construction of a new line into new territory.

But as the City of New York, the mass-transit community, and anyone who recalls fond memories of the Interborough celebrate the centenary of subway service, there is a small but critical stretch of subway tunnel served daily by IRT trains that is new—very, very new.

When the West Side IRT was extended southward from 42nd Street, the center express tracks diverged from the outside local tracks at Chambers Street and made their way under the East River to Brooklyn. The two local tracks continued southward under Varick Street and West Broadway and terminated at the same South Ferry loop that had originally been built for the Contract Two lines in 1905.

The first station south of Chambers Street was Cortlandt Street. Here IRT passengers could transfer to New Jersey-bound trains of William Gibbs McAdoo's Hudson and Manhattan Railroad (H&M), which departed from the nearby Hudson Terminal. In 1962, the H&M left the private sector and was acquired by the Port Authority of New York and New Jersey for operation by a new Port Authority subsidiary called Port Authority Trans-Hudson, or PATH. As part of the arrangement, the Port Authority tore down the H&M's twin office buildings at 30 and 60 Church Street and constructed two massive office buildings that were called the World Trade Center.

When the World Trade Center was attacked and destroyed on the morning of Tuesday, September 11, 2001, the IRT Subway tunnel adjacent to the Cortlandt Street Station was also destroyed. Makeshift service patterns had to be developed for the West Side IRT Line, and service between Chambers Street and South Ferry was necessarily annulled. But then, in an effort that can only be called heroic, the Transit Authority turned to the task of rebuilding the line. There was no time for preparing new specifications. Instead, engineers looked to the past and, using the very same designs as had the Interborough when the line was built in 1918, a totally new subway tunnel was constructed to replace the former structure.

Interestingly, because of the way debris was cleared out of the disaster area in the weeks and months after September 11, 2001, the new IRT Subway tunnel appears to be an aboveground structure. As the WTC site is eventually restored, the subway tunnel will be subsumed within and beneath the new development and assume a proper belowground orientation. But the important fact is that on September 15, 2002, four days after the first anniversary of the attack, IRT trains were again running between Chambers Street and South Ferry—even though the Cortlandt Street Station itself had yet to be rebuilt.[40]

As the celebratory events associated with October 27, 2004, unfold, the newest section of trackage over which IRT Subway trains are operating represents a proud and determined response to the unspeakable evil that visited New York on September 11, 2001. And on that note, the legacy of the IRT—and the legacy of August Belmont—enters its second century of service to the people of New York.

The Metro subway system in Baltimore.

Two generations of cars on Philadelphia's Broad Street Subway.

North of the downtown business district, Chicago features a four-track elevated line that offers both local and express service. All rolling stock shown in this vintage photo from the early 1950s has been replaced by newer equipment.

Cleveland is the only U.S. city where high-platform subway trains share trackage with light rail cars. The PCC car boards passengers from the low-level center platform, while rapid-transit service uses the more conventional outside platforms. Vintage PCC cars have since been replaced by newer light rail equipment.

The original cars that began subway service in Toronto (top) were painted a deep red. Newer equipment (bottom) features unpainted aluminum.

"Hail to the Chief!" There are only two known instances when a president of the United States rode a subway train while in office. President Richard M. Nixon took a ceremonial ride on the then-new BART system in the East Bay area of his native California in 1972 (top), and two decades later, President Bill Clinton greeted passengers aboard the new Metrolink light rail system in St. Louis (bottom).

The Balboa Park Station on the Bay Area Rapid Transit.

Automated rapid-transit lines serve two Canadian cities. One is a feeder line to the basic subway network in Toronto, while the other, shown here, provides basic service in Vancouver.

Atlanta is yet another U.S. city that has elected to build an impressive new subway system.

A new subway in Washington, D.C., now stands as the second-largest rail transit system in the United States.

Among the flexibilities of light rail transit is an ability to board passengers from street-level platforms in residential neighborhoods, then switch to a high-platform configuration at busy subway stations. Photo shows such an operation in San Francisco.

APPENDIX

The following tables identify various classes of electric rolling stock that have provided passenger service over the past century on the Interborough Rapid Transit Company and its successor agencies as well as the various commuter railroads that provide service between New York and its surrounding suburbs. In addition, Table 1C displays information about subway service patterns as well as marker-light codes used by the IRT Division during the winter of 1959 to 1960.

1. THE INTERBOROUGH SUBWAY AND SUCCESSOR PUBLIC AGENCIES

TABLE 1A
INTERBOROUGH RAPID TRANSIT COMPANY

Car Numbers	No. of Cars	Name or Designation	Builder	Date
3340[1]	1	*August Belmont*	Wason	1902
3341[1]	1	*John B. McDonald*	Wason	1902
2000–2159[2, 3]	160	Composite trailer	Wason, Saint Louis, & Jewett	1903
3000–3339[2, 3]	340	Composite motor	Wason, Saint Louis, Jewett & Stephenson	1903–1904
3342[1]	1	First steel car	PRR (Altoona)	1903
3344[1]	1	Private car *Mineola*	Wason	1904
3350–3649[3]	300	Gibbs Hi-V motor	American Car & Foundry	1904–1905
3650–3699[3]	50	Hi-V deck-roof motor	American Car & Foundry	1907–1908
3700–3809	110	Hi-V motor	American Car & Foundry	1910–1911
3810–3849	40	Hi-V motor	Standard Steel	1910–1911
3850–4024	175	Hi-V motor	Pressed Steel	1910–1911
4025–4036[4]	12	Lo-V Steinway motor	Pullman	1915

Car Numbers	No. of Cars	Name or Designation	Builder	Date
4037–4160	124	Lo-V Fliver motor	Pullman	1915
4161–4214	54	Lo-V Fliver motor	Pullman	1915
4215–4222[4]	8	Lo-V Steinway motor	Pullman	1915
4223–4514	292	Hi-V trailer	Pullman	1915
4515–4554	40	Lo-V trailer	Pullman	1915
4555–4576[4]	22	Lo-V Steinway motor	Pullman	1916
4577–4699	123	Lo-V motor	Pullman	1916
4700–4770[4]	71	Lo-V Steinway motor	Pullman	1916
4771–4810	40	Lo-V motor	Pullman	1916
4811–4965	155	Lo-V trailer	Pullman	1916–1917
4966–5302	337	Lo-V motor	Pullman	1917
5303–5377	75	Lo-V trailer	Pullman	1922
5378–5402	25	Lo-V trailer	Pullman	1922
5403–5502	100	Lo-V motor	Pullman	1922
5503–5627	125	Lo-V motor	American Car & Foundry	1925
5628–5652[4]	25	Lo-V Steinway motor	American Car & Foundry	1925
5653–5702[4]	50	Lo-V World's Fair Steinway motor	Saint Louis Car	1938

All cars have been retired; selected units are preserved at various railway museums.

Notes

1. Not used in revenue passenger service.
2. Wooden bodies; transferred to Elevated Division in 1916.
3. Built with vestibule doors only; center doors added later.
4. Cars designated as "Steinway" could operate only in trains composed of other Steinway-type cars (see text).

TABLE 1B

IRT DIVISION—BOARD OF TRANSPORTATION;
NEW YORK CITY TRANSIT AUTHORITY; NEW YORK CITY TRANSIT

Car Numbers	No. of Cars	Name or Designation	Builder	Date
5703–5802[1, 2]	100	R-12	American Car & Foundry	1948
5803–5952[1, 2]	150	R-14	American Car & Foundry	1949

5953–5999; 6200–6252[1, 3]	100	R-15	American Car & Foundry	1950
6500–6899[1, 4]	400	R-17	Saint Louis Car	1955–1956
7050–7299[1, 4]	250	R-21	Saint Louis Car	1956–1957
7300–7749[1, 4]	450	R-22	Saint Louis Car	1957–1958
7750–7859[5, 8]	110	R-26	American Car & Foundry	1959–1960
7860–7959[5, 8]	100	R-28	American Car & Foundry	1960–1961
8570–8805[6, 8]	236	R-29	Saint Louis Car	1962–1963
8806–9345[6, 7]	540	R-33	Saint Louis Car	1963
9346–9769[6, 8]	424	R-36	Saint Louis Car	1964
1301–1625[9, 10]	325	R-62	Kawasaki	1984–1986
1651–2475[9, 10]	625	R-62A	Bombardier	1986–1988
8001–8010[9, 11]	10	R-110A	Kawasaki	1992
6301–7210[9, 11]	910	R-142	Bombardier	1999–2002
7211–7730[9, 11]	520	R-142A	Kawasaki	1999–2002

All R-26 through R-36 units are scheduled for retirement when sufficient numbers of R-142 and R-142A units are in service, although some may be retained until additional new cars are acquired.

Notes

1. Retired.
2. Single-unit cars with motorman's cab at both ends and exterior conductor's controls.
3. Single-unit cars with motorman's cab at both ends and interior conductor's controls.
4. Single-unit cars; motorman's cab at one end, conductor's cab at opposite end.
5. Semipermanently coupled in two-car units with conventional H2C coupler.
6. Permanently coupled in two-car sets.
7. Five hundred cars permanently coupled in two-car sets, plus forty single units with motorman's cab at each end. All two-car sets retrofitted with air-conditioning during midlife rebuild, while single units were not air-conditioned.
8. Retrofitted with air-conditioning during midlife rebuild.
9. Air-conditioned.
10. Built as single-unit cars; later converted into five-car semipermanently coupled sets.
11. Includes cars with motorman's cab at one end, plus cars with no cabs for motormen.

Tables included in Chapter 1 display basic Interborough and IRT service patterns at various intervals over the years. Actual service patterns were a good deal more complicated, however, involving services that operated only a few trains a day or ran only during certain hours of the day. This table attempts to display such complexity. While it shows service at a particular historical moment, the winter of 1959 to 1960, it is indicative of the multiple terminals and various kinds of services that were operated. Marker lights were color-coded devices on the head end of a train to indicate the service being operated.

TABLE 1C
IRT DIVISION—NEW YORK CITY TRANSIT AUTHORITY:
SERVICE AND MARKER LIGHTS: 1959–1960

Service	Northern Terminal	Southern Terminal	Marker Light over Motorman's Cab	Opposite Marker Light
Broadway Line[1]	242nd Street	South Ferry	red	red
Broadway Line[2]	137th Street	South Ferry	white	red
Broadway Line[3]	Dyckman Street	South Ferry	green	red
Broadway Line[4]	242nd Street	South Ferry	yellow	red
Seventh Avenue–Bronx Express[2]	East 180th Street	New Lots Avenue	green	yellow
Seventh Avenue–Bronx Express[5]	Dyre Avenue	New Lots Avenue	green	red
Seventh Avenue–White Plains Express[6]	East 241st Street	Flatbush Avenue	yellow	red
Seventh Avenue–Lenox Express[2]	145th Street	Flatbush Avenue	red	white
Seventh Avenue–Lenox Express[3]	145th Street	New Lots Avenue	red	green
Lexington-Jerome Express[7]	Woodlawn	Atlantic Avenue	green	red
Lexington-Jerome Express[8]	Woodlawn	Utica Avenue	green	green
Lexington-Jerome Express[6]	Woodlawn	New Lots Avenue	green	white
Lexington–White Plains Express[7]	East 241st Street	Atlantic Avenue	white	green
Lexington–White Plains Express[3]	East 241st Street	Utica Avenue	white	red
Lexington–White Plains Express[9]	East 241st Street	South Ferry	red	green
Lexington–White Plains Express[3]	East 241st Street	Flatbush Avenue	white	yellow
Lexington–White Plains Express[10]	East 241st Street	New Lots Avenue	white	white

Lexington–White Plains Express[11]	East 238th Street	Utica Avenue or Flatbush Avenue	red	red
Lexington–White Plains Thru Express[12]	East 241st Street	Utica Avenue	red	yellow
Lexington-Pelham Local[13]	Pelham Bay Park	Brooklyn Bridge	red	red
Lexington-Pelham Local[14]	177th Street	Brooklyn Bridge	white	red
Lexington-Pelham Local-Express[15]	Pelham Bay Park	Brooklyn Bridge	yellow	red
Flushing Local[16]	Times Square	Main Street	red	red
Flushing Local[3]	Times Square	111th Street	white	red
Flushing Local[3]	Times Square	Willets Point Boulevard	n/a	n/a
Flushing Express[17]	Times Square	Main Street	yellow	red
Third Avenue Line	Gun Hill Road	149th Street	red	red
Dyre Avenue Shuttle[6]	Dyre Avenue	East 180th Street	red	red
42nd Street Shuttle	Times Square	Grand Central	red	red
Bowling Green Shuttle[18]	Bowling Green	South Ferry	red	red
Out of Service Deadhead Train	—	—	yellow	yellow
Tail End of All Trains	—	—	red	red

Weekday service patterns.

Notes

1. Does not operate during morning rush hours.
2. Does not operate during after-midnight hours.
3. Operates rush hours only.
4. Operates morning rush hours only; limited stops north of 137th Street.
5. Does not operate during late-evening or after-midnight hours.
6. Operates during after-midnight hours only.
7. Operates during midday hours only
8. Operates only during rush hours and early-evening hours.
9. Operates during evening hours; some rush-hour service as well.
10. Southbound only; operates during evening rush hours.
11. Northbound only; operates during evening rush hours.
12. Express north of 149th Street; operates southbound during morning rush hours, northbound during evening rush hours only.
13. Does not operate during rush hours.
14. Operates rush hours and midday only.
15. Express north of 138th Street; operates southbound during morning rush hours, northbound during evening rush hours only.
16. Does not operate during evening rush hours.

17. Operates toward Times Square during morning rush hours, toward Main Street during evening rush hours.

18. Does not operate when Lexington–White Plains Express service is running to South Ferry.

2. THE NEW YORK CENTRAL RAILROAD AND SUCCESSOR PUBLIC AGENCY

TABLE 2A

NEW YORK CENTRAL RAILROAD

Car Numbers	No. of Cars	Name or Designation	Builder	Date
4000–4123; 4173[1]	125	Motor coach	American Car & Foundry	1906–1907
4124–4172	49	Motor coach	Saint Louis Car	1907
4350–4355	6	Motor combine	Saint Louis Car	1907
4394–4397	4	Motor baggage/RPO	Saint Louis Car	1910
4398–4399	2	Motor baggage	Saint Louis Car	1910
4174–4187	14	Motor coach	Pressed Steel	1913
4356–4361	6	Motor combine	Pressed Steel	1913
4188–4204	15	Motor coach	Standard Steel	1917
4205–4222	18	Motor coach	Standard Steel	1918
4223–4237	15	Motor coach	Standard Steel	1921
4238–4267	30	Motor coach	Standard Steel	1924
4268–4296	29	Motor coach	Standard Steel	1925
4297–4306	10	Motor coach	Standard Steel	1926
4307–4316	10	Motor coach	Standard Steel	1928
4402	1	Motor baggage	Standard Steel	1928
	20	Motor coach	Standard Steel	1929
4500–4599[2]	100	Motor coach	Saint Louis Car	1950
98[3]	1	Trailer club-coach	Standard Steel	1927
4600–4625; 4700–4726[4, 5, 6]	53	Motor coach	Pullman-Standard	1962
4750–4783[4, 5, 7]	34	Motor coach	Pullman-Standard	1965

Except for eighty-seven cars in the 4600- and 4700-series scheduled to remain in service through 2004, all cars have been retired. The designation "RPO" refers to cars equipped with Railway Post Office facilities.

Notes

1. Sixty feet long when built; later rebuilt into sixty-nine-footers.
2. Later renumbered 1000–1099.
3. Built as conventional day coach; converted to unpowered MU trailer for commuter club car service with 4500-series cars in 1951.

4. Air-conditioned.
5. Acquired through New York State leasing program; see text.
6. Later renumbered 1100–1152.
7. Later renumbered 1153–1186.

TABLE 2B
METROPOLITAN TRANSPORTATION AUTHORITY—
METRO NORTH RAILROAD (HUDSON AND HARLEM LINES)

Car Numbers	No. of Cars	Name or Designation	Builder	Date
8200–8377[1]	178	M-1 motor coach; Metropolitan	Budd/General Electric	1971–1972
8000–8141[1]	142	M-3 motor coach; Metropolitan	Budd/General Electric	1977
4001–4180[1] ??	180	M-7 motor coach	Bombardier	[2]

All cars are air-conditioned.

Notes

1. Coupled into two-car sets; each car has engineer's cab at one end.
2. Scheduled to enter service in 2004.

3. NEW YORK, NEW HAVEN AND HARTFORD RAILROAD AND SUCCESSOR PUBLIC AGENCIES

TABLE 3A
NEW YORK, NEW HAVEN & HARTFORD RAILROAD

Car Numbers	No. of Cars	Name or Designation	Builder	Date
1309[1]	1	Open-platform trailer coach	Osgood Bradley	1904
1414[1]	1	Open-platform trailer coach	Wason	1904
4010–4011[2]	2	Open-platform motor combine	Osgood-Bradley	1908
4020–4023	4	Open-platform motor coach	Standard Steel	1909
4200–4215	16	Open-platform trailer coach	Standard Steel	1909–1912
4024–4027	4	Open-platform motor coach	Standard Steel	1912

Car Numbers	No. of Cars	Name or Designation	Builder	Date
4650–4651	2	Open-platform trailer combine	Standard Steel	1912
4010[3]	1	Motor combine	Standard Steel	1914
4028–4040	13	Motor coach	Standard Steel	1914
4216–4237	22	Trailer coach	Standard Steel	1914
4652–4655	4	Trailer combine	Standard Steel	1914
4060–4063[4]	4	Motor coach	Standard Steel	1915
5000–5005[5]	6	Trailer coach/club	Standard Steel	1915
2758	1	Trailer baggage/RPO	Osgood Bradley	1915
2759, 2767	2	Trailer baggage/RPO	Osgood Bradley	1915
4041–4048	8	Motor coach	Osgood Bradley	1921–1922
4238–4251	14	Trailer coach	Osgood Bradley	1921–1922
4049–4051	3	Motor coach	Osgood Bradley	1925
4070–4094[6]	25	Motor coach	Osgood Bradley	1926
4252–4288	34	Trailer coach	Osgood Bradley	1926–1927
4095–4109	15	Motor coach	Osgood Bradley	1929–1931
4289–4313	25	Trailer coach	Osgood Bradley	1929–1930
4660–4661	2	Trailer combine	Osgood Bradley	1930
4400–4488[7]	89	Motor coach	Pullman-Standard	1954
4670–4676[7]	7	Motor combine	Pullman-Standard	1954
5110–5113[7]	4	Motor coach/club	Pullman-Standard	1954

All cars have been retired. The designation "RPO" refers to cars equipped with Railway Post Office facilities.

Notes

1. Used in trailer service with AC-only motor cars.
2. AC-only.
3. Replaced No. 4010, built in 1908, which was destroyed by fire in 1910. Originally AC-only; rebuilt into AC/DC trailer combine No. 4656 in 1934.
4. Rebuilt as AC/DC cars in 1940–1941 and renumbered 4052–4055.
5. Nos. 5000, 5002, and 5003 rebuilt into locomotive-hauled coaches in 1943; No. 5004 rebuilt into trailer combine No. 4657 in 1941.
6. Certain cars in these series used in locomotive-hauled Penn Central suburban service over former Pennsylvania Railroad lines prior to retirement.
7. Stainless-steel-sheathed cars popularly known as "washboards."

TABLE 3B
NEW YORK, WESTCHESTER & BOSTON RAILROAD

Car Numbers	No. of Cars	Name or Designation	Builder	Date
101–128	28	Motor coach	Pressed Steel	1911–1912
201–202	1	Motor combine	Pressed Steel	1912
129–138	28	Motor coach	Pressed Steel	1915
501–505	5	Trailer coach	Pressed Steel	1915
4060–4063[1]	4	Motor coach	Standard Steel	1915
139–140	2	Motor coach	[2]	1922
141–150	10	Motor coach	Pressed Steel	1924
151–170	20	Motor coach	Pressed Steel	1926
171–190	20	Motor coach	Osgood Bradley	1927
191–195	5	Motor coach	[3]	1928

All cars have been retired.

Notes

1. New Haven Railroad AC-only MU cars assigned to Westchester service.
2. Rebuilt from Nos. 201 and 202.
3. Rebuilt from Nos. 501–505.

TABLE 3C
METROPOLITAN TRANSPORTATION AUTHORITY; STATE OF
CONNECTICUT—METRO NORTH RAILROAD (NEW HAVEN LINE)

Car Numbers	No. of Cars	Name or Designation	Builder	Date
8400–8451; 8452–8470[2]; 8500–8551; 8552–8570[2]; 8601–8619[3]; 8651–8669[3]	144	M-2 motor coach; Cosmopolitan[1]	General Electric	1973–1974
8700–8749; 8800–8849	100	M-2 motor coach; Cosmopolitan[1]	General Electric	1975
8900–8953[4]	54	M-4 motor coach; Cosmopolitan	Tokyu Car	1987
9000–9047[4]	48	M-6 motor coach; Cosmopolitan	Morrison-Knudsen	1994

All cars are air-conditioned.

Notes

1. Coupled into two-car sets; each car has engineer's cab at one end.
2. Even numbers only.
3. Odd numbers only.
4. M-4 and M-6 units coupled into three-car sets; end units include an engineer's cab at one end; center units have no cabs.

4. PENNSYLVANIA RAILROAD AND SUCCESSOR PUBLIC AGENCY

TABLE 4A

PENNSYLVANIA RAILROAD

Car Numbers	No. of Cars	Name or Designation	Builder	Date
497–499; 504–617	117	MP-54-E1 motor coach	PRR (Altoona)	1915; 1918; 1922
4546–4551; 4553–4557	9	MPB-54-E1 motor combine	PRR (Altoona)	1915; 1924
5296–5297	2	MBM-62-E1 motor baggage/RPO	PRR (Altoona)	1915
[1]	6	MB-62-E1 motor baggage	PRR (Altoona)	1918
4557	1	MPB-54-E1 motor combine	PRR (Altoona)	1924
[2]	8	MP-54-E2 motor coach	PRR (Altoona)	1926
[2]	49	MP-54-E2 motor coach	Standard Steel Car	1927
[2]	15	MP-54-E2 motor coach	Pressed Steel Car	1927
[2]	15	MP-54-E2 motor coach	American Car & Foundry	1927
[2]	114	MP-54-E2 motor coach	PRR (Altoona)	1927–1930
4561, 4567	2	MPB-54-BE2 motor combine	PRR (Altoona)	1928
5287–5291	5	MB-62-E2 motor baggage	PRR (Altoona)	1927
5292, 5298	2	MBM-62-E2 motor baggage/RPO	PRR (Altoona)	1928–1929

459–496	38	MP-54-E3 motor coach	PRR (Altoona)	1932–1937
4568–4575	8	MPB-54-BE3 motor combine	PRR (Altoona)	1932–1934
1–42	42	MP-54-T trailer coach	PRR (Altoona)	1932–1937
43	1	MP-54-T trailer coach	PRR (Wilmington)	1939
5416–5419	4	MBM-62-T baggage/RPO trailer	PRR (Altoona)	1933–1934
[3]	49	MP-54-E5	PRR (Wilmington)	1950–1953
4549[4]	1	MPB-54-E5	PRR (Wilmington)	1950–1953
409–458[5]	50	MP-54-E6 motor coach	PRR (Altoona)	1950–1951

All cars have been retired. The designation "RPO" refers to cars equipped with Railway Post Office facilities.

PRR, Pennsylvania Railroad.

PRR MP-54 MU cars that remained in service during Penn Central years were reclassified as follows:

MP-54-E1 units became class MA9B;
MP-54-E2 units became class MA9C;
MP-54-E3 units became class MA9D;
MP-54-E5 units became class MA9E;
MP-54-E6 units became class MA9F.

Notes

1. Two MB-62-E1 units known to have been numbered 5969 and 5970; numbers of other four units not known.

2. The entire MP-54-E2 fleet was numbered 618 through 819.

3. MP-54-E5 units rebuilt from thirteen older MP-54-E1 and thirty-six MP-54-E2 units, retaining their original numbers after the rebuilding. One MP-54-E5 unit was rebuilt from an older MP-54-T trailer car and assigned a new number.

4. Rebuilt from older MPB-54-E1 unit, retaining older unit's number.

5. MP-54-E6 units rebuilt from older P-54 suburban passenger coaches and were not previously part of the MP-54 fleet.

TABLE 4B
NEW JERSEY TRANSIT

Car Numbers	No. of Cars	Name or Designation	Builder	Date
100–134[1, 2]	35	MP-85 motor coach; Jersey Arrow I	Saint Louis Car	1968–1969
534–603[3]	70	MA-1G motor coach; Jersey Arrow II	AVCO/General Electric	1974–1975
1304–1333[2, 4]	30	MA-1H motor coach; Jersey Arrow III	AVCO/General Electric	1977–1978
1335–1533[4, 5]	200	MA-1J motor coach; Jersey Arrow III	AVCO/General Electric	1978

All cars are air-conditioned.

Notes

1. Later designated class MA1-A; no longer in MU service; some converted to trailer cars for use in locomotive-hauled service.
2. Single-unit cars with engineer's position at each end.
3. All units retired.
4. Converted to full AC propulsion.
5. Semipermanently coupled in two-car sets.

5. LONG ISLAND RAIL ROAD AND SUCCESSOR PUBLIC AGENCY

TABLE 5A
LONG ISLAND RAIL ROAD

Car Numbers	No. of Cars	Name or Designation	Builder	Date
1000–1133[1]	134	MP-41 motor coach	American Car & Foundry	1905
1200–1204[2]	5	MB-45 motor baggage	Wason	1905
1401–1420	20	MP-54A motor coach	American Car & Foundry	1908–1909
1421–1450	30	MP-54 motor coach	American Car & Foundry	1908
1452–1551	100	MP-54A motor coach	American Car & Foundry	1910
1209–1210	2	MBM-62 motor baggage/RPO	American Car & Foundry	1910
1211–1219	9	MB-62 motor baggage	American Car & Foundry	1910

1350–1364	15	MPB-54 motor combine	Standard Steel	1910
1552–1601	50	MP-54A motor coach	American Car & Foundry	1911
1778–1783[3]	6	MP-54A motor coach	American Car & Foundry	1912
1602–1621	20	MP-54A motor coach	American Car & Foundry	1912
1348–1349	2	MPB-54 motor combine	American Car & Foundry	1912
1365–1369	5	MPB-54 motor combine	American Car & Foundry	1912
1370–1381	12	MPB-54 motor combine	American Car & Foundry	1913
1382–1384	3	MPBM-54 motor passenger-baggage/ RPO	American Car & Foundry	1913
1385–1399	15	MPB-54 motor combine	American Car & Foundry	1913
1622–1636	15	MP-54A motor coach	American Car & Foundry	1913
1677[4]	1	CT-54A trailer commuter club car *Rockaway*	American Car & Foundry	1913
1637–1676	50	MP-54A motor coach	American Car & Foundry	1914
907–926	20	T-54 arch roof trailer coach	Standard Steel	1915
927–951	25	T-54 arch roof trailer coach	Standard Steel	1916
952–996	45	T-54 arch roof trailer coach	Pressed Steel	1916
1678–1777; 1784-1943	259	MP-54B and MP-54C arch roof motor coach	American Car & Foundry	1920–1927
1944–1983	40	MP-54D arch roof motor coach	Pullman	1927
1135–1179	45	MP-54 motor coach	American Car & Foundry	1930
200[5]	1	T-62 double-deck trailer coach	PRR (Altoona)	1932
201	1	CT-70 double-deck trailer coach	PRR (Altoona)	1937
1347	1	MP-70 double-deck motor coach	PRR (Altoona)	1937
1337–1346[6]	10	MP-70 double-deck motor coach	PRR (Altoona)	1947
1287–1336[6]	50	MP-70 double-deck motor coach	PRR (Altoona)	1948
3500–3519	20	MP-70T motor coach; (no controls)	Pullman-Standard	1953

Car Numbers	No. of Cars	Name or Designation	Builder	Date
2501–2522[6]	22	MP-72 motor coach	Pullman-Standard	1955
2601–2674[6]	74	MP-72 motor coach (no controls)	Pullman-Standard	1955–1956
2801–2844[6]	44	T-72 trailer coach	Pullman-Standard	1956
2525–2536[6,7]	12	MP-72 motor coach	Pullman-Standard	1963
2675–2692[6,7]	18	MP-72 motor coach (no controls)	Pullman-Standard	1963

All cars have been retired, although some MP-72 and T-72 units saw additional service as locomotive-hauled coaches. The designation "RPO" refers to cars equipped with Railway Post Office facilities.

LIRR, Long Island Rail Road.

Unless indicated otherwise, all LIRR MP-54-type cars are equipped with railroad-style monitor roofs. Numbers and styles shown represent original "as-built" designation and configuration; no effort has been made to identify and catalog subsequent renumberings or conversions to different styles of service.

Notes

1. Similar to Interborough Rapid Transit Company's Gibbs Cars; see text.

2. Wooden-bodied cars used to haul baggage and express cars; not used in passenger service.

3. Originally built for and owned by Pennsylvania Railroad for third-rail service between Penn Station and Manhattan Transfer; conveyed to LIRR in 1923.

4. Only LIRR commuter club car in MU fleet.

5. First "double-deck" car built for LIRR MU service; see text.

6. Air-conditioned.

7. Acquired for service to 1964–1965 New York World's Fair.

TABLE 5B

METROPOLITAN TRANSPORTATION AUTHORITY—
LONG ISLAND RAIL ROAD

Car Numbers	No. of Cars	Name or Designation	Builder	Date
9001–9620[1]	620	M-1 motor coach; Metropolitan	Budd	1968–1971
9621–9770[1]	150	M-1 motor coach; Metropolitan	Budd-GE	1972

| 9771–9944[1] | 174 | M-3 motor coach; Metropolitan | Transit America | 1985–1986 |
| 7001–7326[1,2] | 326 | M-7 motor coach | Bombardier | 2002–2003 |

All cars are air-conditioned.

Notes

1. Coupled into two-car sets; each car has engineer's cab at one end.

2. Contract for the acquisition of 326 cars included an option for the purchase of 372 additional units; some of the option cars may be used for Metro North service.

NOTES

CHAPTER 1: AUGUST BELMONT AND HIS SUBWAY

1. David McCullough, *Mornings on Horseback* (New York: Simon and Schuster, 1981), 262. McCullough's work is a study of Theodore Roosevelt, whose first major speech as a member of the New York State Legislature in 1882 was a denunciation of Gould and his acquisition of Manhattan Railways. McCullough, *Mornings on Horseback*, 262–65.

2. For additional information about Manhattan Railways and the New York elevated lines, see William Fullerton Reeves, *The First Elevated Railroads in Manhattan and the Bronx of the City of New York* (New York: New-York Historical Society, 1936); see also Robert C. Reed, *The New York Elevated* (New York: A. S. Barnes, 1978). For a detailed chronology of operational milestones associated with the elevated lines from 1867 through 1955, see "New York's El Lines," *Electric Railroads,* 25 (December 1956).

3. In 1889, two years before it was acquired by Manhattan Railways, Suburban's main line was 2.98 miles long, and the company owned thirteen steam locomotives plus twenty-six passenger cars. By contrast, Manhattan Railways included 32.4 route miles, owned 291 locomotives and 921 passenger cars. *Annual Report of the Board of Railroad Commissioners of the State of New York* (Albany, N.Y.: James B. Lyon, 1890), 661, 671.

4. For a treatment of the Tweed era in New York politics and Tweed's dealings with Jay Gould and Manhattan Railways, see Seymour J. Mandelbaum, *Boss Tweed's New York* (Westport, Conn.: Greenwood Press, 1965), 59–73; see also Maury Klein, *The Life and Legend of Jay Gould* (Baltimore, Md.: Johns Hopkins University Press, 1986). Klein believes that Manhattan Railways was the "most incongruous pillar of Gould's business empire" and also suggests that available source materials are insufficient to provide adequate explanation of why he entered the elevated railway business. Klein, *Life and Legend of Jay Gould*, 282.

5. Klein, *Life and Legend of Jay Gould*, 474.

6. Gustavus Myers, "History of Public Franchises in New York City," *Municipal Affairs* (March 1900):172.

7. Ibid., 172–73.

8. Mere days before the election, Roosevelt was thought to be substantially ahead of Hewitt. But there was a third-party candidate in the race, Henry George, the nominee of the Labor Party. When George's campaign appeared to be making serious headway in the final days of the race, there was significant GOP defection from Roosevelt to Hewitt to avoid the possibility of a George victory. For further details, see Edmund Morris, *The Rise of Theodore Roosevelt* (New York: Modern Library, 2001), 339–59.

9. Mayor Hewitt's message was printed in its entirety in the *New York Times*. See "The Mayor's Big Scheme," *New York Times* (1 February 1888):9. No negative implications should be inferred from the newspaper's use of the word "scheme" in its headline. See also "The City's Crying Needs," *New York Herald* (1 February 1888):4.

10. Hewitt believed that two of the railroad's four tunnels under Park Avenue north of Grand Central should be converted into rapid-transit facilities. For additional details about the Park Avenue tunnels, see Chapter 4.

11. "The Mayor's Big Scheme," 9.

12. *New York Times* (1 February 1888):9.

13. For additional information about Sprague and his achievements in Richmond and elsewhere, see Brian J. Cudahy, *Cash, Tokens and Transfers* (New York: Fordham University Press, 1990), 35–50; William D. Middleton, *The Time of the Trolley* (San Marino, Calif.: Golden West Books, 1987), 5, 65–73. For an account of the development of electric railways by Sprague himself, see Frank J. Sprague, "Some Personal Experiences," *Street Railway Journal* (October 8, 1904):566–71.

14. The words are those of Hardin H. Littell, the first president of the American Street Railway Association, delivered on the occasion of the association's second annual convention. *Verbatim Report of the Second Annual Meeting of the American Street-Railway Association* (Brooklyn, N.Y.: Office of the Association, 1883–1884), 8.

15. For a comprehensive chronology of political developments that led to the construction of the subway as well as technical details associated with early phases of its construction, see "The New York Rapid Transit Subway," *Street Railway Journal* (5 October 1901):425–33; for a series of five articles dealing with various aspects of the subway's development, see *Railroad Gazette* (16 September 1904):338–45; for a recent in-depth account, see Clifton Hood, *722 Miles* (New York: Simon and Schuster, 1993), 56–74.

16. In addition to Steinway, there were four appointed members of the commission: John H. Starin, Samuel Spencer, Eugene S. Busche,

and John H. Inman. A sixth member, selected by the original five, was John N. Bowers. For the full text of the Steinway Commission's report, see *New York Times* (21 October 1891):9. "At a special meeting of the Aldermen yesterday the report of the Rapid-Transit Commission was unanimously approved," *New York Times* (29 October 1891):9.

17. "The New York Rapid Transit Subway," 426; see also "Failure to Make a Sale," *New York Times* (30 December 1892):8.

18. "The New York Rapid Transit Subway," 427. After leaving office, Governor Roswell Flower would later play an important role in the creation of the Brooklyn Rapid Transit Company. For details, see Brian J. Cudahy, *How We Got to Coney Island* (New York: Fordham University Press, 2002), 169–74.

19. See *New York Times* (8 November 1894):4.

20. See "Metropolitan Street Railway's Rapid Transit Offer Withdrawn," *Street Railway Journal* (May 1899):334.

21. "The Rapid Transit Commissioners met for the first time in their new offices on the fourth floor of 320 Broadway yesterday afternoon and took the final steps necessary to authorize the advertising for bids from contractors to build the underground road." *New York Times* (14 November 1899):9. See also "Invitation to Contractors for the New York Tunnel Railway," *Street Railway Journal* (December 1899):889–90.

22. In addition to the two contractors who actually submitted bids, until the very last minute the Third Avenue Railway, a New York streetcar operator, was expected to submit a bid to build and operate the new subway. Third Avenue elected to defer, however. See "Bids for Rapid Transit," *New York Times* (14 November 1899):9.

23. See *New York Times* (17 January 1900):1.

24. *New York Journal* (25 March 1900):50.

25. *New York Times* (18 January 1900):1.

26. August Belmont, Jr., was born in 1853. His father had arrived in New York in 1837 as the North American representative of the House of Rothchild and quickly became an important figure not only in the world of finance but also in Democratic Party politics, fashionable high society, and the emerging sport of thoroughbred horse racing. Belmont Park Race Track in Nassau County, Long Island, memorializes the family name. After completing work on the New York subway, Belmont and McDonald joined forces in a nine-year effort that culminated in the opening of the Cape Cod Canal in 1915. August Belmont, Jr., passed away in 1924 at the age of 71. For his obituary, see *New York Times* (12 December 1924):21.

27. See "Manhattan Leased by Subway Company," *Street Railway Journal* (29 November 1902):877–78. The agreement was executed in

late 1902 and became effective April 1, 1903. Under the terms of the lease, "the rental will be 7 per cent per annum on the stock of the Manhattan Railway Company guaranteed by the Interborough Rapid Transit Company," ibid., 877.

28. Quoted in Arthur Schlesinger, Jr., *A Thousand Days* (Boston: Houghton Mifflin, 1965), 733.

29. William Barclay Parsons was born in 1859, graduated from Columbia College, and quickly earned a reputation as a premiere engineer in the field of railway construction. Prior to his assignment with the Board of Rapid Transit Commissioners in New York, for instance, he worked on a railroad project between Hankow and Canton in China. He resigned his subway post soon after the Interborough began service in 1904 and traveled to Panama to prepare a report for President Roosevelt on the feasibility of building a canal across that narrow isthmus. Parsons joined August Belmont in 1905 to work on building the Cape Cod Canal and served as an engineer with the U.S. Army during the First World War. After the war, Parsons retired and devoted his time to writing. His major work is *Engineers and Engineering in the Renaissance* (Baltimore: Williams and Wilkins, 1939). William Barclay Parsons died in 1932 at the age of 73; for his obituary, see *New York Times* (10 May 1932):21.

30. "The Multiple Unit System of electric railway operation enables a train of any number of cars . . . to be operated as a unit, and by one operator." Pennsylvania Railroad, "Syllabus for Class in Railway Electricity," Part I (Philadelphia, 1914). Frank Sprague himself described the system in some detail in "The Sprague Multiple Unit System," *Street Railway Journal* (4 May 1901):537–50; see also Frank Sprague, "The Problem of Elevated and Suburban Electric Railway Transportation," *Street Railway Journal* (July 1899):467–72.

31. There are segments of four-track rapid-transit right-of-way in both London and Chicago that operate local and express service, but they are outdoors and away from downtown areas, not in central-city subway tunnels. As discussed in Chapter 2, there are four-track segments of the Boston subway, but not for the operation of local and express service.

32. F. J. Sprague, "Ideal Rapid Transit," *Supplement to the Street Railway Journal* (March 1891):1–6.

33. "The 'Rapid Transit' Dinner at the New York Electric Club," *Supplement to the Street Railway Journal* (March 1891):7.

34. Sprague, "Ideal Rapid Transit," 4; "The 'Rapid Transit' Dinner at the New York Electric Club," 7.

35. Although trains continue to run through the City Hall station

every day, trains no longer stop there and the station is not used for passenger entry and exit. Its distinctive architecture has been retained, and there are plans to reopen the city's first subway station as part of the New York Transit Museum.

36. For further details about streetcar, cable railway, and elevated train service across the Brooklyn Bridge, see Cudahy, *How We Got to Coney Island,* 157–69.

37. Initial plans called for the Interborough to veer eastward after crossing Spuyten Duyvil Creek and terminate at Bailey Avenue near the Kingsbridge station of the New York Central Railroad's Putnam Division. Plans were changed, however, and the Interborough instead continued north to a terminal at Broadway and 242nd Street, adjacent to Van Cortlandt Park. See Interborough Rapid Transit Company, *The New York Subway: Its Construction and Equipment* (New York: Interborough Rapid Transit Company, 1904; rev. ed. New York: Fordham University Press, 1991), 23–26.

38. Elevated service over this connection began on November 26, 1904. Over the years, it was operated at various times by Second Avenue and Third Avenue el trains; use of the connection was discontinued in 1946. See "New York's El Lines," 7–8; see also "To Connect Tunnel with Elevated Railroad in New York," *Street Railway Journal* (18 July 1903):108–9.

39. *The New York Subway: Its Construction and Equipment,* 42.

40. In at least two instances—at the Belmont Hotel at Fourth Avenue and East 42nd Street and at the New York Times Building at Broadway and West 42nd Street—the new Interborough subway tunnel was built *through* the belowground structure of major New York buildings. Evidence of this interlocking construction can be examined at the western end of the Times Square station on the Times Square–Grand Central shuttle.

41. "Laying Track in the New York Subway," *Street Railway Journal* (21 March 1903):445.

42. See *New York Times* (20 February 1903):1, 2. For a slightly later set of proposals, see "Plans for Extension of New York Subway and 'L' Systems," *Street Railway Journal* (28 January 1908):326–28.

43. For further information about the Brooklyn Rapid Transit Company, see Cudahy, *How We Got to Coney Island,* 169–74.

44. "Brooklyn Tunnel Bids," *Street Railway Journal* (19 July 1902):128.

45. Peter Derrick, *Tunneling to the Future* (New York: New York University Press, 2001), 43.

46. See "Tunnel Franchises," *Street Railway Journal* (2 August 1902):169.

47. See "Ground Broken for Brooklyn Tunnel," *Street Railway Journal* (15 November 1902):818.

48. For details about the Interborough's electric generating plant, see *The New York Subway: Its Construction and Equipment,* 77–116.

49. In Chapter 3 an alternative arrangement used in London is discussed, where a separate "fourth rail" completes the circuit, with running rails playing no electrical role at all.

50. Manhattan Railways began electrifying its elevated lines in 1900, prior to the company's being acquired under lease by Belmont and the Interborough in 1902. The first electric-powered revenue train carried passengers on the Second Avenue Line on December 30, 1901, and all of the Manhattan els were electrified by early 1903. W. E. Baker, who had supervised the earlier electrification of Chicago's Metropolitan West Side Elevated Railroad, was hired to manage the conversion, and L. B. Stillwell was retained as a consultant. For further details, see George H. Pegram, "The Power House and Sub-Station Buildings of the Manhattan Railway Company," *Street Railway Journal* 17 (15 January 1901):2–11. For an account of the ceremonial inauguration of electrified service over the Second Avenue el on January 9, 1902, with such notables as John D. Rockefeller, Jr., H. H. Vreeland, president of the Metropolitan Street Railway, and subway builder John B. McDonald aboard, see *New York Times* (10 January 1902):14.

51. *The New York Subway: Its Construction and Equipment,* 135.

52. See "Cars for the New York Subway," *Street Railway Journal* (20 September 1902):382–83.

53. "Cars for the New York Subway," *Street Railway Journal* (22 August 1903):265. The full article runs from page 264 to page 266.

54. "The New York Subway Cars," *Street Railway Journal* (22 August 1903):248.

55. See "Test of Subway Motors," *Street Railway Journal* (21 March 1903):446–47.

56. For full details of such conversions, see Gene Sansone, *Evolution of New York City Subways* (Baltimore: Johns Hopkins University Press, 1997), 25–27.

57. The order was split as follows: Jewett, 100 cars; John Stephenson, 100 cars; St. Louis Car Company, 200 cars; Wason, 100 cars. Sansone, *Evolution of New York City Subways,* 84.

58. "Cars for the New York Subway," 265.

59. President Alexander J. Cassatt of the Pennsylvania Railroad was the brother of Mary Cassatt, widely recognized as the artist who introduced the impressionist school of painting to the United States.

60. For additional details about this unique car, see "Steel Car for

the New York Subway," *Street Railway Journal* (13 February 1904):260–61.

61. For a description of these events, see George Gibbs, "Origins of the Steel Passenger Car," *Railroad History* (Spring 1978):71–73 (reprint of a news release issued in May 1929 by the Pennsylvania Railroad).

62. John H. White, Jr., *The American Railroad Passenger Car* (Baltimore, Md.: Johns Hopkins University Press, 1978), 132.

63. For additional details, see L. B. Stillwell, "The Electrical Equipment of the New Steel Cars for the New York Subway," *Street Railway Journal* (4 March 1905):422–23.

64. *New York Times* (27 October 1904):1.

65. Ibid., 16.

66. The editors of the *New York Times* were particularly pleased at the restrained nature of the celebration: "It is indicative of civic sanity that New York can celebrate so great an event as the opening of its system of underground rapid transit without the conventional accessories of trumpets and drums, processions obstructing the streets, speechmaking ad nauseam, a spread for the Aldermen with unlimited midday champagne, and the other familiar features of municipal functions." *New York Times* (28 October 1904):8. On the previous day, October 27, the same newspaper ran a lengthy, four-part editorial that can be recommended as a summary of the political developments that led to the subway's construction. See *New York Times* (27 October 1904):8.

67. "The New York Subway Opened," *Street Railway Journal* (5 November 1904):859.

68. In 1903, Mayor Hewitt was memorialized when a new city fireboat was christened the *Abram S. Hewitt* in his honor. Interestingly, the *Hewitt,* as well as other city fireboats of this era, were the work of a distinguished naval architect by the name of Harry de Berkely Parsons, a brother of William Barclay Parsons. For further details about New York fireboats, see Brian J. Cudahy, *Around Manhattan Island and Other Maritime Tales of New York* (New York: Fordham University Press, 1997), 76–119, 243–53.

69. Rail enthusiasts continue to debate the relative merits of various classes of subway cars for viewing the right-of-way from a train's front window. Nothing will ever equal the darkened front vestibule of a typical Interborough car, once the motorman's cab was restricted to the right side of the front vestibule with the design of the deck-roof cars in 1908 to 1909. These Interborough cars featured two large windows, one in the "storm door" and another in the vestibule area opposite the motorman's cab.

70. For details about these new cars, see "Improved Steel Car for the New York Subway," *Street Railway Journal* (14 March 1908):422–26.

71. For comprehensive data about transit patronage, see Boris S. Pushkarev, *Urban Rail in America* (Bloomington, Ind: Indiana University Press, 1982), 199–274.

72. Rapid Transit Commission of the City of New York, *New York Subway* (New York: RTC of NYC 1904), 1.

73. See. "Transit Proposals to New York Commission," *Street Railway Journal* (5 March 1904):384.

74. "Discussion on Side-Door Subway Cars in New York," *Electric Railway Journal* (10 April 1909):699.

75. Ibid., 698.

76. "Rebuilding New York Subway Local Cars for Side-Door Operation," *Electric Railway Journal* (10 October 1912):758.

77. For a full treatment of the Dual Contracts, see Derrick, *Tunneling to the Future*, 153–85; see also Hood, *722 Miles,* 135–61.

78. For a description of the Triborough Subway System, see "A New Subway Line for New York City; Its History," *Engineering News* (10 March 1910):288–89; see also Derrick, *Tunneling to the Future*, 126–30.

79. For details about the creation of the Public Service Commission, see James Blaine Walker, *Fifty Years of Rapid Transit* (New York: Law Printing, 1918).

80. Hood, *722 Miles,* 61–66.

81. Ibid., 125. In 1912, the Interborough's first president, Theodore P. Shonts, decried what he called a developing "attitude of hostility to the welfare of the public service companies." *Christian Science Monitor* (29 May 1912):16.

82. For additional details about the financial arrangements of the Dual Contracts, see Derrick, *Tunneling to the Future,* 186–230.

83. The contemporary Grand Central–Times Square shuttle requires interesting maneuvering when trains are returned to the shops for maintenance and servicing. What was previously the northbound local track has no physical connection to the other shuttle tracks, and trains using this track enter and leave the shuttle via the northbound local track of the Broadway–7th Avenue Line. A pedestrian walkway must be hoisted out of the way to allow such access. The other two shuttle tracks—the former southbound local track and the former northbound express track—are connected to each other by switches and have access to the IRT system via the southbound local track of the Lexington Avenue Line.

84. Under the terms of the Dual Contracts, a six-track subway tunnel was constructed under Brooklyn's Flatbush Avenue between Atlantic Avenue and Grand Army Plaza. Four of the tracks, as described, were for the Interborough's Brooklyn Line. The other two were built for the Brighton Beach Line of the Brooklyn Rapid Transit Company. For further details, see "Reconstruction of the Brighton Beach Line," *Public Service Record* (December 1918):12–15.

85. The bridge used to cross the Harlem River was built in 1882 by the New York and Northern Railroad, a company whose trains connected with Manhattan Railways el trains at 155th Street. See Chapter 4 for additional details about a suburban railroad that is better known as the Putnam Division of the New York Central R.R.

86. The new BRT subway car was based on an earlier design that was developed by the Boston Elevated Railway, as discussed in Chapter 2. For additional information on the BRT car, see "The New Municipal Car—Design," *Electric Railway Journal* (6 June 1914):1261–67.

87. See "Hearing on Car Destination Signs before the Public Service Commission," *Electric Railway Journal* (30 January 1909):199.

88. Ibid.

89. *Electric Railway Journal* (27 July 1918):149.

90. For full details, see "Multiple-Unit Door Control on the Interborough Subway Trains," *Electric Railway Journal* (19 September 1925):433–39.

91. The onset of MUDC, and the fact there would no longer be a conductor or guard stationed at the end of every subway car, prompted the Interborough to print and install maps in all of its subway cars to compensate for the verbal station announcements guards previously rendered. In designing such maps, Interborough cartographers defied convention and displayed Manhattan Island horizontally, placing "north" on the right side of the map. (In the 1930s, the new Independent Subway System would follow the Interborough's lead and orient its maps in a similar fashion.)

92. For additional treatment, see Sansone, *Evolution of New York City Subways*, 30–50.

93. Ibid., 84–110.

94. For additional information about the Steinway Tunnels, see Hood, *722 Miles*, 162–80; see also David Rogoff, "The Steinway Tunnels," *Electric Railroads* 29 (April 1960).

95. The original Dual Contracts plan was for BRT subway trains to reach Queens Plaza via the Queensboro Bridge. Concerns developed over the ability of the bridge to support the heavier weight of that company's trains, so a BRT tunnel was built instead, and the bridge right-

of-way was used by Interborough elevated trains. In addition, because BRT subway trains were wider than Interborough equipment, the BRT used narrower elevated equipment for its joint operation over the Flushing and Astoria lines, with subway trains from Manhattan terminating at Queens Plaza.

96. For additional treatment, see Hood, *722 Miles*, 197; see also Brian J. Cudahy, *Under the Sidewalks of New York,* rev. 2nd ed. (New York: Fordham University Press, 1995), 97–100.

97. For details about the BRT bankruptcy and the early years of the BMT, see Cudahy, *How We Got to Coney Island,* 227–30; Hood, *722 Miles,* 214–39.

98. For additional details about the Independent Subway System, see Frederick A. Kramer, *Building the Independent Subway* (New York: Quadrant, 1990); see also Cudahy, *Under the Sidewalks of New York,* 85–100; Hood, *722 Miles,* 203–13.

99. For additional details, see Sansone, *Evolution of New York City Subways,* 42, 49.

100. Hedley passed away in Yonkers on July 16, 1955, at the age of 91. For his obituary, see *New York Times* (17 July 1955):60.

101. *New York Herald Tribune* (13 June 1940):25.

102. Ibid.

103. Although the Third Avenue Line can correctly be called the last of the Manhattan els, the final operational segment of elevated right-of-way on Manhattan Island that was built during the Manhattan Railways era was the 155th Street Station of the shuttle service that connected with the Jerome Avenue Line across the Harlem River in the Bronx. The shuttle line beyond 155th Street was a Dual Contracts–related effort, but the station itself, located immediately behind the Polo Grounds, was once the northern terminal of both the Sixth Avenue and the Ninth Avenue Lines. The shuttle was phased out in 1958. The abandonment of the Manhattan portions of the Third Avenue Line in 1955 saw the publication of a wonderful retrospective about the Third Avenue Line in particular and New York elevated service more generally; see E. J. Quinby and Freeman Hubbard, "Third Avenue El," *Railroad* (June 1955):12–29.

104. Another technical difference in IRT practice is that track trips associated with automatic signals are located on the right, or train operator's side, of the right-of-way, while on the BMT and IND such devices are on the left side.

105. For details about various classes of new IRT cars acquired between 1955 and 1964, see Sansone, *Evolution of New York City Subways,* 225–28, 231–39, 242–43, 247–51.

106. Although certain IND lines once operated eleven-car trains, in more recent years the busy Flushing Line was the only Transit Authority service to operate eleven-car trains. Since all R-36 units were configured as two-car "married pair" sets, forty R-33 cars were built as single units, painted two-tone blue to match the R-36 cars, and used on the Flushing Line. To compensate for this assignment, thirty-four R-36 units that would otherwise have been used in Flushing service were delivered in a livery similar to the R-33s and used on the basic IRT network. During subsequent rebuilding, the single-unit R-33s lacked sufficient room for the installation of air-conditioning equipment and they were never so equipped. For additional information about IRT service to the 1964-to-1965 World's Fair, see "A First-Class Rapid Ride," *Railway Age* (1 June 1964):22–24.

107. For more details about the New York, Westchester and Boston, see Chapter 4.

108. Although the Dyre Avenue shuttle originally used retired el cars from the Interborough's Manhattan Division, connected with the IRT at East 180th Street, and looked like an IRT operation, in point of fact it was managed by the city's Board of Transportation as part of the IND Division. It was formally shifted to the IRT after the Second World War.

109. The Interborough long used a system of wayside signal indications whose aspects were similar to those on U.S. railroads. More recently, new signals installed on the IRT Division have adopted the same distinctive codes used on the BMT and IND Divisions. Interlocking signals protecting various junctions typically include two separate sets of green-yellow-red signals, arranged vertically. In older Interborough practice, the upper signal displays information about the main track, the lower signal about the diverging track. Thus a "red over green" indication meant proceed on diverging route, next signal is clear, while "green over red" was the equivalent indication for the main track. In BMT-IND practice, the upper signal displays allowable speed, while the lower signal shows whether the switch is set for the main track (green) or the diverging track (yellow). On the BMT-IND, then, "green over yellow" means proceed on the diverging route, the next signal is clear.

110. The South Ferry Station platform long used by the shuttle from Bowling Green was built under the terms of the Dual Contracts and is no longer in service, although the track adjacent to the platform remains active. A parallel South Ferry station was built as part of the Contract Two effort and serves as the southern terminal for Broadway–7th Avenue local trains.

111. Many of the retired cars were loaded on barges, towed out to sea, and pushed overboard to create undersea habitat in the Atlantic Ocean off the mouth of the Delaware River. See "End of Line for Subway Cars: the Ocean Floor," *New York Times* (22 August 2001):B3.

112. The R-62 and R-62A units were originally single-unit cars with an operator's cab at each end. More recently, New York City Transit has reconfigured most of the fleet into semipermanently coupled five-car units.

113. The new R-142 and R-142A cars can be coupled into units of various lengths, as long as cab cars are at either end. In practice, however, five-car units will be standard.

CHAPTER 2: CHANGE AT PARK STREET UNDER

1. For general historical information about rapid transit in Boston, see Robert L. Abrams, "The Story of Rapid Transit; Boston," *Bulletin of the National Railway Historical Society; Part I (Spring 1960):4–17; Part II (Summer 1960):14–22; see also Tony Fitzherbert, "Rapids 'round the World—IV: Boston," *Headlights, Part I (May 1962):5–8; Part II (June 1962):6–10.

2. For a general treatment of Sprague and his work, see William D. Middleton, *The Time of the Trolley* (San Marino, Calif.: Golden West Books, 1987), 5, 65–73; for Sprague's own reflections on his Richmond achievement, see Frank J. Sprague, "Some Personal Experiences," *Street Railway Journal* (8 October 1904):566; for a news account of Sprague's work in Richmond, see "Electric Railway; Its First Day of Operation," *Richmond Times* (3 February 1888):1.

3. For information on the creation of the West End, and the identity of its predecessor companies, see *History of the West End Street Railway* (Boston: Louis P. Hager, 1892).

4. For a full treatment of the cable car era in urban transportation, see George W. Hilton, *The Cable Car in America* (Stanford, Calif.: Stanford University Press, 1982). Hilton provides details about every U.S. cable street railway, including many that were planned but never built. For details about West End proposals, see pp. 471, 472.

5. The West End's first electric-powered streetcar entered service on January 1, 1889. It ran from Allston to Coolidge Corner and then via Beacon Street to Park Square in Boston proper.

6. For an important study that links the development of residential neighborhoods surrounding Boston with the growth of the city's streetcar system, see Sam Bass Warner, Jr., *Streetcar Suburbs,* rev. ed. (Cam-

bridge, Mass.: Harvard University Press, 1978). For a late-nineteenth-century analysis of the same subject, see Louis Bell, Ph.D., "Urban Growth and the Electric Railway," *Street Railway Journal* (January 1896):10–13.

7. George C. Crocker, chairman of the Boston Transit Commission, addressing an annual meeting of the American Street Railway Association; *Report of the Seventeenth Annual Meeting of the American Street Railway Association* (Chicago: Office of the Association, 1898–1890), 1029. For additional information about the conversion of Boston's streetcars to electric propulsion, see "Street Railways Have Certainly Speeded Up Since 'Old Dobbin' Furnished the Power," *Co-operation* (February 1950):7–18. (*Co-operation* was a magazine published for Boston transit employees.)

8. This concern over the prospect of underground travel is treated at some length in Benson Bobrick, *Labyrinths of Iron* (New York: Newsweek Books, 1981), 49–73.

9. *New York Times* (15 August 1897):10.

10. "The legislative act establishing the Boston Transit Commission authorized, but did not require it to build a subway or subways between Pleasant Street on the south, and Causeway Street on the north, with a branch to Park Square"; "The Boston Subway," *Street Railway Journal* (September 1898):493.

11. *New York Times* (15 August 1897):10.

12. *Scientific American* (5 September 1896):135

13. See Interborough Rapid Transit Company, *The New York Subway: Its Construction and Equipment* (New York: Interborough Rapid Transit Company, 1904; rev. ed. New York: Fordham University Press, 1991), 37–66.

14. *New York Times* (10 October 1897):21.

15. *Scientific American* (18 September 1897):184.

16. The editorial views of the *Boston Journal* were quoted by the *New York Times* (10 September 1897):5.

17. *New York Times* (15 August 1897):10.

18. Ibid.

19. *Harper's Weekly* (18 September 1897):934.

20. *New York Times* (29 May 1897):1.

21. *Boston Globe* (1 September 1897):1.

22. "Opening of the Boston Subway," *Harper's Weekly* (18 September 1897):934. For a comprehensive technical review of the Boston subway prepared at the time of its opening, see "The Boston Subway," *Street Railway Journal* (September 1898):494–500; for a detailed description of the project written to commemorate its seventy-fifth anni-

versary, see Burton G. Brown, Jr., "The Boston Subway: 1897," *Bulletin of the National Railway Historical Society* 3 (1973):18–27, 43–46; for a retrospective on the original Boston subway published to commemorate its centenary, see Bradley H. Clarke and O. R. Cummings, *Tremont Street Subway* (Cambridge, Mass.: Boston Street Railway Association, 1997).

23. See Frank J. Sprague, "The Sprague Multiple Unit System," *Street Railway Journal* (4 May 1901):537–50; see also "The Multiple Unit System on the South Side Elevated Railway of Chicago," *Street Railway Journal* (December 1898):763–66.

24. For arguments as to why the West End Street Railway should have remained Boston's primary mass-transit provider, see *History of the West End Street Railway,* 128–32.

25. Less well known than the elevated railway systems of Brooklyn, New York, and Chicago were two relatively small elevated lines that operated for a short time in Kansas City, Missouri, and Sioux City, Iowa. For further details, see Brian J. Cudahy, *Cash, Tokens and Transfers* (New York: Fordham University Press, 1990), 67–69.

26. "The Proposed New Electric Elevated Railway in Boston," *Street Railway Journal* (September 1898):501.

27. *Boston Globe* (1 May 1901):6.

28. *Boston Globe* (10 June 1901):1, 2.

29. See for example, "Alterations at Dudley Street Terminal," *Street Railway Journal* (8 December 1906):1106.

30. *Boston Globe* (10 June 1901):1.

31. Ibid., 2.

32. *Boston Globe* (20 February 1901):8.

33. See "New Power Station and Elevated Railway System in Boston," *Street Railway Journal* (2 March 1901):253–64. In 1908, BERY retained Stone and Webster to evaluate its power situation, and as a result of this study a new generating station equipped with steam turbine engines was built in South Boston in 1911 that produced three-phase, 25-cycle alternating current at a potential of 6,600 volts. This was stepped up to 13,200 volts for transmission, then reduced and converted to direct current at various substations throughout BERY's service area. See "Power Generation and Distribution System of the Boston Elevated Railway," *Electric Railway Journal* (30 December 1911):1313–19.

34. For further details, see "The Boston Elevated Opens Atlantic Circuit," *Street Railway Journal* (7 September 1901):302–3.

35. See *Boston Globe* (16 January 1919):1, 8. On the day of the Boston molasses explosion, the nation was but a single state ratification

vote away from adopting the Eighteenth Amendment to the federal Constitution and the onset of the era known as Prohibition.

36. *Boston Globe* (22 November 1909):1.

37. Ibid. For additional information, see "Forest Hills Extension Opened in Boston," *Electric Railway Journal* (4 December 1909):1162.

38. For a description of various improvements to the Main Line El during its first decade of operation, see "Recent Extensions of the Boston Elevated System," *Electric Railway Journal* (18 December 1909):1214–22.

39. "The new cars of the Boston Elevated have been built without platforms at the end; that is, the platform has been enclosed and the end bulkhead of the car body has been removed, making the platform practically a part of the car"; "New Cars for the Boston Elevated," *Railroad Gazette* (5 August 1904):212.

40. For a discussion of why a dwell time differential of 3.2 seconds per station represents an important improvement in overall performance, see "Station Stops in Rapid Transit Service," *Street Railway Journal* (1 April 1905):589–91. This article provides full documentation of BERY's experiences.

41. For additional details on BERY's early el cars, see "New Power Station and Elevated Railway System in Boston," *Street Railway Journal* (2 March 1901):262–63. For a comprehensive photographic review of the early days of the Main Line El, see Frank Cheney and Anthony Mitchell Sammarco, *When Boston Rode the El* (Charleston, S.C.: Arcadia, 2000).

42. "The New Subway in Boston," *Street Railway Journal* (8 November 1902):960.

43. See "Boston Subway Legislation," *Street Railway Journal* (5 July 1902):45–46.

44. *Boston Globe* (29 December 1904):1.

45. For additional details, see "East Boston Tunnel Improvement," *Street Railway Journal* (10 January 1903):87–88.

46. *Boston Globe* (30 December 1904):4. For a short treatment of ferryboat transportation across Boston Harbor in the years before the East Boston tunnel was constructed, see "Go Through the Tunnel," *Boston Globe* (30 December 1904):1.

47. The Atlantic Avenue Station on the East Boston Line long bore the legend "Atlantic Avenue Under." This was a distinctive Boston expression for the lower level of a two-line transfer station. The route that the East Boston Line was "under" at Atlantic Avenue Under was the alternative waterfront alignment of the Main Line El, although the Atlantic Avenue Under designation was retained for many years after the

el was abandoned in 1938. Atlantic Avenue Under did not open in 1904 when tunnel service was inaugurated; it was not completed until 1906. In 1967, the Atlantic Avenue Station was renamed Aquarium.

48. General Manager Dana also wrote an article describing the change over. See Edward Dana, "Relief Effected by Train Operation in East Boston Tunnel," *Electric Railway Journal* (12 January 1924):61–62.

49. See "Changing Tunnel for Rapid Transit," *Electric Railway Journal* (12 July 1924):39–41; see also *Boston Globe* (21 April 1924):20.

50. For additional information on the East Boston rapid transit cars, see "New Cars for the East Boston Tunnel," *Electric Railway Journal* (13 January 1923):85–86; see also "Reducing Weight of Rapid Transit Cars Saves $108,000 a Year," *Electric Railway Journal* (23 August 1924):269–74.

51. Quoted in "Public Control; Guaranteed Dividend; Higher Fare for Rehabilitation," *Electric Railway Journal* (9 February 1918):272–77. Five years earlier, in 1912, BERY president William A. Bancroft wrote a thoughtful article on the future of electric railways in metropolitan Boston that provides interesting perspective in the light of what eventually happened in 1918. See William A. Bancroft, "Electric Railways—A Look Ahead," *Christian Science Monitor* (29 May 1912):sec. 3, 7.

52. The major provisions of the PSC proposal were: 1) a municipal guarantee of a 5 percent annual dividend to BERY stockholders for two years, 5.5 percent after that; 2) control of the company by a public board of trustees; 3) raising of $9 million in new capital by the sale of the BERY-owned Cambridge Subway to the state of Massachusetts; 4) short-term operating deficits to be underwritten by the municipal government; 5) trustees free to set fare at whatever rate is required; "Public Control; Guaranteed Dividend; Higher Fare for Rehabilitation," 273.

53. Ibid., 275.

54. *Electric Railway Journal* (27 April 1918):796.

55. Brush is paraphrased in "An Epoch-Making Law," *Electric Railway Journal* (1 June 1918):1057. With the appointment of the new public trustees, Brush tendered his resignation. See "M.C. Brush to Turn Over Boston 'L' to State," *Electric Railway Journal* (15 June 1918):1170.

56. For additional details about the center-entrance cars, see O. R. Cummings, *Surface Cars of Boston: 1903–1963* (Forty Fort, Pa.: Harold E. Cox, 1963), 39–47; see also "Low-Floor Multiple-Unit Cars for

Boston," *Electric Railway Journal* (12 May 1917):879; "Boston Elevated's Latest Surface Cars," *Electric Railway Journal* (29 December 1917):1167.

57. Author's notes from a 1974 interview with a veteran Boston transit worker.

58. See "The New 'L' to East Cambridge," *Boston Traveler* (25 May 1912):3A.

59. See *Boston Herald* (2 June 1912):1. Car No. 5287, built in 1912 by the St. Louis Car Company, was classified as a Type 4A unit by BERY.

60. The original Public Garden incline was demolished during the extension project. A new incline was built at the same general location so that cars from Back Bay and Huntington Avenue could continue to enter the Central Subway at this point. The new incline was built in the middle of Boylston Street, not within the Public Garden where the original incline was located. See also "Work on Boylston Street Subway Tears Up Back Bay Thoroughfares," *Boston Post* (5 May 1912):D.

61. The idea of converting the Boylston-Tremont Subway into a high-platform rapid-transit line was suggested in 1918 by John A. Beeler, who had been retained as a consultant by the Massachusetts Public Service Commission. See "Public Control; Guaranteed Dividend; Higher Fare for Rehabilitation," *Electric Railway Journal* (9 February 1918):272–77.

62. See "Horse Runs Wild Through Subway," *Boston Globe* (14 December 1917):3.

63. For a treatment of the general terms of this debate, see "The Cambridge Subway Brings up Questions of Through Trains," *Street Railway Journal* (2 May 1908):763.

64. See "The Question of Stations for the Cambridge Subway," *Street Railway Journal* (16 May 1908):835.

65. *Christian Science Monitor* (11 March 1912):1.

66. *Scientific American* (22 July 1911):76.

67. See *Boston Globe* (11 March 1912):2; see also *Christian Science Monitor* (11 March 1912):1.

68. For a history of public transportation between Boston and Cambridge written to commemorate the opening of the new Cambridge subway, see "From Stagecoach to Subway, Apropos of the Opening of the Cambridge Tube," *Christian Science Monitor* (23 March 1912):2. For a feature story about the architectural treatment of stations along the new route, see "New Subway Brings Harvard Near City," *Sunday Herald Magazine* (24 March 1912):4.

69. *Boston Globe* (23 March 1912):1, 2. For a detailed treatment

of the entire project, see "The Cambridge Subway," *Electric Railway Journal* (11 May 1912):782–89; for a comprehensive photographic review of the Cambridge Subway from 1912 to the present, see Frank Cheney, *Boston's Red Line* (Charleston, S.C.: Arcadia, 2002).

70. By 1912, Boston newspapers had developed expertise in reporting mass-transit developments, and some of their accounts rivaled those of more specialized trade publications. See for example, "New Cambridge Subway Car," *Boston Herald* (24 March 1912):12. For a treatment from the trade press, see "Steel Cars for the Cambridge Subway," *Electric Railway Journal* (13 January 1912):58–61.

71. See "Reducing Weight of Rapid Transit Cars Saves $108,000 a Year," *Electric Railway Journal* (23 August 1924):269–74.

72. *Boston Post* (29 May 1912):1.

73. For additional details, see *Boston Globe* (4 November 1927):25.

74. Commissions of various kinds studied the question of transit expansion in Boston over the years, with perhaps the best known of these being the "Coolidge Commission" of 1945. (It was named after its chairman, Arthur Coolidge, not, as is sometimes thought, Calvin Coolidge, who, prior to being elected Vice President of the United States in 1920, served as governor of Massachusetts.) For an example of the extent of rapid-transit expansion projects under discussion in the years following the completion of the Dorchester extension, see *Report of the Legislative Commission on Rapid Transit* (Boston: Commonwealth of Massachusetts, 1947).

75. See *Boston Globe* (17 February 1941):1, 4.

76. Ibid.

77. For further information on this milestone development, see Stephen P. Carlson and Fred W. Schneider III, *PCC: The Car that Fought Back* (Glendale, Calif.: Interurban Press, 1980).

78. The Brooklyn-Manhattan Transit Corporation (BMT) was the successor of the earlier Brooklyn Rapid Transit Company (BRT).

79. Boston car No. 3001 was built as part of the Brooklyn order but diverted to BERY prior to delivery. Some Brooklyn traction buffs insist that Boston's No. 3001 had been painted in Brooklyn colors by Saint Louis Car Company and assigned the number 1057 prior to its being repainted in BERY livery.

80. For full information about the PCC era in Boston, see Edward A. Anderson, *PCC Cars of Boston: 1937–1967* (Cambridge, Mass.: Boston Street Railway Association, 1968).

81. For additional information on the Boston, Revere Beach and Lynn Railroad, see Robert C. Stanley, *Narrow Gauge* (Cambridge, Mass.: Boston Street Railway Association, 1980).

82. See Carlson and Schneider, *PCC*, 169–70.

83. For additional details about cars used on the Revere Beach extension of the East Boston Tunnel, see *Rapid Transit Cars in Boston* (Cambridge, Mass.: Boston Street Railway Association, 1965), 46–48; see also "The Rapid Transit Extension Will Feature the 'Car of Tomorrow,'" *Co-operation* (December 1949):79–82.

84. *Co-operation,* 26 (September 1947): 54. For a review of the BERY era in Boston written on the eve of the MTA takeover, see "The Life and Times of the Boston El," *Co-operation* (June 1947):6–17.

85. See Anderson, *PCC Cars of Boston*, 36.

86. Conversion of the Highland Branch into the MTA's Riverside Line was one of the final projects that Edward Dana supervised before retiring as the system's general manager on July 20, 1959. Dana has written of the Riverside Line; see Edward Dana, "Riverside Line Extension, 1959," *Transportation Bulletin* (October 1960–July 1961):1–20; see also "The Nation's Newest Trolley Line," *Headlights* (August 1959):3–5.

87. The 01100 series cars had to respect the Main Line El's platform and tunnel clearances, but designers were able to gain additional inches of width by allowing the side walls of the cars to bow slightly outward above the floor. Older Main Line El rolling stock had an 8-foot 7-inch maximum width, but thanks to their extended sidewalls, the 01100-series measured 9 feet 7 inches at their widest point. As a purely technical matter, there were few features in the 01100 cars that required the MTA to pay royalties to the Transit Development Corporation (TDC) for the use of PCC patents. But General Manager Dana was so supportive of the TDC that he insisted on making such payments anyway; see Carlson and Schneider, *PCC*, 169–70.

88. For additional details, see "Boston Operates Alloy-Steel Cars," *Modern Railroads* (December 1963):94–95. By using the same "bowing outward" design that was used for the 01100-series cars in 1957, the new Cambridge-Dorchester cars had a maximum width that was a fraction over 10 feet 5 inches, while BERY's original Cambridge cars were 9 feet 6 inches in width at the belt rail.

89. For details about the MBTA's color codes, see *Design in Transit* (Boston: Institute of Contemporary Art, 1967).

90. I myself played a small role in the selection of the color that identifies Boston area commuter rail service. As the MBTA's Director of Marketing in the mid-1970s, I was supervising the development of a new route map for use by the system's passengers. At the time the commuter rail system had no color of its own, but we needed one for the map. Impressed by a distinctive shade of purple that was then being

used to indicate commuter lines of the Erie Lackawanna Railroad on a map of Northern New Jersey, we decided that henceforth Boston commuter rail lines would be rendered in "Erie Lackawanna purple."

91. For a discussion of the MBTA's expansion program before any concrete steps were taken by way of implementation, see Tom Shedd, "Urban Transit: Boston Shows the Way," *Modern Railroads* (April 1967):97–99.

92. For a complete description of this project, see Bradley H. Clarke, *South Shore* (Cambridge, Mass.: Boston Street Railway Association, 1972).

93. See *Headlights* 39 (October–December 1977):2–16, for a series of articles dealing with various MBTA expansion projects that were then just getting under way and which would became the heart of the system's rehabilitation.

94. There is a considerable body of published material on rapid transit in Boston, much of it produced by a Cambridge-based group of railway enthusiasts known as the Boston Street Railway Association (BSRA). Especially valuable are a series of album-style books that document various aspects of the city's transit history in word and pictures. See, for example, *Transit Boston: 1850–1970* (Cambridge, Mass.: BSRA, 1970); *Rapid Transit Boston* (Cambridge, Mass.: BSRA, 1971); *The Boston Transit Album* (Cambridge, Mass.: BSRA, 1977); *The Boston Rapid Transit Album* (Cambridge, Mass.: BSRA, 1981).

Chapter 3: The World's First Subway

1. For complete details about London's intercity railway terminals, see Alan A. Jackson, *London's Termini* (London: Pan Books, 1969).

2. Charles E. Lee, *Seventy Years of the Central* (London: London Transport, 1970), 9. (Lee has written a series of short works outlining the history of each London underground line. While there are more recent studies, Lee is excellent in his treatment of the origins of the various lines.)

3. For an arresting account of psychological barriers that had to be overcome before underground travel could become practical, see Benson Bobrick, *Labyrinths of Iron* (New York: Newsweek, 1981), especially chap. 2, "Hades Hotel," 49–73.

4. No members of the Royal Family attended the Metropolitan gala. Bobrick notes that the prime minister, Lord Palmerston, excused

himself "because of age," and also because he "wanted to keep above ground as long as he could"; Bobrick, *Labyrinths of Iron*, 101.

5. *The Times* (10 January 1863):10.

6. *The Times* (12 January 1893):7.

7. For a treatment of the Metropolitan, see Charles E. Lee, *The Metropolitan Line* (London: London Transport, 1972).

8. Lee, *Metropolitan*, 10.

9. The City Corporation of London subscribed one fifth of the stock the Metropolitan offered, or 200,000 pounds sterling (Lee, *Metropolitan*, 9). While the City Corporation undoubtedly saw this as a way to promote an important civic betterment, it is not correct to regard this payment as a public subsidy of the railway venture. Barker and Robbins, for instance, point out that the City Corporation later sold its shares in the Metropolitan "at a premium"; T. C. Barker and Michael Robbins, *A History of London Transport*, vol. I (London: George Allen and Unwin, 1975), 113.

10. For photographs of these structures, see Barker and Robbins, *History of London Transport*, vol. I, plates 57, 58.

11. *The Times* (23 January 1863):5.

12. See, for example, Sir Arthur Conan Doyle, "The Adventure of the Bruce-Partington Plans," in *The Complete Sherlock Holmes* (Garden City, N.Y.: Doubleday, 1930), 913–31.

13. J. Graeme Bruce, *Steam to Silver* (London: London Transport, 1970), 5–6.

14. Lee, *Metropolitan*, 19.

15. The new "Metropolitan District Railway [has] five stations, including Westminster, which is conveniently placed for the Houses of Parliament and the Thames Embankment. Trains to and from the City commenced running this morning by way of Paddington and Nottinghill"; *The Times* (24 December 1868):5.

16. Charles E. Lee, "District Line Centenary," *Railway Magazine* (December 1968):698.

17. *The Times* commented that the opening of the Inner Circle "fulfils many long deferred expectations," but the newspaper was also quite dissatisfied with "the complicated network of lines which now exists and which has been constructed without much apparent method or harmony"; *The Times* (7 October 1884):9.

18. This treatment of these matters is necessarily superficial and brief; the relationship of various railway companies with respect to suburban passenger service in the outskirts of London is both lengthy and complex.

19. For additional details, see Bruce, *Steam to Silver*, 30–43.

20. Ibid., 30.

21. For further details about the District's first MU cars, see S. B. Fortenbaugh, "The Electrification of the London Underground Electric Railways Company's System," *Street Railway Journal* (4 March 1905):388–420; see also Bruce, *Steam to Silver*, 30–36.

22. For details about the East London Line, see Bruce, *Steam to Silver*, 44–53. This short narrative about London Underground cannot hope to identify expansion prospects and possibilities, but as just one example of what the future might hold, there are plans to expand the East London Line. See Jonathan Roberts, "ELL—From Shuttle to Metro," *Modern Railways* (September 2001):i–viii.

23. H. F. Howson, *London's Underground* (London: Ian Allan, Ltd., 1951), 57.

24. J. Graeme Bruce, *Tube Trains under London* (London: London Transport, 1968), iii.

25. In responding to a toast raised in his honor at a luncheon reception following a ceremonial ride over the new line, the Prince of Wales said: "Therefore this railway today, this first electric railway that has been started in England (*hear, hear*), will, I hope, do much to alleviate the congestion of the traffic which now exist"; *The Times* (5 November 1890):12.

26. For an extensive description of the new line written at the time of its opening, see "The City and South London Railway," *The Times* (4 November 1890):13; see also Bruce, *Tube Trains under London,* 1–9. For a North American appreciation of the new railway, see "To Run by Electricity," *New York Times* (7 December 1890):20.

27. Howson, *London's Underground,* 27.

28. "The City and South London Railway," *The Times* (4 November 1890):13.

29. See H. A. Bartlett, "Tunneling with a Shield in London Clay," *Railroad Gazette* (16 September 1904):344–45.

30. For information about technical issues associated with tube construction, see H. G. Follenfant, *Underground Railway Construction* (London: London Transport, 1968); see also Follenfant, *Reconstructing London's Underground* (London: London Transport, 1974), 7–41.

31. See Bruce, *Tube Trains under London,* 4–7. In making an early recommendation for an underground railway in New York, Frank Sprague proposed that: "Cars for such an underground system would require no windows"; Sprague, "Ideal Rapid Transit," *Supplement to the Street Railway Journal* (March 1891):3.

32. Howson, *London's Underground,* 28.

33. Bruce, *Tube Trains under London,* 1.

34. For details about the Central's electric locomotives, see Bruce, *Tube Trains under London,* 14–17. For a general account of the new railway written for American readers, see "The Central London Railroad," *Railroad Gazette* (13 July 1900):481–82. While providing technical information about the new railway, the *Railroad Gazette* also opined that the road's management "find mortification in the fact that practically the whole of the mechanical and electrical appliances comprised in the equipment of the line are of American design and construction" (ibid.).

35. The locomotives featured a "gearless" drive with motors effectively mounted on the axles. The weight of the motors thus bore directly on the axles and was not supported by any springing mechanism. The excessive "vibration was undoubtedly due to the pounding effect on the rail joints of the uncushioned load." "New Fireproof Rolling Stock for the Central London Underground Railway," *Street Railway Journal* (11 October 1902):604.

36. See Bruce, *Tube Trains under London,* 18.

37. Ibid., 27–48.

38. The London Underground was also a continual object of interest for mass-transit operators in the United States. See, for example, "Cars, Schedules, Power Consumption, Running Test and Signals in London Subways," *Electric Railway Journal* (6 August 1910):212–18.

39. For details of Yerkes's exploits in Chicago, see Brian J. Cudahy, *Destination Loop* (Brattleboro, Vt.: Stephen Green Press, 1982), 35–38.

40. For an evaluation of underground railways in London written just prior to Yerkes's arrival, see "The London Underground Electric Railways," *Railroad Gazette* (25 May 1900):342–43.

41. For additional details, see Fortenbaugh, "The Electrification of the London Underground Electric Railways Company's System," 388–420.

42. Lee quotes from the diary of Ralph David Blumenfeld, a famous editor of the *Daily Express.* "James McNeill Whistler was over from Paris today and holding forth as usual. His latest grievance is that Yerkes proposes to put up a gigantic power house in Chelsea for the electrification of the Underground, and it is to have enormous chimneys towering into the sky, it will completely ruin the bend in the Thames." Charles E. Lee, *The Northern Line* (London: London Transport, 1973), 12.

43. Charles E. Lee, *The Piccadilly Line* (London: London Transport, 1973), 10.

44. For a description of Yerkes's Underground Electric Railway Company written shortly after the financer began construction work on

the three tube lines, see "London's New Tube Railways," *The Times* (6 June 1903):6.

45. In recent years, the westernmost of the two northern branch lines has been split off from the Bakerloo and incorporated into the new Jubilee Line.

46. Charles E. Lee, *The Bakerloo Line* (London: London Transport, 1973), 11.

47. Quoted in Lee, *Bakerloo Line*, 12.

48. "The car has a motor truck at one end only and in the compartment at that end is mounted all the electrical apparatus, thus concentrating a heavy weight over the adhesion wheels." "Some New Steel Passenger Cars," *Railroad Gazette* (16 June 1905):678–80.

49. Barker and Robbins, *A History of London Transport,* vol. II, 61.

50. For Yerkes's obituary, see *New York Times* (13 December 1905):4.

51. For a treatment of these developments, see Geoffrey Wilson, *London United Tramways* (London: George Allen and Unwin, 1971), 85–88.

52. In raising a toast at a ceremony to mark the opening of what was then the Hampstead Tube but would later be called the Northern Line, British member of Parliament David Lloyd-George hoped this would not be the last new underground railway to be built in London. See "Opening of the Hampstead Tube," *The Times* (24 June 1907):3.

53. For details, see Barker and Robbins, *History of London Transport*, vol. II, 242–60.

54. *The Future of London Transport* (London: Greater London Council, 1970), 9–10. For additional information, see Barker and Robbins, *History of London Transport*, vol. II, 270–82.

55. Ibid., 10.

56. For additional details, see Barker and Robbins, *History of London Transport*, vol. II, 334–58; see also Howson, *London's Underground,* 105.

57. Quoted in John R. Day, *The Story of the Victoria Line* (London: London Transport, 1969), 7.

58. Because automatic train control systems were then starting to be deployed on U.S. transit lines, the opening of the Victoria Line was given considerable publicity in the trade press in America. See, for example, "Queen Elizabeth Opens London's New Victoria Line," *Passenger Transport* (25 April 1969):5. For a treatment in a British journal, see "The Victoria Line Opens," *Railway World* (November 1968):514–15.

59. Day, *The Story of the Victoria Line,* 86.

60. The newest subway line in Paris, the fully automated *ligne 14*, incorporates a similar system of "double doors" for its entire length, as do most automated transit systems in airports. Two fully automated transit lines in North America, one in Vancouver, the other in a suburb of Toronto, lack "double doors" but include pressure-sensitive devices between and adjacent to the tracks that automatically shut the system down should a passenger enter the right-of-way. Vancouver identifies its system with the acronym PIES—Platform Intrusion Emergency Stop.

61. "During the first year of operation nearly 8 million passengers traveled on the Piccadilly Line extension to and from Heathrow Central station," London Transport reported, and "some 20 per cent of all air passengers using Heathrow traveled by the Underground." *Annual Report and Accounts for the Year Ending 31 December 1978* (London: London Transport Executive, 1979), 14.

62. For more recent information about surface and tube rolling stock of the London Underground, see Brian Hardy, *London Underground Rolling Stock,* rev. ed. (London: Capital Transport Publishing, 2002).

63. For additional information, see Alan Pearce, Stephen Jolly, and Brian Hardy, *Docklands Light Rail* (London: Capital Transport Press, 2000).

64. For information about the Glasgow subway, see David L. Thomson and David E. Sinclair, *The Glasgow Subway* (Glasgow: Scottish Tramway and Museum Society, 1964).

65. For a treatment of the rehabilitation effort geared to the interests of North American readers, see "From Cable Drive to Computer Control—Glasgow's 83-Year-Old Subway Gets Rebuilt," *Transportation Research News* (September-October 1979):6–10.

66. For a more recent treatment of the Glasgow subway, see John Wright and Ian Maclean, *Circles under the Clyde* (London: Capital Transport Publishing, 1997).

67. "The Metropolitan Railway of Paris," *Street Railway Journal* (1 September 1900):797.

68. For details about these cars, see Jules Hervieu, *Le Chemin de Fer Metropolitain Municipal de Paris* (Paris: Libraire Polytechnique, 1903). Hervieu's work contains detailed plans and drawings that can be appreciated without any understanding of French.

69. Armand Bindi and Daniel Lefeuvre, *Le Metro de Paris* (Paris: Editions Ouest-France, 1990), 12.

70. For an early comparison of the New York and Paris subways written by a statistician with the New York Public Service Commission, see Robert H. Whitten, "Comparison of Operation of the New York

and Paris Subway Systems," *Electric Railway Journal* (11 December 1909):1178–85.

71. *New York Times* (12 August 1903):2.

72. See "Paris Subway Reforms," *Street Railway Journal* (19 September 1903):599.

73. For recent information about the Paris Metro, see Brian Hardy, *Paris Metro Handbook* (London: Capital Transport Press, 1999); see also "New Generation of Rail Cars Boosts Paris Metro's Capacity," *Metro* (May–June 1978):26–27.

74. For information about the construction of the Montreal Metro, see Dominique Beaudin, *Le Metro de Montreal* (Montreal: Les Editions de L'Action Nationale, 1960); for three articles published at the time the system opened, see *Headlights* (January 1967):2–13. For more recent information, see Benoit Clairoux, *Le Metro de Montréal: 35 ans deja* (Montreal: Editions Hurtubuise HMH, 2001).

75. There is relatively little material available about the Mexico City system. For an article written shortly after the first three lines were in service, see "Moving Mexico City's Millions: The Rail Solution," *Railway Age* (11 October 1976):36–37; see also Glen D. Bottoms and Luis Leon Torrealba, "Metro de la Ciudad de Mexico," *Headlights* (July 1974):8–10.

76. For additional information, see Robert Schwandl, *Metros in Spain* (London: Capital Transport Press, 2001).

77. Although any such book is quickly overtaken by events, and its information becomes out of date, an excellent general resource on world subways is John R. Day, *A Source Book of Underground Railways* (London: Ward Lock Ltd., 1980). For a more recent study of ten important world subway systems, see Stan Fischler, *Subways of the World* (Osceola, Wis.: MBI Publishing, 2000). Updated information about world transit systems is available in a biennial volume published by Jane's Information Systems. For the most recent edition, see Tony Pattison, ed., *Jane's Urban Transport System; 12th Edition 2001–2002.* (Coulson, Surrey, UK: Jane's Information Systems, 2002).

CHAPTER 4: NEW YORK'S ELECTRIFIED RAILROADS

1. In contemporary Chicago, suburban commuter railroad service operated by a public agency called Metra includes an electrified network that was originally built by the Illinois Central Railroad. The Chicago, South Shore and South Bend Railroad runs electric trains between Chicago and South Bend, Indiana, and operates in and out of Chicago

over Metra trackage. This electrified service represents less than 25 percent of Chicago's overall commuter rail service, the rest being diesel-powered. Of three commuter lines operated in the Baltimore-Washington area by a Maryland state agency known as MARC, only one, which provides service between Perryville, Maryland, and Washington via Baltimore, uses electric-powered equipment.

2. See, for example, William D. Middleton, *Grand Central* (San Marino, Calif.: Golden West, 1977); Lorraine B. Diehl, *The Late, Great Pennsylvania Station* (New York: American Heritage, 1985); William D. Middleton, *Manhattan Gateway; New York's Pennsylvania Station* (Waukesha, Wis.: Kalmbach, 1996); Carl W. Condit, *The Port of New York* (Chicago: University of Chicago Press, 1981).

3. For news accounts about the disaster, see *New York Times* (9 January 1902):1–3; *New York Herald* (9 January 1902):1.

4. "New Rochelle Now a Mourning City," *New York Times* (9 January 1902):1.

5. See "The Mayor's Big Scheme," *New York Times* (1 February 1888):9.

6. See "Reversal of Track Running on the New York Central," *Railroad Gazette* (20 August 1907):227–28.

7. *New York Times* (9 January 1902):2.

8. Ibid.

9. *New York Times* (26 July 1901):14.

10. *New York Times* (26 July 1901):12.

11. *New York Times* (25 January 1902):2.

12. For details about the Baltimore and Ohio electrification, see William D. Middleton, *When the Steam Railroads Electrified* (Milwaukee, Wis.: Kalmbach, 1974), 26–35.

13. For a treatment of Wilgus and his career with the New York Central, see Middleton, *Grand Central,* 55–57.

14. William J. Wilgus, "The Grand Central Terminal in Perspective," *Proceedings of the American Society of Civil Engineers* (October 1940):1002. (Wilgus's full treatment is on pp. 992–1024.)

15. Ibid.

16. Ibid.

17. *New York Times* (30 September 1906):8.

18. *New York Times* (16 January 1902):8.

19. Wrote Sprague: "Mr. Westinghouse has a habit, which I fear is almost chronic, of tendering advice to those contemplating advanced methods in electrical transportation to do nothing unless it be to wait until his particular plans have materialized." *New York Times* (18 January 1902):8.

20. The Sprague-Westinghouse dispute continued for many years. See, for example, Frank Sprague, "An Open Letter to Mr. Westinghouse," *Street Railway Journal* (6 January 1906):27–29; see also George Westinghouse, "The Single-Phase Alternating and the Direct Current Systems," *Railroad Gazette* (22 December 1905):578. Sprague's own company, the Sprague Electric Company, had been acquired by General Electric in 1902, while even earlier Sprague had sold his patents and other assets in the field of electric elevators to the Otis Elevator Company. See "General Electric Acquires Sprague Company," *Street Railway Journal* (7 June 1902):664.

21. *New York Times* (27 November 1903):2.

22. In early 1903, the New York legislature passed three laws that impacted the New York Central's Manhattan operations. One gave the railroad legal authorization to depress the right-of-way, another empowered the City of New York to undertake the construction of cross-streets over the terminal area and authorized the city to borrow $600,000 for such work, while it was the third that prohibited the operation of steam locomotives on the Park Avenue Line south of the Harlem River. For information about these three pieces of legislation, see *New York Times* (11 February 1903):3; *New York Times* (19 February 1903):6; *New York Times* (12 March 1903):7; *New York Times* (22 April 1903):3. See also G. R. Wadsworth, "Terminal Improvements of the New York Central & Hudson River in New York," *Railroad Gazette* (20 October 1905):366.

23. For additional information about the New York Central's first electric locomotive, see Robert S. Burpo, Jr., "A Brief History of the First Electric Locomotives on the New York Central Railroad," *Bulletin of the Railway and Locomotive Historical Society* (April 1962):19–23. See also "The New York Central Electric Locomotive," *Street Railway Journal* (4 June 1904):861–62; "Electric Locomotives for the New York Central," *Railroad Gazette* (27 July 1906):77.

24. *New York Times* (21 July 1906):1. The new locomotives were actually a variation on what would soon prove to be a standard electric traction design, a center cab with a lower "hood" on each end, to borrow an automotive term. The NYC locomotives also included an enclosed walkway so that crews could move from one engine to another or from engine to train, and this resulted in a raised section along the centerline of the "hood."

25. Ibid., 2.

26. *New York Times* (1 October 1906):16.

27. *New York Times* (12 December 1906):8.

28. See "Steel Cars for the New York Central's Electric Suburban Line," *Railroad Gazette* (3 November 1905):424–25; see also "New

Steel Motor Cars for the New York Central and Hudson River Railroad," *Street Railway Journal* (4 November 1905):837–38.

29. "Steel Cars for the New York Central's Electric Suburban Line," 424.

30. For an explanation of the notation used to describe the wheel arrangements of electric locomotives such as 1-D-1, see Fred A. Talbot, *Cassell's Railways of the World,* vol. I (New York: Simmons Boardman, 1924), 112–22.

31. See *New York Times* (17 February 1907):1–3.

32. *New York Times* (5 March 1907):1; see also "New York Central Officers Indicted for Manslaughter," *Railroad Gazette* (29 March 1907):462.

33. For examples of technical studies that were conducted in the wake of the accident, see "Stresses in Tracks on Curves," *Railroad Gazette* (15 March 1907):327–29; "Comparative Effects of Steam and Electric Locomotives on a 3-deg. Curve," *Railroad Gazette* (22 March 1907):414–15.

34. "Tractive Power of Electric Locomotives," *Railroad Gazette* (10 May 1907):650.

35. See "Tests of the Effect of Snow on Third-Rail," *Street Railway Journal* (17 February 1906):288–89.

36. See "Under-Running Third-Rail for the New York Central," *Railroad Gazette* (1 September 1905):198–200; see also "Under-Contact Third Rail for the New York Central," *Street Railway Journal* (2 September 1905):336–37.

37. For information about NYC powerhouses and electrical distribution networks, see "Improvements of the New York Central & Hudson River within the Electric Zone," *Railroad Gazette* (17 November 1905):462–66.

38. Over the years it has been common to call Harmon the end of the electrified zone. Harmon is where through-trains exchanged engines—steam to electric or electric to steam. But the third rail continued a mile or so beyond Harmon to Croton, although only suburban trains served Croton. In more recent years the Croton station has been closed and the Harmon station renamed Croton-Harmon.

39. See "Steam and Electric Locomotive Terminals of the New York Central at Croton and North White Plains," *Railroad Gazette* (14 June 1907):824–30.

40. *New York Times* (21 July 1906):1.

41. Ibid.

42. For a treatment of the Putnam Division, see Daniel R. Gallo and Frederick A. Kramer, *The Putnam Division* (New York: Quadrant, 1981).

43. The most famous event in Polo Grounds history took place on the afternoon of October 3, 1951, when Bobby Thomson of the Giants hit a hanging curve ball thrown by Brooklyn's Ralph Branca into the lower-left field stands, propelled the Giants into the World Series, and broke countless hearts from Flatbush to Greenpoint. For a story about the extraordinary cultural impact this home run has had over the years, see Albert R. Karr, "This 50-Year-Old Sees His Idol as Last of the Sports Heroes," *Wall Street Journal* (27 October 1989):1.

44. For information about Grand Central Terminal, see Middleton, *Grand Central,* 63–68; Condit, *The Port of New York,* 54–100; Wilgus, "The Grand Central Terminal in Perspective," 1015–19.

45. *New York Times* (3 February 1913):3.

46. *New York Times* (2 February 1913):1.

47. For additional information about New York Central electric locomotives, see Middleton, *When the Steam Railroads Electrified,* 36–71; Alvin F. Staufer, *New York Central's Early Power* (Carrollton, Ohio: Alvin F. Staufer, 1967), 118–33; "The New York Central's Electric Locomotives," *Headlights* (January-March 1983):1–27.

48. For a report on the New York Central's early experience in maintaining its new fleet of MU cars and locomotives, see F. E. Lister, "Care and Handling of Electrical Equipment, New York Central & Hudson River," *Railway Age Gazette* (3 June 1910):1367–75.

49. One matter of some confusion involves the length of NYC's early MU cars. The cars acquired in 1905 were an even 60 feet long measured over their anti-climbers. See "Steel Cars for the New York Central's Electric Suburban Line," *Railroad Gazette,* (3 November 1905):424–25. Some later cars were 62 feet in length, others were 69 feet long, and all (or most) of the original sixty-footers were later expanded into 69-foot cars, presumably at the same time as the upper window sash was plated over.

50. For details about these new cars, see *New York Times* (23 August 1949):25; see also Stephen Meyers and Herman Rinke, "New M-U Cars Arrive," *Headlights* (May 1950):1–8.

51. The year after NYC acquired the 100 new MU cars in 1950, the railroad rebuilt one of its older, 78-foot day coaches into an unpowered MU trailer which was configured as a commuter club car. Identified as car No. 754 when it was built by Standard Steel in 1927, it was designated No. 98 when it entered MU service in 1951. For further details, see John S. Horvath, "One of a Kind," *Central Headlight* (first quarter 1981):16–18.

52. Before the program could be established, voters in New York State had to approve a constitutional amendment that authorized guar-

anteeing bonds which the Port Authority would issue to pay for the cars with state credit. See "Governor Signs Rail Bonds Bill to Permit Buying of New Cars," *New York Times* (7 April 1962):13.

53. Under Penn Central management, all New York–Boston passenger service was shifted out of Grand Central and into New York's Penn Station via Hell Gate Bridge. When Amtrak was created in 1971, it took over the operation of intercity passenger service over the former New York Central Railroad, and Amtrak trains operated out of Grand Central for several years to such NYC destinations as Albany, Montreal, Buffalo, and Chicago. To consolidate all its New York service at Penn Station, in 1991 Amtrak upgraded the former New York Central West Side Line into Manhattan, and after building a connecting link from this line into Penn Station, Amtrak was able to move out of Grand Central, leaving that terminal as an all-commuter facility.

54. For a treatment of the New Haven's early electrification experiments, see Sidney Withington, "Pioneer Experience in Electric Traction and the New Haven Railroad," *Bulletin of the Railway and Locomotive Historical Society* 26 (1931), 25–32.

55. *Railroad Gazette* (16 August 1907):165.

56. "The power house at Cos Cob furnishes single-phase current for the operation of electric trains over the New Haven road and is also designed to deliver three-phase current to the Port Morris power house of the New York Central to compensate for the energy required to operate the New Haven trains over then lines of the New York Central." E. H. McHenry, "Electrification of the New York, New Haven & Hartford," *Railroad Gazette* (16 August 1907):183.

57. In the summer of 1907, the Fall River Line's nightly sailings were operated by the palatial steamboats *Priscilla* and *Puritan,* one vessel departing from each terminal each evening. Because there is evidence that *Priscilla* was tied up in Fall River during the day on July 11, it is reasonable to conclude that *Puritan* handled the New York departure that evening. See *Fall River Daily Evening News* (11 July 1907):10.

58. See *New York Times* (25 July 1907):14; *Railway Age Gazette* (26 July 1907):105; *New York Times* (5 October 1907):4.

59. See "Lightening Disables New Haven Trains," *New York Times* (15 July 1908):1.

60. A month before revenue service was inaugurated in the new electrified district and while the system was still being tested, at least three New Haven freight brakemen were electrocuted while working aboard freight cars under the AC wires. See *New York Times* (29 June 1907):1.

61. See "New Haven to Electrify Boston to Providence," *Electric Railway Journal* (27July 1912):133.

62. "New Haven Conspiracy Trial Begun," *Electric Railway Journal* (16 October 1915):841.

63. Passengers could walk from the New Haven's Harlem River Terminal to an el station at 133rd Street that was used by both the Second and Third Avenue Lines. At various times in the years after 1886, there was also a shuttle service over a short spur track between the New Haven terminal and the 129th Street el station; the shuttle was permanently discontinued in 1924. For additional details, see Roger Arcara, *Westchester's Forgotten Railway* (New York: Quadrant, 1972), 73.

64. See "Harlem River Branch Improvements; New York, New Haven & Hartford," *Railway Age Gazette* part I (28 January 1910):186–90; part II (4 February 1910):257–60.

65. Prior to the construction of Hell Gate Bridge and the possibility of an all-rail route between Boston and Washington via New York, the New Haven and the Pennsylvania operated such through-trains by using a ferry connection between Port Morris and Jersey City. The "Federal Express," a Boston-Washington overnight train, was one such train, while the "Colonial," which ran by day, was another. Over the years, two ferryboats were primarily used to transport passenger cars between Port Morris and Jersey City, the *Maryland* and the *Maryland (ii)*. For additional details about this unusual operation, see George W. Hilton, "The Steamer Maryland Route," *Steamboat Bill* 95 (fall 1965):87–93.

66. As plans for the Hell Gate Bridge were developing in 1906, the New Haven applied for a franchise to build a line from Woodlawn to West Farms so that its trains might operate to Port Morris. Reported the *New York Times:* "This is taken to mean that the New Haven Road plans to use the Pennsylvania Station instead of Grand Central." *New York Times* (22 June 1906):5. It must be acknowledged as possible, of course, that the New Haven's 1906 action was less a genuine proposal and more part of its negotiating strategy with the New York Central to establish more favorable terms for its electric-powered trains to operate into Grand Central. The fact remains, however, that the New Haven later invested substantial capital in upgrading the Port Morris Branch, although the upgraded section left the main line at New Rochelle, not Woodlawn as earlier proposed.

67. See "Conversion of New Canaan Branch from 500-Volt D.C. to 11,000-Volt A.C. Operation." *Electric Railway Journal* (15 May 1909):900–903.

68. For details about the New York, Westchester and Boston, see Roger Arcara, *Westchester's Forgotten Railway.* See also Karl Groh, "New York Westchester and Boston Railway," *Electric Railroads,* 31 (April 1962):1–16.

69. See "Purchased Power for the New Haven," *Electric Railway Journal* (18 December 1915):1200–1201.

70. See "Motor Cars for the New Haven Suburban Service," *Railroad Age Gazette* (15 October 1909):707–8.

71. The two AC MU units acquired in 1909 for New Canaan service were open-platform cars with wooden bodies, each equipped with four GE No. 603A 125 horsepower motors. See "Conversion of New Canaan Branch from 500-Volt D.C. to 11,000-Volt A.C. Operation," 900–903.

72. See *New York Times* (28 April 1966):1, 58.

73. Interstate Commerce Commission, "Excerpts from Ruling on New Haven," quoted in *New York Times* (28 April 1966):58.

74. See "New MU Deal Off," *Headlights* (October 1964):3–4.

75. Preliminary specifications for the 144-car order were circulated to potential bidders in 1968. *New York Times* (22 March 1968):93. For technical details about the cars, see "Cosmopolitans Are Here," *Headlights* (June 1973):10–11.

76. *Rail Transit Car Costs* (Los Angeles: Southern California Association of Governments, 1975), 117, 119.

77. See "Steel Passenger Cars for the Pennsylvania Railroad," *Railroad Gazette* (14 June 1907):846–60.

78. For details about one such experimental car, PRR No. 1651, see "New All-Steel Passenger Car for the Pennsylvania Railroad," *Street Railway Journal* (18 August 1906):270–71. The *New York Times* called No. 1651 "the first all-steel passenger car to be built in the world," a claim that obviously overlooks earlier achievements of the Interborough Rapid Transit Company. *New York Times* (12 August 1906):16.

79. Ibid.

80. "Steel Passenger Cars," *Railroad Gazette* (14 June 1907):822.

81. "Steel Passenger Cars for the Pennsylvania Railroad," 849.

82. "The Pullman Company has built a sleeping car that is as near all-metal construction as is now practicable to make it." "All-Steel Pullman Sleeping Car," *Railroad Gazette* (19 April 1907):541. The experimental car bore the name *Jamestown*. For additional information, see John H. White, Jr., *The American Railroad Passenger Car* (Baltimore, Md.: Johns Hopkins University Press, 1978), 266–78.

83. *Railway Age Gazette* (18 February 1910):367.

84. For information about the PRR's New York terminal electrification and Manhattan Transfer, see Brian J. Cudahy, *Rails Under the Mighty Hudson,* rev. ed. (New York: Fordham University Press, 2002); see also Middleton, *Manhattan Gateway,* 39–49.

85. For additional information about Broad Street Station, see Harry P. Albrecht, *Broad Street Station* (Clifton Heights, Pa.: Steam Locomotives of Yesteryear, 1972).

86. See "Thousands See Historic Broad St. Station End," *Head-lights,* 14 (May 1952):3; for additional information about PRR stations in Philadelphia, see Allen P. Underkofler, "The Philadelphia Improvements," *Magazine of the Philadelphia Chapter of the Pennsylvania Railroad Technical & Historical Society* part I (May 1979):1–30; part II (September 1980):1–30.

87. George H. Burgess and Miles C. Kennedy, *Centennial History of the Pennsylvania Railroad* (Philadelphia: Pennsylvania Railroad, 1949), 545–46, 606–8; see also Michael Bezilla, *Electric Traction on the Pennsylvania Railroad, 1895–1968* (University Park, Pa.: Pennsylvania State University Press, 1980), 62.

88. In addition to Arsenel Bridge, there were also substations in West Philadelphia, Bryn Mawr, and Paoli. For additional details about the entire project, see "Philadelphia-Paoli Electrification," *Electric Railway Journal* (13 November 1915):981–89; see also "Electrification of the Pennsylvania at Philadelphia," *Railway Age Gazette* (12 November 1915):889–94.

89. George Gibbs, "Progress in Electrification during 1915," *Railway Age Gazette* (31 December 1915):1233.

90. For additional discussion of the advantages PRR expected to gain by the electrification of its Philadelphia surburban services, see Middleton, *When the Steam Railroads Electrified,* 313–20; see also *Centennial History of the Pennsylvania Railroad,* 545, 606.

91. "Further consideration was given during the year to plans for the future electrification of the main line crossing the Allegheny Mountains from Altoona, the foot of the eastern slope, to Conemaugh, on the western slops, by which it is believed large economic economies can be effected and the heavy freight train movement facilitated." "Pennsylvania Electrification Progress," *Electric Railway Journal* (13 March 1915):524.

92. For an explanation of the principles involved in the repulsion starting motor, see "Philadelphia-Paoli Electrification," *Electric Railway Journal* (13 November 1915):982–83.

93. Ibid., 983. We saw in Chapter 1 that under Frank Hedley, the Interborough Rapid Transit Company also equipped its trains with electropneumatic braking.

94. For information about how the Pennsylvania trained its workforce in the operation of the new electric trains, see Clarence Roberts, "Training Steam Railroad Men for Electric Operation," *Electric Railway Journal* (22 May 1915):970–72.

95. The inauguration of electrified service between Board Street and Paoli on September 11, 1915, was not the principal mass-transit

news in Philadelphia newspapers the next morning. Within hours of the arrival of the first revenue train of MP-54 cars in Philadelphia, city officials broke ground adjacent to City Hall for the construction of the new Broad Street subway. The groundbreaking was front-page news, while PRR's accomplishment was relegated to page 4. See *Philadelphia Inquirer* (12 September 1915):1, 4.

96. See "P.R.R. Extends Philadelphia Electrification to Chestnut Hill," *Electric Railway Journal* (27 April 1918):798–803.

97. See "Beam Light Signals on the Pennsylvania," *Railway Age Gazette* (26 February 1915):366–67.

98. For a treatment of the PRR's decision, see J. V. B. Duer, "The Pennsylvania Electrifies," *Scientific American* (1 October 1933):170–71; see also Bezilla, *Electric Traction on the Pennsylvania Railroad*, 56–73.

99. For a comprehensive treatment of the MP-54 car, see Charles Hulick, "A Brief History of the Pennsylvania Railroad MP54 Multiple-Unit Cars," *The Keystone* (autumn 2000):19–28.

100. Author's notes from interview with an Amtrak engineer in 1975.

101. For details about these cars, see "PRR Pioneer III MU Cars," *Headlights* (September 1958):3. The contract with Budd for these six cars contained an option that would have permitted the railroad to acquire forty-four additional units, but the option was never exercised.

102. For details about these cars, see "New Commuter Cars for Philadelphians," *Headlights* (April 1974):14–15. The Reading Company had electrified its Philadelphia-area suburban service in 1929 with an AC system similar to that of the PRR. For additional details, see Middleton, *When the Steam Railroads Electrified*, 306–11.

103. At some point a change in notation practice appears to have been adopted, since the cars designed MP-85 units measured 85 feet in overall length, not between their interior bulkheads.

104. For information about the Jersey Arrow cars, see "The Jersey Arrows Arrive," *Headlights* (October 1968):2–3.

105. Commuter railroad service in the Philadelphia area—over the lines of both the former Pennsylvania Railroad and the former Reading Company—is currently operated by a public agency known as the Southeastern Pennsylvania Transportation Authority (SEPTA). In addition to acquiring new commuter rolling stock, SEPTA has linked the former Reading system with the former PRR network of lines via a new tunnel through the heart of downtown Philadelphia. Commuter service between Washington and Baltimore over former PRR trackage is now operated by an agency of the state of Maryland that is identified as MARC.

106. For details about the DL&W electrification, see Stephen Meyers, "Lackawanna," *Headlights* (January 1949):1–3.

107. For details about the "re-electrification" of the former DL&W lines, see Martin Garelick, "Rail Rebirth for New Jersey," *Progressive Railroading* (August 1984):29–34. In addition to replacing DC catenary on the former DL&W network, New Jersey Transit has extended the former PRR electrification from South Amboy to Long Branch along a route currently called the North Jersey Coast Line, as well as from Bay Street–Montclair to Montclair Heights on the former Erie Lackawanna system.

108. The LIRR was not the only other railroad to use Pennsylvania-designed P-54 suburban passenger cars in DC electrified service. The PRR-controlled West Jersey and Seashore Railroad operated between Camden and Atlantic City and began electrified service in 1906. See "The Electrical Equipment of the West Jersey & Seashore Branch of the Pennsylvania Railroad," *Street Railway Journal* (10 November 1906):928–46. The original cars used by the West Jersey and Seashore featured wooden bodies, but in 1912 the road acquired thirteen MP-54 coaches and two MP-54 combination baggage-coaches. For additional details, see "Red Electrics to the Jersey Shore," *Headlights* (July–August 1972):13–14. PRR's West Jersey and Seashore was merged with the Reading Company's south Jersey operations in 1933, and the DC electrification was eliminated in 1949.

109. *Railroad Gazette* (11 May 1900):305.

110. One pending LIRR proposal that the *Railroad Gazette* was pleased to believe would be off the table with the line's acquisition by the PRR was the construction of a deep-water harbor for transatlantic ocean liners at Montauk, with Long Island trains then providing connecting service to New York. Austin Corbin, the LIRR's president from 1882 through his untimely death in 1896, had championed the plan. "We suppose now that Mr. Corbin is dead no man of any importance thinks that it would be wise." *Railroad Gazette* (11 May 1900):305. For further information about Corbin's plan, see Brian J. Cudahy, *How We Got to Coney Island* (New York: Fordham University Press, 2002), 82–87.

111. For a detailed treatment of the LIRR's Atlantic Avenue improvement project, see Vincent F. Seyfried, *The Long Island Rail Road: A Comprehensive History;* part 7 "The Age of Electrification" (Garden City, N.Y.: Vincent F. Seyfried, 1975), 24–42.

112. *New York Times* (10 October 1897):23. Baldwin was reported as being especially impressed with the Central London Railway, which was then under construction.

113. *Railroad Gazette* (23 March 1900):190.

114. "The Electrification of the Long Island Railroad," *Street Railway Journal* (4 November 1905):829. The full article is on pp. 828–34.

115. In 2003, the aboveground portion of the LIRR's Flatbush Avenue Terminal is being replaced with a completely new structure. The place where one should look for evidence of the planned connection from 1905 is along a curved wall behind the ticket windows belowground at platform level that curves from Track 2 of the LIRR terminal into the Manhattan-bound track of the IRT's Seventh Avenue Line at the north end of the Atlantic Avenue subway station.

116. "The Brooklyn elevated lines have been for some years operated by the third rail, but the location of their rail is 22¼ ins. outside and 6 ins. above the track rail, while the Long Island Railroad third rail is 26 ins. out and 3½ ins. up. This made it necessary to devise some form of adjustable third-rail shoe which would operate with equal facility over both third rails and be able to change from one to the other at reduced speed without requiring attention on the part of the motorman or train crew." W. N. Smith, "The Electric Car Equipment of the Long Island Railroad—I," *Street Railway Journal* (11 August 1906):216.

117. "The Electrification of the Long Island Railroad," *Street Railway Journal* (4 November 1905):929.

118. For additional information, see "The Pennsylvania Railroad's Extension to New York and Long Island—The Long Island City Power Station." *Street Railway Journal* (7 April 1906):536–37; see also "The Electrification of the Long Island Railroad," *Street Railway Journal* (4 November 1905):828–34.

119. A short branch line leaves the LIRR main line just beyond the station at Queens Village and leads to a special terminal station adjacent to Belmont Park Racetrack in Elmont. Although the current terminal is not on the same site as the original one, the LIRR continues to serve Belmont Park with special trains during its racing season.

120. *New York Times* (19 July 1905):3.

121. See "The Electrification of the Long Island Railroad," 833, where a map of the LIRR's electrified district includes the line in question. In fact, the line was equipped with a third rail, although no electrified service ever operated over it.

122. "The only other changes are in the application of a skeleton fender at each end of the car, M.C.B. couplers instead of the Van Dorn style radial drawbar, and a headlight on the roof." "Some New Steel Passenger Cars," *Railroad Gazette* (16 June 1905):680. The misleading photograph appears in the same article on page 679.

123. For comprehensive details about the LIRR cars, see W. N.

Smith, "The Electric Car Equipment of the Long Island Railroad," *Street Railway Journal* part I (11 August 1906):216–26; part II (18 August 1906):250–60. For a general press account of the cars and the electrification project, see *New York Times* (9 July 1905):6. Transit and railroad executives of our own day can be forgiven any envy they might harbor toward the 1905 LIRR over the fact that a contract for 134 new MU cars was signed in January, and all cars were delivered within seven months. Today, advertising bids and executing a contract for new cars can easily require more than seven months of work.

124. See "Combined Steel and Wooden Trains Discontinued," *Electric Railway Journal* (2 January 1915):78.

125. For a review of LIRR maintenance experience with its new MU cars, see "Steel Cars on the Long Island," *Street Railway Journal* (20 March 1915):566–70.

126. "In order to reduce the weight and cost of construction the arch roof was decided upon." "Steel Coaches for Long Island Suburban Service," *Railway Age Gazette* (6 August 1915):242. The full article is on pp. 242–44.

127. "The construction of these cars follows closely the design of the Class T-54 trail cars used by this company, with such modifications as are necessary to adapt them for motors and controls." "Features of New Long Island Cars," *Electric Railway Journal* (2 February 1924):167. The full article is on pp. 167–70.

128. In addition to this extension of third rail service to Babylon via the Montauk Branch in 1925 and earlier electrification to Belmont Park, Valley Stream, and the Rockaways from Brooklyn in 1905, the following LIRR suburban lines were equipped with third rail electrification in the early years of the twentieth century: Floral Park to Hempstead; Jamaica to Long Island City and Penn Station; Valley Stream to Long Beach; Whitepot Junction to Woodhaven; Woodside to Whitestone Landing and Port Washington; Floral Park to Mineola and East Williston; Valley Street to West Hempstead and Mineola; County Life Press to Mitchell Field and Salisbury Plains.

129. *New York Times* (14 August 1932):6. The "Pullman car" reference was not an allusion to luxury accommodations such as drawing rooms and double bedrooms but rather to compartments, as they were called. By night, Pullman porters rigged compartments into upper and lower berths, while by day, passengers rode on fixed seats that permanently faced each other.

130. Two experimental sleeping cars turned out by the Pullman Company in 1933 featured window arrangements that resembled the PRR-built "double-deckers." They were duplex sleepers incorporating

the same "split-level" concept as the LIRR MU cars, but featuring a side aisle and sixteen staggered roomettes. The window arrangement was different on the room side of the cars and the aisle side, and it was only the room side that resembled the "double-deckers." See John H. White, Jr., *The American Railroad Passenger Car,* 278–79. Of this unusual design, White says "with its awkward jumble of staggered windows, [it] had the grace of an armor-plated hen house" (p. 279).

131. For further information about these distinctive LIRR MU cars, see Mike Boland, "Long Island's Lovable Double-Deckers," *Classic Trains* (spring 2003):64–69.

132. *New York Times* (1 March 1949):1.

133. "L.I. Rail Road Files Bankruptcy Plea Despite Fare Rise," *New York Times* (3 March 1949):1, 37.

134. *New York Times* (31 October 1949):9.

135. *New York Times* (23 November 1950):1. The grade crossing elimination project was completed in the summer of 1950, but civic ceremonies marking the opening were restrained. Two injured passengers were still hospitalized on July 19, when the first revenue train carried passengers along the new elevated right-of-way. See *New York Times* (18 July 1950):46.

136. *New York Times* (23 November 1950):1. For a retrospective on the Richmond Hill disaster written many years afterward by a man who was the LIRR's assistant passenger traffic manager in 1950 and was the only survivor from the rear car of train No. 780, see Robert A. Patterson, "Tragedy Recalled," *Trains* (October 1986):38–40.

137. For information about the LIRR's recovery, see William D. Middleton, "The Long Island Comes Back," *Trains* (December 1957):14–32.

138. An ad hoc measure that the LIRR adopted following the twin accidents in 1949 was to require MU crews to keep the rear headlight illuminated, but with a red filter in front of the lamp as a safety measure. In addition, as the gray paint scheme of 1949 evolved, first end doors and eventually the full end bulkhead were painted orange to enhance visibility.

139. For additional details about these cars, see George Eggers and Hugh J. McCabe, Jr., "20 M.U. Cars for Long Island R.R.," *Headlights* (November 1953):2–3; see also "Emphasis on Comfort in M.U. Coaches," *Modern Railroads* (November 1953):57–58.

140. We saw earlier how the New York Central acquired new MU cars under this same program. See *New York Times* (7 April 1962):13.

141. See "World's Fair Service," *Railway Age* (1 June 1964):20.

142. *New York Times* (21 January 1966):16.

143. For an interview with William J. Ronan that focused on the future of commuter rail service in metropolitan New York, see "New York's MTA Puts Railroads in the Picture—In a Big Way," *Railway Age* (12 October 1970):26–27. For information about MCTA and MTA plans for upgrading the LIRR and Metro North, see Robert Roberts, "New York Thinks Big on Transit," *Modern Railroads* (April 1968):60–67; see also "MTA Unveils Its Plan," *Headlights* (February 1968):2–6.

144. *New York Times* (20 August 1966):27.

145. MCTA initially sought bids for 250 cars, but because of the Budd Company's favorable price quotation, the order was increased to 270. The options included in the original contract included alternatives for various quantities of additional cars, and the MTA was able to exercise an option for the maximum number permitted under the contract. See "Application of the Metropolitan Transportation Authority for a Mass Transportation Facilities Grant under the Urban Mass Transportation Act of 1964" (12 April 1968), 2. Pullman-Standard and the St. Louis Car Company submitted unsuccessful bids for this contract.

146. *New York Times* (2 August 1968):35.

147. Comparing the new M-3 units to the earlier M-1 fleet, Lawrence A. Baggerly, the LIRR's Vice President for Operations, said: "The railroad has retained what was reliable in the older equipment, and redesigned what was troublesome." "Moving Ahead with the Long Island Rail Road," *Progressive Railroading* (August 1986):27.

148. For a discussion of phase-in problems associated with the M-1 cars, see William D. Middleton, "Long Island: Back from Looneyville?" *Trains* (January 1971):20–26; see also Middleton, "Deciding the Future of the 5:15," *Trains* (February 1971):40–46.

149. *New York Times* (23 December 1968):78.

150. Prior to the formal transfer of DD-1 electric locomotives from PRR to LIRR in the early 1930s, important trains bound for points beyond the third-rail district, such as the New York–Montauk "Cannonball," would leave Penn Station behind a Pennsylvania DD-1 and switch to an LIRR steam engine at Harold Tower in Long Island City.

151. For many years, conventional electric railway wisdom asserted that direct-current traction motors were superior to alternating-current motors in the kind of start-and-stop service that commuter trains and subways typically operated. More recently, newly developed styles of AC motors, coupled with new kinds of electronic controls, have turned matters quite around, and many properties now specify AC motors for their new equipment, despite the added complexity of converting DC to AC.

152. Per FRA rules, each MU car is subject to the same monthly inspection regimen as are conventional railway locomotives.

153. For a general review of electric-powered rolling stock of the Long Island Rail Road, see Ron Ziel and John Krause, *Electric Heritage of the Long Island Rail Road* (Newton, N.J.: Carstens Publications, 1986).

Chapter 5: The Legacy of the IRT

1. Comprehensive data and information about transit patronage by era, year, and city, is available in Boris S. Pushkarev, *Urban Rail in America* (Bloomington, Ind.: Indiana University Press, 1982).

2. Arnold's 1902 report recommended subway tunnels that would be used solely by streetcars. In a later report submitted in 1911, he recommended replacing the Union Loop with a network of subway lines. See Bion J. Arnold, *Recommendations and General Plans for a Comprehensive Passenger Subway System for the City of Chicago* (Chicago: Chicago City Council, 1911).

3. "The Loop property consists of a franchise, a power station, a double-tracked elevated structure 11,150 ft. long, eleven groups of passenger stations and an interlocking switch and signal system. It owns no rolling stock." "The Union Elevated Railway of Chicago," *Street Railway Journal* (December 1898):766–68.

4. The electrification of the South Side L in 1897 gave Frank Sprague an opportunity to demonstrate the workability of multiple-unit control. For a brief description of his achievement, see "The Multiple Unit System on the South Side Elevated Railway of Chicago," *Street Railway Journal* (December 1898):763–66; for a more detailed description, see Frank J. Sprague, "The Sprague Multiple Unit System," *Street Railway Journal* (4 May 1901):537–50. For another perspective, see George H. Hill, "Some Notes on the History and Development of the Multiple-Unit System of Train Operation," *Street Railway Journal* (4 May 1901):551–54.

5. In the early years of the twentieth century, one will find elevated railways in Boston, New York, and Chicago referred to in short-hand fashion as either an "el," or an "L." In later years, regional differences emerged, and while the East Coast cities talk about their "el" trains, in Chicago the nearly universal usage is "L." Prior to the opening of the Union Loop in 1897, the various L companies terminated their trains at stub-end terminals located just outside the city's central core.

6. Yerkes began with his tenure in Chicago by securing control of the West Chicago Street Railroad. In 1894, he acquired the Lake Street L with an eye toward developing joint streetcar/rapid-transit services in the neighborhoods the two companies served. For additional information about the early years of street railways in Chicago, see Robert David Weber, *Rationalizers and Reformers; Chicago Local Transportation in the Nineteenth Century* (Ann Arbor, Mich.: University Microfilms, 1971).

7. The Dearborn platform is somewhat shorter—2,500 feet from end to end.

8. Chicago Rapid Transit was acquired by the CTA in 1947. The city's streetcar and motor bus operations became CTA responsibilities shortly afterward.

9. One CTA branch line, an operation called the Skokie Swift, uses overhead catenary for most of its length, and a small fleet of cars has been custom-fitted with roof-mounted current collectors for this service. The Skokie Swift right-of-way was once used by interurban cars and trains of the Chicago, North Shore and Milwaukee Railroad that until their abandonment in 1963, reached downtown Chicago over CTA elevated lines. The Skokie Swift was a demonstration project funded under the Urban Mass Transportation Act of 1964, although it has since become a permanent part of the CTA system. For the final report issued about this demonstration project, see *Skokie Swift* (Chicago: Chicago Transit Authority, 1964.) For additional information about Chicago rapid-transit rolling stock in general, see *Chicago's Rapid Transit,* vol. I, *1892–1947* (Chicago: Central Electric Railfans' Association, 1973); *Chicago's Rapid Transit,* vol. II, *1947–1976* (Chicago: Central Electric Railfans' Association, 1976).

10. We saw in Chapter 2 how Boston's MTA was able to squeeze additional inches of width into its transit cars by incorporating an outward bow in the sidewalls above platform level. CTA engineers have done the same thing, and the 9-foot-plus overall width of today's rolling stock contrasts with an 8-foot, 8-inch width of rolling stock designed by the Chicago Rapid Transit Company.

11. For additional information about the development of rapid transit in Chicago, see Brian J. Cudahy, *Destination Loop* (Brattleboro, Vt.: Stephen Greene, 1982); David M. Young, *Chicago Transit* (DeKalb, Ill.: Northern Illinois University Press, 1998); "Chicago: 80 Years of Rapid Transit," *Headlights* (April 1974):2–11; see also Robert L. Abrams, "The Story of Rapid Transit: Chicago," *Bulletin of the National Railway Historical Society* (third quarter 1961):14–32. Abrams has written a series of articles about rapid transit in various North American

cities which, while published around 1960, remains valuable for historical perspective.

12. In addition to the Market Street Line in Philadelphia, the only privately financed rapid-transit subways in the United States were the Cambridge portion of Boston's Cambridge-Dorchester Line, discussed in Chapter 2, and a system of lines linking Manhattan and railroad depots in New Jersey that was known as the Hudson and Manhattan Railroad. For details about this system, popularly known as the Hudson Tubes, see Brian J. Cudahy, *Rails Under the Mighty Hudson,* rev. ed. (New York: Fordham University Press, 2002).

13. For additional information, see Harold E. Cox, *The Road from Upper Darby* (New York: Electric Railroaders' Association, 1967).

14. Subway-surface cars, as the trolley operation has generally been called in Philadelphia, began operating into the new subway on December 18, 1905. See *Philadelphia Inquirer* (18 December 1905):1, 2.

15. The 1939 curtailment was supposedly temporary, and PRT was forced to restore service in 1943. It was permanently discontinued in 1953, and the elevated link down to the waterfront was torn down. See Cox, *The Road from Upper Darby,* 24.

16. The cars acquired to inaugurate Market Street service in 1906 were 49 feet, 7 inches long, and a fraction of an inch over 8 feet, 8 inches wide. Later Market Street cars were 55 feet long and 9 feet, 1 inch wide. By contrast, Broad Street cars were 67 feet long and 10 feet wide. The design of Broad Street cars closely followed specifications used in New York by the BRT/BMT, a design that was originated by the Boston Elevated Railway for its Cambridge Subway. For additional details about the Broad Street subway and its rolling stock, see Tony Fitzherbert, "Broad Street Subway," *Headlights* (January–March 1979):1–14.

17. For an account of the opening of the Broad Street Line, see *Philadelphia Inquirer* (2 September 1928):1, 6.

18. The four-track portion of the Broad Street Line extends from Olney in the north to a point just below the Walnut-Locust Station, south of City Hall. While the Broad Street Subway was opened in 1928, the express service was not inaugurated until 1959.

19. For additional information about the new rapid-transit cars acquired for Bridge Line service, see "Rapid Transit Cars of Improved Type," *Transit Journal* (July 1936):242–47.

20. In 1951, the Delaware River Port Authority (DRPA) replaced the Delaware River Joint Commission, and PATCO is a subsidiary of DRPA.

21. For information about PATCO's Lindenwold Line, see J. Wil-

liam Vigrass, "The Lindenwold Hi-Speed Line," *Railway Management Review* 2 (1973):28–52; Ronald DeGraw, "Lindenwold Line Opens," *Bulletin of the National Railway Historical Society* 2 (1969):52–62; "Good Things Take Time," *Headlights* (July–August 1972):9; Russell E. Jackson, "PATCO: A Decade of Service," *Headlights* (April-May 1979):8–10.

22. For information about new cars that SEPTA acquired for Broad Street service in the early 1980s, see Russell E. Jackson, "The New Broad Street–IV Cars," *Headlights* (November–December, 1983):7–9.

23. For additional information about PRT and rapid transit in Philadelphia, see Robert L. Abrams, "The Story of Rapid Transit: Philadelphia," *Bulletin of the National Railway Historical Society* (first quarter 1961):4–24. For more recent treatment of rail transit in Philadelphia, see Frederick A. Kramer and Samuel L. James, Jr., *PTC Rails* (Flanders, N.J.: Railroad Avenue Enterprises, 1996); see also Mervin E. Borgnis, *An Inside Story of PRT and PTC* (Winchester, Va.: Mervin E. Borgnis, 1995).

24. For information about the Newark subway, see John Harrington Riley, *The Newark City Subway Lines* (Oak Ridge, N.J.: John Harrington Riley, 1987); see also Robert L. Abrams, "The Story of Rapid Transit: Newark," *Bulletin of the National Railway Historical Society* (first quarter 1959):4–9. For information about the Rochester subway, see John F. Collins, Jr., "Rochester's Little-Known Subway," *National Railway Bulletin* 2 (1986):16–25. For information about Pacific Electric's Los Angeles subway, see "Hollywood Subway," *Interurbans Special* (1975):10–20; Donald Duke, *Pacific Electric Railway* (San Marino, Calif.: Golden West, 1958): 34–43.

25. For information about the Hudson and Manhattan Railroad and how it has been transformed into a modern rapid-transit service currently known as the PATH System, see Cudahy, *Rails Under the Mighty Hudson;* see also Paul Carleton, *The Hudson & Manhattan Railroad Revisited* (Dunnellon, Fla.: D. Carleton Railbooks, 1990).

26. Cincinnati is an especially interesting case where almost 2 miles of subway tunnels plus additional miles of at-grade right-of-way were constructed in the 1920s. For a variety of reasons, the project was never completed. For additional information, see David B. Osborn, "The Story of Rapid Transit: Cincinnati," *Bulletin of the National Railway Historical Society* 2 (1965):28–36.

27. The new line in Cleveland was 12.5 miles long, followed an east-west corridor, was built entirely outdoors save for a single underground station downtown, and, like the Revere Beach extension in Boston, utilized overhead catenary for current distribution. On the east side

of Cleveland, the new line shares trackage with the Shaker Heights Rapid Transit, a light rail transit system that links Shaker Heights with downtown Cleveland. For additional information, see James A. Toman and Blaine S. Hays, *Horse Trails to Regional Rails* (Kent, Ohio: Kent State University Press, 1996); see also Robert L. Abrams, "The Story of Rapid Transit: Cleveland," *Bulletin of the National Railway Historical Society* (second quarter 1958):20–32.

28. For information about rapid transit in Toronto, see John F. Bromley and Jack May, *Fifty Years of Progressive Transit* (New York: Electric Railroaders' Association, 1973); see also Robert L. Abrams, "The Story of Rapid Transit: Toronto," *Bulletin of the National Railway Historical Society* (fourth quarter 1959):22–30; see also *Transit in Toronto* (Toronto: Toronto Transit Commission, 1967).

29. Joseph A. Strapac, *Off and Running* (Burlingame, Calif.: Chatham, 1972), 3. For additional information about BART, see a series of eight articles in *Headlights* (October–December 1974):1–27. See also William D. Middleton, "Trouble-Plagued BART Brings in a New Team of Problem-Solvers," *Railway Age* (12 April 1976):24–27, 52; Edward T. Myers, "BART Is New from the Rails Up," *Modern Railroads* (February 1972), 42–71.

30. Boston's MBTA extended Red Line service to Quincy Center in 1971, as described in Chapter 2, while the rapid-transit line in Cleveland, built in 1955, was extended from its western terminal at West Park onto the grounds of Hopkins International Airport in 1968—the first UMTA-funded rail-transit extension and the first instance in North America where passengers could walk from subway train to airline check-in counter. More recently, rapid-transit extensions have been built to serve BWI Airport in Baltimore, Reagan National Airport in Washington, Hartsfield International Airport in Atlanta, both O'Hare International and Midway airports in Chicago, Lambert Field in St. Louis, and Metropolitan International in Oakland. In addition, electrified commuter railroad lines have been built onto the grounds of Philadelphia International Airport and St. Joseph County Airport in South Bend, Indiana, while an automated rail service links Newark International Airport with a station along the Northeast Corridor that is served by both Amtrak and New Jersey Transit. As of 2003, construction continues on a rapid-transit extension to San Francisco International Airport as well as an automated transit line that will link JFK International Airport with both the Long Island Rail Road and New York City Transit's Rockaway Line.

31. For a review of the federal transit assistance program, see George M. Smerk, *The Federal Role in Urban Mass Transportation* (Bloomington, Ind.: Indiana University Press, 1991).

32. In 1991, the Urban Mass Transportation Administration (UMTA) was renamed the Federal Transit Administration (FTA).

33. In addition to the noted light rail transit systems that include elements of subway operation, new light rail systems have also been built in the United States whose operation is either at grade or along elevated structures. These include Baltimore, Denver, San Diego, Salt Lake City, San Jose, Sacramento, and Portland, Oregon. In addition, a new rail-transit system that will include some underground operation is under construction in San Juan, Puerto Rico.

34. For information about WMATA, see Ronald H. Deiter, *The Story of Metro* (Glendale, Calif.: Interurban Press, 1985); see also *Headlights* (April–June 1956) for separate articles about the WMATA system, its rolling stock, and its automated control system.

35. During a typical recent federal fiscal year, FY 2002, the FTA awarded grants of $7.78 billion. Of this total, $1.41 billion was invested in the construction of new "fixed guideway" transit systems, while $2.45 billion was used for the modernization of older systems. *2002 Statistical Abstracts* (Washington, D.C.: Federal Transit Administration, 2003).

36. For information about Vancouver's SkyTrain, see *On Track: The SkyTrain Story* (Burnaby, British Columbia: B. C. Rapid Transit Company, Ltd., 1990).

37. For a comprehensive review of the development of rail rapid transit in America, see William D. Middleton, *Metropolitan Railways* (Bloomington, Ind.: Indiana University Press, 2003).

38. In 1945, there were 273.5 route-miles of rapid transit in the New York metropolitan area. By 1980, this had been reduced to 258. See Pushkarev, *Urban Rail in America*, table H-5. For information on the elimination of elevated lines in New York, see Lawrence Stelter, "Analysis of Demolishing New York City Elevated Transit Lines," *Municipal Engineers Journal* 2 (1990):21–47.

39. As discussed in Chapter 4, the Rockaway Line was where the LIRR operated its first electrified service in 1905. For additional details about this service, including its conversion into an extension of the subway system in 1956, see Herbert George, *Change at Ozone Park* (Flanders, N.J.: RAE Publishing, 1993).

40. See *New York Times* (15 September 2002):38.

BIBLIOGRAPHY

THE INTERBOROUGH RAPID TRANSIT COMPANY AND THE SUBWAYS OF NEW YORK

Cudahy, Brian J. *Under the Sidewalks of New York*, 2nd rev. ed. New York: Fordham University Press, 1995.

Cunningham, Joe. *Interborough Fleet*. Belleville, N.J.: Xplorer Press, 1997.

Derrick, Peter. *Tunneling to the Future*. New York: New York University Press, 2001.

Hood, Clifton. *722 Miles*. New York: Simon and Schuster, 1993.

Interborough Rapid Transit Company. *The New York Subway; Its Construction and Equipment*, rev. ed. New York: Fordham University Press, 1991.

Reed, Robert C. *The New York Elevated*. South Brunswick, N.J.: A. S. Barnes, 1978.

Sansone, Gene. *Evolution of New York City Subways*. New York: New York Transit Museum Press, 1997.

RAPID TRANSIT IN BOSTON

Anderson, Edward A. *P.C.C. Cars of Boston: 1937–1967*. Cambridge, Mass.: Boston Street Railway Association, 1968.

Cheney, Frank. *Boston's Red Line*. Charleston, S.C.: Arcadia, 2002.

Cheney, Frank, and Anthony Mitchell Sammarco. *When Boston Rode the El*. Charleston, S.C.: Arcadia, 2000.

Clarke, Bradley H. *South Shore*. Cambridge, Mass.: Boston Street Railway Association, 1972.

Clarke, Bradley H., and O. R. Cummings. *Tremont Street Subway*. Cambridge, Mass.: Boston Street Railway Association, 1997.

Cudahy, Brian J. *Change at Park Street Under.* Brattleboro, Vt.: Stephen Greene, 1972.
Warner, Sam B., Jr. *Streetcar Suburbs,* 2nd ed. Cambridge, Mass.: Harvard University Press, 1978.

RAPID TRANSIT IN EUROPE

Barker, T. C., and Michael Robbins. *A History of London Transport*, 2 vols. London: Allen and Unwin, 1974–1975.
Bobrick, Benson. *Labyrinths of Iron.* New York: Newsweek Books, 1981.
Bruce, J. Graeme. *Tube Trains under London.* London: London Transport, 1968.
———. *Steam to Silver.* London: London Transport, 1970.
Day, John R. *A Source Book of Underground Railways.* London: Ward Lock Limited, 1980.
———. *The Story of London's Underground.* London: London Transport, 1972.
Fischler, Stan. *Subways of the World.* Osceola, Wis.: MBI Publishing, 2000.
Hardy, Brian. *London Underground Rolling Stock*, rev. ed. London: Capital Transport Publishing, 2002.
Hervieu, Jules. *Le Chemin de Fer Metropolitain Municipal de Paris.* Paris: Libraire Polytechnique, 1903.
Jackson, Alan A., and Desmond Croome. *Rails through Clay: A History of London's Tube Railways.* London: Allen and Unwin, 1962.
Lee, Charles E. *100 Years of the District.* London: London Transport, 1968.
———. *Seventy Years of the Central.* London: London Transport, 1970.
———. *The Metropolitan Line.* London: London Transport, 1972.
———. *The Northern Line.* London: London Transport, 1973.
———. *The Piccadilly Line.* London: London Transport, 1973.
———. *The Bakerloo Line.* London: London Transport, 1973.
———. *The East London Line and the Thames Tunnel.* London: London Transport, 1976.

Thomson, David L., and David E. Sinclair. *The Glasgow Subway*. Glasgow: Scottish Tramway Museum Society, 1964.

Wrottesley, A. J. F. *Famous Underground Railways of the World*. London: Frederick Muller, 1956.

NEW YORK COMMUTER RAILROADS

Arcara, Roger. *Westchester's Forgotten Railway,* rev. ed. New York: Quadrant, 1972.

Bezilla, Michael. *Electric Traction on the Pennsylvania Railroad, 1895–1968*. University Park, Pa.: Pennsylvania State University Press, 1980.

Burgess, George, and Miles Kennedy. *Centennial History of the Pennsylvania Railroad*. Philadelphia, Pa.: Pennsylvania Railroad Company, 1949.

Condit, Carl W. *The Port of New York*. Chicago: University of Chicago Press, 1981.

Cudahy, Brian J. *Rails Under the Mighty Hudson,* rev. ed. New York: Fordham University Press, 2002.

Diehl, Lorraine B. *The Late, Great Pennsylvania Station,* New York: American Heritage, 1985.

Droege, John A. *Passenger Terminals and Trains*. New York: McGraw-Hill, 1916; repub. Milwaukee, Wis.: Kalmbach, 1969.

George, Herbert. *Change at Ozone Park*. Flanders, N.J.: RAE Publishing, 1993.

Harrison, Richard J. *Long Island Rail Road Memories*. New York: Quadrant, 1981.

Hulick, Charles. "A Brief History of the Pennsylvania Railroad MP54 Multiple-Unit Cars." *Keystone* 33 (autumn 2000):19–28.

Middleton, William D. *Grand Central*. San Marino, Calif.: Golden West Books, 1977.

———. *Manhattan Gateway*. Waukesha, Wis.: Kalmbach, 1996.

———. *When the Steam Railroads Electrified*. Milwaukee, Wis.: Kalmbach, 1974.

Nelligan, Tom. *Commuter Trains to Grand Central Terminal*. New York: Quadrant, 1986.

Pattison, Tony, ed. *Jane's Urban Transport Systems: 2001–2002.* Coulsdon, Surrey, UK: Jane's Information Group, Ltd., 2001.

White, John H., Jr. *The American Railroad Passenger Car.* Baltimore, Md.: Johns Hopkins University Press, 1978.

Ziel, Ron, and John Krause, *Electric Heritage of the Long Island Rail Road, 1905–1975* Newton, N.J.: Carstens, 1986.

RAPID TRANSIT IN NORTH AMERICA

Beaudin, Dominique. *Le Metro de Montréal.* Montreal: Editions de L'Action Nationale, 1960.

Carlson, Stephen P., and Fred W. Schneider, III. *P.C.C.: The Car That Fought Back.* Glendale, Calif.: *Interurban Press, 1980.*

Chicago Rapid Transit. Vol. I, *1892–1947* Chicago: Central Electric Railfans' Association, 1973.

Chicago Rapid Transit. Vol. II, *1947–1976* Chicago: Central Electric Railfans' Association, 1976.

Cox, Harold E. *The Road from Upper Darby.* New York: Electric Railroaders' Association, 1967.

Cudahy, Brian J. *Cash, Tokens and Transfers.* New York: Fordham University Press, 1990.

―――. *Destination Loop.* Brattleboro, Vt.: Stephen Greene Press, 1982.

Fischler, Stan. *Subways of the World.* Osceola, Wis.: MBI Publishing, 2000.

Middleton, William D. *Metropolitan Railways.* Bloomington, Ind.: Indiana University Press, 2003.

Pushkarev, Boris. *Urban Rail in America.* Bloomington, Ind.: Indiana University Press, 1982.

Smerk, George M. *The Federal Role in Urban Mass Transportation.* Bloomington, Ind.: Indiana University Press, 1991.

WEB SITES

There are many Web sites one may visit for information about rail rapid transit, including those maintained by the various providers of transit and commuter railroad services. Quality varies, of course, from site to site, and it must be understood that operating transit agencies are more interested in providing basic information about current transit services than, for instance, historical perspectives on older rolling stock.

Two general Web sites can be recommended, however. The first is oriented more toward the subways of New York, although it contains information about transit in other cities as well, while the second is worldwide in scope and contains information about quite literally hundreds of world subway systems.

New York Subway Resources: www.nycsubway.org
metroPlanet: www.metropla.net

INDEX